The Literature of Cinema

ADVISORY EDITOR: **MARTIN S. DWORKIN**
INSTITUTE OF PHILOSOPHY AND POLITICS OF EDUCATION
TEACHER'S COLLEGE, COLUMBIA UNIVERSITY

THE LITERATURE OF CINEMA presents a comprehensive selection from the multitude of writings about cinema, rediscovering materials on its origins, history, theoretical principles and techniques, aesthetics, economics, and effects on societies and individuals. Included are works of inherent, lasting merit and others of primarily historical significance. These provide essential resources for serious study and critical enjoyment of the "magic shadows" that became one of the decisive cultural forces of modern times.

Hollywood:
The Movie Colony
The Movie Makers

Leo C. Rosten

ARNO PRESS & THE NEW YORK TIMES

New York • 1970

Reprint Edition 1970 by Arno Press Inc.
Reprinted by permission of Leo C. Rosten
Library of Congress Catalog Card Number: 74-124036
ISBN 0-405-01636-0
ISBN for complete set: 0-405-01600-X
Manufactured in the United States of America

HOLLYWOOD

THE MOVIE COLONY
THE MOVIE MAKERS

by

Leo C. Rosten

hb

New York

HARCOURT, BRACE AND COMPANY

TO

CHARLES E. MERRIAM

HAROLD D. LASSWELL

FURNITURE AND FURNISHINGS

... FOR THE YEAR FOR:	$		AMT END	$
FLOOR-COVERINGS		PICTURES, CURTAINS, ORNAMENTS		
CHAIRS, TABLES		PIANO, OTHER MUSICAL INSTRUM'TS		
OTHER WOODEN FURNITURE		BEDS, BEDDING, BED-LINEN		
DISHES AND TABLE-WARE		KITCHEN UTENSILS		
TABLE-LINEN, TOWELS		STOVES, REFRIGERATOR		
SUPPLIES FOR SWEEPING AND CLEANING		OTHER		
AMT END. $				$

TOTAL EXPENDITURES FOR FURNITURE AND FURNISHINGS

EQUIPMENT:

(Enumerate the principal articles in each room, designating the rooms as
parlor kitchen, etc. and state the kind of furniture (e.g. folding bed,
lace curtains), and present condition)

ROOM -
- -

ROOM -
- -

RD. ROOM -
- -

4TH. ROOM -
- -

5TH ROOM -
- -

6TH ROOM -
- -

ROOM -
- -

WHAT IS THE STANDARD OF TASTE AND ECONOMY REPRESENTED BY THE FURNITURE AND
FURNISHINGS? -

IS ANY FURNITURE BOUGHT AT SECOND-HAND? - - - - - - - - - - - - -
- -

PREFACE

THE name "Hollywood" provokes either amusement or indignation in those whose conception of Hollywood has been formed by publicity and gossip. This book is neither amused nor indignant. It does not offer deceptively simple answers to extremely complicated problems. It does not confuse the spectacular with the representative. It cannot help disappointing those who would like a study of Hollywood to be either a catalogue of nonsense or a bucket of whitewash.

This book is primarily concerned with putting Hollywood under the microscopes of social science. For Hollywood is an index of our society and our culture. To quote from the first chapter in this study: "The aberrations of our culture are more vivid, more conspicuous, and more dramatic in Hollywood than in New Bedford or Palo Alto. Our values are extended to the strident and the unmistakable in Hollywood's way of life. . . . A study of Hollywood casts the profile of American society into sharper relief."

This volume is the result of over three years of research, observation, and work in Hollywood. The materials were collected by the author and a staff of social scientists which included two sociologists, an economist, a personnel expert, a statistician, a translator, and others. (The members of the staff are credited in the Acknowledgments.)

Some of the conclusions in this book will prove surprising;

v

others will, no doubt, support popular impressions. But the difference between social science and gossip, between systematic analysis and casual journalism, lies not in what is said but in how it was discovered. This study uses whatever methods help to make Hollywood comprehensible, whatever techniques advance the search for clarity. Where measurement is possible, measurement is given; where documentation is possible, data are offered; where objective materials are not available, probability and insights are suggested.

Hollywood has often been attacked on irrelevant grounds, indicted with slipshod materials, and generally harassed by irresponsible commentators. It is one of the ironies of this state of affairs that many of the facts about which the movie people have been most defensive are, in reality, neither as damaging nor as embarrassing as they fear. In few areas of American life is there such a miasma of myths and misconceptions as that which surrounds Hollywood.

All of the existing materials on Hollywood, the movies, and the motion picture industry have been dissected and digested for this study. But the most valuable information was obtained from (1) detailed questionnaires, of which we circulated 4,200 to Hollywood's producers, actors, directors, writers, cinematographers, film editors (cutters), research workers, and others; (2) hundreds of interviews carried on over a period of thirty months in every nook and cranny of the Hollywood scene; (3) the materials which the major motion picture companies made available to this writer, and the documented answers to most of his questions; (4) the knowledge obtained in three years of firsthand work, creation, and research in the movie colony.

The present volume consists of two parts: the Movie Colony and the Movie Makers. The Movie Colony deals with the life, practices, and values of Hollywood; it explores the manners and *mores* of the movie colony, the pattern and spirit of Hollywood which permeates its incomes, spending, homes, parties, ro-

PREFACE

mances, politics, prestige, and so on. The Movie Makers is concerned with the four major groups in Hollywood: movie producers, actors, directors, writers. The following fields of inquiry
must be reserved for a later volume: (a) the economics of
movie making, picture costs, markets, profits, financial practices; (b) the Motion Picture Producers and Distributors Association [the Hays Office]; (c) the production code and censorship; (d) Hollywood's guilds and labor problems.

The entire study was made possible by the Carnegie Corporation of New York, which awarded me a grant for a sociological study of the movie colony and the movie makers. The
research began in January, 1939, as the Motion Picture Research
Project. In the summer of 1940, the Rockefeller Foundation authorized a grant-in-aid which extended the scope and detail of
the research.

In the Acknowledgments, I have expressed my indebtedness
to the Carnegie and Rockefeller Foundations, to the staff of research assistants who labored on the materials, and to the legion
of persons who placed material and expert knowledge at our
disposal. I need only absolve any and all persons from responsibility for the pages which follow. All the writing was done
by myself; the interpretations, emphases, conclusions, and errors
are strictly my own.

LEO C. ROSTEN

August 2, 1941

vii

ACKNOWLEDGMENTS

I AM indebted to the trustees of the Carnegie Corporation, and especially to Dr. Frederick P. Keppel, president, for his faith in the study and for the financial support which made it possible. Charles Dollard of the Carnegie organization helped the project by his co-operation. To John Marshall of the Rockefeller Foundation, and Donald Slesinger of the American Film Center, I express my gratitude for the Rockefeller grant which extended the life and resources of the project.

The following scholars acted as my Advisory Board, and I wish to thank them for their co-operation and support: Robert S. Lynd, Columbia University; Herbert Blumer and Louis Wirth, University of Chicago; Harold D. Lasswell, Washington School of Psychiatry and William Alanson White Foundation.

The materials for this study were collected by the following staff members, whose names it is a pleasure to record in appreciation of their labors and their talents: Dorothy B. Jones, to whom I owe special thanks for the skill and unfailing loyalty with which she took charge of 4,200 questionnaires, put the data into reports, administered the affairs of the office for three months in 1940, and solved many exhausting problems; Mae D. Huettig, who completed an invaluable analysis of the economic and financial structure of the motion picture industry; Ruth A. Inglis, who explored the field of censorship, the Hays

Office, and the Production Code; Philip Keller, who analyzed the trade practices and trade problems of the motion picture industry. Elise McNichol served the Project as secretary for two years and worked with a rare combination of equanimity and application. I should like to express my thanks to the part-time and volunteer researchers: John Western, Michael Hunter, Sylvia Jarrico, and Jean Lyle. T. David Zuckerman deserves special mention for his able statistical assistance.

The following persons gave the writer materials and assistance which were of basic value: John Arnold, Joseph I. Breen, Jack Chertok, Kenneth Clark, Charles Einfeld, Matthew Fox, Y. Frank Freeman, Donald Gledhill, Will H. Hays, Jason Joy, Murray Kinnell, Frederick L. Klay, John Lee, David Lory, Stanley Love, J. R. McDonough, J. P. McGowan, Stewart Mc-Kee, Fred Metzler, Floyd Odlum, Fred Pelton, Tom Petty, Irwin Stalmaster, Kenneth Thomson, Walter Wanger, Harry M. Warner, and the heads of the fan mail, research and certain other departments of the studios. My thanks are due to Winifred M. Hausam, director of Western Personnel Service, a research center of western colleges and universities, who co-operated by making available additional staff for the analysis of questionnaire materials.

Data on motion picture costs, salaries, foreign markets, studio payrolls, and so on, were supplied by Columbia Pictures, Metro-Goldwyn-Mayer, RKO-Radio, Twentieth Century-Fox, Universal, Walter Wanger, Warner Brothers.

The manuscript was read by the following persons, whose comments were of immeasurable value: Harold D. Lasswell, James Allen, Margaret Mead, Saul Padover, Gregory Bateson, Dorothy B. Jones, and Walter Wanger. Special credit is due Gertrude D. Chern for faultless editorial assistance. My wife deserves a tribute for her tenacious insistence upon clarity of style and structure.

ACKNOWLEDGMENTS

The following publishers granted me permission to quote from the books credited:

COVICI-FRIEDE: *History of the Movies* by Benjamin B. Hampton.

E. P. DUTTON AND COMPANY: *Hollywood Saga* by William C. DeMille.

FARRAR AND RINEHART: *I, Candidate for Governor and How I Got Licked* by Upton Sinclair.

HARCOURT, BRACE AND COMPANY: *Middletown* and *Middletown in Transition* by Robert S. Lynd and Helen Merrell Lynd.

HARPER & BROTHERS: *Lords of Creation* by Frederick Lewis Allen.

HOUGHTON MIFFLIN AND COMPANY: *Greenwich Village* by Caroline F. Ware.

ALFRED A. KNOPF: *Profiles from the New Yorker; The American Language* by H. L. Mencken.

J. B. LIPPINCOTT COMPANY: *"King Lehr" and the Gilded Age* by Elizabeth Drexel Lehr.

THE MACMILLAN COMPANY: *History of the Business Man* by Miriam Beard; *The Rise of American Civilization* by Charles and Mary Beard.

MC GRAW-HILL BOOK COMPANY: *Competition and Cooperation Among Primitive Peoples* edited by Margaret Mead.

W. W. NORTON AND COMPANY: *We Make the Movies* edited by Nancy Naumberg.

RANDOM HOUSE: *The Great Goldwyn* by Alva Johnston.

CHARLES SCRIBNER'S SONS: *The Saga of American Society* by Dixon Wecter; *The Movies Come from America* by Gilbert Seldes.

SIMON AND SCHUSTER: *We Saw It Happen* edited by Hanson W. Baldwin and Shepard Stone; *The Life of Greece* by Will Durant.

SINCLAIR: *Upton Sinclair Presents William Fox.*

L. C. R.

CONTENTS

stances the variations indicate merely the taste and habit of a single family rather than a social standard. It would be hazardous on the basis of so small a number of cases to make an estimate of the sum required to maintain a normal standard in each community. It would certainly fall below the amount needed in New York City, but the exact measure of the difference requires a larger induction of cases.

One

THE MOVIE COLONY

1. THE HOLLYWOOD LEGEND

THERE are two Hollywoods: the Hollywood where people live and work, and the Hollywood which lives in the mind of the public like a fabulous legend. Before we can understand the movie colony we must understand its legend; and before we can understand the legend we must glance at a few facts which will give body and structure to the exploration of a fantasy.

Hollywood is the place where movies are made. Hollywood is the creative hub of an industry which reaches into the obscure corners of the globe. Hollywood has carried entertainment from the realm of individual art into the world of big business. This is something new under the sun.

The motion picture industry has a capital investment in the United States alone of approximately two billion dollars—in movie production, theaters, and distribution.

Movie box-office receipts were well over half a billion dollars ($673,-045,000) in 1939. This represented 67.4 percent of the total volume of business done in all the commercial places of entertainment in the land.

The average amount of money spent on movie entertainment in the United States annually is around $5 per person or $25 per family.

Between 52,000,000 and 55,000,000 Americans go to the movies each and every week in the year.

There are 15,115 movie theaters operating in the United States today —one movie theater for every 2,306 families, or for every 8,700 Americans.

There are more movie theaters in the country than banks (14,952). There are twice as many movie houses as there are hotels with fifty or more rooms (7,478). There are three times as many movie theaters as there are department stores (4,201). There are almost as many movie theaters as there are cigar stores and cigarette stands.[1] *

Now let us narrow the facts to Hollywood, where the studios make the movies which are distributed, serviced, and exhibited all over the world.

Hollywood (and its environs) employs from 27,573 to 33,683 persons a month in making films.

Hollywood's annual payroll ranges from $133,000,000 to $145,000,000.

Hollywood spent $186,848,971 in manufacturing movies in 1939.

Hollywood produces about 90 percent of all the films made in America, and the United States supplies about 65 percent of all the films used in the world.[2]

These are the stakes involved in the empire whose favored children we are about to explore. They are impressive stakes. It is, therefore, significant that Hollywood is generally dismissed— by the cynical or the bewildered—as "screwy." The movie colony is believed to be more or less dominated by maniacs, operated under the laws of lunacy, and populated by an assortment of illiterates, "geniuses," divorcees, crackpots, and poltroons. The millions who read the gossip columns or have seen those classic delineations of Hollywood's folly, *Once in a Lifetime* and *Boy Meets Girl,* are quite familiar with the producer who tried to hire Chaucer, the director who wears earmuffs to spare himself from hearing the actors, the actresses who bathe in milk, carry monkeys on their shoulders, and spend their lives shuttling between Yuma and Reno.

The question naturally arises: How can "the madmen of Hollywood" operate a business which spends almost $187,000,-

* All references to sources will be found in the Reference Notes at the end of the book, beginning on page 415.

000 a year in making pictures? How can erratic and undisciplined personalities turn out the 350-400 movies a year upon
which a two-billion-dollar enterprise depends? How can supposedly illiterate egomaniacs make films which take in half a
billion dollars a year at the box-offices of the United States
alone? The answers are spread through the chapters of this
book.

In reality, there is nothing particularly screwy about Hollywood; or, better, Hollywood is no more screwy than other and
less conspicuous parts of our society. The aberrations of our
culture are simply more vivid, more conspicuous, and more dramatic in Hollywood than in New Bedford or Palo Alto. Our
values are extended to the strident and the unmistakable in
Hollywood's way of life. It is for this reason that a study of
Hollywood can cast the profile of American society into sharper
relief.

If we look at Hollywood against the larger context of the
world in which we live, if we compare the motion picture industry to other businesses at a comparable time, in *their* sudden heyday, if we compare the *nouveaux riches* of the movie
colony to the *nouveaux riches* of banking, railroads, or real
estate, we discover startling and conclusive parallels between
the practices of Hollywood and New York, between the mores
of Bel-Air and Oyster Bay, between the chalets of Santa Monica
and the mansions of Newport. Hollywood can be placed under
the microscope of social science like a slide on which we see,
in sharper and isolated detail, the organic processes of the larger
social body. Pathology illuminates the normal.

Hollywood was not created out of a void; its characteristics
were not invented; its people did not descend from Shangri-La.
The men and women who live and work in Hollywood came to
the film colony from other parts of America and the world; and
they brought to Hollywood appetites which have been gratified,
aspirations which have been realized, in this rich and indulgent

5

community on the Pacific. The citizens of Kalamazoo who possess the unique and sometimes distressing temperament of actors, writers, directors, and producers would not behave differently if *they* had the money, the opportunities, and the sanctions afforded the mortals who live in the movie colony. Hollywood can be defined, examined, and understood if we keep asking "Why?" Why do they live this way, talk this way, act this way? Why do they build such homes, give such parties, earn such fortunes? Why do they "go Hollywood"?

When seen as a social complex; when viewed with insight, when studied with patience and analyzed with detachment, Hollywood loses many of its bizarreries. The fallacy of our stereotypes about Hollywood is strikingly illustrated by the fact that whereas uneducated captains of industry are praised as "self-made men," uneducated movie executives are dismissed as "illiterates." Erratic bankers are called "eccentric," but erratic movie makers are called "crazy." Hard-bargaining businessmen are admired for being shrewd; their counterparts in Hollywood are denounced for being "mercenary." And where the private indiscretions of Park Avenue are winked at as all-too-human peccadillos, those of Beverly Hills are paraded forth as proof of movie licentiousness.

Hollywood is a place which has been so ballyhooed that it has become preposterous, and so lampooned that the ridicule ceases to carry credence. Let us therefore study the people of Hollywood and the patterns of movie making as one might study the people and practices of Tahiti. Let us find the facts about the people who constitute that collection of talents and egos called the movie colony. Let us lay bare the social mainsprings and the economic framework of a community which is significant because of the product it manufactures and the symbolic function it serves to millions of men.

Let us search for evidence, and analyze this evidence without undue prejudice or preference. Let us place Hollywood under an X-ray instead of a spotlight. That has never before been done.

The American press is read only where English is read; the American radio is heard only where English is comprehended; but the American movie is an international carrier which triumphs over differences in age or language, nationality or custom. Even the Sumatran native who cannot spell is able to grasp the meaning of pictures which move, and he can love, hate, or identify himself with those who appear in them. Through the movies, a Frenchman remarked, the United States has effected a "cultural colonization" of the world. And trade follows the films as well as the flag.

There are almost four hundred newspapermen, columnists, and feature writers (including a correspondent for the Vatican) assigned full-time to Hollywood. Only Washington, the matrix of our political life, and New York, the nerve-center of our economic system, possess larger press corps.[3] Hollywood has become the Enchanted City; it is not far-fetched to suggest that Mohammedans have their Mecca, Communists have their Moscow, and movie fans (the word comes from "fanatic") have Hollywood. The astonishing interest of the public in Hollywood is too obvious to call for elaboration; but it is important for thinking men to understand the place and the people with which the world's populace is so intensely concerned, and to remember that the movie-going legions are spread across the globe. On the forty-second day of the bombardment of London, the *London Mirror*, no doubt unaware of the ironic significance of its act, cabled its Hollywood correspondent for two hundred weighty words concerning Ann Sheridan's contract dispute with Warner Brothers. In far-off Bombay the magazine *Filmindia* (which regularly denounces Hollywood's portrayals of India) gave exquisite and

7

unforgettable testimony to the influence of Hollywood when one of the advertisements, for a picture made in India, proclaimed: "Brahmin Boy Loves Untouchable Girl!" As the Anzac warriors marched across Libya to attack the Italians at Bardia, they sang a chorus from Mervyn Le Roy's *Wizard of Oz*.[4] And when twenty-two naval chiefs of eleven Central and South American countries visited the United States recently, one of the highlights of their trip and one of the most effective bids for their good will was a dinner at Ciro's, Hollywood's most elegant night club, with three hundred movie luminaries in attendance; the celebrated Norma Shearer was hostess of the evening and the celebrated Cesar Romero was master of ceremonies.*

If four hundred columnists and feature writers were assigned to Detroit or Pittsburgh and were charged with the sole responsibility of writing daily stories about the foibles, diet, and libidinal acrobatics of automobile magnates or steel monarchs, the public would have a different set of stereotypes about these men, and about the circles in which they move. But industrialists are not "glamorous," manufacturers make poor news copy, and the employees of Remington Rand can never rival those of MGM for sex-appeal. The reported malapropisms of a Goldwyn have hit the front pages for a decade; the name of Andrew W. Mellon was not even printed in the New York *Times* until he was sixty-six years old. Zanuck and Warner are names familiar to the public, but the men who bestrode American industry not so long ago—Frick, Reid, Yerkes, Ryan, Schwab—were "astonishingly little known to the nation at large."[5] When 74-year-old Arthur Curtiss James, scion of Phelps-Dodge, one of the twelve richest men in the land, and the largest owner of railroad stock

---

* The next day's photographs showed the vice-admiral of Brazil with Claudette Colbert, a naval commander from Argentina with Miriam Hopkins, and the admirals of Peru, Chile, Uruguay and Ecuador with the Misses Joan Bennett, Ann Sothern, Dolores del Rio, and Joan Blondell.[6] The worldwide influence of Hollywood's movies and Hollywood's stars is discussed in "The Long Arm of Hollywood," chapter 16.

in the nation (over $350,000,000), died in June of 1941, his passing received a column or two in the newspapers.[7] The public had scarcely heard his name; the obituaries were long, formidable, and dull. But when a young actress named Jean Harlow was ill, the press and the radio gave America hourly accounts of her pulse-beat, and when Rudolph Valentino died there was anguish in a million homes.

We must remember from the outset that Hollywood's personnel and Hollywood's business—its salaries, profits, skullduggeries, and mistakes—are recorded for all the world to see. No other community in America is reported upon each day so intensely, so insistently, and with such a deplorable premium on triviality. There are, of course, other industries in the public eye—automobiles, steel, oil. But which of them is so familiar to the public? Which of them is bathed in such romanticism? Which of their employees is offered such foolish adulation? How much does the public know of a Sloan, a Watson, or a Grace, or of that bundle of bagatelles called their "private lives"? (The gossip column of Louella Parsons at one time appeared in 400 newspapers in the United States, England, Canada, France, China, Egypt, and India.) The business giants are symbols of rectitude and prestige; they are figures of shadowy outline; their professional acts are rarely publicized. But the men and women of Hollywood are symbols of glamour and romance, demi-gods and demi-goddesses who are in the forefront of public attention. The affairs of finance are carried on behind oak-paneled doors and a screening battery of public-relations experts; the affairs of Hollywood are carried on in a fish bowl with four hundred pairs of eyes glued to the sides. The struggle for financial power is framed in hieroglyphics so abstract and intricate that none but the experts understand them; the working processes of Hollywood are written in names and acts which a high-school girl can comprehend.

The common man knows—indeed, he can scarcely help know-

9

ing—an extraordinarily diverse and absurd catalogue of facts about the people who live in Hollywood. A random reading of the gossip columns told this writer, in allegations of varying credibility, that Paulette Goddard trimmed a Christmas tree with spare bits of ermine; that Victor McLaglen has a penchant for purchasing wild animals ("I like to keep kangaroos, bears, tropical birds, and other wild creatures to remind me of my days of high adventure"); that Louis Hayward had some rare Irish roses shipped from Dublin to Hollywood via the Atlantic Clipper; that Myrna Loy protected a peach tree in her garden one cold night by wrapping her mink coat around the trunk; and that Cecil B. DeMille, one of the last Romanesque figures in the motion picture industry, poured a quarter of a million dollars into his gardens. The tennis court with which Robert Taylor "surprised" Barbara Stanwyck on her birthday was better known to some citizens than Cordell Hull's reciprocal trade agreement with Brazil, with which it competed for news space. One dare not speculate on the avidity with which readers devour such news items as Norma Shearer's alleged purchase of $1,000 worth of handkerchiefs for Christmas presents, the gesture of George Raft in ordering twenty-one champagne cocktails for the barbers and beauty operators while he had his hair cut, or the purchase by a movie producer of an automobile originally made for the Crown Prince of Denmark.[8] It is a commentary on our society—or, perhaps, on Hollywood's publicity—that a mob of frenzied fans once swarmed through New York's Pennsylvania Station to greet Edward G. Robinson, famed for depicting gangster roles, and failed to recognize his fellow passenger, Herbert Hoover.

The idols of the screen are an international royalty whose dress and diet and diversions are known to hundreds of millions of subjects. Never in history has the public been so avid for information about mortals who earn a living by posturing. The phenomenal popularity of Hollywood's employees is seen in the ecstasy with which people greet a world première in their midst. These carnivals are masterpieces of planned ballyhoo, to be sure, but the hysteria of the populace when it views a movie star in the flesh borders on idolatry. The metropolises of Seattle and Tacoma locked horns in a titanic struggle over which would be sanctified by the première of *Tugboat Annie Sails Again.* The lucky city, Tacoma, decreed an official "Tugboat Annie Day," all the school children were reprieved from education, 40,000 soldiers in nearby army posts were granted a furlough, and the cast of the movie (which did not include one star of the first rank) steamed up the bay with an escort of several hundred local tugs, yachts, and dredges proudly led by a U. S. Coast Guard cutter. When *Northwest Mounted Police* was previewed in Chicago, the Loop saw two days of high jinks, and 12,000 women entered a contest for the privilege of sitting next to Gary Cooper. The première of *Virginia City* attracted the governors of six sovereign states of the Union; and thousands of un-Western visitors from all over the land turned Virginia City into an inferno of cowboy suits, ten-gallon hats, and joy unconfined. And when the Paramount studio suggested that Dorothy Lamour might not be able to appear in Detroit for the opening of *Disputed Passage,* "the mayor, the presidents of two universities, and leaders in the automobile industry bombarded Hollywood with frantic pleas." Miss Lamour did smile upon Detroit, and police officials estimated that the crowd which turned out was the third largest in the city's history.* [9]

The sheer magnitude of this adoration invites awe. Each day millions of men, women, and children sit in the windowless

* A report of the New York Probation Bureau stated that some of the demonstrations for Hollywood's celebrities—in hotels, theaters, railroad stations—are the result of astute organization. Two wise 18-year-olds launched a promising career by building up a staff of 200 "applauders" and autograph hunters who were hired out to interested persons. It was charged in court that the "amazing, spontaneous outbursts" by jitterbugs in the Paramount Theater in February, 1938, a phenomenon referred to in several learned journals, was the work of the 200 "characters," as these delightful *agents provocateurs* came to be known along Broadway.[10]

11

temples of the screen to commune with their vicarious friends and lovers, to ride with Autry, love with Garbo, fight with Gable. These millions devour tons of strange magazines dedicated exclusively to Hollywood gossip and movie personalities.* Each night they read the newspaper pages devoted to the chit-chat, the lingerie, and the petty history of the fabulous community which has captured their imagination. To the public, all things are possible in Hollywood, and most of them happen there.

The legendary Hollywood is a sort of Venice without canals, full of glittering conveyances, dazzling maidens, and men like gods. Everyone has flashing white teeth, shapely limbs, three bank-accounts, and a sun tan. Marble swimming pools abound, there are miles of Byzantine palaces, and champagne flows everywhere. Every lawn boasts a borzoi, every living room a fireplace, every garage two Cadillacs and a station wagon. The skies are always bejeweled with stars and the blaze of preview lights. Romance breathes from the very stones, and each golden sunset is the prelude to a night life more voluptuous than Montmartre's and just short of Gomorrah's.

It is perhaps unnecessary to remark that no city could fulfill these titillating expectations. Yet the very character of the Hollywood legend is charged with meaning, for the public which clings to the conception of Hollywood as a Bagdad-on-the-Pacific is faithful to the values on which it has been nurtured.

Men have always loved the Cinderella story and have always dreamed of magical success. Hollywood is the very embodiment of these. One reason for Hollywood's stars becoming national idols is that they represent a new type of hero in Ameri-

* Each of the following fan magazines has a monthly circulation (Audit Bureau of Circulation figures) of between 250,000-500,000: *Photoplay, Hollywood, Movie Mirror, Screen Guide, Silver Screen, Screenland, Motion Picture, Movie Story Magazine.* Other circulation figures: *Harper's,* 107,770; *Atlantic Monthly,* 105,925; *Nation,* 37,000; *New Republic,* 27,140.[11]

can experience. Hollywood's children of fortune are not the thrifty newsboys of the Horatio Alger stereotype—honest, diligent, pure of heart; here, instead, are mortals known to be spendthrift and Bohemian, people believed to lack impressive brains and given to profligate ways. Yet they have been rewarded with great lucre and honored throughout the land. They represent a new type of folk-hero in a society whose ethos rests upon hard work and virtuous deportment. Furthermore, the public *sees* the actors at their trade; it sees *how* they earn their living. The public never sees Morgan making money or Ford making cars; but it does see Robert Taylor making faces. The visual evidence of the films offers the waitress a chance to compare herself to the movie queen; it gives the shoe clerk a chance to match himself against the matinée idols. It provokes the thought, "Say, *I* could do that . . ." No other industry presents so simple an invitation to the ego.

It is difficult to know how a substantial segment of the American population can *not* hope, however feebly, to be among the blessed whom the magic hand of Hollywood plucks from obscurity. Let us take an imaginary Fanny Jones in any town in the United States. Her talents may be dismal, her features vegetable, her intelligence uninspired. Yet how plausible it is for her to muse, "It might happen to me." And why not? Is Fanny Jones freckled? She knows how easily the Westmores hide the freckles of Joan Crawford or Myrna Loy. Is Fanny Jones astigmatic? She knows that Norma Shearer has a slight squint. Does Fanny Jones lisp? She has read all about the fact that certain words are cut out of Kay Francis's scripts. Is Fanny Jones buck-toothed? They'll put enamel caps on her teeth. Is Fanny Jones short? They can photograph her on a box. Is Fanny Jones tall? They can put her leading man in a trench. Is her voice bad? "They" will change it. Is she fat? They'll put her on a diet. Is she thin? They'll fatten her up. Can Fanny Jones

act? Well! Can Hedy Lamarr? They'll teach her. All that Fanny
Jones really needs for a stab at glory is that elusive, indefinable
quality for which, she has read, movie producers are always
searching in palpitating desperation—"Personality." And Luck.

What fatal blemishes can the Fanny Joneses (or the John
Joneses, for that matter) actually admit which will preclude
them from the new Valhalla? Hollywood's wizards will coach
them, dress them, raise their eyebrows, straighten their teeth,
lift their bust lines, lower their coiffures. Brilliant directors,
writers, and producers will dedicate themselves solely to the
exploitation of hidden talents. The one thing that Fanny Jones
really needs for a chance at glory is—physiological cohesion,
the faculty of remaining intact before a camera. Yes, Fanny
Jones can continue to dream of a contract with RKO, a home
at Malibu Beach, and a shiny convertible with an automatic
top. For Fanny Jones can legitimately feel that all she needs is
—luck. The movie scout happening to stop for a malted at her
fountain. . . . The movie magnate happening to see her face
somewhere, sometime, somehow. . . .

The conclusive point is that these things do happen, and the
movie pages hammer them home to a world which never tires
of the Cinderella story. The Fanny Joneses know that less than
a year before scaling Parnassus, Dorothy Lamour was an eleva-
tor operator in a Chicago department store, Arleen Whelan
was a manicurist, Fred MacMurray was a saxophone player,
Frances Farmer was an usher in a Seattle theater. (This is only
the sketchiest catalogue of miracles.) And if Fanny Jones cannot possibly imagine herself stepping into the role of a Bette
Davis or a Carole Lombard, there are other "types" with which
she can identify herself: a Priscilla Lane, a Martha Raye, a
Zasu Pitts. The symbol roster of Hollywood offers refuge to the
plain and the ungainly, too. All Fanny Jones needs is—luck.

It is easy to understand why the public believes that movie

stars follow the Waitress-to-Movie-Queen pattern. It is interesting that the same stereotype is held for movie executives. In politics, business, or trade, the leading personalities are believed to have come up "the hard way." They are assumed to have labored in their field, served long apprenticeships, climbed the high ladder rung by rung. But the Hollywood producer is vaguely assumed to have jumped from a loft in Manhattan to a lodge in Brentwood in one fell swoop. If you say "Knudsen," the images which appear encompass the total career-line: immigrant boy, factory hand, machinist, foreman, and so on. If you say "Producer" the mind jumps from a humble beginning to a dazzling end—and all that took place in between is left blank. (But 47.1 percent of the movie producers have worked in Hollywood for fifteen or more years; 30.4 percent have worked in the film colony for twenty or more years; and the nature of their occupational backgrounds, the number and kinds of jobs they have held, are impressive.*) The fact that fame and fortune in the movies, unlike other industries, do come overnight to the producer or star or director of a smash hit, reinforces faith in the omnipotence of chance. Hollywood means Luck.

The movies are one of the very few fields of enterprise left in America in which youth is promised high rewards, in which youth is, indeed, an advantage rather than a burden. Acting in films, unlike the theater, is one of the last professions in which inexperience is really of little account. The would-be movie star needs no capital, no training, no skill. (A reviewer once said of a famous movie actress: "She has two expressions—joy and indigestion.") The fortuitous arrangement of facial components may be enough to shoot a name onto the theater marquees. It is no wonder that Hollywood is a magnet which attracts hope.

* See the analysis of the professional experience of 144 Hollywood producers and executives, in chapter 12.

The first premise of our philosophy of education, and the *sine qua non* of our system of values, is that the rewards of our society go to those who have skill, make sacrifices, and behave soberly. Our culture is saturated with the dynamic attributes of what Max Weber called "the Protestant ethic": Work hard, be virtuous, and you will succeed. But our world, particularly in an era of crisis, does not fulfill these promises, and to the degree that our economy fails to reward those who try hard and train themselves and shun evil, the role of luck becomes increasingly important, and the individual becomes increasingly aware that luck is a crucial part of success. The very fact that opportunities have shrunk, that millions are caught in depressions as in an iron trap, that neither ability, intelligence, nor training seems to guarantee success any more—these make the role of luck more desperately cherished, more desperately invoked in fantasy or prayer. There is unconscious point to the dream of Hollywood which millions keep alive in their minds.

To Americans raised in the American tradition, faithful to the American concept of unbounded personal achievement, Hollywood is the last frontier. In the movie colony, as in the content of the movies themselves, romantic individualism, the most compelling idea in American history, has reached the apogee of its glory.

The lexicon of Hollywoodiana has grown fat and formidable; around the very concept of Hollywood there is woven a credo of what the movie colony is supposed to be.

"Nearly everyone in Hollywood has been divorced." But an analysis of 457 cases shows that 75.5 percent probably have never been divorced.

"Most of the *actors* in Hollywood have been married several times." But an analysis of 200 actors (excluding extras) shows that 64.5 percent probably have never been divorced.

"Hollywood is illiterate." But an analysis of 706 cases shows that 57.1 percent of the movie colony have gone to college.

"Hollywood's *producers* are illiterate." But an analysis of 121 producers and executives shows that 57 percent went to college, a higher percentage than movie directors (53.0) or movie actors (49.8).

"Movie producers come from Russia or Poland." But an analysis of 132 executives and producers shows that only 4.84 percent were born in Russia *and* Poland.

"Movie actors and actresses earn over $50,000 a year." But 80 percent of the actors (extras excluded) in Hollywood earn under $15,000 a year, and 45.1 percent earn less than $4,000.*

And so on.

This does not mean that the movie·makers are modestly rewarded, or rarely get divorced, or can be classed among the intelligentsia. They are prodigiously rewarded; they are more frequently divorced than America in general; and they are not intellectuals. But it does mean that popular impressions of Hollywood, sometimes correct and penetrating, are more often foolish and false.

There are historical reasons for the Hollywood legend, and they are enlightening. Hollywood has no official identity; since 1910 it has been a part of Los Angeles. Today only half of the motion picture studios are in Hollywood or Los Angeles; the rest, and by far the more important studios, are located within a radius of some fifteen miles.† Most of the laborers and craftsmen who work in the studios live in Los Angeles and Hollywood proper. But the overwhelming majority of producers, stars, directors, and writers—the high-priced levels of the industry—have long since moved away. Beverly Hills, Bel-Air, Brentwood, Holmby Hills, Van Nuys (in the San Fernando Valley), and

* The data given here are taken from later chapters, where they are analyzed in detail. Also see Appendices C, D, and E.

† The following studios are in Hollywood or Los Angeles proper: RKO, Paramount (which is planning new quarters elsewhere), Columbia, the United Artists group, and the independent "quickie" producers clustering around what is known as "Poverty Row." The huge Warner Brothers plant, Universal Pictures, and Disney Productions are about five miles north of Hollywood; the Twentieth Century-Fox lot is in West Los Angeles; Metro-Goldwyn-Mayer is in Culver City, several miles south of West Los Angeles, along with Hal Roach and Selznick Pictures.

Pacific Palisades are distinguished for their movie residents. Malibu Beach and Santa Monica, on the shores of the Pacific, are crowded with the homes of moviedom's elite. By "Hollywood" we shall mean all of these places, the social (rather than geographical) entity called the movie colony, the area in which the movie makers live and work.

A recent report of the Hollywood Coordinating Council of Social Service Agencies cast a paradoxical light on the community which is officially Hollywood, and which most visitors think is the heart of the movie colony.

Perhaps the most interesting thing [about the Hollywood district] is the difference between popular impression regarding its characteristics and the actual facts. Given a newspaper reputation as a place of gaiety and dissipation it has the lowest crime rate and very nearly the lowest juvenile delinquency rate of any district in the city. Looked upon as the home of "glamorous" moving picture people, the greater part of the population is of a very conservative home-owning type.[12]

But the lurid reputation of Hollywood persists. Let us see how it arose, and let us see what part the movie colony played in the exotic story.

The California gold rush, in the middle of the nineteenth century, brought a mob of miners, settlers, cowboys, gamblers, prostitutes, and desperadoes of various persuasions to the Golden State. For Los Angeles, the long pull of prosperity was climaxed some sixty years later, when a great boom hit the city, a boom which began in 1919 and has not yet abated.* It was a triple bonanza: the sensational flowering of the motion picture industry in Hollywood (where the first film had been shot in 1907), the discovery of oil at Long Beach, and the real-estate boom on every side. Fortunes were made overnight, and with the speculators, the oil men, and the real-estate promoters, another group came to the promised land—the old, the sick, and the middle-aged, largely from the Middle West, who came

* See Appendix A.

18

not to woo Mammon but to sit out their savings in the sun and die in the shadow of an annuity and an orange tree. A mighty publicity campaign—"Come to California!"—fixed millions of eyes on the state.

"Come to California!" was a slogan designed to appeal to people of means; it attracted the jobless and the rootless as well. It was warm in California, and cheaper to live; it was beautiful and new. Los Angeles was a young, growing city of daring promotion and reckless vision. It was a boom town *and* a playground. The tourists and the transients poured through the gates.

The hordes which flocked to Los Angeles included a generous assortment of the déclassé: hard men and easy women, adventurers, race-track touts, quacks and cranks of every delicate shape and hue. Confidence men exploited many who had come to retire; embezzlers fleeced many who had come to invest; "healers" fed on those who had come to recover; evangelists consoled those who had been betrayed. Yogi mystics and swami palm readers, occult fakirs and bold-faced fakers took hasty root in the City of the Angels, and they flourished. Gambling houses and racetracks sprang up to capitalize on the climate and a holiday public eager to reach for the brass ring. The crackpot reputation of the city grew, and this brought more of the unbalanced pouring into the town.

Now, what was said and thought of this fraternity of the foolish was said and thought of Hollywood. The distinction between the new Barbary Coast and the movie colony was not always kept clear. The movies, to be sure, attracted their own grotesque people and added them to the totem pole of Los Angeles culture. Hollywood was a magnet to characters in search of an offer. Strange people knocked on the studio gates, people with queer skills and odder personalities; from vaudeville there came midgets, hoofers, acrobats; from the circus there came bareback riders, elephant trainers, sword swallow-ers; and as the post-war depression of 1919 made jobs scarce throughout the land, fire-eaters, bird imitators, and tattooed females with pin-cushion husbands joined the throng which beat its way to Hollywood. The 1920s were the decade of the great migration.

The triple real-estate-oil-movie boom is said to have brought fifty thousand girls to Los Angeles in the ten years from 1919 to 1929.[18] To cope with the "girl problem" and all its social overtones, the civic fathers began to use California's vagrancy laws with determination, and rounded up the disreputables. An interesting thing happened; hundreds of men and women neatly foiled the law (which required that the suspected vagrant have either a certain amount of cash or a confirmable occupation) by announcing to police sergeants, in firm and righteous tones, that their occupation was "movie extra." Some had been employed as extras—for a day or a week; most had not set foot within a studio gate. But they were recorded as "extras" in the police books, and the nation thrilled to tales of movie "stars" caught in raids on brothels or marijuana parties. "Hollywood," already a glowing and cosmic symbol, was drafted into the service of journalistic sensationalism; the name put an aura of glamour around what was more properly pathetic.

The gaudiness of the life which throbbed in Los Angeles was bruited around the world, and the yellow press regaled its devotees with lurid stories and cockeyed pictures. In justice to Los Angeles, it should be stated that the city never failed those with a mocking eye. It is still a city in which there are real-estate offices shaped like sphinx heads, restaurants built like ice-cream cones, and professional hermits who parade the business streets in whiskers and a loin cloth. It is easy to lampoon a city in which, not so long ago, the police were called out to destroy a wild coyote which had come down from the hills and was cavorting on one of Hollywood's busiest thoroughfares.

The Sunday supplements were enlivened by features on

"Hollywood's" cavalcade of lunacies. To readers whose own lives were drab and routinized, the stories of debauchery read like a contemporary Decameron. And what Hollywood lacked in indigenous eccentrics the country at large was happy to supply; recently the *polizei* rushed to the home of Lionel Barrymore to apprehend a young man from Kingston, Pennsylvania, camped on the front porch with this maxim engraved on his chest: "Movie stars are nuts."

The Mid-Westerners who came to Los Angeles to retire, and the tourists who visited it to relax, were awed by the carnival life of the city. They must have been disturbed by the garish houses and the glittering automobiles, by the abandon of the night clubs and the exhibitionism on the beaches—above all, by the loose and lavish use of money. A community populated entirely by entertainers is a ready-made target for hostility. The theatrical profession has always aroused suspicion in the breasts of the moral; acting is the Devil's game, and actors are children of evil.* Hollywood became a synonym for Sodom; the tourists saw sins, but not skills.

The movie colony by no means played Galahad to the Mephistopheles of Los Angeles. The picture people, young, flush with money, heady with fame, rebellious and self-indulgent by temperament, gave the world occasion for a sense of moral outrage. From about 1919 to 1924, the movie crowd went through a purple era. The legend made it monstrous.

In 1920 the idolized Mary Pickford divorced Owen Moore and married the idolized Douglas Fairbanks. This was transformed into a *cause célèbre* over which lips smacked in a thousand

---

* Hollywood also served as the scapegoat for traditional and familiar hostilities: of the rural for the cosmopolitan, for example. Note that the word "hypocrite" is derived from the Greek word for actor, *hypocrites* ("answerer"—the actor who answers the chorus). The enlightened Solon denounced Thespis, the founder of acting, on the grounds that playing roles is a form of public deceit and therefore an act of outright immorality. In Boston, the very word "theater" was iniquitous until a generation ago, and the social samurai finally found a way to patronize the playhouses by the euphemistic strategy of calling them "museums." [14]

21

hamlets. Countless citizens had obtained Nevada divorces without creating a national uproar; but the attorney general of Nevada, waiting until the two most popular actors in the universe were married, threatened to rescind the Pickford-Moore divorce on the ground that there had been "collusion and fraud," that America's Sweetheart had not been a *bona fide* resident of Nevada, and that both her divorce from Mr. Moore and her marriage to Mr. Fairbanks were, consequently, illegal. The attorney general won world-wide publicity for himself and Reno; the charges died a feeble natural death.[15]

In 1921 the famous Roscoe ("Fatty") Arbuckle case, involving the death of an inconspicuous lady named Virginia Rappe after an "orgy" in San Francisco, exploded in the national headlines.* And then the death, through "dope," of Wallace Reid, the mysterious demise of movie director William Desmond Taylor (1922), the suicide of Olive Thomas in Paris, and a score of lesser *contretemps* followed one another in breathtaking succession. Hollywood's disrepute echoed throughout the world.

Platoons of scandalmongers descended on the movie capital. Silly escapades were inflated into dark orgies; beautiful maidens were ruined in job lots; oceanic amounts of alcohol were supposedly consumed every hour; and dope addiction, it was implied, was almost as common as rheumatism. As the Arbuckle, Reid, and Taylor material ran short, photogenic and obscure "actresses" were hurled onto the front pages with their individual improprieties presented as evidence of communal licentiousness. The activities of the ladies who had flocked to Los Angeles for non-movie purposes served as added grist. for the mill of horror. "Sensational free-lance writers [proclaimed] 'Three beautiful film stars were arrested in a bawdy house,' or, 'A beautiful screen star was in a shooting in a wild gin party.' In very

---

* According to those who have first-hand information on this celebrated matter, Miss Rappe died from a chronic pelvic illness.[16]

22

few of these instances were important personalities involved." [17]
Every actor, producer, director, and writer in Hollywood was
under latent suspicion. There was in this inquisition as much
extravagance as there had been in the prior adulation.

The attack on Hollywood's morals was deliberately abetted
by European propaganda. This is an important point which is
rarely understood. Hollywood was the target of allegations initiated in European countries by European manufacturers, film
producers, and government agencies. The motion picture interests of Europe were eager to rebuild their own industry
after the first World War, during which their production all
but shut down, and they had to break the near-monopoly of
American films on their own and the world market. Foreign
manufacturers, on the other hand, discovered that American
radios, furniture, typewriters, automobiles, and styles were making vigorous inroads in European markets because Frenchmen,
Germans, Italians, and Englishmen saw American merchandise
amid the photographic glamour of Hollywood's films, and came
out of the movie houses with pronounced pro-American tastes.
European business cried out for help against the new Yankee
threat, and certain government press bureaus instituted an ingenious campaign against American pictures (and merchandise) by castigating Hollywood's morals.[18] This oblique attack
was especially forceful in countries with large Catholic or
Lutheran populations; and where this failed, it was charged that
the insidious American businessmen were plotting to corner
international trade by putting their merchandise into Hollywood's movies and pushing the movies into the fatherlands of
the world like Trojan horses.

The temper and thrust of post-war America helped the di-
abolizing process. The notorious "freedom" of *post-bellum* art
and literature was expressed in sexy plays, books, and songs
which swept the world and shocked the elders. It was not surprising that the movies, a medium particularly dependent on

mass appeal, ground out a succession of films which left little to the imagination and less to their credit. The obloquy of Hollywood was reinforced by the movies it made.

From 1920 to 1922 the ministers, priests, rabbis, educators, clubwomen, and reformers of America joined in an attack which rocked the film industry. Resolutions condemning sinfulness in films were passed by the Southern Baptist Conference, the Central Conference of American Rabbis, the General Federation of Women's Clubs, and Roman Catholic, Episcopalian, Methodist, and Christian Endeavor organizations.[19] During 1921 alone, nearly one hundred censorship bills were introduced in thirty-seven states, and were defeated in thirty-three of them.*

In 1922, as a consequence of the mounting pressure and after the producers themselves had failed in earlier efforts to clean up the films,† the Motion Picture Producers and Distributors of America was set up. Will Hays, chairman of the Republican National Committee and Postmaster General in the Harding administration, was made president of this organization, which soon became known as the "Hays office," under a contract which placed his salary at $100,000 a year and was later revised to give him $150,000 a year.[20] The movie colony and moving pictures became the objects of an organized, long-range clean-up.

Hollywood's producers hired detectives to investigate their studios and their employees. For weeks the private life of the movie colony was converted into secret operatives' reports. The results were, on the whole, disappointing. Relatively few first-rank actors, producers, or directors were discovered to be practicing vices different enough from those of the public at large

---

* In Congress, Senator Gore and Representative Herrold introduced a bill which aimed to prohibit the shipment and exhibition of films in which "ex-convicts, desperadoes, bandits, train robbers, bank robbers, or outlaws" appeared. Representative Appleby sponsored a bill which aimed to create a federal motion picture commission to pass on all pictures involved in interstate commerce. Both measures were defeated.[21]

† Notably the National Association of the Motion Picture Industry, which adopted, on March 5, 1921, a 13-point code of morals for films.

to call for drastic measures. Benjamin B. Hampton, the most cogent chronicler of the motion picture industry, estimates that perhaps half a dozen persons "addicted to wild parties" disappeared from pictures.[22] This writer considers the figure too conservative.

The rolls of the movie extras were combed to eliminate ladies of flexible virtue. The Central Casting Bureau and the Call Bureau were established to systematize casting practices, and reduced individual temptations. Certain thespians given to homosexuality slipped from the scene. Certain romances were translated into marriage under pressure from the producers. Conspicuous black sheep were fired, suspended, or given ultimata for reform. "Morals clauses," under which the studios could discharge an employee at the first hint of moral dereliction, were written into all contracts and used as weapons at the first premonition of scandal. The virtues and profits of probity were extolled by studio officials in long, moist appeals to reason. For the first time in Hollywood's history, notoriety became a liability instead of an asset. Discretion became the order of the day when sin and earnings were formally divorced.

Good behavior was enforced, in general, by the merciless lens of the movie camera, which invariably records the telltale lines left by vice, bad habits, or even such carelessness as over-eating. Ambition and business prudence have made the Los Angeles movie colony a class of careful people who hesitate before doing anything that may reduce their earning power.[23]

The props to Hollywood's disrepute were being knocked away. The days of large-scale moral abandonment were at an end. But the legend lived on.

The mad, gaudy days of Hollywood have passed their peak. There is an increased seriousness in the movie colony, and an approximation of dignity. The actors are more versed in their art and less flamboyant in their deportment. The writers are studying their craft, and becoming less defensive about their profession. The directors have passed through the megaphone-and-temper state, and seek recognition for their talents rather than their recklessness. The executives and producers are less indulgent of charlatans, and although efficiency is still a baffling and distant dream, there is a growing intolerance of that extravagance which has neither taste nor point. All through Hollywood there is a rising sense of craftsmanship, a mounting appreciation of merit rather than pretension, an urge and a search for integrity.

The movies, Howard Barnes once said, are "the sleeping giant of the arts." The community which in less than two years gave birth to *Fantasia, Citizen Kane, The Grapes of Wrath, Wuthering Heights, Abe Lincoln in Illinois, Our Town, Rebecca, Gone With the Wind, Dr. Ehrlich's Magic Bullet,* and *The Long Voyage Home* need not be unduly apologetic about its output.* It is worth notice that when we think of Hollywood we tend to think of its *worst* movie product, or of the typical. But when we think of books or magazines, plays or paintings, we recall only the distinguished; we have forgotten the malodorous. The fascination of the movies as a medium is so potent that those of us who would not think of reading a Faith Baldwin novel, for example, do not hesitate to see movies based on Faith Baldwin novels. The people who read the *Atlantic Monthly* also see the Marx brothers' pictures; but how many of the people who see the Marx brothers read anything above the level of *True Confessions?* The history of an art is the history of its masters; it is not a history of its bunglers. If the movies were judged with similar criteria we would understand why the historians of the year 2000 may well write: "In the 1940s, Hollywood experienced a renaissance. Such films as *Citizen Kane, The Grapes of Wrath, Our Town.* . . ."

* Five of the books and plays from which these movies were made were the work of Pulitzer Prize authors; three were original stories written for the screen.

The eight major studios in Hollywood produced 376 pictures in 1939. In the same year only 1,133 new books of fiction were published in the United States.[24] It takes one writer and a modest printing establishment to bring a book to the public. It takes no less than 276 major arts and crafts to make a movie, and the costs are staggering. (Though here again the legend, which has it that most pictures cost a million dollars apiece, is misleading.) Six major studios in Hollywood opened their picture-cost records to this writer; an analysis showed that the 251 movies made by these studios in a typical year fell into the following pattern:

Picture Costs	Number of Pictures	Percent of Total
Over $1,000,000	19	7.6
$500,000-$1,000,000	60	23.9
$250,000-$500,000	40	15.9
Under $250,000	132	52.6
	251	100.0

In other words, almost a third of the movies cost over a half million dollars each, and only half of Hollywood's films cost under a quarter million dollars apiece.*

Costs of such magnitude are possible only because Hollywood commands the patronage of a stupendous number of ticket buyers. Hollywood must continue to satisfy and aim at an audience, in the United States alone, of more than 50,000,000 people a week. (Or it should reduce its costs beyond recognition, which would mean revolutionizing the star system and the production system, and abandoning the ferocious competition for talent and stories—at which point the Department of Justice might step in.) An audience of this gigantic size means that, unlike book publishers or magazine editors or play producers, Hollywood must appeal to mentalities ranging from six

* The six studios were Loew's Incorporated (MGM), Twentieth Century-Fox, Warner Brothers, RKO Radio, Universal Pictures, Columbia. Data are for 1938. For a more complete list of production costs see Appendix B.

to sixty, from stevedores to seminary students, from barmaids to dowagers.*

If we contemplate the tastes and the pressures of a market so immense and so variegated, Hollywood's problems become clearer. The total output of movies certainly does not stand comparison with the total output of the Theater Guild or the publishing houses on Madison Avenue. But the total output of movies certainly does not suffer by comparison with the total output of popular magazines. It is certainly superior to the quality of comic strips. As for the radio, it is for the reader to decide whether the average movie is more banal than the average radio program. Hollywood is geared to a mass market, yet it cannot employ the *methods* of mass production. Each picture is a different picture and presents unique demands; those who say that movies are merely variations of Boy meets Girl, Boy loses Girl, Boy gets Girl would not suggest that symphonies are merely rearrangements of the same noises.

If for no other reason than the magnitude of the economic stakes involved, the Hollywood of the legend was doomed. Hollywood had to produce thousands of pictures for millions of people in dozens of lands. You can't run a factory, or even a studio, in a three-ring circus operated by the Ritz brothers. The movie colony was affected by the requirements of the motion picture industry. The manufacture of movies substituted the problem of selling a commodity for the problem of "having wonderful time." Hollywood was forced—more or less—to shift its attention from the Arabian Nights to Dun and Bradstreet. The search for pleasure gave priority, if not way, to the pursuit of box-office receipts.

Hollywood still boasts an abundance of egomaniacs, buffoons, semi-literates, and persons of surpassing obnoxiousness. Its life

* In a speech delivered to the Authors' League conference in 1941 R. C. Sherriff, author of *Journey's End,* said that his play, which ran for a year and a half to packed houses, would have had to run thirty years to reach the number of people which the movie reached.

is still syncopated. The inanities of movie production could still fill a hilarious volume. The malicious can select facts and anecdotes to lend verity to even the more outlandish yarns about Hollywood, and the visitor can quote producer-malapropisms which recall Renan's quip about the proud families of French society: "Their ignorance gives one a rough sense of the infinite."

There is the producer who walks around his office with his shoes off, and insists that in the movies every time a husband comes home he must kiss his wife on the forehead "or else the audience won't believe they're married."

There is the titan who declared that a melodrama "has to be full of airplanes." ("Before the airplane was invented, a melodrama had to be full of automobiles.")

There is the man who judged all stories by their resemblance to his ideal tale: "A story about two brothers in love with the same girl, or two sisters in love with the same boy."

There is the philosopher who insisted, "You can't do pictures about married people. Married people don't like them, and single people don't want their illusions broken."

There is the executive who spent $20,000 preparing to re-shoot an entire scene because one of the characters used the word "din": "The public won't understand the word 'din.'"

There is the producer who, when told that a set would cost $40,000, lamented: "Forty thousand here—forty thousand there. Say, it adds up!"

And there are the other kind: men of great insight and occasional wit, men with an instinct for what is dramatically true, men with an urgency to put their visions on the screen.

The judicious, in search of truths wider than the latest tidbit about Hollywood's folly, would agree with Douglas Churchill of the New York *Times:*

. . . there is much in the town to command respect. For every ten knaves and fools there is an artisan of unexcelled competence. Certainly Hollywood is over-run with characters . . . who create as ridiculous a pageant as is available to the American eye, and certainly they predominate. But those producers, writers, directors, performers, photographers, publicists, make-up artists, and members of a hundred other crafts who are skilled and who are responsible for the best that is on the screen are earnest, talented men and women who would stand out in any company. They are in the minority and those who are rascals and posers dominate the scene—a condition that accounts for the industry's reputation.[25]

The chapters which follow are something of a postmortem, for they deal with the movie colony in 1938-41. That was, perhaps, the end of Hollywood's lush and profligate period; it was, perhaps, the last dramatic manifestation of a lush and profligate world. Hollywood today is uncertain and insecure because it senses the approach, if not the shape, of things to come.

Most of the foreign markets are gone, and in the countries where Hollywood's movies are not *verboten* the revenues of American film companies are frozen and impounded. The costs of making movies have risen so sharply and have reached so insupportable a level that surgical operations are in the offing.* The salaries of movie stars and producers, directors and writers, have reached a summit from which there is only descent. The onslaught of taxes will tear larger and larger gaps in Hollywood's estate. The enforcement of the anti-trust laws has already challenged—although in a compromise consent decree— the old structure of guaranteed markets and trade agreements which for years cushioned the eight major movie companies against the consequences of their failures. The rise in Hollywood of executives trained not in movie production but in theaters and movie exhibition is an omen of the future. The place and strength of the talent guilds (actors, directors, writ-

* In 1921 Hollywood's total production costs were $77,397,000; by 1937 they had risen to $197,741,000. The average cost per picture, at one studio whose records were analyzed, was $488,063 in 1934; four years later, the average cost per picture was $715,634.[26] More figures will be found in Appendix B.

ers) and the unions will recast Hollywood's employee-employer relations and labor policies. The internal crises which grip motion picture corporations must one day hit some of the personnel and most of the canons of movie making. The number of pictures being manufactured in Hollywood is so wasteful that, when double-features disappear (as they will), violent unemployment will run a scythe through the ranks of the movie makers.*

The historical repercussions of the New Deal will be felt in Hollywood, no less than in other areas of our land, through the impersonal operation of the law and through the cumulative pressures of a public opinion geared to the expectation of new equities in the distribution of security, wealth, and prestige. The legacy of World War II must profoundly affect the world in which we live, and Hollywood (to the perennial surprise of some of its inhabitants) is but a small part of that world. Only the shortsighted or the hopelessly naive can believe that the Hollywood which we are about to explore will continue in the tradition and the spirit of the Hollywood that is already a legend.

* In 1936 there were 20,000 extras in Hollywood; in 1937 there were 11,000 extras; on August 5, 1940, there were 6,534 extras in the Screen Actors Guild (and therefore in Hollywood) after 2,000 extras had been dropped from the rolls of the Guild because they were ninety days or more delinquent in their dues, which come to five cents a day.[27]

31

2. THE MOVIE COLONY

THE dazzling spotlight which Hollywood turns upon its Personalities throws into shadow the thousands who work in the movie studios—technicians and craftsmen, musicians and sound engineers, painters, carpenters, laboratory workers. These, plus the thousands of extras whose faces are used in an agglomerate mass, are the anonymous people who swarm over the sound stages, the lots, and the offices wherever pictures are fabricated. They are movie workers, as distinguished from what we shall call movie makers.

The movie workers lead ordinary lives; they live in middle-class homes or apartments; their incomes are sometimes higher and often lower than those of their relatives in Cleveland or St. Paul.* They go to church, play golf, crowd the beaches. They are no more or no less attractive, secure, or neurotic than America at large. They are never seen at the fashionable night clubs or restaurants. They never set foot in the majestic homes.

* Annual earnings (1938) of the following groups averaged:

2,906	carpenters	$1,066	533 sound men (all classes)	$2,919
1,695	electrical operators	1,575	299 wardrobe people	1,255
1,312	"grips"	1,738	278 still photographers	2,347
957	painters	1,426	136 hair-dressers and	
948	prop makers	1,215	make-up appliers	3,477

And so on. Furthermore, in 1940 only 3.1 percent of the extras *who were employed* averaged $150 or more a month; only 9 extras earned $2,500-$3,000; only 45 earned $2,000-$2,500; 579 received $1,000-$2,000; the rest earned less than $1,000 each.[1]

They may affect the manners and the superlatives of Hollywood's elite, but they are not a part of the Hollywood which is the symbol of affluence and allure. They may boast of their proximity to the gods, bask in reflected glory, or cherish their identification with the fabled world of the screen. But they enjoy no social status within the movie colony, and they have no individual identity to the world beyond. They are in Hollywood, but they are not of Hollywood.

Hollywood is composed of three concentric circles. The largest circle embraces all of the thirty thousand movie workers and movie makers; the middle circle encompasses the movie makers alone ("the movie colony"), the producers, actors, directors, and writers who participate in Hollywood's social and professional life; and the smallest circle, the one at the center of power and prestige, encloses the movie elite, some two hundred and fifty persons who, to set an arbitrary but useful index, earn $75,000 or more a year.

This book will say little about the great mass of movie workers. It is chiefly the producers, actors, directors, and writers of Hollywood who will occupy our attention. For it is they who shape Hollywood's profile and set its values; it is they who create the content and the implications of the films. They earn the high salaries; they enjoy the most prestige; they are an integral part of the professional order and the social life of the movie colony. In the next chapter we shall concentrate on Hollywood's elite; in this chapter let us examine the movie colony.

It is often said that Hollywood has no sense of reality, and spins its fables in some Nirvana out of space and time. One of the less original aphorisms with which we are all familiar is, "Hollywood is only a state of mind." Hollywood is in the southwestern nook of the United States, only a hundred odd miles from Mexico. But it is 2,741 miles from Washington, 2,901 miles from New York, 2,219 miles from Chicago, 1,925 miles from St. Louis, 1,938 miles from New Orleans.

These are not simply figures; they are signs of psychological as well as geographical distance. The climate of Hollywood is like that of Capri or the Riviera, not the East or the South or the Middle West; and the mental climate complements the weather. Upheavals in Washington, droughts in Kansas, convulsions in Wall Street, seem muffled and remote in a town where the sun is felicitous and the houses are brightly colored, a town where the daily energy is exhausted in slashing at the Gordian knot of a fictitious Story. The Los Angeles papers offer scanty international news compared with the newspapers of the East, and New York newspapers and national political journals arrive in Hollywood four to five days late. Even the radio is less immediate in its impact; some national programs do not come through at all; others are rebroadcast from disks at inconvenient hours. The salubrious climate and the pervading sense of isolation led one melancholy screen writer to say, "Hollywood is a warm Siberia."

There are other reasons for the antipodean character of the movie colony. Hollywood is a one-industry town. Its people sleep, eat, talk, and think movies. They are engaged in the creation of symbols rather than of material goods. Movie making is one prolonged, involuted fantasy. It is often said that the movies are an escape for the masses; it is rarely suggested that they are also an escape for the movie makers. When a movie producer or actor, director or writer, goes to sleep he leaves the world of fantasy and enters the world of reality.

It is stories, roles, dramatic artifices, which tyrannize Hollywood's attention, not goods or crops or machines. And this preoccupation with the fanciful must tend to blur perceptions of the real. To personalities lost in fantasy, reality passes through a distorted receiver; either it ceases to seem as threatening as it ought to, as in the case of children, or it becomes absurdly ominous, as in the case of psychotics. In either case, the real world—of men and things and events—loses its proper proportion and becomes exaggerated at an extreme. The singular anxiety of some of the movie makers, and the singular indifferentism of others, are end points on Hollywood's psychological horizon. If Hollywood is a community of people who work and live in fantasy, then it is to be expected that their life should take on the attributes of the fantastic. The greater wonder, one visitor exclaimed to this writer, is that Hollywood is sane.

The movie colony's intense engrossment in its work gives Hollywood a feverish, self-fascinated quality, and lends a despotic priority to its own values. This can be illustrated by a few classic examples. When Tom Mooney was released from San Quentin—an event which was front-page news on the seven continents—a columnist in the *Hollywood Reporter* solemnly announced: "The labor activities of Tom Mooney have very likely cost him a picture contract." [2] When Mussolini's legions marched into Ethiopia and the world waited for the League of Nations to act, a producer was asked by a breathless friend, "Have you heard any late news?" To which that child of Hollywood replied hotly, "Italy just banned *Marie Antoinette!*" And in the week in which Mussolini raped Albania, Louella Parsons, correspondent for all the Hearst papers and dean of Hollywood's gossip writers, began one of her extraordinary columns: "The deadly dullness of the past week was lifted today when Darryl Zanuck announced he had bought all rights to *The Bluebird* for Shirley Temple." *

Let us examine this escapist haven more closely.

* Miss Parsons, called by one commentator "the most consistently inaccurate reporter who ever lived to draw $600 a week," announced on various occasions that RKO was in the process of negotiating with W. H. Hudson to do a screen version of *Green Mansions;* that Paramount intended to remake *Peter Ibbetson,* "by Henrik Ibsen"; and that D'Annunzio's inamorata was a famous Italian actress named Il Duse. She (Miss Parsons) once burst into verse in her column with this line: "Oh, to be in England now that it's May," and lightly corrected the *faux pas* the next day by writing: "Oh, to be in England now that May is here." [3]

Hollywood is young. The movie colony itself is barely thirty years old, and its people are young—not as young as the public seems to think, or as the publicity would have it. But compared with other industries or professional groups, Hollywood would probably show a marked youthfulness. An analysis of 707 cases * showed that 46.2 percent of the movie colony are under 40 years of age; over a third are between 30 and 40. If we break the data into groups, we find:

Producers: Over a fourth are under 40; over half (52.6 percent) are under 45; three-fourths are under 50. The median average age is 43.

Directors: Over a third are under 40; over two-thirds are under 45; less than a tenth are 50 or over. The median age is 42.

Actors: Almost a third are under 35; 37.6 percent of the actresses are under 30 and over a fifth are under 25. The median age for actresses is 34, for actors (including veteran "character" players) 46, for both, 42.

Writers: 31.7 percent are under 35, well over half (57.6 percent) are under 40; 70.9 percent are under 45, and 84.2 percent are under 50. The median age is 37.

Assistant Directors: Over a third are under 35; almost two-thirds are under 40. The median age is 37.

First Film Editors (cutters): Over 85 percent are under 45. The median age is 37.

There is more striking evidence of the role of youth in Hollywood. The history of the movie colony and the motion picture industry is crammed with the saga of "boy geniuses." Movie production at the studios, involving the millions of dollars that were cited earlier, is often placed in the hands of very young men. In few other industries are comparable power and freedom delivered into such callow (and gifted) hands. The late Irving Thalberg, for instance, was in his twenties when he began to soar through the movie firmament and was breaking precedents and box-office records before he was thirty. At 22, Darryl F. Zanuck was writing scenarios for Rin Tin Tin; but at 26 he be-

---

* 271 actors and actresses, 92 producers, 20 executives, 66 directors, 120 writers, 79 assistant directors, 41 first film editors, 18 directors of photography. See Appendix D.

came the head producer at the big Warner Brothers plant; and at 30 he was one of the most influential figures in Hollywood, tore up his $5,000-a-week contract, and within a year was put into the top production chair at Twentieth Century-Fox as vice-president. David O. Selznick was vice-president in charge of production at RKO when he was 29; he was a vice-president and producer at MGM when he was 31. Hal B. Wallis stepped into the chief executive-producer post at Warner Brothers when he was 32. Matthew Fox became assistant to the president of Universal when he was 29. Pandro Berman took over the reins at RKO when he was less than 32. And a 26-year-old like Garson Kanin directed top-flight pictures, the budgets for which were around $750,000. Youth is at a premium in Hollywood, and those who are not so young spend a conspicuous amount of effort in offering visible indications of their rejuvenescence.

The emphatic youthfulness of many of Hollywood's central personalities brings up a point which is not generally given the attention it deserves: The movie people—famous, pampered, rich—are very young to be so famous, so pampered, and so rich. Probably never in history has so immature a group been accorded such luster, such sanctions, and such incomes. "Youth on the prow, and Pleasure at the helm . . ."

Hollywood's wealth is first-generation wealth, possessed by people who have not inherited it, spent by people who have not been accustomed to handling it, earned as a reward for talent (or luck) rather than heritage. It is not surprising that the movie colony has not achieved stability or integration: it is too young, too new, and too uncertain. The people of the movie colony are characterized by showmanship, not breeding; glibness, not wisdom; audacity, not poise. Of Hollywood it might be written, as was written of the America of the 1880s, here is "a society that for the first time found its opportunities equal to its desires, a youthful society that accounted the world its oyster and wanted no restrictions laid on its will." [4]

37

In a professional community which is itself young, and whose population is weighted towards youth in its composition, one would expect optimism to flourish; and when the dominant industry in that community demands buoyant, creative types, then we would expect optimism to be at a maximum. Hollywood is optimistic. Hollywood demands optimism. Hollywood's restaurants, parties, and offices are characterized by much levity and verbal horseplay. Despite the perennial crises in the motion picture industry (labor strife, wholesale lay-offs, shrinking box-office receipts) Hollywood possesses a sense of insulation from the electrical displays of our economy.

To Hollywood, economic reversals seem to be but passing fevers. The long trend of the movie business has been one of phenomenal prosperity and expansion, with greater and greater profits to the industry and higher and higher rewards to most of its personnel.* The Hollywoodian therefore suspects that when a producer complains that business is not good he means that it isn't as superlatively good as he had hoped it would be, or that it isn't as good as it was last year (when it was unusually good), or that although it is fine at the moment it *may* get worse. And secretly, the producer generally does not believe his own lamentations either; his mind is focussed on a smash hit just around the corner.

"You've got to be an optimist to be in pictures," a New York film executive told this writer. "It is wild, unbeatable optimism that built the industry. The way Hollywood makes pictures and the fortunes they cost would terrify ordinary businessmen—but Hollywood makes profits. Enthusiasm pays huge dividends in the motion picture industry."

Wherever optimism is too conspicuous and too determined, the observer has reason to doubt its appearance. Along with the

---

* A studio such as MGM has made net earnings well over seven million dollars a year in each and every year from 1935 to the present date (1941). In one year, 1937, the net earnings were $14,334,000. See Appendix B.

insistent optimism, there is in Hollywood a vague, restless fear that "it can't go on," that the mighty structure is impermanent, that its foundations are unsound. From many choirs in the movie colony this uneasy refrain ascends: "It can't last. Pictures cost too much; producers get too much; actors ask too much; writers earn too much; directors make too much. It *can't* go on this way."

[Hollywood] is a serene principality on its surface, but one need not scratch deep to discover that it is afraid of its shadow, still more afraid of the shadow it casts upon the world's screens. Fear is behind its production code, a fear of giving offense which might, in turn, produce an offensive onslaught on the box-office. Fear is behind its players, writers, and directors—a fear that one bad picture will wipe out the memory of all their good ones. Fear is what makes [Hollywood] the unreal world that it is, fear far more than glamour, far more than wealth and beauty and the Southern California sunshine.[5]

Optimism and insecurity run through the movie colony side by side. This is no paradox, for optimism is often a narcotic to deaden anxiety, and in Hollywood anxiety serves as a restraint on excessive elation and as a kind of penance for extravagances of income, spending, conduct, or business operations. There seems to be an unconscious *need* for anxiety in the movie colony, and anxiety is provoked, nursed, and kept alive (note the popularity of gambling, for example) in a manner which suggests self-punishment for obscure and disturbing guilts.

Hollywood tries to resolve its anxieties by keeping other people anxious about the same things. It is for this reason that conclaves in the movie colony—whether at the Brown Derby or a Guild meeting—tend to keep attention focussed on a threatening future. "Something's going to crack up at MGM. . . . Such-and-such a studio is headed right for bankruptcy. . . . It can't last. . . ." These points help to explain the constant "suffering" of Hollywood, the morbidity and self-deprecation which the movie people cultivate—and, if you please, enjoy. Optimism

39

is the desideratum of Hollywood, but Cassandra is its prophet.

Hollywood's chronic dissatisfaction has impressed many visitors. The comedians want to play parts with social significance; the tragedians yearn for a chance at farce; the directors complain about their scripts; the writers fondle dreams of the Great American Novel. One columnist, impressed by Hollywood's variations on the lachrymose theme, exclaimed:

I doubt if any town in history ever had as many carpers, cry babies, belly-achers, and habitual self-pitiers as does this "gay and glittering" city of Hollywood. To tour a studio, one must wade through a sea of tears. My desk is piled high with letters, my telephone is kept buzzing with calls and my reception room is crowded with visitors—all with complaints. . . .[6]

There are many reasons for the perennial complaints, as we shall see. One of the most important is that dissatisfaction is inevitable in a place where there are *no fixed goals*. It is natural for the actress who earns $20,000 a year to envy the actress making $50,000, who envies the actress getting $100,000. In a community where one can make $350,000 a year, $75,000 is not especially impressive—either to the group or the self. Where there is no reasonable point at which to fix "success," where salaries are as well known and as widely discussed as they are in Hollywood, where the scale of rewards against which people measure their success and their prestige is so long and so extensible—there the ego suffers many rebuffs. In the movie colony, there are few places for the ego to rest in peace, except at the very top—and the top in Hollywood is very high. "In this town," one unhardened soul said, "I'm snubbed socially because I only get a thousand a week. That hurts."

The personalities who make pictures are impulsive, volatile, and creative. They always will be; movies can't be made by punch-press operators. And the fact that the movies, as a business, are exposed to a daily ballot of dimes and quarters means that the expectations of months can be smashed or galvanized by the box-office returns of a day. The vicissitudes of movie studios can be illustrated by a few striking examples:

The net earnings of Paramount skyrocketed 820 percent in one year (1935-36).

The net earnings of RKO plummeted 110 percent in one year (1938-39).

The *deficit* of Warner Brothers was $7,918,605 in 1931, and $14,095,054 in 1932; in 1935 the *net earnings* were $674,150; in 1936 they were $3,-177,313 (a jump of 371 percent); in 1937 they had jumped to $5,876,183, and in 1939 they had dropped to $1,741,000.*

The record of many movie individuals reflects the record of the motion picture companies. In Hollywood, men who have earned several thousand dollars a week can go unemployed for years. The writers of several pictures which won Academy Awards were not able to get jobs a week later. Actors who enjoy majestic salaries may become "box-office poison" before they quite understand what has happened. Mae West earned $326,-500 in one year, but found it difficult to get a contract the next. The late John Gilbert's career collapsed overnight, when sound pictures came in; so did Ramon Novarro's. Luise Rainer won two Academy Awards and the fame which attends them, then dropped out of movies because her drawing power had vanished. The rolls of the Motion Picture Relief Fund and of the Los Angeles bankruptcy courts are studded with once dazzling names.

There are few places in our economy where fluctuations in earnings and security can be as violent and unpredictable as they are in Hollywood. We have heard of the startling rapidity of movie success. (One actor, for example, received a weekly salary of $100 and earned $3,100 in 1928; the next year his salary jumped to $1,000 a week; and in 1939 he got $3,000 a week and earned $180,000 for the year.) But there are ample cases to

* See Appendix B.

illustrate the rapidity of the collapse of movie careers. Note the earnings of the following movie directors, for example: *

	1936	1937	1938
A.	$30,000	$75,000	none
B.	80,000	40,000	$7,000
C.	15,000	4,500	1,500
D.	63,000	42,000	none

The volatility of fortune in Hollywood subjects its personalities to a severe and persistent strain. "You're only as good as your last picture" is a by-word in the movie colony, and an hour after a picture is previewed the solemn consensus that "Griffiths is slipping" or "Rogers is through" races through the town. This is scarcely a climate conducive to psychological serenity or efficient digestion. The movies require creative—hence temperamental—personalities; the objective conditions of the business are hazardous; and the combination of an erratic milieu and quivering personalities intensifies the insecurity of both.

The pace is too swift, things change too fast, success and failure are too close together. You can't expect people to gait their lives to the pace of the world outside. Normally a man builds all his life; he may succeed, enjoy a few easy years, and then he is ready to retire. Here success may come overnight and vanish overnight. How can you have that happen and expect to find people living as they do elsewhere? [7]

The movie colony gets a curious satisfaction out of drumming these facts home—to itself. The stories which begin, "You see that man over there—the one in the shiny serge suit? Well, two years ago . . ." serve to remind the movie makers of the precarious foundation of their careers. The movie makers frighten themselves into caution. They also feel less frightened when they see someone more frightened. They also keep anxiety alive by their identification with the sad fate of others.

The reckless and flamboyant acts for which the movie makers are renowned betray their absymal insecurity. Bravado typifies

* The cases are taken from replies to questionnaires.

Hollywood, bravado in its publicity, its manners, its romances. And bravado is a revealing trait, for it is an attempt—like whistling in the dark—to cover up uncertainty. If Hollywood is afraid "It can't last . . ." then the defiant conduct and compulsive spending of the movie makers represent an effort to act as if it *will* last. The psychic game of "as if" is played by those who are haunted by a suspicion that their extraordinary fortune is unreal or undeserved, subject, in any event, to the caprices of luck; they act *as if* it will last. This kind of behavior is partly designed to negate doubt; it is also a form of magical thinking, an effort to make reality conform to wish. The bravado which is rooted in deep-seated fears drives the movie people to commit acts which, to the outsider, seem to defy the fates, and these are another manifestation of the effort to impress, to spur, to challenge the self: "Now that I've bought this big house (or built this big swimming pool), I'll *have* to do better work, I'll *have* to succeed, I'll *have* to get a higher salary and a long-term contract . . ."

Hollywood is famed for its "individuality" and "temperament," and these, too, spring from the bravado which shields the ego. There is a juvenile tone in the extremes to which the movie colony resorts in order to flaunt its individuality. One actor for years won attention by wearing a sweat shirt to formal parties. Another actor followed the quaint whim of driving to the studio in a cavalcade of seven Cadillacs, each chauffeured, and with a secretary, maid, hair-dresser, and trainer ensconced in station. The director who dresses like a cross between an African explorer and a polo player is familiar to the public. These puerilities are symptomatic of several things: the desire to attract attention and gain exhibitionistic gratification; the urge to "show them"; and the need to release the rebelliousness in which so many of Hollywood's personalities are steeped. The psychological protests of the movie colony are often expressed in the violation of unimportant customs—especially in garb and deportment. The movie makers are given to acts of pointless defiance—but the meaning is not to be found on the surface of their acts. Like children, who assume that age brings peace and maturity, the movie makers are disturbed when they discover that getting older does not mean getting more adult.

The movie makers are engaged in an endless search for deference—from the world, their colleagues, themselves. They seem to be lost in a long, unhappy effort to win respect from symbolic juries. The hunger for praise is marked in Hollywood, and the hunger for orientation amidst the confusion of the world. In an epoch charged with catastrophic crises and violent social change, the people who play the game of movie making are periodically overcome by the urge to "do something important." For Hollywood is plagued by a vague contempt for itself, a revulsion against the make-believe of its life and work. The movie makers always devalue what they have achieved, and continue to set greater and greater goals for their talents. This perennial dissatisfaction, this relentless comparison of what they are or what they are doing with utterly utopian desires heightens the discontent in which they are lost. People of this type are driven to surround themselves with a human and indulgent environment, because they demand constant response—to maintain their inner security and their professional output.

This helps to explain the profusion of "yes-men" in the movie colony. To say that "yes-men" are unnecessary in Hollywood is like saying that gondoliers are unnecessary in Venice. The "yes-men" are quite necessary to those executives and producers who cannot function without consistent admiration. The "yes-man" buttresses the ego and the confidence of his superiors; he shields them from doubt and indecision. The "yes-man" is not really superfluous; he is simply overpaid. There is a functional niche in Hollywood for those who carry the banner of confidence and forever cry: "Swell! That's great! It'll roll them in the aisles!" They may be wrong, and generally are; but they counterbalance the congenital uncertainty with which Hollywood's creators are cursed. They pour ebullience into those who cannot create without it.

Hollywood needs face-to-face stimulation. The movie colony is highly gregarious. The craving for company at almost every hour of day or night exposes the great loneliness which lives under Hollywood's façade of gaiety. The movie makers make a career out of their neuroses and their anxiety. They are overcome by depression when they are alone; hence they do not like to be alone. Anxiety, like misery, loves company.

Hollywood is exhibitionistic. Its mansions, its clothes, and its conduct are devices for conspicuous display. Now, exhibitionism is to be expected among actors, who earn their living in an occupation which maximizes vanity and is devoted to the exploitation of the self; and in a community dominated by actors —"every producer, director, or writer has a bit of the ham in him"—unconventionality becomes as common as ulcers. The picture people have created a milieu in which uniqueness thrives; they infect one another with their narcissism and with their exhibitionism. (Someone has said that the movie colony is governed by the rule of "an I for an I.") In Hollywood, which is populated by temperamental and egocentric personalities, the inhabitants exacerbate each other's abnormalities. In Rome, the Romans make Romans more Roman.

There is an amusing aspect to the devious ways in which exhibitionism rears its head in the movie colony. Movie stars cannot shop or walk down the street without precipitating a parade. They love this, on the whole, but they experience occasional irritation with their fishbowl fate and yearn for anonymity— partial anonymity, at least. One solution of the dilemma was found in the widespread use of sunglasses—but sunglasses with large white rims. These novel blinders concealed identity, but attracted attention. They identified the wearer as a movie star, but forbade recognition of which movie star it was. They were a triumph of conspicuous anonymity. White-rimmed sunglasses won special popularity in Hollywood because they served two powerful and contradictory forces with exquisite efficacy: they announced "Celebrity!" and simultaneously signaled "in search of privacy." When waitresses and extras took up the fad, Hollywood became a baffling sea of Celebrities Hiding Identity.

The movie colony is full of those who, lacking character, become characters. The California climate encourages exhibitionism, and a community full of actors is certain to be full of exhibitionists. In subtropical Hollywood, exhibitionism has free rein. The dress seen on Hollywood Boulevard, the Peacock Alley of the movie extras, is wondrous to behold. Fur coats are worn over lounging pajamas, slacks, or, so far as this author can judge, shorts. The girls, a species renowned for pretty faces and an astonishing resemblance to one another, affect colors in their coiffure which quite defy description. The movie men are alarmingly comfortable in slacks, scarves, and sandals, and specialize in jackets with shoulders which are a tribute to their tailors rather than their physiques.

Exhibitionism is by no means unique to Hollywood, though it is rampant and inescapable there. William James put it down as a postulate of human nature that "we have an innate propensity to get ourselves noticed, and noticed favorably, by our kind. No more fiendish punishment could be devised . . . than that one should be turned loose in society and remain absolutely unnoticed . . ." [8] (Modern psychiatrists hold that there is a period of "infantile exhibitionism" through which all of us—hermits as well as strip-teasers—pass.) In Hollywood, exhibitionism is simply more dramatic, conspicuous, and widespread than it is in, say, Fort Dodge.*

* When a banker buys a car, it is long, impressive, and black; when an actor buys a car, it is low, sleek, and colorific. The difference is symbolic; but the differences in tradition were not always so. The history of the *haute monde* of the Nineties is full of tales of glittering phaetons and brightly caparisoned lackeys. One

The Hollywood of today is popularly supposed to be a community of unconventionality, of individualism and of general personal freedom; just a gay, carefree lot of youngsters having a perpetual good time. But a glance beneath the surface of the gaiety soon convinces a careful observer that in Hollywood, as in other places, conformity rules with an iron hand. If you would be considered a part of it you must follow its customs; if the fashion is unconventional clothing you, too, must wear it or be thought of as a reactionary. . . . You must drive a costly car and live expensively or be condemned as unimportant or, worse yet, as reflecting upon the studio which pays you so generously. Above all, you must go to Sunday cocktail parties, particularly those given by prominent executives, where nothing is talked but shop and nothing is played but cards.[9]

Hollywood fosters and encourages exhibitionism: eccentric deportment makes excellent publicity. Publicity is, of course, good business in the world of entertainment, but the fanatical craving for publicity, to which so many of Hollywood's people are enslaved, suggests a *need* for self-dramatization. Not all the applause or attention of the outside world can sate the publicity-hunger of those possessed by implacable drives for self-dramatization. One producer admitted that he takes advertising in a certain trade paper in order to guarantee flattering comment. "Of course I pay for the praise—but a fellow likes to read nice things about himself in the papers."

The student of design is struck by the blurring of sex lines in the film colony's dress. Women's clothes are masculinized; men's clothes are feminized. The vogue for color in men's clothes (green trousers, orange sneakers, pastel neckerchiefs) and for masculinity in women's attire (slacks, tweeds, socks, shorts) lends an epicene quality to the garb of Hollywood. This applies to manners and language as well as dress. Hollywood uses "dear" and "darling" with a sanguine disregard of sex. The theatrical tradition has long encouraged the wholesale use

celebrated dowager wrote: "The most childish and insane ways of showing off met with the approval of Society . . . I recall seeing one matron driving down Bellevue Avenue in her Victoria. She had a monkey on each shoulder and a plump, well-washed pig on the seat beside her." [10]

of affectionate lingo—but "dear," "sweetheart," "darling," and "honey" are bandied about in Hollywood with a frequency which confirms the suspicion that jealousies are often cloaked in the phrases of flattery.

Hollywood talks and thinks in superlatives. Movie people do not "like" things; they are "mad about" them. They do not dislike things; they loathe or detest them. All phenomena, from filigree brooches to tidal earthquakes, can be marvelous, terrific, colossal, or stupendous—or, in reverse English, cute, cunning, or chic. In its language, as in its behavior, Hollywood reveals a strenuous effort to deny doubt, by self-induced elation. The excessive use of adjectives such as "terrific" or "sensational" sets a Gresham's Law to work as inexorably in vocabulary as it does in money—superlatives drive sobriety out of circulation. The revealing story is told of two movie producers meeting on the street: "How's your picture doing?" asked the first. "Excellent." "Only excellent? That's too bad!" *

Hollywood, it was said earlier, sleeps, eats, thinks, and talks movies. The remarkable point is that the chief concern in Hollywood is not movies, but making movies. Shop talk is paramount in the movie colony—and it is an intriguing topic, packed with amusing dilemmas and astonishing personalities. But almost no attention is paid to the film as an entity, a force, a factor in society. One explanation for this lies in the uneasiness which besets Hollywood wherever theories are involved. The movie makers work with hunches, not logic; they trade in impressions rather than analyses. It is natural that they court the intuitive

* Hollywood has a vocabulary of its own, and the argot is rich and expressive. *Flesh peddlers* and *ten percenters* are agents; *juicers* are electricians and *grips* are property men. *Switcheroo* denotes a change (switch) in plot structure; *double take* refers to the facial expressions which accompany delayed comprehension (a pleased smile, a pause, a sudden look of consternation). The vernacular of the trade journals is equally rich in abbreviation and ingenuity. *B.O.* means box-office; *biz* means business, and *pix* is shorthand for pictures. *Meggers* (from "megaphone") are directors. *Stinkeroo* refers to a flop and *smasheroo* to a hit. The classic headline, "Stix Nix Hix Pix," from *Variety* some years ago, announced, in its own way, that rural audiences were disinclined to patronize pictures of the unsophisticated genre.

and shun the systematic, for they are expert in the one and untutored in the other.

But there is another reason why the movie people like to talk of movie making and do not like to talk about movies. "Hollywood," one story editor remarked, "is sitting on a powder keg of talents and possibilities and the unrealized scope of the screen." The concentration on talk about making movies is, in part, a defense mechanism, an escape from a recognition of the enormous potentialities of the screen and therefore of the enormous *responsibilities* of the movie makers. Hollywood is a little afraid to face those responsibilities. So energy is used up in an endless elaboration of stories and problems which deal with the technique of picture-making, the curious impasses, the hilarious *culs de sacs,* the colorful clashes of temperaments. Hollywood is nervous about the power of the screen, because the movie makers are not sure how to use it.*

Where talk in Hollywood leaves the primary zone of shop talk, it is concerned with gossip and anecdotage. Conversation and gossip are synonymous in the movie colony. The salaries and feuds, plans and romances of all the generals and most of the lieutenants in the production army are manna to a town overrun with magpies and agog with news of contracts and kisses, options, droptions, careers, and debacles. A thousand tongues are loyal to the cause of rumor and for all the skepticism about the gossip columns, they are followed with more avidity and credence than anyone likes to admit.

The talk about pictures is endless, and picture talk is endlessly absorbing. After-dinner conversation and studio talk are very similar: story problems, production problems, new pictures, old pictures, what Goldwyn said and what Curtiz didn't, who is working where, the purge at Paramount, the shakeup at RKO, and—above all—who is doing what with, for, or to whom. No phrase is so common in Hollywood as the titillating "I heard

* See "Politics over Hollywood," chapter 6.

. . ." Gossip, in Hollywood as in Waco, is a disguised and sanctioned form of slander. Derogatory anecdotes, Hollywood's largest noncommercial export, compensate their purveyors for inferior status and power. Derisive stories and insinuating revelations are safety valves for envy and frustration. The movie people talk to each other about each other, and they infect each other with the sweet virus of rumor.

Most people in Hollywood tell a story well, and few other communities are as rich in story material. But the concentration on anecdotes serves to distract attention from more relevant—hence disturbing—social or interpersonal problems. A Hollywood party quickly resolves itself into a tournament of anecdotes, and the earnest competition in storytelling is heightened by those who *must* perform for deference, who depend upon plaudits for their sense of security, who interpret the social success of others as a rebuff to themselves.

Hollywood has the greatest collection of mimics on earth, and the actors have by no means a monopoly on the talent—as any conference with a producer, director, or writer will prove. Now, skill in mimicry is a revealing characteristic. Children practice mimicry as a means of playing "grown up"; they also use it as a device to master fears by imitating threatening objects. Adults who devote excessive energy to imitating seem to be driven by the urge to test themselves in other roles, other identities which may be more pleasing to the self than the protean personality which mimics usually possess. Mimicry, in children, ends when a definite identity is chosen for the self. Adults who prolong, cherish, and refine their talent for playing someone else are, we might say, still exploring the world to discover other characters they might like to be.

Our society stresses specialization, and frowns upon those who continue to postpone the acceptance of a functional identity for themselves. A striking thing about Hollywood is that it is full of so many characters in search of a character; they remain a combination of many. It is this which makes them seem insincere; it is this, in part, which makes them colorful, unpredictable, and "irrational." For here are adults who sustain their juvenility (and their creative fantasy), who lend their profession that infantilism which is so typical of the screen and the stage. Here are creators in search of a stable personality. Here are the rich in fantasy.

When Orson Welles (of whom someone said, "There, but for the grace of God, goes God") was first shown through a studio he exclaimed, "This is the biggest electric train any boy ever had!" The remark is acute and revealing. Movie making is a game; the movie makers play it with great zest and, as in all games, the players surrender to periodic impatience with the game's illusory significance. An interesting refrain runs through Hollywood: "This is a crazy business. It ruins your digestion. It undermines your self-respect. It drives you nuts. But I wouldn't be doing anything else for the world!" This hymn of woe, which might be dubbed the Hollywood Lament, always ends with an emphatic, "I wouldn't be doing anything else for the world!"

The movie makers love their work. The actors complain about their stories and their directors; the directors complain about the producers and the scripts; the producers complain about their directors and their writers; the writers complain about the producers, the directors, the actors, and the industry. But they all love making movies.* There is no tedium in making pictures, except for the repetitive "shooting" on sound stages. There is no serenity, either. Hollywood takes immense nervous energy

* The antagonisms of the movie makers, their complaints and suggestions, were analyzed from replies to questionnaires which contained several questions intended to encourage the expression of grievances: "What are your chief complaints about working as a [director, writer, etc.]?" "In what specific ways could your working relationship be improved?" For a discussion of complaints and suggestions, see chapters 12-15. For the occupational preferences of assistant directors, directors of photography, and film editors, see Appendix F.

out of those caught in the controlled delirium of movie making. Weeks of tension follow weeks of semi-indolence; there is no encompassing routine into which life can fall, no certain progression in which personalities can find long-range equilibrium.

The movie people cannot stay away from Hollywood without falling into boredom and uneasiness. Time and again a producer or a director will announce that he is going away for a six months' vacation—and is back in Hollywood within six weeks. The movie makers do not seem to be able to endure extended residence in the world outside the movie colony. This can be understood; what other environments are as indulgent as Hollywood's, or as variegated, or as distracting? What other places offer such exhilarating conflicts, such opportunities for self-dramatization? Where else are there so many aggressive people who by their hostility excuse counter-hostility? Where else can narcissism be so richly fed? "I always bragged of the fact that no second of those contained in the twenty-four hours ever passed but that the name of William Fox was on the screen, being exhibited in some theatre in some part of the world." [11] A movie director confessed: "When the credits dissolve on that screen and the music comes up and it says 'Directed by'—I get a lump in my throat."

The movie makers enjoy making movies and, for the most part, they like the jobs they hold. Sample comments from several hundred answers to questionnaires illustrate the point:

> I feel happier at directing than anything else.
> No two days are alike.
> I actually enjoy the work.
> Greatest medium of self-expression.
> Thrilling, exciting.
> Most creative of all branches.
> I love the work.

This presents a point of the utmost importance. Most Americans live in two separate universes, the world of work and the world of play. Our schools, our churches, stress the idea that play *follows* work, that work is something unpleasant which sanctions play. But in Hollywood the work is a form of play, and the people love their work, and they are paid handsomely for having fun. The movie makers are paid to dream their dreams and exploit their reveries. They are paid for doing things which other people would like to do without being paid. Is it any wonder that the movie makers are plagued by ambiguous guilts? In a society where work means sacrifice or the performance of distasteful routines, those who are rewarded for having fun may be expected to be ridden by remorse. And where the rewards are as high as they are in Hollywood, and, in addition, are coupled with adulation from the populace, the guilts would be all the greater. Is it for this reason that so many people in the movie colony jump at the chance to impress the listener with how hard they work? They seem to be defending themselves. They seem to be trying to convince themselves. They seem to think that no one believes that they do work hard; and they themselves, when they look at their bank books and their homes, their press clippings and their social calendars, can't believe that they worked *that* hard.

Love of work is especially noteworthy in a society in which work has become increasingly dull, routinized, and mechanistic. The best comment on the morale of the movie factories is that they have the atmosphere of a high-school dramatic club. The joy of craftsmanship, which characterized prefactory work and was swept away by the Industrial Revolution, still thrives in Hollywood's plants.* The movie maker gets personal attention and individual approbation; in few other fields are men so encouraged to "express yourself," in few other fields does the

* Even the carpenters, property men, and messenger boys get a certain amount of awe from their wives and friends because of their proximity to the wonders and demigods of the sound stage. Such envy is not accorded to most laborers in our society. Two union leaders told this writer that studio painters and electricians feel quite superior to painters and electricians in the Los Angeles locals.

ego receive such sustained and deferential rewards. Psychological income is high in Hollywood.

No one retires voluntarily in Hollywood. There is no precedent or expectancy that the attainment of a given age or a certain estate will be followed by professional retirement and a life of leisure. This is partly because of the absence of fixed goals, partly because movie making is forever fascinating, partly because the kind of people who make movies can never rest in the effort to prove their skill and potency to the world, and partly because the expiation of guilts is a lifelong proposition. Those who retire from Hollywood are forced to retire and those who have been forced out plan desperately to get back. In the movie colony, the champ never retires undefeated; if he did, everyone would say knowingly, "No wonder . . . he was going blind!"

The ex-romantic star tries character parts; the ex-glamour girl accepts matron roles; the producer organizes a small company; the director takes less attractive jobs. The simplest explanation is that the comparative inaction and anonymity of the world outside are intolerable after the exhilarating work and life of Hollywood. True enough—but there are more penetrating reasons. The movie makers depend upon praise for their inner security; they are driven by an urgency to keep on working; their need for testimonials to their talent is bottomless; their need for support to their ego is infinite; their need to remain preoccupied with problems outside themselves is ubiquitous. Hollywood is almost Japanese in the value it places upon "face," and saving face is a double-sided matter—the preservation of prestige in the eyes of the community, and the retention of a sense of value by the self.

So it is that the aging Adolph Zukor, once the most powerful man in films, and more recently relegated to positions of high-sounding vacuity, continues to fight for activity and power in the Paramount plant. Harold Lloyd, who could retire for life, produces pictures now that he has passed the apex of his popularity as a comedian. Gloria Swanson and Richard Barthelmess, after years of retirement and travel, have embarked on comeback careers. Mary Pickford continues to plan productions which she will finance, and yearns for a chance to act. Winfield Sheehan, once head of the Fox studio, drifts in and out of studios in secondary production capacities. Dozens of men and women in the movie colony who have ample money and fat scrapbooks cannot face the prospect of life outside the gratifying realm of movie making.

. . . no one ever retires on his laurels. . . . The minute that a man is no longer an active participant he loses all standing in the community and may even be taunted with the fact that he was once a big man. . . .

The only recognized, valid motivation . . . is the desire to succeed and to continue to succeed. A successful man must always continue the game, which is played for no fixed prize. Retirement is without honor, and means that such an individual is henceforth to be ignored as a nonentity. The whole of the social life is integrated into this one pattern; no field of social life is exempted from it.

This quotation, so pertinent to Hollywood, was written by Dr. Margaret Mead—about the Manus tribe in the Admiralty Islands.[12]

Hollywood is cosmopolitan. A random inspection of movie biographies disclosed actors from Tasmania, Brooklyn, Stockholm; directors from Pasadena, Tiflis, Sicily; writers from Budapest to Wapakoneta, Ohio; cameramen from China to New York; producers from Minsk to Wahoo, Nebraska. The largest collection of Indians outside of a government reservation is said to reside in Hollywood. On the social margins of the movie colony there are such fugitive groups as the Indian Actors Association, the Latin Writers Association, the Malayan-Filipino Club, the Chinese Screen Actors Association, the Hawaiian Actors Association and others.

The endless search for new faces and rare skills has brought people to Hollywood from the unnumbered places of the world. There are almost as many accents in Hollywood as in Shanghai, and the assemblage of skills surpasses the collection of nationalities. Within the circumference of the movie colony one has no difficulty in finding deep-sea divers, snake charmers, hog callers, dust manufacturers, walrus trainers, glass blowers, Cossacks, Yogis, Foreign Legionnaires, and so on and on.

The potency of "Hollywood" as a symbol of quick opportunities and lavish rewards, like the symbol of "America" a generation earlier, has become a giant magnet to the world. The stream of actors, technical advisers, movie hopefuls, and tourists, the swarm of new faces and new careers, the sporadic changes in personnel, give Hollywood (as Washington) the character of a hotel lobby. In the movie colony, everyone seems to be from somewhere else.

In the days of silent pictures, a foreign accent may have presented a problem on Broadway, but not in Hollywood. The dislocations of post-war Europe impelled many entertainers and movie technicians to migrate to Hollywood, and the catastrophic impact of Hitler over Europe drove hundreds of artists off the continent, to strike out for new careers in South and North America.

How large a proportion of the movie makers are foreign-born? An analysis of 555 cases (producers, actors, directors, writers) showed that 78.2 percent were born in the United States and 21.8 percent outside the United States.* (80.2 per-

* 221 actors and actresses, 132 producers and executives, 108 writers, 94 directors. The percentage of foreign-born whites 21 years old and over in the United States is 11.6. The 21.8 percent foreign-born of Hollywood's movie makers is a smaller proportion than the foreign-born whites in the following cities: Boston (29.4), Cambridge, Mass. (28.4), Waterbury, Conn. (27.8), Providence, R. I. (25.5), Detroit (25.5), San Francisco (24.2), Rockford, Ill. (21.2), and so on (1930 census figures).[13] But the concentration within one area, one profession, one general social group, and one field of identification, gives the movie colony a more cosmopolitan flavor than is found in the cities mentioned.

cent were born in the United States and Canada.) About a fifth of the four major skill groups in Hollywood, therefore, were born outside of the United States. Foreign birth does not, of course, imply alien status. Many of the movie makers who were born abroad, like many other Americans, came to the United States at a tender age and were raised and educated here. By countries, the origins of the movie makers are:

		Percent
United States		78.20
Great Britain and Dominions		12.25
Great Britain	7.03	
Canada	1.98	
Ireland	1.98	
Union of South Africa	.54	
Australia	.36	
India	.18	
British West Indies	.18	
Russia		2.53
Germany		1.98
Hungary		1.26
Austria		1.08
France		.72

Under one-half of one percent each: Sweden, Poland, Japan, Italy, China, Mexico, Norway.

The distribution of foreign-born among the four major groups offers a little surprise:

	Percent
Directors	28.7
Actors and actresses	25.3
Producers	17.4
Writers	13.9

The high proportion of movie directors of foreign birth is explicable by the fact that European directors were more expert and inventive than other film groups on the Continent; they found a readier market in Hollywood for their experience and skills. Besides, the director, unlike the actor or writer, needs little command of English; he works, as we shall see, with visual rather than verbal techniques.

It was Dorothy Parker who said, "Authors and actors and artists and such, never know nothing and never know much." The educational background of Hollywood presents another surprise to those who hold the impression of widespread illiteracy in the movie colony. An analysis of 706 cases,* ranging from executives and actors to film editors and cinematographers, showed:

57.1 percent went to college
38.5 percent went to high school but not to college
9.2 percent undertook postgraduate work beyond the four-year college level
4.4 percent did not go to high school

In later chapters we shall analyze the education of the various groups in the movie colony.

Hollywood is characterized by sudden wealth and sudden success; it is typified by brash personalities and assertive behavior; it seems dedicated to ostentation and self-indulgence.

With all the opulence and splendor of this city, there is very little good breeding to be found. I have not seen one real gentleman, one well-bred man, since I came to town. At their entertainments there is no conversation that is agreeable; there is no modesty, no attention to one another. They talk very loud, very fast, and all together.[14]

This statement, oddly enough, was not made of Hollywood. It was made by John Adams, second President of the United States, and he was referring to the Society of eighteenth-century New York. It is a particularly fitting quotation here, since it epitomizes the reaction of the Brahmin to persons who lack lineage and decorum. Hollywood—new, thriving, socially am-

* 251 actors and actresses, 121 producers and executives, 133 writers, 66 directors, 17 directors of photography, 79 assistant directors, 39 first film editors. For a breakdown by groups, see Appendix D.

bitious—lacks both. The disdain with which Hollywood is customarily regarded is, in its essence, similar to the scorn which Cabot Lodge cast upon the vulgarity and intellectual poverty of the elite of the Nineties. It is similar to the icy contempt which the patricians of Southampton held toward Newport (!) because that celebrated spa worshipped "cash rather than culture, arrogance rather than aristocracy." [15] The condescension with which the movie colony is generally discussed is, it would seem, a contemporary version of an ancient snobbery. Hollywood lacks urbanity. Its people are characterized by notoriety, not pedigree; its position rests on money, not birth; its fame depends on publicity, not ancestry. To paraphrase the words of a *grande dame* who despised the merchant princes of her day, Society represents a wealthy aristocracy, but Hollywood represents an aristocracy of wealth.

For Hollywood is *nouveau riche*. Its magnificos are young, untrained in the art of the good life, untempered by old codes of behavior. In the movie colony there is being formed an amusement-aristocracy, to use Miriam Beard's phrase, and Hollywood is assuming the social function of European royalty —"that of luxuriously diverting itself in public and diverting others . . . In such an elite, gradually enlarged and diversified . . . the people sees itself mirrored and seeks its models." [16]

3. THE MOVIE ELITE

THE movie colony is the high court of Hollywood; the movie elite is the regency council. An elite is that group, in any society, which possesses most of the wealth, exerts the preponderant influence, and enjoys maximum prestige. The leading producers, actors, directors and, to a lesser extent, writers, form Hollywood's elite. Any extended discussion of the movie capital must revolve around those who sit at the top of Hollywood's pyramid of income, power, and prestige. The upper ranks are highly mobile, accessible, and democratic. You are "in" when you occupy a certain position and make a certain amount of money; you are "out" as long as you don't. Buddy de Sylva was discharged from RKO in 1939, left Hollywood, produced three plays on Broadway, and returned to the movie colony as chief producer at Paramount in 1941. The portals are never bolted.

Hollywood's elite, we may say, consists of about 250 producers, executives, actors, directors, writers, publicity experts, and miscellaneous key men. If we were to take an annual income of $75,000 or more as our gauge, we should find a minimum of 200 persons in this impressive circle.*

Power is by no means jointly held by the 250, nor equally distributed among them. Five movie executives, for example, outweigh all of Hollywood's directors, writers, and stars in the

* See "The Big Money," chapter 4.

60

power of decision-making. The men who make up the Association of Motion Picture Producers (a California corporation nominally independent of the Hays office) are the monarchs of Hollywood's policy and practices with reference to movie production, labor disputes, wage scales, the guilds, the unions, and so on. An executive-producer such as Darryl F. Zanuck, Louis B. Mayer, Y. Frank Freeman, or Jack L. Warner controls the administration and policy of his studio with unmistakable authority. The circle of final and central control in Hollywood reflects the power structure of the motion picture industry at large. Suppose we glance at that structure, and those who enjoy cardinal authority in it.

The economists of the Temporary National Economic Committee, which was established by a resolution of the Seventy-fifth Congress to investigate the concentration of power in American business, concluded that the motion picture industry has grown "from an activity in the hands of a large number of small and financially weak individuals to an industry controlled by a few large companies which dominate its policies and control its actions." [1] Starting with the first groups which controlled patents on film equipment—Edison, Biograph, Vitagraph—power in the industry has gravitated toward a few huge organizations. Today, the empire of the screen is dominated by eight major organizations: The Big Five—Loew's, Inc. (of which Metro-Goldwyn-Mayer is the production subsidiary), Twentieth Century-Fox Film Corporation, Paramount Pictures, Inc., Warner Brothers Pictures, Inc., Radio-Keith-Orpheum (RKO) Corporation; and the Little Three—Universal Corporation, Columbia Pictures Corporation, and United Artists Corporation.

The eight major companies produce approximately eighty percent of the total production *value* of all the feature pictures made in the United States.* The Big Eight do a total volume of

* According to the *Motion Picture Almanac*, there were 74 companies purportedly engaged in the making of movies in 1940. But the Big Eight released (in addition

business (movie production, distribution, and exhibition) of almost half a billion dollars annually. For the past five years, the Big Eight have received 95 percent of all the rentals paid by the theaters of America for the exhibition of films (movies are not sold to the theaters, but rented out on a percentage basis); only 5 percent of all the film rentals in the United States did not go to the eight major companies.[2]

These data underline what is well known to all the movie makers, and to all who study the motion picture industry: The Big Eight dominate the making of movies; they dominate the distribution of movies; they dominate the exhibition of movies in theaters.[*] "The integration of the motion picture industry is complete," says the TNEC, "from the inception of an idea for a picture through to the actual exhibition of the film."[3]

How is power distributed within the hierarchy of the Big Eight? The answer is clear. Loew's Incorporated (total assets $168,618,000), which consists of approximately 123 subsidiary organizations in the amusement business, is king of the Big Eight and of the motion picture industry of America. For the past six years, Loew's net profits have ranged from 23.8 to 55 percent of the total net profits of seven of the eight major com-

to their own product) the films which 17 other companies made. 49 companies might be called independent motion picture producers. But only 4 of these 49 companies actually made and released movies—Monogram, Republic, Victory, and World Pictures Corporation; and of these only Republic Pictures can be considered a large motion picture organization.

[*] It is important to observe that the investment in exhibition (motion picture theaters, buildings, real estate, etc.) is far greater than the investment in the Hollywood studios which produce films. The following sums are invested in the three branches of the motion picture industry: exhibition, $1,880,000,000; studios, $112,000,000; distribution, $20,000,000. The Big Eight own about 2,800 theaters out of the 17,000 in the United States (16 percent); but these theaters are of critical importance. More than 80 percent of all the metropolitan first-run houses in the country are affiliated with the Big Eight. Out of 92 cities with a population of over 100,000, the Big Eight control exhibition in 73. The Big Eight and their affiliated exhibitors control movie exhibition in *all* cities in the United States with populations of over 1,000,000. As we shall see in a later volume, several motion picture companies are primarily in the real estate business; and they produce films in order to supply their immense theater structure with product.[4]

panies.* Second only to Loew's are three other companies; their potency may be seen in the following résumé of the movie business in 1939:

Loew's and Twentieth Century-Fox collected 71.61 percent of the total net earnings of seven of the eight major companies (United Artists excluded).

Loew's, Twentieth Century-Fox, and Paramount received 86.04 percent of the net profits.

Loew's, Twentieth Century-Fox, Paramount, and Warner Brothers received 95.15 percent of the net profits.

It would be expected that power and prestige in Hollywood, as in the motion picture industry at large, would revolve around the men who operate the four leading companies. That is the case. There can be no disagreement with the statement that the key people in Hollywood are found in the executive groups of the four companies which enjoy a prepotency of size and profitability: Louis B. Mayer and Edgar F. Mannix of Loew's (MGM); Y. Frank Freeman of Paramount; Darryl F. Zanuck and Joseph M. Schenck of Twentieth Century-Fox; Harry M. Warner and Jack L. Warner of Warner Brothers. Authority in the production apparatus of Hollywood is brought to a final focus in these men, and in their associates and satellites; the figures of secondary rank in Hollywood include George Schaefer of RKO, Samuel Goldwyn, Harry Cohn of Columbia. Other movie executives appear in the inner circle when and as needed, but they operate on the periphery of power, their position is marginal, and their influence is subordinate: Clifford Work

---

* Loew's Incorporated enjoyed net earnings of $9,538,000 in 1939—or 49.91 percent of the net earnings of seven of the eight major companies. (Figures on earnings for United Artists were not available.) In one year (1935) Loew's received 55 percent of the total profits. In 1939, Loew's did a total volume of business of $112,489,000—or 23.8 percent of the total volume of business of the Big Eight. And so on. Figures on the total assets, net profits, and total volume of business of the major motion picture companies will be found in Appendix B.

(Universal)', David O. Selznick, Hal E. Roach, Walter F. Wanger, and others.

Around this nucleus of executives and producers, organized as the Association of Motion Picture Producers, there is the larger elite of Hollywood—the ranking producers, actors and directors (plus a few writers) who earn the big money, enjoy high prestige, possess the "contacts," and occupy a place more or less near the center of gravity of power.

Hollywood's elite is racked by jealousies and torn by dissension. Suspicion, conflict, and hostility run through the town; power is jealously guarded and vigorously exercised. The struggle for hegemony on the upper levels (producers, executives) is carried on by men who have a phenomenal drive for power, a flair for dramatic collision, and a capacity for epic feuds. Implacable guerilla warfare has fashioned the history of the motion picture industry, and business collaborations which might have proved immensely profitable have been (and are) thwarted by vendettas which arose from the endless fight for power and the endless battle of egos. The movie colony hums with gossip about who is knifing whom, and the young in heart forever bewail the cannibalistic ethos of their elders. Frederick Lewis Allen made an observation on the financial oligarchy he called "The Lords of Creation" which applies with equal validity to Hollywood:

Ordinary trade agreements between business rivals on prices and on the division of markets were usually made only to be broken; as a big industrialist testified many years later, they often lasted only until one of the conferees could get to a telegraph office or a telephone. . . .[5]

It is not surprising that the virtue which is most often mentioned and courted in Hollywood is "loyalty." William C. DeMille (not Cecil B.) looked back upon his thirty years in the movie colony and wrote:

. . . when times are hard . . . everyone is asked to show his loyalty by accepting a salary cut. . . . I have heard one of the biggest [producers] speaking with tears in his eyes to a mass meeting of the studio personnel, begging them to help him tide the company over a financial stringency, and nobly offering to cut his own immense salary drastically. . . . When money was lopped off [the employees'] salaries it was gone forever, but when it was taken from the producer's weekly check in the same proportion, it finally came home to roost in the shape of profits and bonuses. In fact, if the producer had been able to achieve a fifty percent cut among the loyal comrades, he could easily have cut his own salary down to zero and, by so doing, very probably have tripled his yearly income. Still, his speech on loyalty, was extremely moving and, in its climax particularly, suggested the Gettysburg oration.[6]

Hollywood deplores the chicaneries of its overlords. Month after month, pleas for "co-operation" run through the trade papers and those periodic luncheons held to cement good will. Not the least wistful call for amity was an editorial by W. R. Wilkerson, publisher of the *Hollywood Reporter,* who broke a lance in the cause of "some kind of Moral Re-Armament here in the studios":

. . . a rearmament of work and play that will bring all creators closer together . . . [and give them] a more sympathetic attitude towards the success or failure of their fellow workers. . . . As it is, almost every studio hates the other; all are jealous of the success of the other; individuals gloat over the failure of their fellow-workers—even in their own studio. . . . Everyone is too self-centered; each striking out to stop the other.[7]

Hollywood's executives vow eternal friendship at frequent banquets, and each *Pax Romana* is heralded with moving oratory and unction. Then some cunning maneuver, some startling squeeze-play, some betrayal of a word solemnly given, sends heads shaking sadly all over the movie colony. Let us bear in mind that business perfidy is not a practice either invented by or confined to Hollywood. Adam Smith, in the very *Wealth of Nations* which became the philosophical foundation of the world's economy, warned his readers that commerce is "the most fertile source of discord and animosity"; he deplored "the impertinent jealousy of merchants and manufacturers . . . the mean rapacity, the monopolizing spirit . . ." [8]

In motion pictures, as in aviation or canned goods, the sheer momentum of competition leads to violent and enduring hostilities, and the very nature of competition fosters predatory tactics. Our economy has long encouraged what might be called the modified murder of competition. The strategy of most businesses —in Hollywood or in Jersey City—is closer to the laws of war than to the Sermon on the Mount.

In the race for profits one [is] driven to do the same tricks which the other man did or be beaten. In competitive business, bad practices tend to drive out the good. If I don't . . . Jones will. . . . We'd better get in there first. We can't afford to be squeamish. Business is business. In the memorable words of H. H. Rogers, "We are not in business for our health." [9]

It has been suggested, in an earlier chapter, that the affairs of finance and business are shrouded in mysterious and technical symbols. When one group of Wall Street operators squeezes another group to the wall, the methods employed are so intricate, and the facts so hidden from public view, that the personal aspects of the fight are concealed, and the drama remains unexploited. But when the movie magnates lock horns, it is on a figurative street corner; it is news, because they are colorful people, and they are quarreling over world-famous personalities, and the nature of their deadly schism can easily be written and understood.

Hollywood's feuds are scarcely *sui generis*, though Hollywood believes that the bitterness and intrigue of its maneuvers for power are peculiar to the motion picture industry. They are not. John Pierpont Morgan, for example, could neither coax nor force John D. Rockefeller and his allies into the amenities of co-operation; they fought to the end. The business *rapport* which existed between E. H. Harriman and Stuyvesant Fish was smashed partly because of a remark which Mamie Fish made about Mary Harriman at a tea party, and the board of the Illinois Central Railroad was treated to the enlightening spectacle of Harriman invading Fish's company in order to ruin him—so that he could avenge the affront his wife had suffered.[10] But in Hollywood the clash of personalities is better known, better publicized, and recorded with unequaled relish. Any gossip column is an archive on the tempests (mostly in a teapot) which rage among the elite of the movie capital.

It is of major importance to remember that many of the original promoters and pioneers of the screen are still active in Hollywood. And the men who laid the foundations of the industry were vigorous and unyielding. Respectable businessmen and respectable financiers shunned the movie infant for fifteen years; the movies were vulgar knickknacks, as all sensible people knew; they could never be more than a passing fad; they were cheap amusement, patronized only by the poor and the immigrant, the illiterate and the unwashed.

The men who built the motion picture industry (Fox, Laemmle, Zukor, Selig, Loew, Goldwyn, Lasky, Warner, Mayer) were not drawn from the supposedly farsighted ranks of American business. They came, instead, from the marginal and shabby zones of enterprise, from vaudeville, nickelodeon parlors, theatrical agencies, flea circuses, petty trade.* There were tough-minded, hardworking, aggressive men—rude in manner, quick in their hunches, with an instinct for ballyhoo and a genius for showmanship. They were men whose prototype was Phineas T. Barnum, whom Parrington described as "a vulgar, greasy

* This is a source of constant embarrassment to Hollywood. When you say Henry Ford was a garage mechanic you are paying him a compliment, but when you say a producer was a glove salesman you are hurling an insult. In no other industry is humble origin interpreted as a skeleton in the closet rather than a proof of admirable success.

genius, pure brass without any gilding, yet in picturesque and capable effrontery the very embodiment of the age." [11]

The movie pioneers were men of demoniacal energy and a striking variety of talents. They had brains, confidence, and a phenomenal capacity for work. William Fox, for example, who began in the motion picture business at the age of twenty-six with a capital of $1,600, who twenty-five years later was operating movie companies with assets well over $400,000,000, and who soon after was forced out of Hollywood entirely by investment groups, has made this illuminating confession:

> For more than thirty years I avoided carrying a watch. I never wanted to know what time it was. My day ended when my day's work was completed. Again and again, I didn't go to bed at all during the twenty-four hours. . . .
>
> I was acquainted with every story that was selected by my companies. I read every story they ever produced. I made suggestions in the majority of the stories produced by our companies. In the early years I wrote most of the scenarios. No picture ever produced by the Fox Film Corporation was permitted to be viewed by the general public, until every title it contained had been approved and passed by me. . . .
>
> I knew the condition of every nation we traded with. I knew the value of every currency of every nation we traded with. I thought I knew the politics of every nation we traded with.[12]

The first producer-executives were promoters and showmen; they combined the talents of craftsmen, impresarios, and circus barkers.* They did not cater to small, cultivated circles. They were sensitive to mass desires, for they were of the masses themselves. They had the virtues and the failings of pioneers. They were accused of being vulgar, and with justice; yet it was their very unrefinement which fitted them so perfectly for their function. As Bernard Shaw put it, "Universality of character is impossible without a shade of vulgarity." [13] It was the promoters and the showmen, not the graduates of proud preparatory

---

* Samuel Goldwyn once launched a personal campaign against bobbed hair, which he detested, by instructing his publicity office to cable to Rome and try to get the Pope to join him in the great crusade.[14]

schools, who sensed and satisfied the entertainment demands of a nation into which Europe's millions were pouring—millions who could not understand English but were enchanted by pictures—a nation in which an immense laboring class found no arts within its cultural span and few diversions cheap enough for its pocketbook.

These were the men who forged an instrument which entertained more people at lower prices, for longer periods, than ever before in history. They stamped a vaudeville spirit onto the motion picture industry, and it still bears evidence of their crudity and strength. They were masters of "the visceral cliché." [15] They infused a driving, bombastic spirit into the movies, and they breathed that spirit into the Hollywood which has become the capital of the screen.

The promoters and their lieutenants still dominate Hollywood. This explains, in part, the flashy spirit—and profits—of movie making, the maudlin content of many pictures, the willfulness with which authority is exercised, the resistance to economies (in an industry approaching stabilization) by men who pushed it forward by indifference to economy, the paternalism with which motion picture companies are operated. The stubborn, grandiose seeds which generated the movie giant are deep in the soil of its production and management today.

We should pause to observe that many of the bankers and merchants and magnates whose names spell dignity in America were also once peddlers, shopkeepers, barbers—or their sons. They were driven by the same appetites which characterized the ex-salesmen, nickelodeon operators, and furriers who hacked a movie empire out of the entertainment wilderness. They were. characterized by the same foibles and given to the same impulsive deportment. For the cellulords, like the pork barons, respond to social values they have not examined, and reach for symbols they had no hand in fashioning. Hollywood, despite its surface uniqueness, is faithful to social patterns of which it is not aware. It is society, not man, that sets the molds of prestige and establishes the methods of achieving it. Society canalizes the ways by which power can be won, status achieved, wealth enjoyed.

There are striking resemblances between the founder of the House of Vanderbilt and the founder of the House of Mayer, between the first Warner and the first Astor, between the ethos of Wall Street and that of Hollywood, between the spirit of Newport and that of Malibu Beach. In fifty years, names like Zanuck, Mannix, and Selznick may well be great, and those who possess them may find entree to circles which were closed to their grandparents. "Honour," says an old English proverb, "is but ancient riches."

The remarkable point is that Hollywood's elite has no respect for itself. Here is a rich skill-group which feels inferior, which accepts with embarrassment the derision of others. The businessmen of any community automatically gain prestige and political influence. The businessmen of Hollywood—partly because of their personalities, partly through their own shortsightedness, more through the snobbery of Los Angeles—are largely ignored in the business-politics of their community. Hollywood's elite takes a marginal role in both the social structure and the commercial regime.

Hollywood is singularly deferential to the prestige of others; it is almost craven before politicians, professors, or playwrights. (Playwrights who cannot be hired, that is; the unhirable playwright is an artist; the hired playwright is an employee.) The movie paladins revere, and surely overvalue, the old, the traditional, the accepted. They have no real sense of their own importance; they have no real confidence in their own right to respect. Their hunger for social recognition is pathetic. Their hunger for information, knowledge, "culture" is abysmal. If for no other reason, this would divide Hollywood's elite from the nabobs of other times and places. The "big people" of other

70

communities and other industries are, in general, smug, opinionated, arrogant in their wealth and convinced of the supernal wisdom of their accidental philosophies. The "big people" of Hollywood are insecure, defensive, and filled with a propelling desire for information which can offer them roots and moorings among the mysteries of a complex world. Hollywood's elite is, at bottom, dissatisfied with its own culture and envious of others.

Hollywood's elite is beholden to Veblen's "sense of costliness masquerading under the name of beauty." [16] Here is a grave and unconscious aping of the higher elites in American life. Here is a naive dedication to conspicuous expenditure. Here is the ludicrous spectacle of prestige sought by purchase and of a spurious, synthetic culture. Here are men and women who have become dizzied by sudden riches, living boldly and spending recklessly in an effort to forget and deny that not so long ago they were poor, anonymous, déclassé. They live in great, fine houses. They wear excellent fabrics. They ride in sleek automobiles. They have spacious offices and beautiful spouses. As someone said of an earlier generation of *arrivistes,* they try to play the Medici and only capture the spirit of Maecenas. They are caught in the curious trap of unaccustomed wealth, and spend nerves and energy in trying to achieve ease in conforming to expectations, their own and those of their fellow parvenus, to which they have become enslaved. Bright, bold, undisciplined, and crude, they are driven by unconscious urgencies, prodigal of their health, torn by rancor, possessed by rivalry; and beneath all the desperate display they remain lost in their own magnificence, disturbed and uncertain in the false paradise of pecuniary success.

The *nouveaux riches* of Egypt and Greece, Rome and Antwerp and London, also built marble swimming pools and tiled gymnasiums, gorged themselves with rich foods and took on the physical dimensions of importance. They tipped lavishly, entertained on a fabulous scale, and were fond of risqué stories. There were scandalous corners in the avenues of their living. They gambled freely, kept beautiful mistresses (or gigolos), bred costly horses, and fed useless dogs. And the notoriety of their spas and their pleasure resorts crept into the gossip and the verse of their time. "One might believe," Plutarch sighs, "[that] Lucullus thought his money really captive and barbarian, so wantonly and contumeliously did he treat it." [17] Were it not for chronology, one would say that every Four Hundred has "gone Hollywood."

Hollywood presents a marked parallel to the lavish and exuberant decades of history, and especially to that epoch in American life which Mark Twain dubbed the Gilded Age. For Hollywood is a boom town, and there is a striking resemblance—in living, manners, values, and wealth—between the lords and ladies of Hollywood and the railroad, oil, or iron barons at that time in *their* history when prodigious prosperity carried them up the intoxicating profit-curve. In the heyday of American prosperity, as in Hollywood today, there was a premium on the sheer amassment of riches, and unbounded fortunes were accepted by a public with its own munificent aspirations.

The Gilded Age was an era of acquisition and greed, a robust epoch in which the power-crazed—indifferent to social costs, corrupted by egoism, contemptuous of the consequences of their predatory desires—rode roughshod over a nation. It was the day of the robber barons—rapacious, headstrong, vulgar, builders of a buccaneer economy and a grotesque culture, exponents of an Epicurean morality with crude rationalizations.

Diamonds were set in teeth; a private carriage and personal valet were provided for a pet monkey, . . . a necklace costing $600,000 was purchased for a daughter of Croesus; $65,000 was spent for a dressing table, $75,000 for a pair of opera glasses. An entire theatrical company was taken from New York to Chicago to entertain the friends of a magnate

and a complete orchestra engaged to serenade a new-born child. . . .
At one function the cigarettes were wrapped in hundred-dollar bills.[18]

But the Gilded Age is gone. The sanctions of our society have changed. The old myths have passed away, stripped of force, barren of conviction, wrecked by an era which negated their promises and their pretensions. Men today have repudiated the creed and the gods of the Gilded Age, and they discharge their disenchantment against those whose millions only accentuate their own frustration and despair. Our economic elite is, perforce, on the defensive. They have not read Daniel Webster: "It is too much to expect that the universal franchise and inequitable distribution of wealth will lie peacefully together for long."

The great fortune of Hollywood's elite is, accordingly, out of historical context. For Hollywood's wealth has flowered in a time when the rest of our economy has been contracting; and the very fact that Hollywood's fortune burst forth during the years of economic and social dislocation has exaggerated its aberrance and increased its vulnerability, by singling it out for public resentment. It is not that the things which are happening in Hollywood are really unique; they are simply happening in Hollywood at a time when they are not happening elsewhere in our society. Greater fortunes have been made in a shorter time; extravagance has been more idiotic; business practices have been more ruthless and more picaresque; profligacy and waste have been more widespread.* But in contemporary America the prosperity and the conduct of the movie makers stuck out like defiant peaks on the long, dull plain of the Great Depression. A nation torn by crises, unemployment, industrial strife, and the terrible, overwhelming demands of defense, may be expected to turn its anger against two-million-dollar movies, $7,500-a-week

---

* In 1924, Mrs. John King Van Rensselaer declared: "It is doubtful whether there are more useless and empty ways of spending money than can be found in Newport." [19]

actresses, $100,000-a-year film directors, and $6,000-a-week producers; for these, despite the reasons for their existence, are mocking affronts to the common man, vaguely wicked and unnatural manifestations of social inequity. Hollywood's elite is rich and famous; but it is also guilty and insecure, and this the lords of the Gilded Age were spared.

During the Roaring Twenties the movie colony was not so convenient a scapegoat for the larger distress. In the upsurge of our prosperity, the movie people symbolized all that prosperity promised Everyman: luxury, fame, and, in a subtle sense, superiority to the stricter provisions of the moral code. The nation was buying and spending wildly; the service and luxury trades mushroomed; speculation and its twin, extravagance, reigned in the land. The movie colony participated in the Era of Wonderful Nonsense, the half-dollars poured into the box-offices in a torrent, and the movie elite rode on the crest of the giddy wave, doing more of whatever was done and doing it more conspicuously. The American philosophy of the Big Money was magnified, glorified, and woven into the publicity about Hollywood, which hammered its people, its product, and its way of life into the mind of the world. Hollywood climaxed the expectations of an epoch with its own fabulous conduct.

The rich have always been given license for behavior denied to others. The line between morality and immorality is never as sharply drawn among the Four Hundred as in the middle or lower strata. It is the middle-class which is the moral guardian of society; the elite is worried not by immorality, but by scandal.[20] Let us listen to Adam Smith again; he was a moral philosopher before he was an economist:

> In every civilized society . . . there have been always two different schemes or systems of morality current at the same time; of which the one may be called the strict or austere; the other the liberal, or, if you will, the loose system. The former is generally admired and revered by the common people; the latter is commonly more esteemed and adopted

by what are called people of fashion. The degree of disapprobation with which we ought to mark the vices of levity, the vices which are apt to arise from great prosperity, and from the excess of gaiety and good humour, seems to constitute the principal distinction between those two opposite schemes or systems.[21]

This was true of Alexandria or Paris or Long Island, and it applies to Hollywood.

The parallel between the elite of Hollywood and other prosperity-intoxicated groups is rooted in economics and branches out into deportment. Mrs. John King Van Rensselaer, an *arbiter elegantiarum* of the distinguished circles of the East, declared with commendable candor that even in the ranks she led "prudery was not a synonym for chastity . . . The much deplored, frequently assailed morals of current Society are no bit worse than they were in the prim and prudish half century ago . . . Vice was not rarer in those years, but the whole social organization conspired to conceal its existence." [22]

To the detached observer, the private life of a movie star is hardly more lurid than that of the railroad magnate, Jim Fisk, who poured a ransom "into the laps of wantons." The parties for which Hollywood's nabobs are famed are not wilder than were the yacht parties of William Astor, with which all New York rang. If the business offices of Hollywood provoke smiles, one might recall the offices of the Erie Railroad, which were situated in a converted opera house and were used for nightly gambling and historic carousing.[23] And one might balance the divorces of the movie stars with those of the Vanderbilts or the Manvilles; or the tax evasion of a Joseph Schenck with the defalcations of a Richard Whitney.

The comparison might be carried further, for hallowed American names offer the satirist material as rich as Hollywood at its weirdest. A movie producer may play host at a dinner party while wearing slacks, polo shirt, and sport jacket; but Oliver Belmont received his guests while seated on a carved throne with an Egyptian in a zouave jacket and an embroidered fez standing behind him. A former president of the Baltimore & Ohio Railroad spent his declining years insisting that he was the Prince of Wales: he bought a complete set of medals and uniforms for "state occasions," hired actors to impersonate ambassadors to his "court," and imported an expert on protocol from London. The illustrious Joseph Leiter once brought a monkey, attired in full evening dress, to a Stuyvesant Fish dinner, and the dinner was carried on with the monkey seated in the place of honor. The wife of a former publisher of the *Washington Post* kept a llama among her pets and once spent $5,000 for a Great Dane; and when Lord Balfour and Lord Lee, during a dinner in their honor, admired her tablecloth, she summoned a servant to fetch her a pair of scissors and "as these two British gentlemen stood pop-eyed, [I] whacked off for each of them a square of yellow cloth." Walter P. Chrysler, whom one would scarcely call an eccentric personality, arrived at a Stotesbury party in Palm Beach at the head of a fife and drum corps, uniformed and resplendent.[24]

Hollywood cannot surpass these bizarreries; nor can Hollywood's elite hope to match the strident lavishness with which William Randolph Hearst has lived nor the childish greediness with which he combed the world for Spanish castles and Renaissance fireplaces. The movie magnates, like the shoe or lumber barons, ape their peers; whether they know it or not, their values are derivative, their conduct has been stereotyped, and their search for self-expression ends in gestures which are flamboyant, familiar, and imitative. The producers or actors of Hollywood, like the bankers or merchants of Philadelphia, are children of their society.

The behavior of Hollywood's elite, like the behavior of America's elite, has changed considerably in the past few years. Those who "belong" in Hollywood reflect the transformation

which has occurred in the mores of the moneyed. The luxury
and ostentation which once dominated plutocratic behavior are
neither so widespread nor so conspicuous in American life. The
arrogance which once typified those who sat in the seats of
power has given way to uneasiness and circumspection. The
taste of the parvenus, for one thing, has improved; they have
learned more refined standards of expenditure and less ludicrous values for living; they have come to suspect, if not recognize, the vulgarity of lavishness. Above all, the captains of
industry are not reckless enough to echo the historic "The public be damned!"

This desire for prudence is especially noticeable among the
leaders of Hollywood. Hollywood is lost in a curious paradox:
its business thrives on publicity, but its reputation and security
are directly threatened by the kind of publicity which wins the
widest attention. When the President of Dartmouth College addressed the annual dinner of the Academy of Motion Picture
Arts and Sciences in 1940, Hollywood deplored his "lack of
showmanship" and the publicity men and reporters complained
about the lack of "news" in his speech. Hollywood has an incomparable talent for publicity and a startling ignorance of
public relations.

The desire for circumspection is particularly marked in Hollywood today because of the pitiless publicization to which the
movie colony is exposed; because of the precarious health of an
industry whose heart's blood can be choked off overnight by
sudden shifts in public taste, by organized pressure groups, or
by international politics; because of the salaries which flaunt
Hollywood's fortune while the rest of the land is constricted
with crisis; because of the conduct which parades indiscretion
before the eyes of a public wracked by social fevers and ready
to find whipping-boys for its rage; because actors and showmen
have always been easy targets for demagogues and crackpots;
because those movie leaders who are Jewish are easy prey for

HOLLYWOOD: THE MOVIE COLONY

the manipulators of anti-Semitism, those who are Catholic are easy targets for the purveyors of anti-Catholicism, and those who are Protestant are alarmed by the mounting demands of anti-movieism.

The movies are exposed on a dozen more fronts than most enterprises in America today; the business is more vulnerable, and the Hollywood elite knows it. If Hollywood, for example, produces a picture dealing with the war, it is accused of "warmongering"; if Hollywood doesn't, it is accused of feeding pap to the public and putting profit above the national welfare. When Hollywood released *The Grapes of Wrath*, the simpletons of reaction cried "Communist!" (because of the picture's content) and the simpletons of revolution cried "Fascist!" (because of the picture's ending). When Hollywood produced *Confessions of a Nazi Spy*, the Nazis cried "Bolsheviks!" When it produced *Ninotchka*, the Communists cried "Fascists!" When it produced *Mr. Smith Goes to Washington*, the Bourbons cried "Trouble-Makers!" When it produced *Maytime*, the liberals cried "Escapists!"

Hollywood is uneasy, uncertain, possessed by apprehensions of the future—and with good reason. For the social and governmental controls which have already invaded the empires of finance, shipping, mining, manufacture, utilities, are just beginning to cast their shadow on the movie industry. Other businesses have experienced onslaughts against their profits and hegemony; but the drive against Hollywood is just beginning. No moving picture leader can be sanguine before the steady challenge of unionism, collective bargaining, the consent decree (which brought the Department of Justice anti-trust suit to a temporary armistice), the revolt of the independent theater owners, the trend toward increased taxation, the strangulation of the foreign market, and a score of frontal attacks on the citadels of the screen.

Hollywood does not yet realize that it is facing decades of history compressed into months. The changes and challenges which have hit other industries in the long thrust of American progressivism are sweeping into Hollywood in one prolonged whirlwind. Hollywood and its elite are punch-drunk.

4. THE BIG MONEY

TWENTY-FIVE years ago Mary Pickford received a $300,000 bonus for signing a Hollywood contract which netted her $10,000 a week. In 1924, a movie star at United Artists earned $1,200,000—in salary and a percentage of the profits. In 1931, Constance Bennett got $300,000 for making two motion pictures. In 1937, the production head of MGM, Louis B. Mayer, received $1,296,503 in salary and bonuses. Since 1938, when she earned $465,000, Carole Lombard has free-lanced at $150,000 a picture, which means around $18,000 a week. In 1941, Bing Crosby closed a deal with Paramount for nine pictures at $175,000 a picture, an arrangement which guaranteed the celebrated crooner $1,575,000 for his services over a three-year period. Mr. Crosby reserved the right to make one film a year at any other studio at any price he could get.[1]

Everyone knows that Hollywood's top talents are handsomely rewarded, but their full good fortune is difficult to comprehend even when framed in the sharp and indisputable language of statistics. Thirty years ago a movie director got from $35 to $200 a week; in 1938, forty-five directors earned over $75,000 each. Thirty years ago a newspaperman named Roy McCardell took a job with the Biograph studios as a scenario writer at $10 a scenario; recently another ex-newspaperman, Ben Hecht, had a contract which netted him $5,750 a week, and as a free-lance writer earned $100,000 in a month for turning out two screen

80

plays.[2] In 1938, more than seventeen Hollywood writers earned over $75,000.

The glittering sums secured by the movie makers are woven into the economics of movie making and the social fabric of Hollywood. Prestige varies with the size of the pay check; and prestige means bargaining power. John Stahl, the film director, expressed the point pungently when he informed a reporter that he was employed at $4,000 a week:

Hollywood's large salaries are unnecessary, except for one thing. That is respect. If you don't earn a king's ransom in the movie business, nobody respects you. And if they don't respect you, you can't get work. So you've got to demand a tremendously stiff fee for your services, or you don't make movies. Then you give most of this money back to the government and you worry about your financial affairs, and you'd be a lot better off if you earned only a fraction of your weekly check.* So would the movie industry.[3]

In the same vein, screen writer Mary C. McCall, Jr., has gone on record:

I look forward to the day when my salary will be very high—fantastically high. I want that big salary not because I need it. . . . There's nothing about a $2,000-a-week salary which is at all relevant to my way of life except this one thing—it will give me authority. Then when a producer says, "Look, sweetheart, I have a terrific angle on this opening; we fade in on a bed," I can say, "That's silly," and he will listen to me because I will be so very expensive. I say "That's silly" now, but he rarely listens to me.[4]

Let us make a systematic excursion into Hollywood's Big Money. We shall not discuss the *reasons* for the high salaries; in this chapter we are simply interested in establishing the salient facts. But it should be borne in mind, in our trip through the land of six-digits, that according to the first premise of our economy a person's "value" is the amount he can get in the open market. Outstanding personalities are monopolies on them-

* This is a common and whimsical misconception in Hollywood.

81

selves: a Deanna Durbin, a Leo McCarey, or a Spencer Tracy contains unique attributes and talents for which there is no exact substitute. The fact that their pictures are immensely profitable to the organizations for which they work serves, in Hollywood, as *ex post facto* justification of the salaries they get. In subsequent chapters we shall consider the earnings of the talent *groups,* so that average incomes and typical patterns can be ascertained. At this point let us focus our attention on Hollywood's top earners. How much do they make? How much do they spend? How much do they save?

At least 738 persons in *six* motion picture corporations earned $20,000 or over in 1939. These 738 persons include actors, producers, executive-producers in Hollywood, movie directors, writers, publicity men. (The officers and directors of the corporation are not included.) They received an aggregate of $42,356,578 from six companies: Loew's, Paramount, Warner Brothers, Twentieth Century-Fox, Universal, Columbia.* If similar information were available for RKO, United Artists, and smaller organizations, this writer would judge that at least 850 persons in the movie business earned $20,000 or over in 1939 (or in 1941).

Now if over 800 persons make $20,000 or more a year in the movie business, that healthy sum is obviously not a signal re-

* The officers and directors of motion picture corporations (most of whom are in New York) are not actively engaged in the *production* of movies; they are primarily concerned with finances, administration, theater operations, sales and distribution, revenues, foreign markets, trade problems, and so on. The movie executives in Hollywood are, more properly, executive-producers, and are actively engaged in making movies (Zanuck, Freeman, Schaefer, Mannix, Lichtman, etc.). Our 738 include *executive-producers* in Hollywood, but not corporation officers and directors who do not participate directly in the production of movies. A later volume, which will deal with the motion picture industry as a whole, will deal with the motion picture corporations. Some producers are called "executive-producers," although they are not executives of the corporation, e.g., Hal B. Wallis of Warner Brothers; L. B. Mayer, the active head of MGM, is called "executive employee" and is not an official executive of the corporation. See chapters 11, 12. For a breakdown by studios of salaries over $20,000, see Appendix C.

muneration; third-rate actors and actresses earn over $20,000 per annum, or second-rate directors and writers. Let us ask how many movie-makers earned $75,000 or more in one year. In 1938, at least 217 persons in the motion picture business earned $75,000 or over, and 200 of these were in Hollywood: *

> 80 Actors and Actresses
> 54 Executives and Producers
> 45 Directors
> 17 Writers
> 4 Musical Directors

How many persons in Hollywood earned over $100,000 (in 1938)? Answer: 134.

> 54 Actors
> 42 Executives and Producers
> 34 Directors
> 4 Writers

How many persons in Hollywood earned over $150,000? Answer: 71.

> 31 Actors
> 22 Executives and Producers
> 16 Directors
> 2 Writers

How many persons in Hollywood earned over $200,000? Answer: 31.

> 19 Actors
> 9 Executives and Producers
> 3 Directors
> 0 Writers

How many persons in Hollywood earned over $250,000? Answer: 20.

* The names of those who earned $100,000 or over will be found in chapters 12-15. Also see Appendix C. Seventeen executives in New York earned ·$75,000 or over, in addition to the fifteen given here for Hollywood. The United States Revenue Act authorized the publication of annual salaries above $15,000. In 1939, a Congressional amendment raised the figure to $75,000.

14 Actors
5 Executives and Producers
1 Director
0 Writers

How many persons in Hollywood earned over $300,000? Answer: 12.

9 Actors
3 Executives and Producers
0 Directors
0 Writers

How many persons in Hollywood earned over $400,000? Answer: 4.

3 Actors
1 Executive
0 Directors
0 Writers

How many persons in Hollywood earned over $500,000? Answer: 1.

1 Executive-Producer

From this dazzling record it is clear that Hollywood's top actors, actresses, executives, and producers enjoy especially high salaries; directors fall off around the $200,000 mark, and writers drop sharply after $100,000. It should be observed, once more, that the figures do not attempt to suggest the earnings or welfare of occupational *groups;* since there are fewer executives and producers in Hollywood than actors, directors, or writers, the *percentage* of producers in the Big Money is markedly higher than any other group.

The fifty-four executives and producers who earned over $75,000 in 1938 (in six studios) represent almost one-third of the 159 producers, associate producers, and executives in the entire movie colony.

The forty-five directors earning over $75,000 (in six studios) represent about one-fifth of the 235 directors in all of Hollywood.

The eighty actors securing over $75,000 (in six studios) represent a small percentage (6.4 percent) of the total number of actors available —around 1,250, excluding extras.

The seventeen writers who secured over $75,000 (in six studios) represent a very small percentage of the 600-800 writers in Hollywood.*

This volume is concerned with Hollywood, and not with the motion picture industry as a whole; we shall not discuss in any detail the earnings of the officers and directors of the motion picture corporations, who are paid phenomenally well. But a glance at the pattern of executive remuneration, and a few comments on its meaning, will be more than enlightening—especially since many of the executives are executive-producers in Hollywood.

An analysis of Securities and Exchange Commission data on eighteen of the leading industries in the United States (involving 2,100 companies registered with the SEC) revealed that:

The motion picture industry ranked *fourteenth* among the eighteen industries in terms of annual *volume of business.*

The motion picture industry ranked *eleventh* among the eighteen industries in terms of the size of *total assets.*†

But the motion picture industry paid its executives (officers and directors of the corporations) remuneration which amounted to 1.59 percent of its total volume of business—second only to cement manufacturing, which paid its executives 1.61 percent of the total volume of business.

In 1939, the seven major companies of the motion picture industry paid their 188 executives $6,085,659—or 18.96 percent of their *net profits* —a proportion second only to the department stores, which paid their executives 32.10 percent of their net profits. (Nearly 35 percent of the total executive remuneration paid by the seven major motion picture companies went to twenty-four Loew's executives.)

---

* For complete data on the earnings of producers, directors, actors, and writers, see part two, chapters 12-15.

† "Volume of business" is a better index of the size of a business or a company than "total assets"; it is a simple, accurate, and checkable figure, ·whereas "assets" involves different and arbitrary accounting estimates of the "value" or "book value" of intangible properties. Data on the eighteen industries analyzed will be found in Appendix B.

For every dollar of dividends which the motion picture companies paid to the stockholders, they paid their executives twenty-four cents. (Loew's paid thirty-four cents for every dollar of dividends.)

Movie profits go to the movie elite—in Hollywood and New York—and not to the stockholders. The conflict of interests between stockholders and management is an old and time-honored one in American business. In the field of movies, this conflict is complicated by the fact that the New York film executives are themselves in perpetual warfare with Hollywood's executives, producers, and talents. The movie executives, for the most part, and the movie boards of directors are in New York; the management is in Hollywood. Management gets big money for itself and big money for the talents it employs. This raises production costs, which prevents profits from rising. Movie profits are drained off and channeled into the hands of the movie elite— the producers, the executives, the ranking talent. Because of the scarcity of first-rank movie talent and management, their power to command great salaries is unchallengeable. No movie company has solved this dilemma.*

When the salary lists of American corporations are published each year, the movie people figure most prominently. Now, salary lists are misleading; they are not an index of total incomes; they do not include dividends from stocks, interest on bonds, trust funds, profits from investments or business operations, and so on. The Treasury Department recently reported that in 1939 forty-one persons paid taxes on incomes of $1,000,-000 or more; but none of these persons was included in the list of salaries published by government agencies.[5] The great annual incomes of the Mellons, Dodges, Harknesses, Fords, Huttons, Winthrops are never publicized.† But in 1940 five out of

---

* See the discussion in chapters 11 and 12.

† And there are at least 73 du Ponts of adult age, 53 Goulds, 31 Mellons, 28 Harrimans, 27 Rockefellers, 22 Winthrops, 21 Vanderbilts, 18 Drexels, 16 Harknesses, and so on.[6]

the fifteen highest salaries in the United States went to movie people. If there were an annual catalogue of *incomes*, Hollywood's mighty salaries would be completely overshadowed by those whose fortunes come from property, industrial profits, trust funds, and other forms of unearned increment.

Hollywood's elite are employees. They work for salaries (plus bonuses or profit-shares, in some cases). The movie people derive their wealth from current incomes, not established properties; they are not people of property at all in the sense that the oligarchs of America are. (Professor Sorokin of Harvard demonstrated in 1925 that 52.7 percent of the current generation's millionaires were wealthy by the time they reached their majority.[7]) One or two of the very wealthiest of the movie crowd may be worth five million dollars; but that, a financial expert remarked, is "chicken feed" when compared to the truly potent estates of our samurai. A comparative unknown like Ella Wendel left $75,000,000 worth of real estate when she died ten years ago. Payne Whitney was worth $186,000,000 when he departed this mortal vale; the death of John T. Dorrance (Campbell Soup) divulged an estate of $120,000,000; Richard B. Mellon left $200,000,000; Thomas Fortune Ryan's leavings were officially estimated at $135,000,000; and nineteen women each possess wealth of $25,000,000 or more, which probably provides them, year in and year out, with incomes of more than a million dollars a year.[8]

An accurate arrangement of American Croesuses would put the movie elite at the relatively modest end of the scale of Fortunatus. It would place them even lower in the pyramid of industrial, political, or financial power. No movie magnate, and surely no movie star, can remotely approach the economic leverage exerted by a Lamont or a Stillman, an Aldrich or a Baker, a Mellon or a du Pont.

Hollywood occupies a high and conspicuous place on the roster of salaries *per se*. In 1940, five of the fifteen highest salaries in the land went to 2 movie executives, 1 producer, 2 actors, each of whom received over $200,000. Nineteen of the twenty-five highest salaries in the United States, in 1938, were received by picture people: 13 actors, 4 Hollywood executives and producers, 1 New York movie executive, and 1 movie director. (The salaries ranged from $265,000 to $688,369.) In 1937, fourteen of the leading twenty salaries in the country went to movie people: 8 actors, 5 New York executives, and 1 Hollywood executive.[9]

At this point it is worth quoting Justice Valente of the Supreme Court of New York, who dismissed a stockholders' suit against the executives of Loew's, Inc., by citing "undisputed evidence as to the . . . scarcity of talent to fill positions of producers and executives, and the intense competition among the companies for their services":

The evidence is replete with instances of lucrative offers received by these executives in an effort to lure them away from Loew's. . . . I am convinced . . . that the only way he [Nicholas Schenck] kept his unique organization intact was by the payment of generous compensation. That this policy has been successful is indicated not only by the standing of the company, and the profits which it has earned over the years, but by the testimony of every single witness, including that of the president of one of its chief competitors, who frankly stated that he would like to get this executive group for his own company, and that their loss would be disastrous to Loew's, Inc. So many other large concerns in the business went through reorganization or suffered other losses and passed through crises [but] Loew's, in the worst period of depression, paid its dividends. . . .[10]

This opinion should be compared to the findings of Professor John C. Baker of Harvard, who studied executive compensation in one hundred American industrial companies and concluded: (1) executive salaries are so inflexible that they become "fixed charges on the companies"; (2) statistical evidence does *not* support the argument, commonly heard, that corporations increase their earnings by paying their executives a higher proportion of compensation to earnings. Professor Baker discovered that, contrary to popular belief, in both large and small corporations "those companies which show a high percentage of (executive) compensation to earnings secured less satisfactory results than those with a low percentage." [11]

One school of thought maintains that the movies, by paying astronomic sums to talent, are the largest profit-sharing enterprise in America. Hollywood is emphatically opposed to pouring its profits into the laps of idle stockholders. "Those who make pictures deserve the big money. What does the stockholder contribute, anyway?"

No one company can break the iron ring of Pactolian salaries so long as its personnel can get as much, or more, at any other studio. And that, in present-day Hollywood, is precisely the case. Such personalities as Cary Grant, Claudette Colbert, Ronald Colman, Carole Lombard, Bing Crosby, Gary Cooper have no difficulty in receiving from $100,000 to $150,000 for appearing in a single picture, and have been awarded such ransoms for their services at various studios. Top directors—John Ford, Frank Capra, Leo McCarey, Gregory La Cava—can get from $75,000 to $150,000 for a single film. Out of a representative sample of sixty-two movie directors, 18 (29 percent) earned $50,000 or more in 1938; 14 (22.5 percent) earned $75,000 or more; 12 (19.3 percent) earned $100,000 or more; 6 (9.6 percent) earned $125,000 or over.*

The Big Money is not a recent phenomenon for movie producers and executives, and we have seen that over twenty-five years ago Hollywood's actors and actresses were living under a golden providence. In recent years, the directors and, to a much smaller degree, the writers have begun to enter the circle of princely sums. The prosperity of the films has been immense and continuous, and profits have consistently been funneled off

* See chapter 13.

89

into high salaries. Hollywood would maintain that it is the high salaries which create the profits. The stockholders feel that if the salaries were lower, the profits would be higher.

Taxes, Taxes, Taxes

The movie people complain that everyone gasps at their salaries but no one bothers to gasp at their taxes. Louis B. Mayer reported that he paid $1,108,352 in Federal and states taxes in 1937. (A tax of this amount, however, suggests a total *income* greater than the $1,296,503 salary and bonus which Mr. Mayer received that year.) Nicholas M. Schenck, who received $541,-602 in 1937, stated under oath that he had had to borrow money to meet his tax payments for several years when his salary was over $400,000.[12] Actors, producers, directors, and writers often lament their tax plight, but the emotion strikes one as generated by bewilderment rather than wrath, irritation rather than righteousness.

The movie people suffer several disadvantages in the field of taxation. The stars complain that because their earnings vary sharply from year to year, the tax paid in a year of high earnings is excessive. They suggest that their earnings be prorated over a period of years to arrive at an equitable average income and tax. The earning power of stars, it is alleged, is short-lived; hence actors are penalized in taxes for short-spanned careers. The Associated Actors and Artistes of America, the A. F. of L. organization which embraces all professional entertainers, has campaigned for a revision of income-tax laws, urging that the surtax on entertainers' incomes be based on a three-year average. (This method, incidentally, has been adopted in England.)

Actresses protest that they do not get proper tax allowances for clothes, parties, entertainment, which, they maintain, are essential to their prestige and therefore to their earning power.

One character player petitioned Uncle Sam to allow a deduction of a thousand dollars which he had spent on a new set of false teeth, insisting, with some justice, that there was a direct correlation between his denture and his income.

The resentment of Hollywood's people against their taxes has curious overtones. They feel *personally* offended by the law; they dramatize their income tax returns no less than their ailments. Actors and writers and directors are not accustomed to figures; they live in a world of emotional rather than numerical symbols. Hence the vocabulary of financial counters is instantly strange and threatening; statistics don't "belong" in their universe; figures are unnatural interlopers. The Hollywoodian's reaction to taxes is not that he pays a sum, established by law, for governmental services and necessities; he feels, instead, that there is a conspiracy of envious politicians who are deliberately singling him out for reparations. Around March of each year, Hollywood is full of sounds dimly reminiscent of the second act of a melodrama: "I don't *deserve* this . . . They can't do this to me . . ."

One distinguished actor declaimed to this writer: "I tell you, it's Communism. Let's face it—Communism! I won't make a nickel this year, not a nickel! Every cent I make will go to Washington to pay the taxes for last year." When the actor was asked how much he had made, he said, "Over $240,000." When asked how large all of his taxes were, he said, "About $75,000." When asked what had happened to the difference between $240,000 and $75,000, he cried, "Well, if you're going to count living expenses and the purchase of government bonds for *defense* . . . !" The story is revealing; this child of Hollywood considered his living expenses as "necessary," therefore not subject to discussion (or tax); he considered the purchase of government bonds a sacrifice, nobly endured, for the public good. The fact that he had lived very well and purchased bonds on which he would get 2.9 percent cumulative interest did not really impress him. It was a sincere ignorance; the actor was lost in the role he was playing—honest Eliza being pursued across the financial ice by a pack of voracious tax wolves.

How large a tax load do those in the Big Money in Hollywood carry? This writer was able to obtain sixteen complete case records, for movie makers who earned between $16,721 and $220,000 in 1938. These cases include a producer, ten actors and actresses, two directors, and three writers. Sixteen cases are, of course, too few to permit generalization; it was impossible to obtain more. The material is not presented as a statistical sample, but as a series of case studies.

Case	Income (1938)	Total Taxes Federal and State, Income and Property	All Taxes as Percent of Income
A.	$ 16,721.42	$ 1,406.70	8.4
B.	19,200.00	400.00	2.1
C.	25.589.77	2.672.68	10.4
D.	31,484.22	1,455.68	4.7
E.	38,545.92	3,896.68	10.1
F.	39,307.52	2,983.18	7.6
G.	40,077.08	2,206.52	5.5
H.	41,997.45	6,900.89	16.5
I.	46,000.00	5,100.00	11.1
J.	78,250.00	8,444.58	10.8
K.	104,096.19	20,667.92	19.9
L.	105,554.90	8,379.21	7.9
M.	121,492.95	24,255.19	20.0
N.	129,000.00	13,400.00	10.4
O.	134,739.70	29,791.60	22.1
P.	220,000.00	75,110.00	34.1

Income taxes are, of course, assessed after agents' fees, business expenses, charitable contributions, outlays to dependents, and other deductions have been subtracted from gross income. Since these deductions vary widely from case to case, there is no graduated pattern in the table given above. The California income tax, incidentally, works out roughly to one-fourth of the amount which goes to the Federal government; the community property law in California permits an annual income to be split between husband and wife and reported as two separate incomes; this reduces the state tax load to the movie makers in the high-income brackets.*

Federal and state taxes of all kinds, for our sixteen cases, ranged from $400 to $75,110, or from 2.1 to 34.1 percent of annual earnings. The average amount which went into taxes was 12.6 percent of annual earnings.

The tax load has, of course, risen substantially since 1938 (25-50 percent), and under the pressures of the defense program will continue to rise for years to come. One of our cases paid $18,238 in federal and state income taxes in 1938, and $26,577 in 1940; the case earning $78,250 paid $7,681 in income taxes in 1938, and $10,904 in 1940. (The increased taxes were proportionately much higher than increased earnings.) In 1940, Bing Crosby paid an income tax of $377,000.[13] The income tax on a Hollywood salary is not to be laughed off lightly—but neither is the amount left after taxes have been paid.

Agents, Agents, Agents

"In this world," said Benjamin Franklin, "nothing is certain but death and taxes." In Hollywood nothing is certain but death, taxes, and agents. Agents, like producers, are the sacrificial goats of the movie colony, which confuses their personalities with their functions. They are the salesmen and professional representatives of actors, directors, and writers. They sell talents and stories; they get their clients jobs, contracts, raises, or concessions. They guard prestige and bargaining power. They are experts in marketing anything from a pair of legs to

* As this volume goes to press, Congress is considering sharp revisions in the community property law exemptions.

an unwritten synopsis. Agents get ten percent of the salary of their clients, by whom they are generally resented, and haggle, coax, plead, or fight with producers, by whom they are generally disliked.

No one can prove whether a Hollywood agent, mordantly dubbed "flesh peddler," is worth ten percent. Some are; some are not. Some draw a fat ten percent for a service performed years earlier; others create magical opportunities and boost the salaries of their clients with brazen ingenuity and a sublime indifference to contractual arrangements. Myron Selznick, one of the leading agents in Hollywood, whose organization is reported to have done a gross annual business of $15,000,000 at its peak, won the suit he brought against Carole Lombard when he demonstrated to the satisfaction of the court that he had raised her salary from $750 to $18,000 (a week) in less than ten years.[14] Every actor, director, and writer in Hollywood has an agent, which means that ten percent is automatically subtracted from the salary. It would be almost impossible to operate the movie business without agents. Some agents, sensitive to the nature of their tasks and the onus of their standing, like to call themselves "talent representatives."

The rise of the business manager, as distinguished from the movie agent, is a significant development in the movie colony. The business manager takes over all the financial affairs of his clients; he pays bills, issues checks, puts funds aside for taxes, and acts as investment counselor, conscience, watch dog, trouble-shooter, and lord of the exchequer. Business agents place their clients on a budget to prevent them from living up to their means—to say nothing of beyond them.

Among [a business agent's] clients are scatter-brained artists to whom money is a golden dream, producers who can handle a studio's money but not their own, executives who are too busy to handle their own affairs as well as he can do it for them. So when he takes a client he takes over every phase of that client's life which is not strictly personal.[15]

The business manager stands between his client's quixoticism and his income. He clamps down on generous follies and zany investments. He forces his clients to save. One business manager stated that his clients save forty percent of their incomes. Another revealed that in ten years one actress under his management will have saved and invested enough money so that, even at a modest three percent interest, "she will be able to live almost as well as she does now if she never works any more." [16]

Business agents do not get a flat ten percent; they receive anywhere from one-half of one percent to five percent of their clients' earnings, and in many instances they work for a monthly fee or a fixed annual stipend.

There are other occupational expenses in a movie career which deserve mention. Some stars employ a publicity agent to get them into the news or keep them out of it, to propitiate belligerent columnists, to build them up as personalities. Advertising is considered wise—or inescapable—in Hollywood, and the pages of the trade journals are studded with congratulatory messages, artful sentiments, flattering photographs, and celebrated names. A personal secretary is almost imperative for those in the limelight—to answer fan mail and correspondence, to refuse requests for money tactfully, to send out autographed photographs, supervise social functions, or remember important birthdays. Most top-flight actresses employ personal maids to help them with hair, clothes, make-up, and morale while a picture is being shot. Directors and writers sometimes maintain private offices and personal stenographers.

How much do all these occupational expenses (agents, business managers, publicity, secretarial assistance) take out of a Hollywood income? In one of our sixteen cases, the total ran as high as $58,000, or 26.6 percent of a $220,000 income. The highest percentage was 28.8 ($7,371 out of an income of $25,589). Secretarial assistance did not run above 2.6 percent in any instance. The maximum spent on publicity services was .4 percent of income, and for advertising .6 percent. Dues to organizations and guilds never went above .3 percent. The average outlay for all occupational expenses, in our sixteen cases, was 16.3 percent of annual earnings. The agents' ten percent was, of course, the major item.

Now, if we combine the amounts the movie makers pay out in taxes, agents' fees, business expenses, and so on, we can determine how much net or usable income is left. In our sixteen cases, the minimum percentage for all the above expenses was 15.1; the maximum was 60.7! The average outlay was 29.64 percent of annual income.

There are, undoubtedly, many persons in Hollywood who spent much more or much less in these categories.* But from the evidence available to us, it appears that anywhere from 15 to 60 percent of a movie maker's gross earnings is drained off for agents, taxes, and necessary business expenses. On the average, and it is a rough estimate at best, 30 percent must be deducted from a Hollywood income in order to ascertain the amount available for living, spending, and saving.

"Yes, we make a lot, even after you deduct taxes and agents and business expenses," Hollywood admits, "but we have to spend a lot." How do the movie makers spend it?

* Joseph M. Schenck, for example, claimed necessary business expenses (and tax deductions) of more than $87,000 in one year, and $44,000 in another. The Federal government prosecuted and convicted Mr. Schenck for income-tax evasion, and presented evidence to show that these deductions included an extraordinary array: hotel expenses, flowers, gifts to dancers, entertainment, parties, half the cost of renting a yacht which rarely left the harbor (because most of the guests were fearful of seasickness), Christmas presents, and so on. Mr. Schenck's attorney admitted that Mr. Schenck had entertained on a lavish scale, but contended that it was done for business reasons. He maintained that Mr. Schenck had actually spent $400,000 on entertainment in the year he deducted only $87,000 (1937), and $200,000 in the year for which he deducted only $44,000 (1936). The Federal government was willing to allow Mr. Schenck only $1,600 out of the $87,000 claimed as deductible, and only $400 out of the $44,000.[17]

Houses and Food, Servants and Furniture

Rent or mortgages, food, servants, repairs, and the sundry details which may be called household expenses range widely in the movie colony—from 3.8 to 40.9 percent of annual income in our sixteen case-studies. Both figures are untypical; in the latter case the purchase of a house and furniture in one year accounts for the size of the expenditure. The second highest percentage was 29.3. The median average for our sixteen cases was 13.3 percent.

A more vivid picture may be obtained from absolute sums. The actress who earned $220,000 spent $18,300 on her household, servants, and furniture, and $23,000 more on mortgage and repairs. This awesome total, $41,300, represented 18.8 percent of her income. A director who earned $129,000 spent $13,000 on hearth and home, food and domestics—over 10 percent of his earnings. The person who earned $40,000 spent over a fourth ($10,508) on household operations. The smallest percentage was 3.8, in the case of an income of $104,096, but other expenses were inordinate and help explain the modesty of the figure.

Clothes, Wives, Children, Doctors

How much is spent on "personal care"—the category used by the Bureau of Labor Statistics—which includes clothing, medical services, and miscellaneous spending by husband, wife, and children? Our material shows that in Hollywood these expenses range from 2.9 to 24.6 percent of annual income. The median was approximately 12.5 percent. The maximum spent for clothing alone was 7.8 percent. The median for wardrobe was about

4.3 percent. The $220,000-a-year actress spent $6,300 (2.9 percent) on clothes; an actress earning $121,492 spent $6,093 (5 percent of her income) on her wardrobe.

Automobiles

The automobile is essential to life in Hollywood, where distances are vast, good residential areas remote, and social pressures demand new models of reputable comfort and costliness. Since wives, servants, and children are hopelessly stranded without a gasoline conveyance, nearly everyone in the Big Money owns two cars, and in many instances three. Convertibles are popular; station wagons, which lend a suburban or "estate" tone to living, enjoy a strong vogue.

Automobile expenses (gasoline, maintenance, repairs) ranged from .4 to 6.1 percent of the annual earnings of our group. The highest sum spent was $4,904. The average percentage was 2.6. In this connection it is interesting to observe that according to a survey made by the Department of Labor wage earners in Los Angeles spend more money on automobiles than on clothes.[18] This is not the case for the upper levels of the movie colony.

Relatives and Dependents

The wags say that one-half of Hollywood pays alimony and the other half supports relatives. Like most witticisms, this is inaccurate. How much do the movie makers lay out for dependents and relatives?

In some instances the load is heavy. An actor who earned $31,484 spent $6,030 on dependents and relatives—19.2 percent of his income. Another, earning $78,250, spent $11,987, or 15.3 percent of his income. The actress whose income was $220,000 dispensed only $500 (.2 percent) on dependents. But four of our sixteen cases carried no burden in this field. Of the remaining twelve, monies paid to relatives and dependents ranged from .2 to 19.2 percent of annual income. The average was 6.4 percent for these twelve. If we include those who spent nothing on family obligations, the average was 4.8 percent for our entire group.

Charities

The gossip columns are replete with references to Hollywood's charities, and the movie colony prides itself on the scope of its philanthropies. The Motion Picture Relief Fund, headed by Jean Hersholt, does an admirable and efficient job of relief for the needy who were once attached to the movies, or the hard-pressed who work on the fringes. The Fund dispensed $345,677 on relief in 1940 and provided for 2,024 cases (representing approximately 5,060 persons).* The Gulf Oil-Screen Actors Guild radio show, to which actors, writers, and directors contribute their talents freely, has netted the Fund $800,000 to be used for a home and building for the aged.

The Community Chest is the most widely heralded of the philanthropies in which the movie colony engages; in 1940, Hollywood contributed $465,708 to the drive.[19] In 1939, unhappily, the movie colony's quota was $500,000, and only $319,-816 was raised. Harry M. Warner found at the close of one drive that the movie colony was over $100,000 short of its quota, and

---

* The Motion Picture Relief Fund is supported by contributions from the studios ($80,000 in 1938-39) and from some five thousand movie people who donate one-half of one percent of their salaries. All members of the Screen Actors Guild contribute to the Fund; the Society of Film Editors has enforced a one-half of one percent tax on those earning $100 a week or more. The Will Rogers Memorial Fund, a nation-wide philanthropic organization for the entertainment world, has agreed to aid the Motion Picture Relief Fund by donating $100,000 to a Los Angeles hospital for the permanent endowment of ten beds.

quietly made up the deficiency himself. Walt Disney contributed an expensive movie short to one Community Chest drive, besides contributing a sizable sum. The contributions of stars range from $100 to $5,000, according to the individual or the degree to which he contributes to charities and dependents outside the Community Chest proper. Many actors do not contribute more than the most nominal of sums; some neglect charities entirely.

The roll of welfare organizations in which the movie makers take an active part includes the Red Cross, Ann Lehr's Hollywood Guild, the Assistance League, the Children's Hospital, the League for Crippled Children, the Home for the Aged, Mount Sinai Hospital, the Hollywood Studio Club, the National Infantile Paralysis Fund ($126,504 in 1939) and many others. Hollywood committees have contributed more or less liberally to the migratory workers, Spain, Finland, Holland, refugee organizations, exiled writers, and a dozen political welfare organizations. The aid-to-Greece campaign was run with especial energy by a Hollywood committee chairmanned by Samuel Goldwyn, and over $400,000 was raised from individual donations, benefit performances, and collections in the movie theaters. The movie makers and workers at the studios gave the Red Cross and British war relief agencies a sum estimated to exceed $300,000. On regular occasions Hollywood puts on benefit nights at its night clubs for the Nazareth Home for Boys, and Boys Town in Nebraska. Because of the active leadership taken by the movie colony, California has contributed more than twenty-five percent of the money raised in America for the fight against infantile paralysis. The committee of movie and movie-theater people has raised $890,000 since 1938 from donations and "March of Dimes" collections in the movie houses.[20]

The benefactions of individual producers, actors, directors, and writers would be expected to show great variety. Norma Shearer is reported to have pledged her entire life's radio earnings to the National Foundation for Infantile Paralysis, paying in advance the $15,000 which she was to receive from one series of broadcasts.[21] Harry M. Warner built a fine gymnasium for the inmates at Sing Sing. Sometimes movie mercy takes a droll form. One actor launched his aging Chinese valet on a career as a laundry proprietor by staging a "world première": a microphone and spotlights were installed in front of the laundry, shiny automobiles pulled up, stars and chauffeurs dropped packages in a huge basket on the sidewalk, and the actor performed as a master of ceremonies with florid speeches to the startled bystanders. A movie director inaugurated a drive-in hamburger place for a friend, whom he had helped set up in the enterprise, by attending in white tie and tails while a hired orchestra encouraged dancing on the pavement.

How much do the movie makers spend, in all, on charity and philanthropic contributions? Our sixteen cases—again, not numerous enough to justify generalization—show donations ranging from $20 (!) to $2,100 for the year, or from .1 to 1.6 percent of annual income. The median sum was $385, the median percentage approximately 1.2. The player earning $220,000 a year contributed $1,200 (.6 percent) to charity. The director earning $129,000 spent $2,100 (1.6 percent), the highest amount in both absolute and percentage terms.

Allowing for a legion of open-handed souls in the movie colony, the philanthropic record of Hollywood's individuals as a whole is not spectacular. It unquestionably improved in 1940 and 1941, when aid to Britain and Greece won wide support in the movie colony. (Cary Grant, for example, has contributed at least $150,000 to British war relief and is said by some to have given as much as $300,000.) The personal services which Hollywood's talents contribute to worthy causes do not, of course, appear in any monetary record of benefactions; many actors make personal appearances at benefit performances (especially at army camps), many writers contribute skits and scripts, many directors donate their time and skill to philanthropic enterprises.

But, on the whole, Hollywood is only moderately generous, and is more liberal with its time and talent than its money. Why is this? Partly because Hollywood's people are insecure, and forever entertain dreads about disasters to their careers or savings. They are not accustomed to wealth; they have a deep-seated fear that their good fortune is evanescent—it came overnight and it may vanish overnight.

Philanthropy presents torturous problems to the Hollywoodian. If asked for money by an organization, he is generally overcome by a sense of depression as to the amount he is *expected* to give. He snipes at that figurative amount, questioning the value of the charity itself or "the percentage that will go into administration and overhead." Soon he resents the amount he thinks he is expected to give. Yet he cannot lose face—with others, with himself—by offering a sum disproportionate to his fame and income. And so he tosses between the Scylla of generosity and the Charybdis of anxiety. He ends either in a panic-ridden flight from donation, or by giving a moderate sum with a too-apologetic letter about "the many other requests to which we in Hollywood must respond." He never feels he has given enough; he always has moments when he wishes he had given a little more. The happiest solution, for many of the picture people, lies in putting the entire matter in the hands of a business agent, who then serves as a protecting buffer between the demands of charity and the pangs of apprehension.

But movie people are generous to people whom they know. This is a curious and significant point. In Hollywood, private philanthropies—to people down on their luck, old friends from home, beggars—are probably more frequent, though not necessarily larger, than public donations. The theater has always had a deep and sentimental tradition of benefactions to persons with whom there is a sentimental bond. But with reference to outside groups and organized charities, the psychological defenses go up, in suspicion of hostile and threatening Philistines. Many causes or organizations are instantly branded as "rackets" in the mind of the movie colony.

Movie people probably find it difficult to believe that acute poverty and need really exist. For they live in a make-believe universe in which the unpleasant is reduced to the smallest possible minimum. The movie people "write the scripts" of the world in which they move. They do not write in disturbing problems or challenging things. They tend to reject unpleasant thoughts because they have lived in a world in which unpleasant thoughts can be rejected.

There is a basic difference between giving and spending. Hollywood spends freely; it gives cautiously. The spending is often defended to the self as a social contribution: "Look at all the clerks and shopkeepers I'm helping by spending my money." Our society interprets spending as a demonstration of power, a testimonial of self-confidence in the amount of money which one has and the amount one is sanguine about making. Not to spend easily, therefore, may suggest to the world a fear of not being able to make money. The movie people, like the Joneses, spend partly to put up a front and partly to buttress their faith in themselves.

"Hollywood," said the comedian Ken Murray, "is a place where you spend more than you make, on things you don't need, to impress people you don't like." It is not enough to be wealthy: wealth must be put into material evidence, in forms determined by the canons of prestige. Money is a tool with which to create social distance between those who possess it and those who do not. Expensiveness becomes a mark of prestige in itself, and in time the expensive *ipso facto* becomes the beautiful. The whole philosophy of spending was expressed with memorable finesse in a cartoon which appeared some time ago in the *New Yorker,* that sensitive barometer of our follies: a Park Avenue matron is in a swank millinery shop, holding a hat from which a $1.98 price tag dangles; her expression is triumphant as she asks the salesgirl: "Can you copy this for $30?"

Hollywood's spending tends to become compulsive, as if the exorbitant amounts earned by the movie elite are "hot money." One is tempted to remark that the spending of the movie makers shows a striking resemblance to the spending of gamblers or those who obtained money by means which precipitated guilt in themselves. Spending becomes a mechanism by which one part of the personality pays off another.

How Much Do They Save?

How much is left to the movie makers after they have paid their agents and their taxes, lived in their homes and consumed their victuals, bought their clothes and automobiles, paid their servants, supported their dependents, and made their donations to charity? The money which goes into bank accounts, life insurance, annuities, stocks, bonds, or stables offers us a picture of Hollywood's estate. Again, needless to say, our data show extreme variations. One producer earning $150,000 lives with reasonable care, pays his taxes, and saves $75,000. An unmarried writer who earned $1,000 a week managed to corral over $35,000 in one year for his trust fund. But some in the movie colony ride on the roller coaster of extravagance; their sybaritic life, their horses and gambling, their flyers in investment and romance, make staggering inroads on their income. Yet when persons reach the $100,000-a-year bracket it is difficult to see how they can *avoid* saving thumping sums.

In our sixteen cases, the lowest percentage of annual income left after meeting taxes, living expenses, charities, and so on, was 9.5; the next lowest was 12.4 ($27,300 out of $220,000). The highest percentage left was 60.8 ($64,256 out of $105,554); the next highest was 54.9 percent ($70,800 out of $129,000). Twelve of our sixteen cases had more than a quarter of their annual income left after all taxes, expenses, and living costs; only four had less than a quarter; two had well over half. The average of saving for our group was exactly 33.3 percent.*

Hollywood, to bring this statistical foray to a close, earns much, spends much, is taxed heavily and burdened with sizable expenses; yet after all their spending and living, their inescapable disbursements and their optional luxuries, the movie anointed have enough left for their coffers to make foolish any dirge about the state of their good fortune.† *Omnia vincit amor.*

How to Spend $100,000

Several cases may be of interest to those eager to know how to live on an income of $100,000. Let us look at the books of an actress whose talents are assessed at $3,000 a week and whose earnings in one year of grace reached the sum of $220,-000. Her agent, business manager, personal maid, publicity counsel, and private secretary took $58,600. Taxes to Uncle Sam and the State of California ran up to $75,100. She paid $23,000

---

* Since our sixteen case records came from the files of business managers, it is to be expected that the savings are more substantial than those of movie people who do not engage a business agent to control their spending and plan their saving. In fifteen of the sixteen cases, the great bulk of the monies available for saving went into bank accounts, government bonds, insurance and annuities; minor amounts went into interest payment, loans, the payment of old notes or debts, and so on. In the sixteenth case, the director who earned $129,000, $70,800 (54.9 percent) was available after all taxes and expenses, and a total of $10,800 (8.4 percent) went into a ranch and stable. Those who engage a business manager do not necessarily lead thrifty lives; they are simply more thrifty than they would be without one.

† A complete table on the income, spending, and saving of our sixteen cases will be found in Appendix C.

on her home, and $18,300 went to servants, food, furnishings, and all the items involved in maintaining a large household. (Our lady lived well.) Her automobiles cost her $4,300. Her clothes and her children's wardrobe took a slice of $6,300. Dependents were, happily, a small burden and required only $500. Personal expenses, which includes doctors' bills, dentists' fees, lunches, and pin money (for herself and children), reached the $5,400 mark. No Lady Bountiful, our actress relinquished $1,200 to charity. And so, at the end of the year, she was left with $27,300, which was salted away in savings, life insurance, an annuity, and other investments.

A more favorable record of thrift is found in the case of an actor who earned $134,739. His house, household, victuals, and servants came to $9,253. Personal expenses for his wife and himself totaled $5,122. The children cost him $1,659. Clothing accounted for only $2,384. Medical expenses for the family ran up to $2,314. Automobiles took $1,776 and $1,900 was given to charity. Agents and necessary business expenses came to $20,106 and the tax load was $31,956. This left our thespian the healthy sum of $58,266 for savings, a trust fund, and the proverbial rainy day.

Lastly, let us glance into the life of one who earned less than either of the two cases we have examined—and saved much more. This movie person earned $105,554 and saved no less than $64,256. Rent payments represented a modest outlay of $1,885, and hearth and home, including servants, took $7,125. Clothing and wardrobe for husband, wife, and children amounted to $1,168. The sum of $3,154 went to dependents. The children's education, and medical expenses for the family, ran to $1,401. Automobiles required $2,272. Charity got $1,509. Agents and business expenses ran up to $13,876—very close to the minimum ten percent. Government took $8,379 for taxes. And so, when the last grim bill was paid, $64,256 was still there, strong and untouched.

THE BIG MONEY

A Note on Investments

The movie makers have learned how to invest their money. No longer hypnotized by oil wells, gold mines, and wild-cat speculation, as they were in the early days, they are investing their money in government bonds, real property, or orthodox enterprises. The movie colony has a high stake in local real estate. One realtor estimates that the stretch of ocean front at Santa Monica, populated almost completely by movie people, represents a million-dollar investment. Marion Davies owns thirty lots of beach front and eleven acres in Beverly Hills. Norma Talmadge, Richard Barthelmess, and Corinne Griffith, stars of a bygone day, have large holdings in residential property. Constance Bennett, Cecil B. DeMille, Charles Chaplin, Mary Pickford, L. B. Mayer, and Clarence Brown own bungalow courts and apartment houses, office buildings and warehouses.

The entire board of directors of the $2,000,000 Arrowhead Springs resort, a spa in the mountains two hours from Hollywood, is comprised of movie people and includes the Messrs. Joseph Schenck and Darryl Zanuck (two of the largest stockholders), Edgar Mannix, William Goetz, Al Jolson, and the Misses Claudette Colbert and Constance Bennett. Those who invest in ranches, groves, and livestock—either as part of their estates or as a business proposition—form a distinguished roster: Gable, McLaglen, Warner, Taylor, Tracy, Jolson, Wallis, and many others. Bing Crosby, Paul Whiteman, and Harold Lloyd are large stockholders in radio station KMPC. Movie people have bought into the Hollywood Baseball Club. Constance Bennett is the proprietor of a growing cosmetic business, in addition to her substantial holdings in real estate. Other celebrities of the screen own dress shops, furniture stores, antique shops, florist shops, and have invested in enterprises ranging from night clubs to trade papers.[22]

Cecil B. DeMille owns a large fruit ranch in California and a cotton plantation in Alabama. Reginald Denny is head of the largest model airplane factory in the United States. Frank and Ralph Morgan are scions of the family which makes Angostura Bitters. Al Jolson is part owner of Henry Armstrong, the champion prizefighter. Charles Bickford owns a string of gas stations. Donald Crisp is on the board of directors of a great bank. Jean Hersholt is on the board of directors of two banks and has investments in this country and in Denmark.

Some picture people deliberately become entrepreneurs in an effort to reduce their tax load; some list and operate their horses and stables as a business enterprise, and deduct the losses from their gross income. It is a common misconception in the movie colony that losing money on investments is a pastime carried on strictly at "the government's expense." [23]

Making money with their money magnifies the prosperity of the picture people who are in the Big Money. Joseph M. Schenck received an annual salary of $100,000 from Twentieth Century-Fox, but in three years his total income, from all sources, was $2,014,000.[24] Bing Crosby, who earns $175,000 per picture and does three pictures a year, also receives $7,500 for one hour's broadcast each week, got $77,000 in one year from the sale of 3,500,000 phonograph records, is the major stockholder in the profitable Del Mar race track, owns a 100-acre breeding ranch, seventy-five fine horses, an office building, real estate, and an untold variety of holdings in the corporation called Bing Crosby, Ltd.[25] The size of Louis B. Mayer's total income is a matter of conjecture, but the fact that he paid out $1,108,352 in income taxes in one year suggests the magnitude of his earnings.

In Hollywood, as in Cedar Falls, money breeds money, and wealth begins to accrue to those who possess it and put it to profitable use.   108

5. EROS IN HOLLYWOOD

> AS in all times, the incomes of leading actors [in ancient Greece] are very high . . . and the morals are what might be expected of men moving from place to place, fluctuating between luxury and poverty, and too high-strung to be capable of a stable and normal life. . . . They lived with characteristic superiority to the morals of their time.[1]

Hollywood is a synonym for wealth and glamour; it has also become a synonym for sin. As a symbol of sin, it should be noted, Hollywood is a scapegoat for traditional hostilities, the embodiment of Bohemia to all the Philistines on the face of the globe. The pious dismay with which ordinary folk regard the wicked movie people is precisely that which the country feels about the city, which the Umbrians felt about Rome, or which the backwoodsmen of America once discharged against the first families of Charleston. Back in 1789, the *Boston Gazette* rejoiced that "our beloved President stands unmoved in the vortex of folly and dissipation which New York presents."[2]

In recent years, Hollywood has produced singularly few scandals of really noteworthy proportion; yet the movie makers enjoy a reputation for moral turpitude and the movie colony is celebrated as "the vortex of folly and dissipation." Part of this may be traced to the popular assumption that actors are the natural children of Priapus, and follow sinful, libertine paths. Part of it is due to the fact that show people do tend to live

"with characteristic superiority to the morals of their time."
Part of it may be found in the public's remembrance of Hollywood's past. Part of it is a displaced reaction to salaries too
startling to go unresented and luxury habits too conspicuous to
be ignored.* Part of it is precipitated by the daily barrage of
sedulous gossip in movie columns and radio chit-chat. But, most
decisively, Hollywood's disrepute may be traced to the divorces
and remarriages which parade before the populace like wanton
violations of our moral code. Even if there were fewer divorces
in fact, the frenetic "romances" and elopements of Hollywood,
and the impression of free-for-all courtship, would give the
movie colony a questionable reputation.

The first thing to remember is that happy marriages and
normal lives, in Hollywood as elsewhere, do not get publicity.
The second point to remember is that a good many of Hollywood's amorous acrobatics are deliberately engineered by publicity offices or press agents. Romantic hoopla is unequaled as
a method of building up personalities quickly; and the infatua-
tions of fledgling actors and actresses are often plotted with as
much care as their personal appearance tours. *Life* states that
Victor Mature, "a beautiful hunk of man," discovered that he
photographed to best advantage when snapped beside small,
blonde damosels, and appeared in public with eighty different
small blondes in one recent year.[3] In Hollywood, leading men
in need of ballyhoo are ordered to escort movie queens to night
clubs, and promising actresses are maneuvered into the limelight which surrounds matinée idols; then reporters and photographers are "tipped off" to the budding enchantment, and the

---

* Charges of corruption and depravity have traditionally been hurled against
the wealthy; the pattern runs through history. Diodorus Siculus, an early Greek
historian, chastised the Romans for abandoning their "frugal and continent lives"
and blamed the Marsic War on their "disastrous luxury and insolent self-assertion."[4]
Dante, Boccaccio, the Christian philosophers, the Puritans—our forebears of every
nation and epoch—lament the evils assigned to riches. Aspersions fly more convinc-
ingly when the rich are actors or show people.

presses of the nation swing into action. The studios often pay the food and entertainment bills involved in these spurious romances.

The gentlemen of the press know full well that these are phony affinities, but that does not make them any the less newsworthy. A movie Lorelei's presence at Ciro's with a recruit from the Pasadena Players may be as cold a business operation as her luncheon for the 4-H Club, but her fame demands news space regardless of her motivations or her boredom. One actress, Judith Barrett, recently protested to her studio about the number of ardent swains she was being allotted by the press agents and refused to be an accessory to further "romance publicity tie-ups"; she contended that "loving" three gentlemen in four months bordered on promiscuity and, besides, made her look silly in the eyes of her public.

When a Roland Worthington and a Diana Blake begin to appear together in public, the event wins publicity for each through the fame of the other. This is invaluable to Roland Worthington if he is a new actor and Diana Blake is a star, or to Diana Blake if she is a new actress and Roland Worthington is a star. The conjunction of names arouses interest in the picture Roland Worthington has just completed and in the classic to which Diana Blake is about to lend her talents. Gossip and the natural momentum of even a counterfeit *affaire du coeur* do the rest. Columnists are expert at exploiting the pseudo-machinations of Eros in Hollywood, and the news is kept hot and palpitating for weeks—especially since shrewd brains are employed to spread alarums of impending marriages, stormy separations, rapturous reconciliations, and generally impassioned carryings-on. The movie columns record the epochal sequence for weeks on end, in this too-familiar manner:

What's this about Roland Worthington and Diana Blake? . . . Roland and Diana dancing cheek to cheek at Mocambo. . . . Roland and Diana are that way about each other. . . . Roland and Diana are quarreling. . . . Roland and Diana have made up. . . . Don't be surprised if Roland and Diana elope. . . . Roland and Diana feuding. . . . Roland and Diana making eyes again. . . . Diana burned up because heart-throb Roland is dating Mona Latour, starlet soon to make her movie bow in *Memory at Midnight*. . . . Roland in a dither because pulse-quickener Diana is holding hands with William Loring, collar-ad due to appear in *Memory at Dawn*. . . .

The variety of phrasings by which journalists can hint at amour without supporting data is a triumph of linguistic virtuosity.

Unmarried actors are at a premium in the film colony, and they are drafted by their studios for service in the cause of conspicuous romance. David Niven, until he left for service in His Majesty's forces, was one of the most welcome party-goers and one of the most fully reported bachelors in the movie capital, and was alleged to be enchanted by at least three maidens per month. James Stewart's statistical average, though not so high, was nevertheless imposing. (Jimmie Fidler, the maestro of quidnuncs, metaphorically asserted that Mr. Stewart, before he left Hollywood for the army, had "dated 263 glamour girls.") [5] As for the actresses, no unmarried female of star stature can see a month go by without being reported as pursued by at least one bewitched cavalier of appropriate fame or promise.

There is method as well as madness in the romantic whirligigism of Hollywood. This becomes surpassingly clear if we make a systematic examination of the love market. Let us take one young, popular movie star, Tyrone Power for example, and record all the romances he was reported to have had in one year of his bachelorhood. Let us take a not too recent year in order to gain perspective and to let the facts take on that unconfused quality which time alone endows. Let us see, in some detail, what Mr. Power's sentimental history was said to have been in the 1937-38 movie season (September to September).

During that year, the movie columns and *Photoplay* magazine solemnly reported Mr. Power to be enamored of

> Loretta Young
> Sonja Henie
> Janet Gaynor
> Simone Simon
> Arleen Whelan

Scarcely a week went by without hints of the infatuation existing between the versatile Mr. Power and one or another of these charming maidens, each of whom, during this fecund period, was also reported to be profoundly jealous of at least two of the others. Wonderful to relate, it turns out that Mr. Power and the Misses Young, Henie, Gaynor, Simon, and Whelan were all employees of the same ingenious studio, Twentieth Century-Fox!

Now let us list the attachments officially credited to each of Mr. Power's alleged sweethearts in the same year:

Loretta Young:
Tyrone Power
Cesar Romero
Richard Greene
George Brent

Sonja Henie:
Tyrone Power
Cesar Romero
Richard Greene
Michael Brooke

Simone Simon:
Tyrone Power
Cesar Romero
Richard Greene
Gene Markey

Arleen Whelan:
Tyrone Power
Cesar Romero
Richard Greene
Michael Brooke

Janet Gaynor:
Tyrone Power
Cesar Romero
Douglas Fairbanks, Jr.
Adrian

It would appear that the Messrs. Power, Romero, Greene, and Brooke were engaged in a libidinal round-robin with the

113

Misses Young, Henie, Simon, and Whelan. And oddly enough, all these gentlemen as well as these ladies were employees of the same studio, Twentieth Century-Fox! Nor is that all. Gene Markey, mentioned apropos Miss Simon, was also employed at the same studio; George Brent, cited in re Miss Young, was acting in *The Rains Came* for Twentieth Century-Fox at the time; and Douglas Fairbanks, Jr., linked with Miss Gaynor, was about to appear with her (a Twentieth Century-Fox star) in Selznick's *The Young in Heart*. The hand of engineered love becomes even more apparent if we note that George Brent's other attachments for the year were reported to be Bette Davis, Olivia de Havilland, and Ann Sheridan—all, oddly enough, Warner Brothers stars, as, again oddly enough, is Mr. Brent.

It is too much to believe that actors and actresses are so fanatically devoted to their studios that they love as well as work for them. A simpler explanation is that Twentieth Century-Fox and Warner Brothers (other studios did not happen to figure in Tyrone Power's reported love-life for the 1937-38 season) are remarkably prolific in the manufacture of romance for and among their personnel. Mr. Power, incidentally, finally married Annabella (of Twentieth Century-Fox, by genuine coincidence) and was dropped out of the tournament of amour. Since Mr. Power was his studio's leading matinée idol, this represented an unfortunate blow to the publicity wizards; they thereupon drafted the reserve Lotharios of Twentieth Century-Fox for double duty. Richard Greene, a relatively unknown English actor, Cesar Romero, a dashing Latin bachelor, and Michael Brooke (the Earl of Warwick), for whom the studio had cinematic hopes, became veterans under fire in the restaurants and night clubs of Hollywood; and the sentiments of the Misses Young, Henie, Gaynor, Simon and Whelan again managed to follow the trajectory of press-agented romance. The tenacity with which this coterie continued to exhibit deep passion for each other was nothing short of miraculous.*

The moral to be drawn from this whole quaint analysis is simple: the romances, scandals, and inter-personal complications of Hollywood often involve *the same individuals* week in and week out; and this leads to a somewhat lopsided impression of love and heartbreak in Hollywood. All is not true that appears in the gossip columns—to put it charitably.

The publicity philosophy of Hollywood has long rested upon the premise that almost any news is good news. Keeping a name before the public is the first goal of ballyhoo; the contexts in which the name appears are a secondary consideration. This strategy may be effective for the moment, but it does not help to give the public the impression Hollywood is simultaneously trying to disseminate: that the movie colony is a community of normal, hardworking human beings with, perhaps, slightly more pliable emotions. This would be difficult enough to achieve, considering Hollywood's composition and reputation; when coupled with the strenuous activities of the fourth estate in the film colony, the task is well-nigh impossible.

Where Hollywood is concerned, journalistic license is as elastic as taffy. One female oracle of the press recently announced: "I wasn't surprised when the Mary Healy-Peter Lind Hayes engagement was called off." This world-shaking information appeared in an early edition of the columnist's papers, but was hastily replaced the same day with this item: "Mary Healy and Peter Lind Hayes . . . were on their way to Yuma last night."[6] There was no apology to the readers for this bland metastasis.

Accuracy is no problem in covering Hollywood; neither is good taste. The "Rambling Reporter" column in the *Hollywood*

---

* Miss Young finally married Tom Lewis, Miss Henie wedded Dan Topping, Miss Whelan married Alex D'Arcy, Miss Gaynor married Adrian, and Miss Simon remained unwed.

Reporter recently informed the world that Henry Wilcoxon and Joan Woodbury have "a six-month option clause in their wedding contract," and two weeks later the same Pepys wrote: "The would-be divorcées [of Hollywood] are looking up Las Vegas hotel accommodations instead of . . . Reno, because Las Vegas is only an hour and a half by plane and they can come into Hollywood for 23 hours once a week." * 7

The *Los Angeles Times* ushered in a New Year by publishing a story which surveyed the year's divorces in Hollywood, and proudly listed the names of ninety persons (forty-five couples) who had been disespoused during the preceding twelve months. The caption read:

DIVORCE ROLLS LIST NOTABLES
Big Names of Hollywood on Court Journals of 1940, Review Discloses

The divorces were listed in monthly order, as a sort of almanac. The roster of blighted romance included such battle-scarred warriors for Cupid as John Barrymore and Florence Rice, and such celebrated names as Ginger Rogers, Alice Faye, and Hedy Lamarr. But it also embraced persons who could scarcely be considered either "notables" or "big names." Radio comics, dancers, song writers, band leaders, dubious actors, and obscure cameramen were all poured into one newsy brew; for example, Edmund Ruffner, Charlotte Buford, William Mellor, Irene Colman, Edward Cherkose, Otto Linkenhelt, and so on. These names evoke no recognition in the cinema-seasoned soul of this writer and are surely as unfamiliar to the reader. But Hollywood, that ensign of the dissolute, was credited with their combined conjugal defections.⁸

Hollywood's indiscriminate publicity leads to the invention of minor scandals which a news editor is almost compelled to

---

* The divorce laws in Nevada require six weeks of continuous residence in the state; *twenty-four* hours of absence would break the continuity.

pass on to his culture-starved public. Certainly press agents, as well as the press, must accept responsibility for a whacking share of the idiotic stories to which movie names are linked. Perhaps the most glaring example of this practice is found in a story concocted by some publicity man at Paramount to the effect that almost everybody connected with *I Want a Divorce*, a Paramount picture, had been through the divorce mill at least once. This epic of maladroit publicity "accidentally" leaked out, and the United Press correspondent in Hollywood gave it nation-wide space in his syndicated feature column, listing the divorce-laden cast: actors Joan Blondell, Dick Powell, Conrad Nagel, Frank Fay, Gloria Dickson; producer George Arthur; director Ralph Murphy; author of the original story, Adela Rogers St. John (who resides several thousand miles from Hollywood); writer of the screen play, Frank Butler; and even the press agent, Jean Bosquet. "Only exception is Mickey Kuhn, aged six." [9] This ballyhoo boomeranged, as should have been expected, when civic and religious groups threatened to boycott the film.

The role of the gossip columnists in inflating romantic trivia into news, in inventing love where Cupid never aimed a dart, or in reheating tepid emotions until they appear to give off warmth, must figure prominently in any analysis of Hollywood's libido. Consider this bit of reportage, culled from one issue of Ed Sullivan's gossip column:

. . . What's this about Lya Lys and her hubby? . . . Whether Orson Welles, after his divorce is final, weds Dolores Del Rio, after her divorce is final, is anybody's guess, but they're very much in love. . . . Tony Martin is due to set up bachelor quarters, if he can tear himself away from that blonde and lovely model. . . . Ona Munson is flirting with Raymond Burr. . . . Bonita Granville and Rand Brooks are running a super-temperature. . . . Jane Frazee has Arnold Kunody selling love insurance to himself. . . . The Marlene Dietrich-Tim Durant attachment is building into a bonfire. . . . Madeleine Carroll can't wait to get back to Paris, where her husband-to-be is a political biggie. . . .[10]

A banker or a merchant can dine and dance with a goodly number of attractive females without precipitating an international furor, but when a movie celebrity attends a fully chaperoned party with the wife of his cousin from Seattle, that epochal event is recorded, interpreted, embellished, and splashed across the print and rotogravure pages of the world. Ponder, for example, these items taken from one of Sidney Skolsky's daily columns:

... Jimmy Stewart's and Olivia de Haviiland's intimates are making bets that the pair will elope. . . . Rose Hobart and Walter Grosenor will be divorced. . . . Jeffrey Lynn has a "crush" on Ginger Rogers, whom he never met. . . . Dorothy Lovett and Jack Hively are in the Torrid Zone. . . . Garbo has put Dr. Gaylord Hauser on a diet. . . . Anatole Litvak is giving off-the-set direction to Barbara O'Neil. . . .[11]

When the current gossip market is low, the fires of the past are raked and re-raked for glowing embers. Jimmie Fidler often reminds his readers of the glorious past, as in the following, which appeared in September of 1940:

... In September, 1937 . . . Tyrone Power had switched to Janet Gaynor. . . . Gloria Blondell and Ronald Reagan were an item. . . . Ginger Rogers and Lee Bowman were romantic. . . . Norma Shearer's preferred escort was young Doug Fairbanks. . . . Three years later, we find . . . Tyrone is married to Annabella, and Janet Gaynor is wed to Adrian. . . . Gloria Blondell is now serious with Cubby Broccoli, and Ronald Reagan is married to Jane Wyman. . . . Norma Shearer will marry George Raft, and Doug Fairbanks, Jr. is waiting for Sir Stork. . . .[12]

Where historical scholarship fails to unearth *outré* tidbits about movie people who are still in the spotlight, Mr. Fidler resorts to the revival of gossip about names that have faded into semi-obscurity, as in this column of June 26, 1941:

Eleven Years Ago in Hollywood: . . . Billie Dove, just divorced from Director Irvin Willat, was rumored to be the secret bride of Howard Hughes . . . Bebe Daniels and Ben Lyon were wed . . . Lina Basquette and Cameraman Peverell Marley took their marital woes into court . . . Dolores Del Rio and Cedric Gibbons assured reporters "theirs was the perfect, enduring marriage" . . . Cowboy Star Rex Lease was fined $50 for blacking Vivian Duncan's eye during a Malibu Beach party . . . Betty Compson and Director James Cruze were divorced.[13]

And so on and on.

Hollywood's penchant for dramatic elopements contributes mightily to its reputation for easy virtue. Elopements are an index of impulsiveness, and in a community where elopements occur with excessive frequency the tolerance of impetuous conduct must be high. It is not surprising that the abrupt execution of matrimonial vows provokes disturbing murmurs in the public conscience. Marriages which are consummated without warning, and at a substantial distance from the habitat of the enamored couple, challenge the mores of a public which has been taught that marriage is a holy ceremony requiring thought and solemnity on the part of those who venture into it.

Now, elopements are charged with a particularly strong publicity potential. They are surprise attacks, like *blitzkrieg*, and merit special attention in the press. Elopements are dramatic, and dramatic acts appeal to dramatic personalities. It is the business of actors to dramatize their roles, and it is the practice of actors to dramatize themselves as well. Self-dramatization, either the typical neurosis or the occupational disease of Hollywood, is one reason for the picture people's weakness for elopements. Where the parties to a marriage are not impetuous, and where their preference may be for a quiet union *sans* photographers, parades, and collective hysteria, the familiar hand of publicity still likes to pull the strings.

The movie colony's attitude toward the Hollywood representatives of the press embraces a combination of cunning, fear, hate, and propitiation. The ubiquitous Louella Parsons, whose phone bill averages $200 a month, "can spot a story at 500 paces . . . will employ every known means and pressure to get it—but exclusively—and she is ruthless and terrifying in the clinches."

The echo of Miss Hedy Lamarr's shy "Yes" had hardly died away on the soft night air before Gene Markey was on the phone notifying Louella. When Miss Claudette Colbert decided to elope to Yuma at 1:30 in the morning with Dr. Joel Pressman, it was Lolly whom she thought of first. . . .

To neglect her in such matters is to ask for such a barrage of petty sideswipes in her column as no actor feels he can weather. Joan Crawford tried to give the news of her forthcoming divorce from Douglas Fairbanks, Jr., to a fan-magazine writer, and for years she was picking Louella's buckshot out of her neck. Louella manifested the same resentment when Ronald Colman and Miss Benita Hume failed to notify her of their marriage.[14]

There has been something of an actors' rebellion against the demands of ballyhoo; some stars have gone so far as to demand privacy in the time and manner of their matrimonial ceremonies. The unions of Clark Gable and Carole Lombard, Robert Taylor and Barbara Stanwyck, Ronald Colman and Benita Hume, Laurence Olivier and Vivien Leigh, and Joan Bennett and Walter Wanger set grave precedents in Hollywood for weddings which were neither staged nor spectacular. Gable and Lombard drove to a small Arizona town, were admitted to holy wedlock, and phoned the studio to announce a *fait accompli*. Taylor and Stanwyck tried to be married secretly in San Diego, were apprehended in this heinous effort, but got their quiet wedding elsewhere. The Wanger-Bennett and Olivier-Leigh nuptials were executed with simplicity and dispatch. One daring pair of actors eloped to Santa Barbara, to the astonishment of their respective studios, but they were ordered home for pictures for the fan magazines; they posed in the photograph gallery for half the night, then left for a secluded honeymoon.[15]

These routine ceremonies stand in striking contrast to the matrimonial carnivals of a decade ago, when Hollywood weddings were conducted on a scale reminiscent of the battle of

Balaclava. Recent years have seen nothing fit to compare to the Vilma Banky-Rod La Rocque hymeneal, a landmark of connubial opulence, at which frenzied thousands lined the streets, women fainted, the police used physical persuasion on hysterical fans, and Hollywood's elite was split asunder in the fight for ringside admission. The entire celebration was conducted by the publicity department of the Goldwyn studio, which footed the bill happily. A brave stab at the old majesty was made in the Jeanette MacDonald-Gene Raymond nuptials in 1938, but the blasé shrugged or disapproved of the whole display. A desperate effort at novelty occurred in the fall of 1939 at the union of one Marjorie Kelley and one Ed Maltby; Major C. C. Moseley flew his plane over the garden, dropped a bouquet of orchids and gardenias on an admiring tableau, then blazed two smoky hearts pierced by an arrow across the heavens.[16] This cosmic gesture elicited virtually no approbation (or publicity) in the new Hollywood.

Actors and actresses are handsome people and they work with many other handsome people; if Hollywood were run by a Puritan *Gestapo,* temptation would still thrive. As long as the making of films requires beautiful women and arresting men, especially men and women who can turn emotion on and off at the click of a camera shutter, Hollywood's amorous sentiments will be characterized by flexibility. Movies, we have said, cannot be made by mechanics; movie making demands the activity of creative temperaments, the fructifying interplay of unrestrained personalities, of people with a flair, people who can act or direct or write, people who can exploit their neuroses and their fantasies. The making of films is itself a kind of prolonged fantasy, and picture makers must be rich in reverie and capable of externalizing their inner fables. Such people are not distinguished for emotional consistency. In the trenchant phrase of Gilbert Seldes, movie people have a high "potential capacity for disaster." [17] In Hollywood, mercurial personalities are concentrated in one tight little colony, and they aggravate and maximize one another's inconstancy.

Actors use their emotions as masons use bricks. "Reactions that occur in more normal employment after five o'clock in the afternoon . . . are discernible on the sets at nine o'clock in the morning. It may be only play-acting, but it cannot but exert some effect on the participants." [18] The general tension of movie making adds additional hazards to an already parlous situation, for the exploitation of nerves—by the self and by others—is part and parcel of the picture making process.

Persons skilled in professional make-believe have an extraordinary capacity for private make-believe; how "genuine," indeed, can an actor believe his own emotions to be when he is so expert in fabricating emotion? Acting is a form of deception, and actors can mesmerize themselves almost as easily as an audience. So it is that actors in quest of an undying love are saddened when they discover that, like other roles, the conjugal loses freshness and conviction with the mere passage of time.

Actors are notoriously egoistic. Their careers rest upon either pulchritude or a talent in simulation; both require consistent attention to the self by the self. The actor's world is dominantly egocentric, and in such a world vanity thrives and narcissism is well nourished. The fight for close-ups, one of the most common pastimes in Hollywood, is the simplest illustration of competition between self-oriented personalities. And this is only natural, since an actor's face and physique are his assets and he is compelled to devote as much attention to them as a glass-blower to his respiration.

There is a saying that the typical Hollywood triangle consists of an actor, his wife, and himself. The self-centered personality makes a difficult enough spouse; when two supreme egotists take the wedding vows the prognosis can hardly be sanguine. Many Hollywood romances founder on the cold rocks of professional competition, for sometimes the clash between careers is inescapable. The success which one mate enjoys is often an implicit rebuke to the other. Psychological security in Hollywood is inextricably allied to prestige, and few movie makers can endure continuous blows to the ego. It was just this point which was dramatized with great skill in the best of the films on Hollywood, A Star Is Born.

The subordination of one's own interests to the demands of another is seldom easy; it is impossible when both husband and wife are making the demands. The Hollywood husband fears he will become the appendage of a glamour girl; the wife sees her own career dimmed by the brilliance of her husband's. When the first Mrs. Lawrence Tibbett sued her husband for divorce, she remarked that "fame and family happiness are not consistent." [19] The movie wives who have professional careers retain their own names and their own careers after marriage, and this reaffirms the psychological autonomy which actors bring into the state of marriage.

Hollywood's people, moreover, cease to be individuals and become business institutions. They are guided, protected, and surrounded by a staff of agents, lawyers, business managers, press agents, secretaries, maids, yes-men; and it becomes increasingly difficult, even for their helpmeets, to cut through the court in order to reach the sovereign. "I've got to make an appointment to see my wife," one Hollywoodian bitterly told this writer. Nor does the disordered schedule by which the movie people live encourage domestic serenity. During the hectic periods of production, directors, producers, or writers may cease to go home, and forget they are married; nights, Sundays, weekends, holidays are burned on the altar of "the picture."

The general temper of Hollywood presents a further challenge to domestic tranquillity. Hollywood is profoundly cynical; movie gossip is cruel and disruptive. The movie colony has a bumper crop of babblers who specialize in tales of marital high-

123

jinks. Romances are subjected to an onslaught of rumor and innuendo; courtships are put to the acid test of calumny; and marriages need stout walls to survive the cannonade of prattle. Nothing rolls off the tongue with more relish than the low-down on Hollywood's love-life. With almost four hundred reporters (in addition to Hollywood's own corps of gossips) on the twenty-four-hour alert, sniffing the air for breezes of love, divorce, or infidelity, filling their columns with the most intimate chit-chat, there is no haven for privacy, even of sentiment. The daily repetition of hints about a dying romance may have little basis in fact, but they keep doubt in the spotlight of attention. Could Caesar's wife have remained above suspicion if suspicion were elevated to print in each issue of the *Acta diurna?* For that matter, could Caesar?

Movie stars, we have suggested, are America's royalty. The aristocratic role not only permits but encourages a certain amount of philandering. The nobility of a society are expected to symbolize its virtues; they are also tacitly charged with the duty of violating the stricter taboos from time to time. This makes the high-born more "human," more endearing to the public, and it provides vicarious gratification to the millions who dare not indulge in the transgressions they may secretly cherish. It is striking that there is at least one black sheep in most of the families of the British aristocracy, and that both the families and the truants are the more fondly regarded because of it. In the same fashion, the movie fan is privately delighted by the romantic acrobatics of his idols. The domestic scandal which involved Mary Astor several years ago and won national attention did not ruin her career (as her frantic producer feared); on the contrary, it increased her fame and popularity. An actor's fan-mail generally rises after a divorce, according to the heads of several fan-mail departments in Hollywood studios. The divorce creates sympathy for a loved object which has suffered;

the divorced star becomes "available" symbolically, offering less guilt and more verity to dreams of possession.

Aristocracies, whether political or cinematic, have generally not been distinguished for moral rectitude. In 1622, Henry Peacham, author of *The Compleat Gentleman,* bewailed the fact that cursing, drinking, and flagrant wenching were no bar to recognition at the court of England.[20] The staunch defense of morality and the consistent expression of virtue are the responsibility of the middle-class. Only the naive identify social status with probity.

Moral elasticity, in short, has never been an obstacle to position, either in Hollywood or Mayfair or Potsdam. And the jeremiads on Hollywood's iniquity are identical with those intoned about actors and actresses all through history. Professor Arthur Livingston of Harvard traced this classic phenomenon and concluded that "the argument of sexual immorality usually brought against the acting profession is an afterthought"—to rationalize their exclusion from the halls of those who "belong." [21]

The movie colony conforms to the pattern of a quasi-royalty in another respect. Members of a nobility marry within the ranks of the high-born; this preserves and perpetuates caste. The movie elite favors professional endogamy for somewhat the same reason. Movie fame and success impose subtle obligations which, if violated, endanger prestige; and the high court of Hollywood cannot escape being influenced by considerations of the alliance between marriage and prestige. Producers, agents, and publicity experts are quick to suggest the risks involved in marrying below one's station.

Marriages in Hollywood thus aim towards the endogamous; the romantic ideal of the movie colony, as of the movie fans, is one of marriage between persons on the same economic-prestige level. The Gable-Lombard, Olivier-Leigh, Wanger-Bennett, Taylor-Stanwyck alliances are the most recent examples of this phenomenon; historically, the Fairbanks-Pickford, Thalberg-Shearer, Banky-LaRocque, Fairbanks, Jr.-Crawford unions remain memorable examples.* Picture people are inclined to take helpmates from the movie colony for other reasons: because of the insulated sphere in which they live and work, because their social life is circumscribed by the film colony, and because of a natural community of interests. Outsiders remain emphatically outside the intensely specialized, self-preoccupied universe of movie making.

The counterpart to all that has been said so far is that the movie people do tend to fall in love genuinely, easily, and frequently. Their search for security is, like that of all of us, profoundly libidinal; but their inhibitions are less conventional. Impulsive by temperament, they fall in love impulsively. Self-dramatizing, they dramatize their affinities. Uncertain, they rush into marriages partly to force themselves into "irrevocable" circumstances, because they fear that time and reason may undermine the foundations of the love for which they desperately yearn and which they urgently wish to give. Elopements often follow hard upon the most tormenting doubts as to whether the great love can last.

It is a grave mistake to assume that Hollywood's people marry cynically. If they were really cynical, or indifferent to the moral power of matrimony, why would they marry at all? They have the money, the circumstances, and the tacit immunity to carry on extended *liaisons intimes* without creating connubial problems or responsibilities. Hollywood's marriages represent efforts to fulfill the marital expectations current in

---

* There are, of course, prominent exceptions to this generalization. Claudette Colbert, Irene Dunne, Bette Davis took husbands from outside the movie colony; Spencer Tracy, Edward G. Robinson, James Cagney, and other male stars are married to women who had no screen careers. Incidentally, the movie stars who married before they became stars are mated to relatively plain spouses; but those who marry after achieving movie fame are influenced by Hollywood's stereotypes of beauty and generally select beautiful or handsome partners from within the movie colony, or persons of high social standing in the world outside.

our society. To the movie star no less than the waitress or the shoe clerk, marriage is a mysterious panacea for inner misery. The picture people are not sufficiently secure to assume their right to aberrance, or to live counter to the mores. The members of a stable elite, or of a profession like the stage, to which has been accorded ancient and broad sanctions for living, can marry in haste without repenting at leisure. But the picture people marry as America marries—out of love, confusion, hope, and despair.

What are the facts about marriage and divorce in Hollywood? To begin with, there are no published data on the subject. The biographies of movie people, in the *Motion Picture Almanac*, the *Film Daily Year Book*, *Who's Who in America*, or other compendiums, are uncluttered by precise information on marriage and divorce. The material to be found in newspapers is incomplete, and newspaper morgues encompass neither a wide nor representative enough segment of the film colony for our purposes. It would be impossible to examine court records in all the places the movie people may have been married or divorced.

No other information was so difficult to obtain in Hollywood as information on divorce. There are no objective sources; the movie makers are sensitive about their disespousement; there was resistance to the effort to ascertain the facts with reasonable accuracy. The information which follows is derived from 686 questionnaire returns, extensive research materials, plus the collated evidence of a panel of experts; it presents the most accurate data *which were available;* it suggests the *probable* pattern of marriage and divorce in Hollywood.*

* A lengthy description of the methods used in obtaining and handling marriage and divorce data is given in Appendix E. The 686 questionnaires comprised 294 actors and actresses, 17 producers, 105 writers, 68 directors, 105 film editors (cutters), 79 assistant directors, 18 directors of photography. The data refer to

127

How many persons in the movie colony are married? From 686 replies to questionnaire inquiries, checked carefully for internal consistency and for representativeness, it was discovered that 73 percent (501) were married and 27 percent (185) were single.

For producers, actors, directors, and writers alone, the groups with which this study is primarily concerned (484 cases), exactly three-quarters were married and one-quarter unmarried (1939-40). Actors and actresses show an inordinately high percentage of single persons (almost a third), as compared to producers, directors, and writers. (Since more actors have been divorced, as we shall see, more of them are single today.) Furthermore, 74.1 percent of the actors are married, as compared to only 54.7 percent of the actresses; conversely, only 25.9 percent of the actors are single, as compared to 45.3 percent of the actresses. In other words, almost twice as large a proportion of actresses are single; almost half of the actresses in Hollywood are unmarried. This may be explained by the fact that actresses, as a group, are markedly younger than actors (37.6 percent of the actresses in Hollywood are under thirty years of age, as compared to only 6.8 percent of the actors).

How many times have how many persons in Hollywood been divorced? Out of 200 actors and actresses studied, 35.5 percent have probably been divorced; out of 79 producers analyzed, 30.3 percent have probably been disespoused. For the professional groups in the movie colony as a whole (457 cases *):

1939-40, when the information was collected. For the complete tabulation, see Appendix E. The sample is both large enough and representative enough to permit generalization.

* The 457 cases include 200 actors, 79 producers, 55 directors, 63 assistant directors, 48 film editors, and 12 directors of photography. Note that *writers* are not included. Although questionnaires were filled out and returned by 167 writers, the Screen Writers Guild withheld the information on number of marriages, salaries, annual income, and so on. Our divorce data on 200 actors and 79 producers are not based on questionnaire returns, as they are for directors, assistant directors, film editors, and directors of photography. The actor and producer divorce materials were derived from an expert scoring method, which is described in Appendix E.

19.3 percent seem to have been divorced at least once.
3.9 percent seem to have been divorced at least twice.
1.3 percent seem to have been divorced at least three times.

‚his means that about 24.5 percent of the professional groups ɩ the movie colony have probably been divorced.* These fig-ᵣes cannot be compared with data for the United States as a ₁hole, because census figures and other studies, such as those ₒnducted by Stouffer and Spencer (*American Journal of So-iology,* January, 1939), deal with divorce *rates, i.e.,* the num-er of marriages and divorces in a given year. No figures are ₐvailable for the number of persons in the United States over ᵢghteen years of age who have been married or divorced once, ₜvice, and so on—which is what our data on Hollywood show. ɩ the United States, in 1937, there were 250,000 divorces ᵣranted and 1,426,000 marriages consummated. Stouffer and ₚencer estimated that in 1935 there were 16.4 divorces per ₕundred marriages.[22]

One more figure is worth recording: of those in Hollywood ʳho are or have been married (if we exclude, that is, those ʳho have never married), 29.3 percent seem to have been mar-ₑd more than once.† For the actors, producers, and directors, ₕis percentage is slightly higher—30.6 percent of the 288 *who*

* Except for the actors and producers, the figures given above were of necessity ₑrived from questionnaire data on the number of marriages; *i.e.,* where two or ₒre marriages were acknowledged, divorce may reasonably be inferred. (A check ₒwed that, for our group, remarriage following the death of, rather than divorce ₒm, a spouse was so infrequent that it could affect our figures by less than one ₑrcent.) Now, since many of our questionees may have been married once, di-ᵥrced, but *not* remarried, the divorce would not appear in our data. (See Ap-ₙdix E.) So many questionees refused to answer whether they were single or ₐrried, and our questionnaires showed so many blank spaces for the question on ₙmber of marriages, that it became clear that those who did not write in their ₐnswer declined precisely because they preferred to conceal the fact that they ₗd been divorced.

† 74 of our cases had never married: 37 actors out of 200, 2 producers out of ', 7 directors out of 55, 18 assistant directors out of 63, 9 film editors out of ₚ, 1 director of photography out of 12. This left 383 cases out of the total of ₇. 112 (29.3 percent of 383) had been married two or more times.

took the marriage vows * appear to have been married mor
than once. This means that, according to our sample, almos
one out of every three marriages among Hollywood's actor:
producers, and directors, has probably ended in divorce.

Let us round out this excursion into the statistics on blighte
romance with a happier accounting, which shows how man
children the subjects of this study have had. Three-fourths c
Hollywood's producers, actors, and directors have children; a
most 40 percent have one child, and over a third (34.7 percent
have more than one child. These proportions are almost exactl
those which prevail if we include assistant directors, film ed
tors, and directors of photography.

American society began to sanction divorces among its men
bers as early as 1875, and in the words of one celebrate
dowager, "all at once it became fashionable to divorce yo
helpmeet, and Newport followed the fashion with amazing er
thusiasm." [23] One evening in the late '80s the distinguishe
James van Alen gave a dinner for a dozen guests, all ornamen
of the *crème de la crème,* and lamented, "This dinner has almo
driven me mad. I thought I should never be able to seat m
guests properly without putting some former wife by her e:
husband. It took us literally hours to make a seating plan. . .
Each year Southampton, Bar Harbor, Tuxedo Park, and oth:
citadels of the wellborn are "compelled to revise [their] know
edge of family ties in accordance with the matrimonial altera
tions brought about during the preceding winter by divorce an
re-marriage." [24]

Our figures on divorce and remarriage strongly underline tl
remarks on the temperament and instability of the movie peop
with which this chapter was begun. Entertainers anywhere, ar
the kingdom of show business at any time, are governed l

---

* 163 actors, 77 producers, 48 directors.

drives which foster inconstancy, whether in observing a diet or maintaining a household. In New Jersey, for example, far from Hollywood and as long ago as 1887-1906, there were substantially more divorces among actors and show people than in any other occupational group.[25]

Professors Ernest W. Burgess and Leonard Cottrell, Jr., of the University of Chicago made a "happiness ratings" of 526 couples, and also drew upon Lang's study of 17,533 couples; their analysis arrived at several conclusions which are pertinent here: first, the higher the degree of control which a community exercises over the conduct of a person in a given occupation, the more frequently will satisfactory marital adjustment be found in that occupation; second, the higher the degree of personal mobility required in an occupation, the less is that occupation associated with good marital adjustment. Burgess and Cottrell found that the nature of an occupation is a more significant factor in influencing marital happiness than are economic factors.[26]

This strongly supports the interpretation of the data on marriage and divorce among the movie makers which this writer has given. The nature of movie making and the kind of people and skills it demands, attract creative and volatile personality types to Hollywood. The professional temper of Hollywood— charged with quick change and unpredictable vicissitudes— heightens instability in already insecure psyches. The syncopated social life tends to increase the waywardness of its individuals. The indulgence of a public enamored of its movie gods offers tolerant sanctions to the violation of taboos, and encourages transgression upon the stricter codes of amour. The moral climate of a community composed of and dominated by show people abets the fickle and the aberrant. It is scarcely strange that there is matrimonial vacillation among such people in such a setting.

Divorce is not a lark, and the disruption of marriages represents far more than the whim of spoiled people who "cannot get along with each other." Divorce means suffering; divorce is an index of personality strife, of conflict within the individual and between two personalities.* The national divorce rate is mounting year by year, and experts predict that if the present trend continues, one-half of all marriages will end in divorce by 1963.[27]

Matrimonial discord reaches into the highest and lowest strata of our society. It was a portentous sign of the times when a King of Great Britain and Ireland and of the British Dominions Beyond the Seas, Defender of the Faith and Emperor of India, abdicated his throne to take unto his heart a lady who had been twice divorced. In the United States, the roster of the multiple-married includes many of the proudest names in our social aristocracy. Consider the historic changes epitomized by names such as Mrs. J. Widener-Leidy-Holden-Wichfeld, Mrs. Margaret Emerson-McKay-Vanderbilt-Baker-Amory-Emerson, Mrs. Delphine Dodge-Cromwell-Baker-Godde, or Mrs. Millicent Rogers-Hoogstraeten-Ramos-Balcom.

The Four Hundred exercise a potent influence on the values of a society, and the example they set has wide repercussions. The old stigma attached to divorce is losing its might; our moral barometer—rightly or wrongly—has a higher tolerance level than ever before. All this buttresses Hollywood's natural urge for libidinal hoopla. Here again, as in other fields we have discussed, Hollywood does what is "done," does more of it, does it less discreetly, and gets it into all the papers.

---

* The Catholic Church, for example, has modified the Augustinian position that marriage is indissoluble; Papal canon law today permits separation on such grounds as cruelty, infidelity, impotence, or adultery.[28]

6. POLITICS OVER HOLLYWOOD

DURING the world crisis in September, 1939, four movie producers had teletype machines installed in their offices to clatter out the minute-by-minute pulse beat of Europe; Hollywood parties rang with fevered talk and were gripped by dark apprehension; committees sprang up to aid Poland, France, Britain, China; and through every nerve of a community reputed to be somnambulistic there raced the throbbing pains of the world's agony. Those who knew Hollywood twenty years ago, or fifteen, or ten, would have been dumbfounded by the tension which electrified the men and women of the movie colony. "Hollywood," someone cried, "has put on political long pants."

Hollywood's rise to political consciousness is dramatic and revealing. Before 1934, roughly, the movie colony was dismissed as a never-never land of sunny skies, Sleeping Beauties, and ivory towers. The movie makers were elf-like creatures fondly believed (and expected) to behave like the fairy-tale princess who only knew she was blessed and thought of nothing but love. The harsher view found Hollywood politically indifferent, innocent, and ignorant, populated by rich children who lolled in an Arcadia of swimming pools and bonbons. The only "ism" in which Hollywood believed, Dorothy Parker remarked, was plagiarism.

In one sense, the movie makers—directors and writers as well

133

as actors—were not considered real people at all. To the public, they were characters out of folklore who lived under symbolic glass-bells. They were fair of face and full of grace, above want or care or concern. They were timeless, not contemporary. They had emotions, not ideas. They could love, but they could not think. Such mundane events as elections and tariffs, wars and blockades could not, presumably, touch their charmed and unreal existence. It is not surprising that when Hollywood became articulate about war, unions, Fascism, boycotts, or the New Deal, a murmur of anguish rose in the land.

The public's consternation did not arise from what the demigods of the screen said, but from the fact that they talked at all. They were violating the pretty role to which they had been assigned in a million fantasies. They were breaking a spell. They were betraying public faith by stepping out of the romantic function they were supposed to serve and in which—precisely because it was exclusively romantic—they were adored. When a Joan Crawford denounced the invasion of Ethiopia, when a Fredric March pleaded for ambulances for Spain, it was like harsh voices destroying a cherished dream. It was easy and natural, at first, for the rudely awakened to cry "Communism!" Congressmen and editors, themselves subjects in the kingdom of the screen, expressed dismay at Hollywood's perfidy, and made headlines by smearing red herrings across the gossamer gowns of Beverly Hills. The loyal drudges of Earl Browder, on the other hand, saw visions of Lorelei on the barricades and foolishly allowed their hopes to soar into regions where common sense was exiled.

Ironically enough, it was the movie executives, who most feared any participation in politics by their glamorous employees, who gave Hollywood its first lesson in the school of hard political reality. The occasion was the bitter Merriam-Sinclair campaign for the governorship of California in 1934. This campaign represented Hollywood's first all-out plunge into the waters of politics. It is a case-study of Hollywood's political activism. Let us describe the history of the organizations and the salient political movements in the movie colony, and then analyze their meaning.

The candidates for the gubernatorial chair of California in 1934 were Frank E. Merriam, a dull Republican wheelhorse lacking in public appeal, and Upton Sinclair, *l'enfant terrible,* muckraker, radical, vegetarian, agnostic. Upton Sinclair had astonished everyone by a campaign which won him the Democratic nomination and threatened to storm the election heights as well. The movie executives were frightened; Sinclair was an outspoken critic and opponent of the motion picture industry, and his tax program threatened to hit Hollywood's studios harder than they had ever been hit before. It looked as though California, which had not had a Democratic governor in thirty-five years, might elect a reformer-Socialist who attacked big business, was dedicated to "production for use, not profit," and was the apostle of a messianic program built around the slogan, "End Poverty in California!"

The movement to beat Sinclair and EPIC took on the attributes of a crusade which bordered on panic. *Time* wrote that the campaign had become "a phobia, lacking humor, fairness, and even a sense of reality." When election betting reached even money on Sinclair's chances, the stocks of six leading California enterprises fell $60,000,000 in one day.[1] The movie magnates joined the anti-Sinclair forces with desperate vigor. Louis B. Mayer of MGM, Republican State Committee vice-chairman, commanded the Hollywood sector; William Randolph Hearst hastened home from Bad Nauheim, Germany, to marshal his newspapers for the fight.

The movie leaders announced that they would be forced to take the entire motion picture industry out of California if Upton Sinclair were elected, and Joseph M. Schenck, a steadfast Democrat, declared in Miami: "If Florida is on the alert, it will benefit to the extent of $150,000,000 a year on the film industry if Sinclair is elected." [2] (Oddly enough, the threat to leave California was followed by the construction of costly new sound stages—in California.) The legislature of Florida hurriedly welcomed the motion picture business by passing a law to exempt them from all taxes if they would migrate, and the incubus of a real-estate boom hovered once more over Florida.

The studio heads did more than issue sensational pronunciamentos. These alarums were, on the contrary, the least effective contribution Hollywood made to the Merriam cause. The producers raised a campaign fund of half a million dollars, partly by assessing their high-salaried employees one day's salary! The assessment was, of course, not so designated officially; it was a "request," but it was accompanied by delicacies of pressure and persuasion which left no room for doubt that refusals would be inexpedient. (The California papers did not publicize this singular tactic, but the *London News-Chronicle* managed to find news in the fact that it had been intimated to Katharine Hepburn that her studio might dismiss her if she came out in open support of Sinclair.) [3] Many in Hollywood refused to be stampeded; Jean Harlow and James Cagney led an actors' rebellion against the "Merriam" tax, writers Gene Fowler, Jim Tully, Frank Scully, and Morrie Ryskind organized an Upton Sinclair committee; but most actors, directors, writers, and producers paid one day's salary into the Republican campaign chest.

Nor was this the big gun in Hollywood's attack on Sinclair. The producers' main barrage was a series of fabricated newsreels of appalling crudity and immense effectiveness. Motion pictures were taken of a horde of disreputable vagrants in the act of crossing "the California border" and prepared to expropriate the God-fearing the moment Upton Sinclair was elected. The pictures were taken on the streets of Los Angeles with cameras from a major studio; the anarchists were actors on studio payrolls, dressed in false whiskers and dirty clothes, and wearing sinister expressions. These "newsreels" were distributed *gratis* to theater owners, and were spread across the screens of leading theaters in every city in the state. The *Los Angeles Evening Herald & Express,* a Hearst paper, printed a large picture of a terrifying mob of young hoboes in front of a freight car, apparently arriving in Los Angeles to launch the Sinclair revolution. Unfortunately, these harbingers of the Terror were recognizable as Frankie Darrow, Dorothy Wilson, and other reasonably familiar actors, and the picture itself was identified as a still from the film *Wild Boys of the Road.*[4] Hollywood's "newsreels" deserved citation as *tours de forces* of propaganda; the New York *Times* printed a two-column description of their content:

In one of the melodramas recently filmed and shown here in Los Angeles, an interviewer approaches a demure old lady, sitting on her front porch and rocking away in her rocking chair.
"For whom are you voting, Mother?" asks the interviewer.
"I am voting for Governor Merriam," the old lady answers in a faltering voice.
"Why, Mother?"
"Because I want to save my little home. It is all I have left in this world."

In another recent newsreel there is shown a shaggy man with bristling Russian whiskers and a menacing look in his eye.
"For whom are you voting?" asks the interviewer.
"Vy, I am foting for Seenclair."
"Why are you voting for Mr. Sinclair?"
"Vell, his system worked vell in Russia, vy can't it work here?"[5]

No comment on this prostitution of the screen * can be more indicting than the editorial which appeared on the front page of the *Hollywood Reporter* eleven days before the Merriam-Sinclair election:

* The California movie houses run short "scare" films on their screens whenever daylight-saving amendments appear on the ballot; daylight saving would give people more evening time for outdoor recreation, and would therefore cut down movie attendance.

When the picture business gets aroused, it becomes AROUSED, and, boy, how they go to it. This campaign against Upton Sinclair has been and is DYNAMITE. It is the most effective piece of political humdingery that has ever been effected. . . . Never before in the history of the picture business has the screen been used in direct support of a candidate . . . never has there been a concerted action on the part of all theaters in a community to defeat a nominee. . . . Maybe our business will be pampered a bit, instead of being pushed around as it has been ever since it became big business. . . .[6]

It was the producers who gave the *coup de grâce* to Sinclair and elected Merriam. But in doing so they shocked the movie colony into a sudden awareness of movie politics and pressure. The Stop-Smash-Smear Sinclair campaign, and the producers' tax on studio personnel, coincided with the rise to power of the Screen Actors Guild and the fight of the Screen Writers Guild for recognition. The juxtaposition of events drove home a lesson in realism to Hollywood's talent groups.

Four years later, in May, 1938, when Governor Merriam was running for re-election against Culbert L. Olson, a group of movie celebrities met at the home of Miriam Hopkins and set up a "Studio Committee for Democratic Political Action." A letter signed by Melvyn Douglas was sent to Hollywood's actors, writers, directors, and technicians calling for members to join "a committee . . . working within the Democratic party, to support and extend the New Deal nationally and, primarily, to bring a new deal to California."

Many of Hollywood's writers, directors, and actors flocked into the organization, which took the title, Motion Picture Democratic Committee. The committee raised money for Olson, pamphleteered, held mass meetings, put on radio shows, sponsored a score of personal appearances and, in a classic gesture, asked Governor Merriam to contribute one day of *his* salary to the Olson campaign fund. Articulate, energetic, with a quick dramatic sense, the Motion Picture Democratic Committee played an important part in the campaign and helped score a

ignal victory in California politics, the election of a Demo-
ratic governor, Culbert L. Olson, for the first time in forty
years. One producer summarized the movie colony's role in the
938 election by remarking sadly, "I guess we started some-
hing in 1934."

Hollywood's earlier political gestures had been of the comic-
opera genre. A Colonel Arthur Guy Empey had organized the
Hollywood Hussars (in 1935), a band of knights prepared to
gallop on their steeds to any emergency—flood or invasion,
earthquake or revolution. Several movie stars were lured into
his staunch regiment, notably Gary Cooper, but resigned when
its proto-Fascist leanings became clearer. Victor McLaglen organized a Light Horse Cavalry with a program as vague and
penny-dreadful as the Hollywood Hussars. Both organizations
aroused wide protest in the movie colony because of their vigi-
ante overtones.*

The political sympathies of Hollywood crystallized into less
melodramatic patterns when, in 1936, several hundred movie
celebrities attended a mass meeting and pledged themselves to
a campaign against Fascism, Nazism, Communism, "and all
other dangerous isms." Prominent in the crusade were David
O. Selznick, Mrs. Fredric March, Herman Mankiewicz, Edwin
Knopf, and others.[7] The American Legion was strongly supported by film luminaries; the 1936 state convention was in-
augurated on a sound stage which the Warner studio turned
over to the Legion, and in 1939 the Legion created a Motion
Picture Division of its Americanism Committee, with movie
producer Walter Wanger as its chairman and a dozen Hollywood Legionnaires as members.

* Of the picture people who were involved in these political romances, only
Mr. McLaglen's name continued to appear in unflattering connections. The big
South African (his father was Bishop of Clermont; his brother was deported from
the United States in 1940 for shady political activities) continued to show a predilec-
tion for movements which featured fine horses and bright uniforms.

When Spain was torn by Civil War, and while the Japanese were raping China in the name of a "new order" for the East a group of movie people organized the Motion Picture Artists Committee. Headed by Dashiell Hammett and allied with international organizations sponsored by Lloyd George, the Duchess of Athol, and President Cardenas of Mexico, the Motion Picture Artists Committee threw itself into drives to aid China and Loyalist Spain. This Hollywood organization conducted an energetic campaign for the boycott of Japanese goods and an embargo on arms shipments to Nippon, urged the removal of the Spanish embargo so that the government at Madrid could buy arms and supplies, and shipped medical supplies, food, clothes, and toys to the wounded and the homeless in China and Spain. The championing of China won general approbation for the committee; its support of Loyalist Spain was another matter. This tragic conflict, so bitterly debated in the United States, was certain to make the Motion Picture Artists Committee the target of violent opposition and to invite the ubiquitous charge of "Communism."

It was the Hollywood Anti-Nazi League which brought the Communist issue to a clear and fateful head. The Anti-Nazi League, the most aggressive and controversial organization in Hollywood's history, was sponsored in 1936 by a group catholic enough to include such widely separated politicos as Rupert Hughes, Donald Ogden Stewart, Eddie Cantor, Dudley Nichols, Viola Brothers Shore, Gloria Stuart, and others. Republicans, New Dealers, movie producers, one hundred percenters, and liberals found a common ground for action in a movement designed to combat Nazi influence and Nazi propaganda. The Hollywood Anti-Nazi League was actively headed by Donald Ogden Stewart, Herbert Biberman, Alan Campbell, and Marion Spitzer; it claimed a membership of five thousand (probably an overstatement) at its peak, and in three years deposited almost $90,000 in its bank account.[8] The league campaigned for a boycott of Nazi goods, published a weekly paper, put on a weekly radio program, and held mass meetings with speakers such as Congressman Jerry O'Connell, Thomas Mann, and Dr. John R. Lechner, chairman of the American Legion's Americanism Committee. The organization scored two memorable *coups;* it exposed Leni Reifenstahl, Hitler's emissary who had come to Hollywood to peddle a Nazi film version of the Berlin Olympic Games, and it so successfully mobilized opposition to Vittorio Mussolini, who popped up in Hollywood fresh from his bombing expedition in Ethiopia ("highly diverting . . . the bombs strike and the ground is thrown up in waves like the unfolding of a rose"), that the son of Il Duce was whisked out of the country by the infuriated Italian embassy.[9]

The Hollywood Anti-Nazi League became a *cause célèbre* when the Dies Committee, the *Motion Picture Herald,* and the local press accused the organization of being used as a Communist "front" agency operated by a clique which followed the Communist party line with remarkable fidelity. No one charged the members of the league with Communist affiliation; even Congressman Martin A. Dies declared that "the great majority of the members are not Communists."[10] It was an inner circle that was indicted as either members of the Communist party, party stooges, or fellow-travelers of more than innocent cast. The leaders of the Hollywood Anti-Nazi League were challenged to clarify their position on Communism when anti-Communist resolutions were introduced from the floor. They reacted promptly; they fought down efforts to put the question to a democratic vote; they raised a hue and cry that the matter of Communism was irrelevant; and, using the classic *argumentum ad hominem,* they accused their critics of being everything from "wreckers" and "saboteurs" to "Fascist lackeys."

Now if the Communist issue was really irrelevant, the leaders of the Anti-Nazi League made it conspicuously relevant by the desperation with which they sidetracked it. They could scarcely

have ignored the fact that each maneuver to squash the accu
sations only magnified their importance and validity. The Anti
Nazi League could have broadened its scope and heightened
its efficiency by taking formal steps to allay the mounting sus
picion that the leaders and spokesmen of the league were in
cahoots with the Communist party or the Communist party
line. The ruling cabal knew that by refusing to meet the issue
they were sacrificing the power of the Anti-Nazi League. They
knew that by mollifying the Communists they were undermin
ing the unity and conviction of the non-Communist majority
They were more determined to hold to the Communist party
line than to further the purpose—anti-Nazi—for which they were
organized.

For weeks the local press carried editorials, letters, and news
stories about Communist domination in the Hollywood Anti
Nazi League. But the guiding faction of the league continued
to suppress efforts to air the controversy in open meetings of
the membership. If the purpose of the leaders could be con
cealed, their methods could not: they were precisely the meth
ods being used on a national scale by the handy men of the
Communist party. The accusations raged; national anti-Com
munist feeling was flaring up; the sponsors of the league fled
and the membership began to fall away, hamstrung by the tac
tics and bewildered by the casuistry with which the executive
board evaded the issue.

The Berlin-Moscow pact threw the Hollywood Anti-Naz
League into internal convulsions. The pro-Stalin faction in the
league, like the pro-Stalin factions in other parts of the land
suddenly de-emphasized their anti-Nazism. When Soviet Russia
invaded Finland, and still the Anti-Nazi League's mentors fol
lowed the party line, the death-rattle of the organization began
to shatter the political air. And when the leaders of the league
notably the engaging humorist, Donald Ogden Stewart, and the
energetic Herbert Biberman, an orator of great passion, at

tacked the President (hailed only a week earlier for his emphatic anti-Fascist stand) as a "war-monger," fought American aid to England, and opposed a national defense program—with Hitler at the gates of Paris—the cat was let out of the bag. The captains of the league were simply following the policies enunciated each week in the *New Masses,* and each day in the *Daily Worker.* The record was clear, the facts were undeniable, and the implications were obvious. The power and support of the Hollywood Anti-Nazi League disappeared overnight. The organization changed its name; it changed the name of its publication; it issued desperate proclamations defending its "true democracy"; and it vanished from the Hollywood scene—stubborn, impotent, and discredited.

The Motion Picture Democratic Committee suffered a similar fate for similar reasons, and taught Hollywood a second lesson in Communist tactics. The committee had allied Democrats, progressives, New Dealers, and liberals around Roosevelt and Governor Olson; as was inevitable, the organization was clamorously supported (at first) by the same small clique which clung to the Communist party line in all its acrobatic contradictions. After the Soviet-Nazi alliance, Melvyn Douglas, chairman of the Motion Picture Democratic Committee and its most influential figure, presented a resolution which denounced Nazi aggression and Soviet perfidy. Douglas was maligned, the resolution was defeated, and Douglas and others resigned* Philip Dunne, the movie writer, became chairman to save the remnants; in several months he, too, was the target of familiar epithets from the pathetic faithful of the Left. Deserted by its most effective leaders and its most important names, the Motion Pic-

---

* When Melvyn Douglas appeared in Ernst Lubitsch's *Ninotchka,* a satire on Soviet Russia, the *New Masses* excoriated him for the horrendous deed; Mr. Douglas told the press: ". . . these last few years I've been dabbling in politics, on committees with some other people, and the C.P. boys have been claiming us. . . . So *Ninotchka,* besides being a good picture, is also a chance to show the C.P. boys just where I stand. . . . If I hadn't agreed with it, I would never have appeared in it." [11]

ture Democratic Committee struggled along for a while, and expired. As in the case of the Hollywood Anti-Nazi League, a small, aggressive, well knit faction, skilled in power tactics and character assassination, had squashed the majority and wrecked an organization.

It is elementary logic to distinguish Hollywood from Communists-in-Hollywood, but when public opinion flared up against the methods and the purpose of Communist "front" organizations, the entire movie colony was smeared for the politics of a handful. Hollywood is a perennial springboard to the front pages; when Hollywood and "Communism" were linked, sensational publicity was sure to fall into the laps of the demagogues. It was not surprising that "Reds in Hollywood" became a theme song of the German-American Bund, the Silver Shirts, Father Coughlin, the Ku Klux Klan, and Fascist oracles of every hue. When Congressman Martin A. Dies made a careless attack on the film colony, suggesting that even Shirley Temple was being used by the Communist party, he gave the signal for the witch hunt.

All through 1939, especially whenever he asked Congress for funds, Mr. Dies declared that Communism was thriving in Hollywood; unfortunately for his case, he presented neither names nor evidence to support the charges. Mr. Dies sold two articles to *Liberty* in 1940, and the magazine printed a boxed notice over the articles which read: "For his statement of his case, [*Liberty*] has allowed him the fullest latitude within the laws of libel." The exposé proved to be tendentious and feeble. The farthest Mr. Dies would go was to assert that "forty-two or forty-three prominent members of the Hollywood film colony either were full-fledged members of the Communist Party or active sympathizers and fellow travelers." [12] No names were given. Mr. Dies admitted that movie producers "appeared to be very anxious to cooperate through their films in exposing and combating un-American activities"; but he suggested that "Communist influence was responsible for the subtle but very effective propaganda which appeared in such films as *Juarez, Blockade,* and *Fury.*" [13] (We shall analyze these pictures later in this chapter.)

All through the summer of 1940, too, Mr. Dies's accusations made the front pages of the land; all through the summer he promised that he would hold a hearing in Los Angeles which would expose Communism in both Hollywood and the films. Mr. Dies had stated that "a mass of verbal and documentary evidence" showed that less than fifty persons in Hollywood were Communist either formally or by sympathy [14]—but the entire movie colony, the movie industry, and the movies were tarred with the red brush.

Buron Fitts, Los Angeles County district attorney, seized the golden opportunity. Fitts, running for re-election after three terms in office, jumped into the headlines with a smear campaign which rested on the testimony of one John L. Leech, a former member of the Communist party. Leech, appearing before a Los Angeles grand jury that was investigating a five-year-old murder case, unexpectedly announced that he had a red-hot "list" of eighteen movie Communists. Dean James Landis of the Harvard Law School had all but called Leech a pathological liar, and had dismissed Leech's testimony in San Francisco (at the first hearings on the deportation of Harry Bridges) as a mélange of "evasion, contradiction and qualification." * But Buron Fitts was running for re-election. He hailed the Leech "evidence," began beating the drum of "Red Menace in the Movie Colony," and promised to "blow the lid off" Hollywood.

---

* In a formal report to the Department of Labor (December, 1939)* Dean Landis had written: "It is impossible even to summarize this . . . testimony by Leech. In evasion, contradiction and qualification it is almost unique . . . one would be tempted to regard Leech's evasionary tactics as pathological in character, were it not that behind this screen of verbiage was a motive—Leech's desire . . . to conceal . . . that he fraudulently had been accepting relief with the knowledge and aid of Mrs. Leech." [15]

To appreciate the full irony of this, the reader should be informed that the movie magnates had supported Buron Fitts for twelve years, had contributed heavily to his campaigns, and *were electioneering for him* in the very campaign in which he was smearing Hollywood.[16] The *Hollywood Reporter's* publisher, W. R. Wilkerson, a steadfast echo of the movie producers, wrote long editorials eulogizing Mr. Fitts and his "understanding" of the picture business.* Some political sophisticates suggested that Buron Fitts had arrange beforehand for Leech to drop his bombshell in the Grand Jury rooms; certainly the swiftness and volubility of Fitts's reaction suggested classic election strategy. Mr. Fitts quoted Leech as having identified Fredric March, James Cagney, Humphrey Bogart, Melvyn Douglas, Franchot Tone, and thirteen less distinguished personalities as either Communists, Communist sympathizers, or dangerous fellow-travelers. And so the headlines screamed of Bolsheviks in Beverly Hills, and a new movie scandal raced across the teletype machines of America.

The New York *Times* weighed the Leech-Fitts charges and editorialized:

... the [movie] persons ... run the danger of impairment in their main property and capital—their standing in the public eye. Since no formal charge lies against them they cannot put their cases to a jury and

* The film leaders were old friends and allies of Mr. Fitts, who, as district attorney of Los Angeles County since 1928, had befriended the movie makers on many occasions. L. B. Mayer contributed $2,000 to one of Buron Fitts's primary campaign funds; Jack L. Warner contributed $3,000 to the same cause.[17] An industry as large and vulnerable as the movies engages in political maneuvering to protect its interests. The Hollywood studios maintain a close liaison with the politicians of Los Angeles and Sacramento; the movies and the film industry are easy targets for taxation, political attack, and crackpot reformers. Locally, the industry has efficient contacts with the Los Angeles city council, police department, sheriff's office, and district attorney's office. Movie power long was felt in the Governor's office and the State legislature. The ubiquitous threat of state taxes affects not only the movie executives but the high-salaried actors, directors, and writers as well. Hollywood's movie agents are in the same position; in July, 1938, a grand jury investigation revealed that Arthur Samish, a lobbyist, had collected $5,000 in 1935 and $10,000 in 1937 from the movie agents "to watch assembly bills 403 and 1226." [18]

must count on their denials to outrun the original Leech statement. In a race of that sort the lie, if any has been told, has a long head start. . . . What is sinister in the present episode is not the possible drop of Communism in the vast sea of mass entertainment, but the misuse of supposedly correct legal machinery to give irresponsible witnesses a chance to smear reputations.[19]

The Fitts-Leech irruption threatened to steal Mr. Dies's thunder; the congressman from Texas left Washington and hastened to Hollywood. Fitts held the initiative, however, by issuing a dramatic subpoena for fourteen members of the Screen Writers Guild who, he implied publicly, were "reds." Fitts held a secret hearing, giving the fourteen writers no opportunity either to defend themselves in public or deny the charges. The executive board of the Screen Writers Guild branded the charges as "capricious and unfair," and demanded that the accused be allowed to answer the charges openly and legally.[20] District Attorney Fitts quickly shifted his attack, and now gave the public to understand that it was the movie *actors* who were working hand in hand with Moscow. The Screen Actors Guild promptly announced that it had called Fitts's hand a few weeks earlier and had received the following statement from him:

The membership of the Screen Actors Guild has never for one moment ever been questioned as to their loyalty, patriotism, and their fine citizenship. Quite the contrary, if any group in this country contributes more to the pleasure and happiness of our people in these troubled times, I do not know the organization.[21]

Any lingering doubts as to Fitts's political integrity vanished. The Screen Actors Guild issued a statement which attacked "Communism, Nazism, and Fifth Columnists," and called the public's attention to the fact that the Dies-Fitts policy was playing directly into the hands of "the real fifth columnists:"

To smear prominent persons without any reliable evidence is to play into the hands of Hitler and Stalin by confusing the innocent with the guilty, so that the public distrusts everyone. It should be remembered that no formal charges had ever been brought, that no proof had ever

147

been offered, and that there was no court in which the movie people could either meet the accusations or clear their names.[22]

The movie colony had for years endured sensational slanders in silence. The counterattack was something of a turning point in Hollywood's conduct. Y. Frank Freeman, president of the Association of Motion Picture Producers, led a delegation of movie people to Mr. Dies's hotel room as soon as he arrived in Los Angeles. There Mr. Freeman gave the following statement to the press:

> Thirty-two thousand motion picture workers in Hollywood are not willing to yield to anyone in their true Americanism. . . . We welcome a complete and impartial investigation. . . . It is and always has been the desire of all loyal Americans in this industry to cooperate with the government's representatives. . . . If a true impartial investigation discloses that there are those who, by their actions and conduct, have brought discredit upon this . . . industry and its . . . workers, then there will be no attempt to protect those individuals or groups of individuals. However, whether such accusations . . . are true or not is yet to be proven, and we know that, in fairness, public decision will be withheld until a complete and impartial investigation can be made. . . .[23]

Mr. Freeman expressed the anger of Hollywood when he declared, "The screen industry insists that these people be either cleared or found guilty—one or the other." To which Mr. Dies replied publicly: "Mr. Freeman and the other gentlemen came here to tender me their fullest cooperation, to have the guilt or innocence of anyone connected with the film industry established. They agreed that those guilty of subversive activities should be exposed." [24]

It is important to observe that in his private meeting with Mr. Freeman and the Screen Actors Guild delegates, Mr. Dies "did not make intemperate accusations against Hollywood people. He said there was a group, including twelve actors, with whom he would like to talk." [25] The Screen Actors Guild promptly notified the twelve actors. Fredric March, James Cagney, Humphrey Bogart, Franchot Tone, Melvyn Douglas, and other movie stars instantly denied the Fitts-Leech charges and offered to prove that the allegations were lies. They insisted that Mr. Dies hold a prompt hearing at which they could testify.

Mr. Dies finally held several secret hearings, in Los Angeles and San Francisco. He announced that the movie actors and writers "were very frank and submitted their books and records for our inspection"; he announced that the accused had testified under oath as to their record, politics, and political faith. And to the amazement of a public prepared for the most dastardly revelations, Mr. Dies declared that the Messrs. Cagney, March, Bogart, Douglas, *et al.* "are not or never have been Communists or Communist sympathizers." To add further confusion to the travesty, Mr. Dies denied that he had ever accused Hollywood's actors of Communism. He said that *some* movie stars had contributed to humanitarian causes through organizations which they did not realize followed the Communist party line. Mr. Dies's last word was judicious: "The chair feels that those people of prominence and influence, who through worthy and commendable motives have desired to aid worthy causes, should be careful in selecting the vehicle through which to extend their help." [26] With this finale, Mr. Dies left for Kansas City.

As for Buron Fitts, he was defeated in the election by John Dockweiler and ruefully returned to private life. Even the standby of political strategy, red-baiting, and the Old Faithful of moral crusades, unholy Hollywood, had failed to rescue Mr. Fitts from the displeasure of the voters. The movie producers added the crowning touch of bathos to *l'affaire Fitts* by echoing "Billy" Wilkerson, who took the *Hollywood Reporter's* front-page editorial space to limn a farewell to Fitts:

The King is dead. Long live the King. . . . Buron Fitts was a great friend of the picture industry . . . and gave our industry and its individuals protection against . . . one shakedown after the other invented by phonies in their effort to grab some money from our people. Now the electorate has supplanted Fitts with Dockweiler and many here in the studios are a bit nervous . . . because ALL the financial support handed out by the industry for the campaign went to Fitts and nothing to Dockweiler.

. . . John Dockweiler may feel a bit peeved . . . but that peeve . . . would never be reflected in his office because he is entirely too high a type gentleman. . . . Our industry supported Buron Fitts because Buron Fitts supported our industry. . . . John Dockweiler . . . has a knowledge of the . . . efforts of crooks to shake [movie people] down and will give equally as great protection as did Buron Fitts. . . . Our people will learn to admire his work as much as they did Mr. Fitts and the same fine understanding will exist, one for the other.[27]

There was no reference in the editòrial to poor Yorick.

It is a vindication of Hollywood that the Dies committee failed to produce more facts to support the alarums anent movie Bolsheviks. This is not to say, of course, that there are no Communists in Hollywood. There are—just as there probably are in Orange, Texas. But to malign all of Hollywood because of the suspected politics of eighteen persons (according to Leech) or forty-three (the maximum Mr. Dies admitted suspecting) was an act of supererogation which deserved the quip "loaded Dies." The New York *Herald Tribune* editorialized: "The palpable injustice done . . . condemns the whole effort as a smear campaign." [28]

The irony of the Fitts-Dies attack lies in the fact that Hollywood's leaders have for years been bitter and vociferous in their denunciation of Communists. Any other conception of the record and public declarations of the Messrs. Warner, Mayer, Schenck, Freeman, Zanuck, Schaefer, Wanger, *et al.* betrays a dismal ignorance of the facts. The movie people's fear of Communism, like the fear of so many others in the land, had become a phobia which at one time tended to blind them to the Fascist threat.* When Hollywood turned out full force, in rapid suc-

---

* Hal Roach played host to Vittorio Mussolini in Hollywood, in 1939, and gave a ball in his honor which was attended by many who later regretted their action; no movie magnate would have been foolish enough to play host to the son of Stalin or Browder.

cession, for aid to Poland, Finland, the Netherlands, and Greece, the charge of wholesale Communism in the movie colony became patently inept. The final joker lies in the fact that Hollywood's leaders probably stand to the right of Mr. Dies and make even less distinction between a liberal and a Bolshevik. The representative from Texas has never denounced the New Deal with as much animus as some of the movie leaders have done in the presence of this writer.

It will be remembered that Mr. Dies asserted that "Communist influence" had injected "very effective propaganda" into *Juarez, Blockade,* and *Fury.* (Mr. Dies might have argued just as logically, as many Communists have done, that Hollywood is "Fascist" because of *Ninotchka, Comrade X, He Stayed for Breakfast, Public Deb Number 1,* and half a dozen more films which lampooned Communist theology.) Suppose we examine the content of these films, and then the political record of the studios and the men who produced them.

Juarez dramatized the fight of Benito Juarez against the ambivalent tyranny of Maximilian, whom Napoleon III had set up on the throne of Mexico. The picture eulogized Abraham Lincoln, and was almost overloaded with affirmations of democracy. The Communists attacked *Juarez* because of its sympathetic portrayal of Maximilian and Carlotta, and accused the writers of having falsified history. (The film deliberately ignored Juarez's anti-clericalism; Juarez had expelled the Papal Nuncio and other ecclesiastics who resisted his decrees.) Mr. Dies was apparently unfamiliar with these facts, or with the statement Lincoln made when he received Juarez's envoy: "You [enjoy] the respect and esteem of this government, and the good will of the people of the United States." [29]

Blockade, the next movie on the list, was a melodrama about the Spanish Civil War which painfully avoided any reference to either the Loyalists or the Franco rebels. The meaning of the movie, in effect, was to appeal to "the conscience of the world";

it favored the shipment of food to Spain. If the cause of the legal government of Spain—with which the United States maintained sympathetic diplomatic relations to the end—was "Communist," then we should ask whether the majority of the American people who supported the Loyalist position were "Communists." (The adhesion of Generalissimo Franco to the Berlin-Tokyo-Rome axis soon convinced the doubtful that the democracies should have been on the side of the legal government.)

We come to the third movie indicted, *Fury*. *Fury* was a classic dramatization of mob violence. It contained no political characters, no political setting, and no political overtones. The assertion that this movie showed Bolshevik influence leaves this writer utterly nonplussed. The only group which could consistently denounce *Fury's* portrayal of lynching is the Ku Klux Klan.

Now let us examine the politics of the men who produced the three films. *Juarez* was produced by Warner Brothers, whose leaders, pictures, and politics have been cited by many scrolls and resolutions of the American Legion and the Daughters of the American Revolution. Mr. Dies had himself singled out the Warners as being strongly anti-Communist.[30] The Warner Brothers' patriotic shorts have for years been produced at a loss to the studio, and cast and filmed on a scale which has attested that the Warners have known they could not recover their costs.[31] It was the Warner Brothers, furthermore, who gave free radio time each week for a year on their station (KFWB) to "America Marches On," one of the first anti-Nazi, anti-Communist programs in the country. Each dramatization featured an address by Dr. John R. Lechner of the American Legion, and the formal sign-off of the program was the statement, "Americans are opposed to Nazism, Communism, and Fascism."

Blockade was produced by Walter Wanger, who had organized and chairmanned a private group which refused to cooperate with the Hollywood Anti-Nazi League until it cleared itself of the charge of Communism. Mr. Wanger resigned from a New York organization because of its failure "to make clear its position with reference to Fascism AND Communism." In an open letter printed in the *Hollywood Citizen-News,* he had stated:

> . . . I can see no excuse for intellectual straddling on this point. There can be no compromise between Fascism and Democracy. There can be no compromise between Communism and Democracy. There can, in short, be no compromise between Dictatorship and Democracy. The current controversy is between Dictatorship and Democracy, and I am on the side of Democracy.[32]

Fury was made by MGM, whose chief, Louis B. Mayer, is a power in the Republican party, national Republican committeeman, and an old friend of Herbert Hoover, who played host to Mr. Mayer at the White House. The producer of *Fury,* Joseph L. Mankiewicz, was a moving spirit in the Aid-to-Finland drive and voted for Wendell Willkie in 1940.

These were the men accused of financing and producing "Communist" movies.

Anyone who attends the movies regularly must be impressed by the fact that Hollywood's output is to an overwhelming degree distinguished by utter political innocuousness. Hollywood shuns the political (and the realistic) because it must appeal to the widest of mass markets, and it dare not risk offending any substantial part of that market. Patriotic stories have always been at a premium in the motion picture industry. The Army and Navy pictures, a staple commodity from Hollywood's production lines, led pacifists to accuse Hollywood of militarism long before demagogues accused it of Communism.

The statement which Walter Wanger presented on a "Town Meeting of the Air" program puts the case for Hollywood trenchantly:

Hollywood made 350 pictures last year. Fewer than ten of these pictures departed from the usual Westerns, romances, and boy-meets-girl story. . . . I say the motion pictures can aid in national defense by giving us more, many more than ten out of 350 pictures which deal with democracy in the world crisis. . . . Where does Hollywood get its material? From popular books, plays, and magazine stories. Note the word "popular." Yet when we make a story which has already appeared in a national magazine, when we film a book which has already become a best seller, there are those who cry, "The motion pictures are beginning to propagandize.". . . The *Saturday Evening Post* . . . published a serial, *Escape*. Nobody accuses the *Saturday Evening Post* of warmongering. But when Hollywood put this story on the screen . . . the cry went up, "Hollywood is going in for propaganda!" [33]

The farce of "Communist Hollywood" was conceived in the days when political innocents assumed that any and all opposition to Fascism was Communist in origin or purpose. It will be to Hollywood's credit that its anti-Fascist activities predated the swing in American public opinion and diplomacy. It will be to Hollywood's credit that it fought the Silver Shirts, the German-American Bund, and the revived Ku Klux Klan at a time when few realized their ultimate menace.

"Causes" are always suspect, and humane acts can easily be attacked by the shallow and the ignorant as symptoms of dark, conspiratorial purpose. The movie people who donated funds to the migratory workers of California, to the wives and children of lettuce workers at Salinas, suffered the usual calumnies before the public came to believe the facts which cried for public action. Melvyn Douglas, Helen Gahagan, and half a dozen others who founded the Committee to Aid Migratory Workers were, of course, sticking their necks out; but they did send food, clothes, toys, and money to Americans whose welfare and liberty had been shockingly mistreated. James Cagney spoke for many picture people when he declared:

We are accused of contributing to radical causes. When you are told a person is sick or in need, you don't ask him his religion, nationality,

154

or politics. . . . I am unequivocally opposed to subversive organizations of any kind. I am for this government and for American principles.[34]

There was a time, not so long ago, when the charge "Communism!" was hurled against anyone—in Hollywood or in Boston—who held that Nazi Germany was a threat to America, that labor unions were legal organizations, that civil liberties should be protected with Jeffersonian courage, that the dispossessed in a free nation have a right to speak and live as free men and citizens. The nation now agrees with many of those who were labeled "un-American." *

Despite its tennis courts and swimming pools, Hollywood was infected by the social insecurity of the times. Even the most sanguine apostles of escapism in the movie colony could not close their ears to the thunder of national change. Wherever men could read the papers or hear the radio, wherever they could sense the unrest which roared around the very foundations of their homes—there men cast worried glances at the political scene. It is naive to assume that this was the work of malcontents or "agitators"; the political awakening of Hollywood was one small part of the political awakening of America.

In Hollywood, naturally, politics is more dramatic than in Shamokin. Hollywood politics is played by the most famous cast in the world. Hollywood politics is publicized by a brigade of publicists and newspapermen rivaled only in Washington. It was said earlier that dramatic acts appeal to dramatic personalities. Hollywood's politics is dramatic, too. The movie makers react dramatically rather than politically. They react not simply as voters and citizens, but as virtuosos aware of the

---

* Soon after the Munich pact, for example, fifty-six leading Hollywood personalities drew up a petition modeled after the Declaration of Independence (which had fifty-six signers) and called upon the people of America to boycott all Nazi goods. The Committee of Fifty-Six was promptly branded as "radical" or "Communist" by the Nazis and their allies, conscious or unconscious, in the United States. The Committee of Fifty-Six, incidentally, was the organization which first attracted movie people who had not figured in Hollywood's political renaissance—Don Ameche, Alice Faye, Bette Davis, George Brent, Rosalind Russell, Henry Fonda, and others.

potency of their names and their influence. Show people do not test out their opinions, study political issues, or ponder the total implications of a political position. They rush into politics as into a benefit performance. They sign petitions with a flourish, make eloquent speeches, and send out batches of long and defiant telegrams. Hollywood reacts to politics as it does to anything else—with fervid emotion and an infinite capacity for suffering. No chamber of commerce or civic league can produce either the breast-beating or the oratory of a Guild meeting or a Bel-Air living-room. "When Hollywood gets aroused, it gets AROUSED."

In the early stages of Hollywood's political awakening, it was *fashionable* to go left—with the right people. In the movie colony, said Frank Nugent, "affluence breeds ennui" and social consciousness is "a form of entertainment." [35] Actors who had gone in for antiques, or actresses who had fancied the rumba, discovered the attraction of politics when political discussion began to dominate Hollywood's dinner tables. There was social pressure to familiarize one's self with the current world, and a new kind of deference was accorded those who performed as political experts. The radio talks of H. V. Kaltenborn and Raymond Gram Swing became almost as popular in Hollywood as the Jack Benny program. The level of political disputation in the movie colony was painfully immature, but the important point was that it was political.

. . . there are honest crusaders in Hollywood. Many of them have fought for an existence in other fields. . . . Circumstances have placed them where the horn of plenty is spilling its goodies, but, while they may be leading Cinderella lives, they do what they can to lessen the burden of others. Hollywood regards them with suspicion and comments maliciously upon their "radical" activities. They have committed the unpardonable sin . . . they have been flirting with reality.[36]

In a world of war, unemployment, and social conflict, those who spend their time in spinning the pretty fables of the screen are troubled by a vague feeling of contempt for themselves, by a revulsion against the falsity of their purpose and the make-believe of their security. The movie people are obsessed by conscience; they are groping to participate in man's fight; they are driven by the urge to do "something significant."

The ivory towers of Hollywood have been undermined by the guilt and the frustration of those who inhabit them. The weekly amassing of immense salaries creates a disturbing sense of inequity in the souls of the movie colony's ex-salesmen, chorus girls, or lumberjacks. The Hollywoodian is haunted by the suspicion that his breath-taking fortune is not truly earned—*i.e.*, is not really deserved or morally justified. There are enough has-beens and might-have-beens floating around the movie colony to plague the children of fortune with the thought, "There, but for the grace of God, go I."

Political activity, Professor H. D. Lasswell has demonstrated, often serves as a form of individual therapy.[37] Emotional insecurities are reduced when personalities set up heroes to love, villains to hate, devils to *blame*. The hostilities generated in the personality can be discharged with economy against symbolic objects. Hitler or Churchill, Roosevelt, the New Deal, the Reactionaries, the Radicals—all these may become metaphorical Nemeses, and individuals preserve their inner equilibrium by discharging hate, fear, or tension to things outside the self. Let us not forget that identification with an heroic cause is eminently attractive to men in a culture like ours, which drives men into small and lonely universes.

To the personalities of Hollywood, lost and isolated in their own empty glory, profound gratification is to be found in organizations or causes which help them feel part of a significant movement, which help them feel at one with "the people." The gnawing doubts of egoism can be denied by the championing of altruistic creeds. Politics offers heroic roles, and what actor can resist an heroic part? Politics offered Hollywood the fresh and inspiring experience of martyrdom. Political activity sustains anxiety, and anxiety is a form of atonement for obscure remorse. Politics satisfies masochistic impulses. Politics is a legitimate way of getting into a bang-up fight, hurling great slogans and bitter anathemas, attacking old authority symbols, releasing inner rage against the figurative demons of the political world. Politics is a legitimate way of provoking that opposition in heated arguments which justifies and sanctions violent counter-aggression. Politics was made for the movie makers, once they discovered it.

But it was foolhardy to worry about genuine or dangerous revolutionists in Hollywood. The inhabitants of the movie colony are scarcely fit to accept the discipline and deprivations of a fanatical cause. The movie makers cannot remain consistent for long, personally or politically; they need quick and dramatic rewards. The stirring language and bravado gestures of protest movements are irresistible to the self-dramatizing, but actors become as bored with a political role as with a stage role if the rehearsals are prolonged and the big show is postponed.

The Hollywood Communist scare betrayed naïveté, a talent for headlines, and an abysmal incomprehension of movie personalities on the part of those who pinned red labels on the movie colony.

The conflicts which dominated America reached into Hollywood as inexorably as anywhere in the land. The New Deal, public relief and public works, the persuasiveness of Franklin D. Roosevelt, the rise of unions and the crucial issue of collective bargaining—these won allegiance from glamour girls no less than from manicurists, from matinée idols as well as coal miners.

Hollywood was carried on the wave of the times—*despite* the omnipresent lures of escapist living. Something happened in the movie business which surprised the executives: the actors and writers and directors were forced to the realization, after long and sad experiences, that in the last analysis they were employees. It seemed ludicrous, at first sight, to think of Clark Gable or Marlene Dietrich, Frank Capra or Gene Fowler as members of movie unions, paying union dues, pledged to a labor organization and ready to strike for it. It became less preposterous when one realized that even the movie makers who earn $1,000-$5,000 a week are *hired* men and women selling their services in a market which, despite its surface romance, is still a market. The Wagner act was a tocsin to Hollywood no less than to Pittsburgh. The movie makers, for all their generic individualism, moved toward the organization of their crafts because organization offered professional advantages and solved professional problems.

The years of unchallenged producer sovereignty, the tradition of draconic executives, the assumption that high salaries negated contractual status, the high-handed exercise of power by those who possessed it, provided fertile soil for the organization of Hollywood's employees. The concept of unionism and the meaning of organization seeped upward into the highest-paid levels of the film colony. The Screen Actors Guild, by threatening an industry-wide walkout, won higher basic rates for extras, greater security, and, above all, gave several thousand actors an outlet for their individual complaints and a channel for their common demands. The movie directors and writers, cameramen and publicists, organized themselves into occupational groups with common goals and protective purposes.* Guilds—the choice of the word in preference to "unions" reveals the professional distaste for proletarian language—sprang up in Hollywood with bewildering speed, and the issues which gripped the nation as a whole were recapitulated in the industry of film making. Hollywood's guilds would not and could not

* The analysis of Hollywood's guilds and unions must be left for a later volume.

have arisen had there not been a need for the functions they offered to fulfill.

Just before the Roosevelt-Landon campaign of 1936, a trade paper poll found Hollywood 6 to 1 for Roosevelt. Movie directors supported the President 8 to 1, actors 7 to 1, writers 5 to 1, laborers 8 to 1, agents 24 to 1—and executives, be it noted, 5 to 1.* In the Roosevelt-Willkie campaign, Hollywood, like the rest of the country, was less emphatically Democrat and New Deal. The powerful Hollywood for Roosevelt Committee conducted a remarkable radio campaign in behalf of the President's third-term, and featured such movie celebrities as Pat O'Brien, Joan Bennett, Douglas Fairbanks, Jr., Alice Faye, Edward G. Robinson, Rosalind Russell, Henry Fonda, and many others. But a formidable battery of picture people supported Mr. Willkie: Louis B. Mayer, Bing Crosby, Walt Disney, Mary Pickford, Gary Cooper, Wallace Beery, Hedda Hopper, William Powell, Robert Montgomery, Harold Lloyd, Joan Blondell, Lionel Barrymore, Ann Sheridan, Adolphe Menjou, Morrie Ryskind, and a hundred more. The producers and executives were, on the whole, strongly pro-Willkie.

In the realm of international politics, Hollywood is more sensitive and more responsive than most communities in the land. There are several understandable reasons for the hypersensitivity. European politics cannot be ignored by an industry which, as a whole, derived from thirty-five to forty percent of its revenues from abroad (before the war broke out), nor by individual producers and studios that got as high as fifty percent of their income from outside the United States. Every time a nation was crushed under the juggernaut of Berlin or Rome, Hollywood felt the blow in its pocketbook. No other American

* The following, to select the larger donors, contributed to the Democratic campaign fund: Nicholas M. Schenck, $10,000; Joseph M. Schenck, $10,000; Sidney R. Kent, $3,500; William Goetz, $2,500; Winfield Sheehan, $2,000; Stanton Griffis, $1,500; Al Lichtman, $1,000; John Considine, $1,000; Charles Chaplin, $500.[38]

product was strangled so quickly and automatically by the con-
quering regimes.

American movies, unlike American typewriters or washing
machines, were *ipso facto* a threat to the Caesars. Goebbels
hurled a systematic propaganda attack against Hollywood's
films, and Hitler once honored Hollywood with special hatred
in a radio harangue heard around the world. Wherever the
Nazis and the Fascists moved, they cut the arteries of Hollywood's income. American movies became pawns in the gigantic
game of power and conquest. Hollywood's product was outlawed in Germany, Italy, Soviet Russia, and in the nations
which fell under the heel of conquest.

Foreign censorship taboos had for two decades familiarized
Hollywood with the politics of entertainment (many American
movies had been denied admittance to Spain, Poland, Turkey,
Hungary, Brazil, Japan), and as the world plunged toward war,
censorship became more severe and film quotas more oppres-
sive. Hollywood's markets were crippled or obliterated by dic-
tatorial action. Foreign propaganda films were taking over the
markets closed to Hollywood by political fiat; and in those
markets which remained more or less free—notably the South
American countries—German and Italian films, made and used
as deliberate instruments of foreign policy, were destroying the
trade which Hollywood, in free competition, had enjoyed.

There was another and powerful reason for the movie colony's political sensitivity. Hollywood, we have said, is cosmopolitan. The movie people have friends, relatives, and memories
which make Europe near and real. To Hollywood's British,
French, German, or Hungarian colonies, the cold news of political events means mothers, fathers, sisters, friends. It is one
thing to read about the cremation of Rotterdam; it is another to
telephone your uncle in Holland and get no reply. It is one
thing to hear of blood terror in Rumania; it is another to receive
no answer to the frantic cables you send to the staff you met

there last year. A substantial percentage of Hollywood had traveled and had known the life of a Vienna which was conquered, a Paris which was overrun, a London which was bombed. And even had the network of their personal lives been less wide, the malevolence of the new Caesars constituted a *personal* threat to the movie makers; after the Nazis smashed Warsaw they arrested the movie theater owners who had ever shown films distasteful to the Third Reich, hanged them, and rolled them through the streets on portable gallows.

The fact that the movies are an international commodity drove politics home to Hollywood with a hard, unyielding impact. The paroxysms of power politics flung the impending chaos of the world into Hollywood's lap. The war on Hollywood antedated the firing of cannon. The political advertency of Hollywood preceded the political awakening of America.

7. THE FIGHT FOR PRESTIGE

AT a recent Hollywood party, the following illuminati dined, wined, and danced with the elite of the movie colony: [1]

Prince Rospigliosi	Mrs. Roberta Mullineaux
Mrs. Gladys Peabody	Princess Conchita Pignatelli
Count Oleg Cassini	Admiral Arthur J. Hepburn
Lady Furness	Mr. Walter Van Pelt
Mr. Alfred Vanderbilt	Miss Cobina Wright, Jr.
Baroness Tamara de Kuffner	Mr. John Hay Whitney
Mr. Atwater Kent	Mrs. Reginald Vanderbilt
Count Claude Zapponi	Prince Raphael Hakim
Lady Mendl	Mr. Howland Paddock
Miss Pamela Paine	Mrs. Morley Vennuly
Mr. Philip Kellogg	Mr. William Wickersham

This is a far cry from the day when the picture people were pariahs, hopelessly beyond the pale of the wellborn. It suggests the remarkable change which has taken place in Hollywood's prestige in the larger world of Society. It was something of a revolution when the panjandrums of Georgia Society made the première of *Gone with the Wind* a Social Event of the first magnitude and exercised the right of deciding who would be invited to the opening in Atlanta. [2]

Aristocracies have always detested the *nouveaux riches;* the war between Society and the parvenus has run through history. Self-made men have never "rated" in the rarefied circles of

163

pomp and prestige; even the mighty Count Jacob Fugger, the most powerful financier of his day, a Catholic "embraced by the Pope," a friend of kings and a factor in dynasties, was snubbed by the patricians of his home town, Augsburg, who would not allow him to hang his newly designed escutcheon next to theirs. The rich English merchants yearned for knighthoods and baronetcies; the rich German burghers craved social recognition from the aristocrats of Paris; and in America the cattle princes and business barons of the West, after storming New York and Newport, cast wistful eyes toward the courts of Europe. "They schemed and contrived and paid through the nose to break in," said Ward McAllister.[3]

Hollywood, the very quintessence of the *nouveau riche*, is the most fertile incubator of parvenus in our time. As such, it symbolizes all that is obnoxious to the old and austere social cliques of the land. Movie stars and movie producers are viewed with acute distaste in the next-door bailiwick of Los Angeles Society. The better clubs in the City of the Angels have long had an unwritten rule barring picture people from membership. For years there were sections of Los Angeles and Beverly Hills in which movie people could neither rent nor buy homes. The citizens of the old guard labored to keep the movie colony "segregated like a leper colony."[4] The annual charity ball of Los Angeles' upper crust, the Las Madrinas Ball, has snubbed the movie colony with consistent frigidity.

There are no film people among the officers or directors of the Hollywood Bowl Association or the Breakfast Club; few movie wives are active in the Assistance League or the Junior League; and the list of sponsors of the Los Angeles Symphony Association shows a conspicuous absence of movie names. The newspapers in Los Angeles run two Society columns, one for the film colony and one for Society. But the columns on movie Society are beginning to mention old settlers, and the Society columns are being sprinkled (lightly) with film names. To the chagrin of Old Californians, visiting celebrities often reject their invitations, and hasten to break bread with "someone in Hollywood."

In the struggle for the honorific, Hollywood adopted the practices and hobbies with which prestige is associated. A polo set grew up in the movie colony, and the haughty Montecito and Midwick (now defunct) clubs were unable to ignore it entirely.* The movie people had the money to buy fine horses, the physiques and physiognomies to look right on them, and the recklessness with which to play the hardy game. Polo tended to encourage wider social recognition; one Old Californian remarked: "The movie folk fitted in perfectly. They were rich, if only for a short time; they lived in the grand manner, if only for a while. They never counted costs; they played extravagantly; they gambled on a colossal scale. Even if they were a bit phony, they were fun." [5]

Hollywood's star is rising in the larger social heavens of America. Hollywood is, indeed, supplanting Society in the public mind as a symbolic royalty.

. . . Hollywood can supply more glitter than a Society which has grown a trifle weary of its past magnificence and also a little timorous of its future. Hollywood's strings of pearls are longer, its Cattleyas rarer, its Hispano-Suizas newer, and its divorces bigger and better. And to some extent it has stolen the show—for that, in this era of specialization, has become the cinema's particular business.[6]

Statesmen, scientists, noblemen, and politicians have accepted Hollywood hospitality. Persons of great rank have hobnobbed with Hollywood's elite: Prince George of Great Britain, Prince George of Denmark, Prince and Princess Sigvard Bernadotte of Sweden, the Grand Duchess Marie, the Maharajah of Indore, Prince Amara of Kapurthala, the Duke and Duchess of Alba, the Duchess of Westminster, Lord and Lady Beaverbrook,

---

* Polo devotees: Walt Disney, Spencer Tracy, Darryl Zanuck, Walter Wanger, Robert Montgomery, Frank Borzage, Gary Cooper, Hal Roach, Clarence Brown, Jack Holt, Leo Carrillo, Michael Curtiz, Wallace Beery.

the Duchess of Sutherland, Prince di San Faustino. Those impressed by talent rather than rank will observe that Bernard Shaw, H. G. Wells, Albert Einstein, Salvator Dali, Diego Rivera, and Somerset Maugham have put up in movie homes. Those who enjoy Society's comedy of manners will note that Randolph Forrest Burke won his spurs by engineering a meeting between Gloria Vanderbilt and—Mickey Rooney.

Hollywood's prestige, in Society's terms, has been greatly enhanced by the connubial alliance of movie personalities and social luminaries; one cites the marriage of Gary Cooper to Veronica Balfe, Randolph Scott to Mariana du Pont, Sonja Henie to Dan Topping, Douglas Fairbanks, Jr., to Mary Lee Hartford, Andrea Leeds to one of the California Howards, Johnny Weissmuller to Beryl Scott of San Francisco. The union of actors and members of European courts is even more impressive; actress Virginia Cherrill became the Countess of Jersey; the late Douglas Fairbanks espoused England's Lady Ashley; Constance Bennett gained a title by marrying the Marquis de la Falaise de la Coudraye, to whom Gloria Swanson had been previously wedded; and writer James K. McGuinness married Baroness Lucie von Ledermann-Wartberg of Silesia. When royalty succumbed to Hollywood's lure, Society was not far behind. *

The movie elite is today being accepted—aye, courted. We might ask if statesmen and scientists would so readily welcome the hospitality of ketchup kings or cereal barons? The movie makers, unlike their bourgeois precursors, have access to the great; they find doors open to them which are still closed to the parvenus of trade and commerce. Even Society is intrigued by Hollywood's glamour; even scholars are titillated by Holly-

* The great hunger of Society for foreign titles is suggested by the fact that by 1909, according to Gustavus Myers, over five hundred American heiresses had become the wives of titled foreigners. Consuelo Vanderbilt married the Duke of Marlborough, Vivien Gould married Lord Decies, Anna Gould became the Countess Boni de Castellane, and so on.[7]

wood's shop talk. How did the accolade of status come to fall upon the movie colony?

In the 1930's, the big money in the United States was made by people in the luxury industries and in the empire of entertainment. New names shot into the income-tax lists; new faces adorned the front pages. It was the screen, the radio, and the theater which were springboards to fame and pelf at a time when the old fortunes were shrinking. But the chasm between Success and Society is not easily bridgeable; fame is no substitute for pedigree, and though money can make magnates only lineage can create Families.

It was Café Society that bridged the gap between Hollywood and Park Avenue. In the night clubs and restaurants of New York, the scions of the East met the gay, bright people of Broadway and Hollywood—persons whose names would make a dowager shudder. Café Society gave new money the social contact for which it yearned, and old money the escape from stagnation which it desperately needed. It was something of a landmark when, in 1930, the best man at a Whitney wedding was a magazine humorist, Robert Benchley, and the ushers included a Broadway tap-dancer, Fred Astaire, and a Hollywood writer, Donald Ogden Stewart.* In the Stork Club, 21, the Colony, El Morocco—Society and Show Business gazed upon each other, and each found a new affinity. Debutantes and playwrights, *bon vivants* and radio singers, millionaires and movie queens formed a new and fluid social set, a set which embraced the continental and the *nouveaux riches,* a social circle centered in New York but with a circumference which included London, Long Island, Biarritz, and Beverly Hills.

---

* It was a milestone in the earlier history of Society when Geraldine Farrar appeared as a guest in the home of Mrs. William Osgood Field; New York Society blinked its eyes. "Today the social hostess is highly flattered to have her invitations accepted by an operatic star like Lucrezia Bori or a great actress like Katharine Cornell; distinguished artists are now in a position to snub social lights, and not infrequently do." [8]

Fortune analyzed Café Society (December, 1937) and listed a "Regency Council" and a catalogue of those who are "In" and those who are "In and Out." The "In" group contains such celebrated names as Mrs. Vincent Astor, the William Rhinelander Stewarts, Prince Serge Obolensky, in juxtaposition to the Irving Berlins, Beatrice Lillie, Dorothy Parker, the Cole Porters, and the David O. Selznicks. The Bakers, Wideners, and Prince and Princess Chlodwig Hohenlohe-Schillingsfürst are cheek by jowl with Hollywood's Countess di Frasso (née Dorothy Taylor), the Schwartzes (A. Charles and Morton L.), and the Louis Bromfields. The "In and Out" group runs from the Jerome Napoleon Bonapartes, the S. Stanwood Menkens, and Grand Duchess Marie to Constance Bennett, Peter Arno, and A. C. Blumenthal. Errol Flynn, Lily Damita, Loretta Young, Bruce Cabot, Dolores del Rio, Marlene Dietrich, Brian Aherne, Douglas Fairbanks, Jr., and many other movie people are welcome in Café Society's set, and are familiar to the night-lifers of New York who cluster around it.[9]

The flowering of Hollywood Society may be seen in such an organ as *Town & Country,* of which one recent issue (chosen at random) contained the following in its proud pages: a picture of Mrs. Averell Harriman dining at Sun Valley with Darryl Zanuck, Pandro Berman, and Mrs. Milton Bren; a "Social Calendar" page which paired a niece of Lady Astor and a Van Pelt with the son of Victor McLaglen; a picture of "Gloria Swanson and friends" at the Flamingo in Palm Beach; a snapshot of the Toscaninis with the Samuel Goldwyns, the Ernst Lubitsches, and the Edward G. Robinsons; and a picture of a ball in San Francisco where the daughters of the oldest families masqueraded as—movie stars.[10]

The occupation of movie making, not so long ago regarded with ridicule or disdain, has made enormous strides in prestige. It could hardly have remained wholly déclassé after the Earl of Warwick (Michael Brooke), John Hay Whitney, James

Roosevelt, Whitney Bourne, a Lodge of Boston, Cobina Wright, Jr., and other representatives of Society's sectors actively undertook careers in Hollywood.

The movie colony of horse-operas and custard pies is lost in the past. The coming of sound to the silent screen, around 1928, represented more than a revolution in the technique of motion pictures; it revolutionized Hollywood's creative personnel and values as well. New talent was imported to the movie colony: dramatists from Broadway and Budapest, novelists from New England and London, actors from the Theater Guild, the Moscow Art Theater, the Abbey Players, writers and humorists and poets from the legitimate stage and the Pulitzer Prize ranks, directors from the finest theaters of America and Europe. Sound imposed new problems and new demands on the film, and battalions of creative minds poured into the studios of Hollywood. And when darkness fell over Europe, blotting out the arts, internationally famed artists gravitated toward the movie colony.

Today Hollywood includes in its professional ranks such writers as Aldous Huxley, Somerset Maugham, Christopher Isherwood; such playwrights as Robert E. Sherwood, S. N. Behrman, and Maxwell Anderson; such composers as Ernst Toch, Kurt Weill, Erich Korngold; such musical luminaries as Jascha Heifetz and Leopold Stokowski. Occasionally it occurs to enthusiastic souls that Hollywood is destined to be the Athens of the screen.*

The florescence of Hollywood's prestige is typified by such random facts as these: the Messrs. Mayer, Schenck, and Zukor are Chevaliers of the Legion of Honor; Jack L. Warner is entitled to wear the purple ribbon of the French Academy's

---

* The distinction of Hollywood's employees has also proved to be a boomerang, as was inevitable: it is the high creative spirits who have been the most cogent and articulate of Hollywood's detractors. This has many historical parallels; in the sixteenth century, for example, the scholars, poets, and painters whom rich merchants subsidized cast contempt upon the persons and businesses of their patrons.

169

Palmes Académiques, and Mr. Mayer received the highest honor of the Republic of Czechoslovakia, the Order of the White Lion. Academic honors have also flowed to the movie elite. Walt Disney boasts an honorary degree from Harvard; Spencer Tracy has a Doctorate of Dramatic Arts from Ripon College; Edgar Bergen and Charlie McCarthy were accoladed by the Northwestern University School of Speech; Bing Crosby received a Doctor of Music degree from Gonzaga College; L. B. Mayer received an honorary LL.D. from the University of Toronto; and a division of New York University conferred a degree on Dorothy Lamour, the siren of the sarong. The final tribute to Hollywood's prestige came from Elsa Maxwell; the queen of Café Society received a telegram from Norma Shearer which read, "Elsa Baby, expecting you on the eleventh," and replied breathlessly, to the world, "You haven't lived in vain if Norma Shearer calls you 'baby.'"

"Hollywood," said Dudley Field Malone, "is the town where inferior people have a way of making superior people feel inferior." Within the borders of the movie colony, social standing depends upon income and fame, and usually the two are in close correlation. When they are not, Hollywood shows an uncanny preference for current earnings as against recent repute. This is another manifestation of the movie colony's *nouveau riche* philosophy: in old and stable Society, money and status are not inextricable. In Boston and New York, many people of high status are almost bankrupt; in Charleston, certain inmates of the county poor farm are regularly invited to the St. Cecilia Ball, but the Lamonts and Wigginses of Long Island, who own estates in South Carolina, are never invited.[11] Status, like water, tends to find its own level.

A [Hollywood] hostess applies the Crossley rating to her friends. She doesn't want a failure to bob up among her successful guests; it would be embarrassing. That's why you always see the same faces at Holly-

wood parties; only the successful members of the colony are eligible.
. . . An actor or an actress is known by the company he or she keeps,
and there is no clowning about it. . . . The chap who gets $500 a week
associates only with others who get $500 a week. The $1,000-a-week per-
former mingles only with other $1,000-a-week individuals. . . . Failures
are outcasts. . . . A few weeks later one of these outcasts becomes
newly successful as the result of a picture or radio program, and immediately you see him or her at all the parties.[12]

This petty snobbery is not peculiar to Hollywood; * but it is
conspicuously clear, swift, and brutal in the movie colony. It
is a form of self-protection: the vicissitudes of movie fortune
are so great, the composition of the social pyramid is so protean,
the mobility of the movie elite is so pronounced, that the struggling and insecure people engaged in the chase for prestige are
under almost irresistible pressure to run with the pack.

The social barometer is remarkably sensitive in Hollywood,
and it is in evidence wherever the citizens of movieland gather.
The major-domos of the restaurants and night clubs enforce
the unwritten laws of social rating with a skill wondrous to
behold. When Lew Ayres, for instance, was first enjoying stardom he was automatically given choice seats at restaurants and
night clubs; when his film popularity (and income) declined,
he was shepherded to the third and fourth rows; when Mr.
Ayres made a comeback in pictures, he once more began to
rub elbows with the elect on the prized edge of the dance floor.
The case of Dick Powell and Joan Blondell (Mr. and Mrs.
Powell) is equally revealing. The day the trade journals announced that their contracts were not to be renewed by Warner
Brothers, these two stars called a night club for reservations
and were told that the best table "available" was in the second
row off the dance floor. Shortly after, when Miss Blondell and
Mr. Powell signed a contract with another studio, they were
according front-row privileges as naturally as of yore.[13]

* Lorenzo Delmonico refused to admit guests to his world-famous restaurant in
New York unless their social standing was acceptable.[14]

One blasé. inhabitant of the film colony maintained to this writer that the table arrangement at restaurants is an accurate and up-to-the-minute chart on Hollywood prestige; a glance at who is sitting where, this gentleman asserts, is enough to tell him who is out of a job, who has had an option lifted, who has been given a raise in increment, whose pictures are "clicking," whose careers are slipping. The Vine Street Brown Derby is believed to reserve the booths near the front and against the north wall for the true elite, and proximity to these hallowed places is in direct correlation to success and standing. Physical and social distance are thus equated with finesse.

The intangible apparatus of prestige operates in every corner of a studio lot. The hairdresser who attends a movie actress enjoys a subtle deference not accorded the electricians or prop boys. When a star enters a sound stage with her battery of attendants, a spirit of protocol is introduced; when the star leaves, the atmosphere relaxes and the labor crews feel free to indulge in horseplay. In the studio restaurants there are informal prestige zones; special dining rooms for executives and top producers; tables in the commissary tacitly reserved for actors, for directors, for writers; sectors to which bit players and extras gravitate; areas for sound men, art men, choruses.

There is no *Social Register* in Hollywood, but residents of the movie colony have no difficulty in enforcing the nuances of social rating. Directors of photography do not rate as high socially as minor comedians; writers are not so sought after as directors; stars are at a premium everywhere. Producers, of course, have the most advantageous position on the social battlefield, because of their wealth, the pattern of their living, and the fact that their invitations cannot be rejected with impunity. Producers' parties "are never ill-attended and their stories find an appreciation seldom accorded to other raconteurs." [15] The wives of movie producers find their levees crowded with stars, celebrities, and the platoons who keep an eye on the main chance.*

Producers may lack confidence in the social circles beyond Hollywood, but they employ the artifacts of prestige freely and lavishly on their own terrain. The *sanctum sanctorum* at MGM is the executive dining room and gymnasium on the top floor of the administration building, where special cooks, masseurs, steam baths, ping-pong tables, and elaborate devices for vicarious exercise are dedicated to the task of guarding the health of the MGM elite. The saga of Hollywood is not complete without one reverent reference to the occasion when a male secretary at a large studio asked for a raise and instead was given a key to the executives' washroom.

The prestige of movie people is not limited to the stars; anyone connected with Hollywood is granted some measure of popular envy. The waitresses at the Brown Derby feel quite superior to those at downtown hotels. The man who paints a garage wall can scarcely hope to get the awe accorded the man who painted a wall on the set for Irene Dunne's next picture. At a recent dinner dance of Hollywood's domestic servants (an annual event), James T. Till, chauffeur for Harold Lloyd and president of the Staff Service Bureau, told the press, "We're the elite among domestics." The newspapers dutifully reported that "among the socially elite of the evening were Constance Bennett's butler, Andrew Schultz; Richard Barthelmess's butler, Tom Cook, and maid, Sera Raknus; and Myrna Loy's entire retinue." [16]

There is a constellation of prestige among the studios, too, and potent distinctions separate the personnel employed on the various lots. A writer or a director at Universal does not "rate" with a writer or a director at Twentieth Century-Fox, and there is as wide a hiatus in rank between United Artists and Mono-

* See "The Night Life of the Gods," chapter 8.

gram as between Harvard and Dropsie College (Pennsylvania). The studio of highest repute in Hollywood is unquestionably Metro-Goldwyn-Mayer. This institution, sometimes called "the country club," possesses the largest and brightest galaxy of stars and creative talent; it pays the most lavish salaries; it produces the most costly pictures; it offers the most indulgent working atmosphere; it makes the most money; it is king in the hierarchy of movie prestige. Five hundred and fifty answers to the question, "Indicate the studio whose pictures you most admire," give us striking evidence of MGM's pre-eminence in the movie colony; and there is a very close correlation between professional and social rating.

POLL ON STUDIO WHOSE PICTURES ARE MOST ADMIRED

	Actors	Directors	Writers	Directors of Photography	Assistant Directors	Film Editors	Total
Metro-Goldwyn-Mayer	83	29	26	10	34	27	209
Warner Brothers	32	13	60	4	12	9	130
United Artists	54	10	30	3	12	6	115
Twentieth Century-Fox	19	4	8	3	5	9	48
Columbia	8	1	2	1	4	4	20
Paramount	7	2	0	1	2	3	15
RKO	2	1	1	0	2	1	7
Universal	4	0	0	0	2	0	6
Total	209	60	127	22	73	59	550

All the movie groups, with the exception of the writers, placed MGM first by sizable pluralities. The writers ranked Warner Brothers first, with twice as many votes as were received by the next studio, United Artists. The preference of movie writers for Warner Brothers' pictures, many of them indicated in their answers, rests upon the fact that Warner Brothers "are not afraid to do films on current political topics."

This studio has produced such memorable films as *The Story of Louis Pasteur, The Life of Émile Zola, Dr. Ehrlich's Magic Bullet,* and such bold political experiments as *Confessions of a Nazi Spy.* The unsaccharine realism and substance of Warners' general output elicits more respect from writers than the florid spectacles with star-studded casts produced by other studios.*

Hollywood's sensitivity to the nuances of prestige accounts for such amusing phenomena as the self-conscious use of "motion pictures" instead of "movies." The movie colony is mildly annoyed by such phrases as "the movie colony." Nor is this purist vanity restricted to the upper levels of Hollywood. The leaders of several labor unions objected to the word "movie" in questionnaires which were to be mailed to their membership, and insisted that "motion picture" be substituted. "'Movie,'" said one union official, "is hick talk."

The threads of prestige run through the entire social and professional fabric of Hollywood. Many of the difficulties which exist between the producers and the actors, directors, writers, or cameramen are traceable to demands for greater recognition, rather than higher salaries. Twenty years ago R. H. Tawney wrote: "It is more and more evident today that the crux of the economic situation is not the technical deficiencies of industrial organization, but the growing inability of those who direct industry to command the active good will of the *personnel.*" [17]

The history of the guilds and the complicated disputes between movie management and movie talent often suggests that in many cases the central issues are concerned with pride and prestige as much as with economics. When one movie writer

---

* The United Artists' figures in the poll, incidentally, combine the votes cast for the independent producers who release their pictures through United Artists: Selznick, Goldwyn, Wanger, and so on. In the questionnaire returns, no other *individuals* were singled out by name as often as David O. Selznick, Samuel Goldwyn, and Frank Capra, in the order named. The votes cast for Columbia Pictures were predominantly intended for the films which Mr. Capra directed for that studio, as most of those who voted for Columbia made clear. John Ford and Walter Wanger were also cited for individual praise.

was asked what the Screen Writers Guild policy would be, he replied: "To keep writers from being pushed around. This is a fight for self-respect." The movie cameramen resolved to change their title to "Director of Photography," and were successful in getting the studios to make the appellation official. The cameramen derived no monetary profit from this nominal metamorphosis, but the increase in their psychological income was substantial. A social worker testifies that certain impoverished movie extras, who have not worked in pictures for years, are reluctant to apply for relief: "It would be a blow to my professional standing."

The Motion Picture Relief Fund, to take a last example, synchronizes its charity to the individual reputation-needs of its cases: private hospital rooms are provided for those whose professional standing would be impaired if they were bedded in wards; an actor may be given a fifty-dollar suit so that he may make a good appearance in his search for work at the studios. To the perplexity of public-relief agencies, the Motion Picture Relief Fund does not want an unemployed actress or singer or dancer to accept a job below his or her customary standard of pay.

Prestige is carefully guarded in Hollywood, for its monetary complements are exact, obvious, and inescapable.

Hollywood, more than any other community in the United States, is the symbol of sudden success, sudden fame, sudden fortune. The pattern of rags-to-riches overnight is fondly cherished in American lore, but time disguises the economic foundations on which our great families were built, and contemporary scions do not dwell on the occupations of their forebears. "Pride of ancestry," someone has said, "increases in the ratio of distance."

American Society prefers to de-emphasize its middle-class origins and its mercantile roots. The proudest names of our social elite rose from the sometimes grubby ranks of commerce and trade. The settlers of America, including the Mayflowerites and the F.F.V.'s, were enlisted from the lower classes—in Dixon Wecter's words, "from the aggressive, the dissenter, the ne'er-do-well, the under-privileged, and the maladjusted." The historian John Fiske explored the ancestry of the leading families of New England (Lowell, Cabot, Saltonstall, Peabody) and the aristocracy of the South (Randolph, Cabell, Lee) and found them all recruited from the parvenu middle class.[18]

Let us cite a few distinguished cases. The first of the Astors was "a jovial, good-for-nothing butcher" (according to his earliest biographer), an immigrant who hoarded his pennies, sold debased liquor, and, for all his twenty million dollars, could barely read and write. The Vanderbilts are descendants of a prodigiously profane and egotistic "Commodore" who read only one book in his life, was considered too uncouth to be invited into the parlors of the wellborn, and proposed that the citizens of New York erect the tallest monument in America "to George Washington and Cornelius Vanderbilt." The Fisks are grandchildren of a tin-and-notions peddler who ran contraband cotton during the Civil War and sold blankets to the Army at outrageous prices. The Goulds are descended from Jay Gould, a conniving, plundering man who moved like an evil spirit through the railroad systems of the country.[19]

The names of Hollywood's leaders are less sonorous, but their origins are far better known: Louis B. Mayer was a movie-theater owner, the Warners were a butcher's sons, Samuel Goldwyn was a glove salesman, the Schencks were drugstore owners, Eddie Mannix was a "bouncer" at an amusement park. The names originally associated with the motion picture industry, but gone from Hollywood now, were also plebeian: Adolph Zukor and Marcus Loew began as furriers, Colonel William Selig was an upholsterer, William Fox and Carl Laemmle were clothing merchants, Lewis J. Selznick was a jeweler.[20]

177

Hollywood is not fortunate in the sheer sound of its patronymics. Movie names do not gain the automatic deference given to names like Schuyler, Cabot, or Farnsworth. There is a widespread assumption that the movie men are "foreigners," and even those of old native stock are believed to have "Jewish" names. Some of the most important people in the movie hierarchy—Darryl F. Zanuck, Y. Frank Freeman, Sidney Kent, George Schaefer, Eddie Mannix, Joseph I. Breen, William Le Baron, Hal Roach, Cecil B. DeMille—are erroneously believed by many to be of the same faith as the mother of Christ.*

It is worth taking a moment to comment upon the malapropisms attributed to the producers, whose diction is considered the most famous and amusing attribute of the movie colony. Mr. Goldwyn's immortal expressions have threatened to pass into the language, and well they might, if one studies the unsurpassed aptness of "Include me out," "A verbal contract isn't worth the paper it's written on," "The trouble with Hollywood is the dearth of bad pictures," "They're always biting the hand that lays the golden egg," and the immortal "In two words —Im possible." A joke about an illiterate movie magnate is always good for a laugh—even among movie magnates. And hoary stories, brought up to date by shifting the locale to Hollywood and the identity to "a movie producer," unfailingly win public favor and credence. Example: The yarn about the hill-billy who couldn't write and signed his name "XX." One day he began signing his name "XXX." "I chose a middle name," he explained. This story was resurrected recently, the hill-billy became "a Hollywood producer," and it was published in *Reader's Digest* (November, 1940).[21]

The significant point is that every American city has its

---

* Mr. Zanuck is of Czech descent and comes from Wahoo, Nebraska; Mr. Freeman is a Methodist from Atlanta; the Messrs. Kent, Le Baron, Roach, and DeMille are Protestants from Lincoln (Neb.), Elgin (Ill.), Elmira (N. Y.), and Ashfield (Mass.) respectively; the Messrs. Schaefer, Mannix, and Breen are Catholics from Brooklyn, Philadelphia, and Fort Lee (N. J.).

legend of a great Malaprop. Washington still chuckles over the dowager who talked of her fine "spinal staircase" and her "sexual bookcases." Detroit Society smiles over the verbal mutilations of John Kelsey, head of the $13,000,000 Kelsey Wheel Company, who bewailed the plight of "the poor pheasants who work in the fields" and thought the national anthem of France was the "Mayonnaise." A Western city cherishes the accidental *bon mots* of a lady who lamented that she spent her days "running pro and con," and said that her famous husband's remarks "ought to be taken with a dose of salts." [22] Hollywood, it would seem, is not *sui generis* in its malapropisms, and even Mr. Goldwyn has his peers. But Hollywood is news. . . .

The whilom salesmen, chorus girls, theater operators, and vaudevillians who fill the upper ranks of the movie colony, long treated with condescension, long ridiculed for being uncultured and gauche, are hot on the trail of social recognition. They build fine homes and hire many servants. They buy fine race horses and frequent tony race tracks. They collect pedigreed dogs and cats; they fancy Sheraton or Chippendale furniture. Hollywood's devotion to pedigreed animals and its craving for antiques are, in one sense, a form of compensation for genealogical inadequacy. Old furniture, old paintings, and old curios are part of an effort to acquire a symbolic history. Hence the mansions in the film colony where the rafters are carefully "antiqued," the fireplaces "aged," the picture frames drilled with "wormholes," the walls and glass studded with coats of arms. The search for ancient objects has become a cult in Hollywood, and passes into what Veblen called "an exaltation of the defective." The well-to-do can buy expensive modern things, but only the rich can buy antiques.

The author may be forgiven for closing this chapter with a quotation from an earlier chapter in this book:

There are striking resemblances between the founder of the House of Vanderbilt and the founder of the House of Mayer, between the first

179

Warner and the first Astor, between the ethos of Wall Street and that of Hollywood, between the spirit of Newport and that of Malibu Beach. In fifty years, names like Zanuck, Mannix and Selznick may well be great, and those who possess them may find entrée to circles which were closed to their grandparents.

A club at Oxford blackballed the Duke of Windsor when he was an undergraduate at Magdalen College; his family, after all, had not set foot on England's soil until the comparatively late date 1066.[23]

8. THE NIGHT LIFE OF THE GODS

> ONE sees continually marriage festivals, banquets, and dances, and everywhere one hears merry song and music, in a word, in every nook and corner one sees the richness, the power, the pomp, and the magnificence of this city.
> —GUICCIARDINI (1483-1540), *commenting on Antwerp.*[1]

There is little distinction between Hollywood's social and professional life. The movie colony works and relaxes with those in its own charmed circle, and the social amenities are semiprofessional in content and purpose. Constance Bennett is credited with the comment that Hollywood tends "to appreciate only persons of influence who might be of . . . professional assistance."[2] Hollywood's parties are more than occasions for conviviality; stories are sold in patios, deals are cemented over rumpus-room bars, contacts are initiated during the glow of Scotch and soda. The power lines of Hollywood run through its restaurants and game rooms, its dining rooms and dens.

The night life of Hollywood is neither so alluring nor so wicked as the legend has it. The "wild party" has left Hollywood's social calendar. Discretion and sobriety have taken root in the movie colony. This is by no means intended to suggest that all of the adults who work in pictures are discreet, pure, and sober, or that the twelve hundred actors, several hundred directors, half a thousand writers, and a hundred odd producers are paragons of virtue. But the scandals of the past have left their imprint; purity leagues, pressure groups, and religious Hawkshaws have taught Hollywood a lesson in the economics of morality. The press is on the alert for blatant misbehavior and is adroit in detecting it; and the requirements of a movie career discourage too-dangerous escapades. In its mores, as in its economics, the movie colony is moving toward stabilization.

For the most part, Hollywood's social life revolves around small, informal parties. The greatest proportion of leisure time is spent in private homes at private dinners; the salient characteristics of these assemblages are good food, competent service, movie anecdotes, and Scotch and soda. Game fads sweep film circles, achieve a social despotism which lasts for weeks, vanish, and are replaced by newer appeals to jaded senses. "Indications," a modernized charade, held dominion in Hollywood's social life for months, and teams of players spent countless hours in practicing weird signals to improve their proficiency. A later version of this mass obsession took the form of a game in which competing teams of Hollywood's elite burst into the frenzied drawing of pictures at a signal from the umpire. Bridge, backgammon, and stud poker have their acolytes in Hollywood no less than Denver, but as these pages are being written "gin rummy," a broad modification of the old card game, is the most effective time killer in Hollywood.

We ought to cast a glance at "theme" parties, which enjoy a perennial popularity in movie-land. The "Come As You Are" frolic was a special favorite for a while; in this strenuously novel procedure, the host and hostess delivered their invitations to their friends at all sorts of embarrassing hours, and the guests were obliged to appear at the party dressed just the way they were when the invitations were delivered. So it was that a movie queen, caught breakfasting in bed, had to attend a party in her nightdress; a screen Don Juan, apprehended in the act of shaving, had to appear in his undershirt and remain freshly lathered all through the gay night; other distinguished guests, caught in off-guard moments, were forced to appear in gardening clothes, bathing suits, and hair-curlers. This provided no end of merriment.

Robert Young invented a party in which the guests were asked to bring baby pictures of themselves, and spent the evening in a prize competition guessing at infantile identities. Edgar Bergen recently scored a great success with a "Come As Your First Ambition" party, which provided the glamorous people of Hollywood with an opportunity to disguise themselves as firemen, houris, locomotive engineers, ballerinas, bareback riders, baseball pitchers, and lion tamers. The Marx Brothers, earnestly incorrigible, staged a farewell party for two guests by taking *hors d'oeuvres* at the Trocadero, rushing out after a fake battle with the waiters, sipping soup in a garage, partaking of Hungarian chicken in the print shop of the *Hollywood Reporter,* and having their dessert in the ring at the American Legion stadium while two wrestlers tossed each other about with professional abandon.[3] This episode had no lasting effect on Hollywood's diversion pattern. Another strained stab at conviviality was a birthday party which a movie writer, Edgar Allan Woolf, gave for his dog; those who admired Mr. Woolf's originality did not know that "King" Lehr gave precisely the same kind of affair, to celebrate his dog's nativity, over forty years ago.[4]

The talented movie elite can entertain almost anyone interested in anecdotes, pantomime, or gossip. Some have applied themselves to the mastery of more esoteric feats. Chester Morris, Orson Welles, Frank Morgan, and Harold Lloyd are magicians, especially versed in the abracadabra of card tricks. Hugh Herbert has won an understandable fame in Hollywood through his genius in putting a half-dollar through the neck of a pop bottle. Norma Shearer, generally called "The First Lady of Hollywood," has regaled a group of friends by balancing a glass of water on her head, sinking to the floor, and rising without spilling a drop on her gown. There is no point in extending the catalogue of secret talents beyond these inspiring samples.

There is a more ambitious aspect to night life in the movie colony—the grandiose, all-out soirées, with hired orchestras, opulent decorations, and enormous guest lists. These large-scale parties are "the thing to do," at fairly regular intervals, for those in the social swim. In Hollywood, huge parties are a tradition, a challenge, a responsibility, and a business investment. You must entertain those who entertain you, and you entertain (or offer to) those into whose homes you wish to tread. The kind of party you throw is a demonstration of the kind of party you can afford to throw. Parties are a barometer of prestige, so party competition in Hollywood becomes as pronounced as rivalry in clothes, guests of honor, homes, or salaries.* And this suggests social exigencies which make the movie colony very much like other wealthy, distraction-hungry groups. The unforgettable wail of the Philadelphia blueblood who is now Lady Decies might have come from any one of Hollywood's reigning hostesses:

> Newport again! Another season; the same background of dinners and balls, the same splendours. The same set, the same faces, here and there a few lines on them carefully powdered out—no one could afford to get old, to slip out of things. New jewels, new dresses, new quarrels, new ambitions. All the old forms of entertainment had been exhausted, grown stale through repetition. Why not give something quite different? [5]

Hollywood works miracles in conjuring up "something quite different." The most "different" parties are those staged by Mr. and Mrs. Basil Rathbone, the hardiest hosts in Hollywood today. The Rathbone revels remain unmatched for scope and grandeur. Mrs. Rathbone is a party-giver of indescribable energy; a Rathbone season of costume balls, charity bazaars, tropical fêtes, garden parties, formal receptions, and Louis Quinze convocations would exhaust a lesser spirit. To commemorate their

---

* The Kwakiutl Indians of Vancouver Island express their social rivalry in feasts at which they burn enormous quantities of blankets or candlefish oil.[6]

wedding anniversary, the Rathbones took over the Victor Hugo restaurant, converted it into a papier-mâché cathedral, and banqueted some two hundred and fifty costumed guests—with Mr. Rathbone dressed as Emperor Franz Josef and Mrs. Rathbone masquerading as Empress Elizabeth.[7] This was the highest point to which relaxation in the film colony had aspired since the memorable occasion when Kay Francis rented a restaurant and had it redecorated as a ship, or since the time Carole Lombard contracted for the exclusive use of the "Fun House" at Ocean Park and invited hundreds of fun-lovers to disport themselves with mechanical pranks for one glorious night. (It was in describing the Lombard party that an observer said helplessly to this writer, "The truth is simply that the people in Hollywood are children.")

Mrs. Rathbone is the former Ouida Bergère, and her parties, one of which *Time* irreverently labeled *Folies-Bergères*, "detonate in something pyrotechnic, exotic, ingenious, and rare. At their most grandiose, they combine the best elements of annual maneuvers, a meeting of the Soviet of Nationalities and the New York World's Fair." To honor Leopold Stokowski, Arthur Rubinstein, and besieged Poland, a Rathbone dinner was carried off with historic éclat. The repast was served to sixty-four guests, including Princess Pignatelli, Sir Victor Sassoon, and George Raft. The sixty-foot dining hall was cleverly extended into the garden by a canopied extension, and the décor for the evening, created by a professional decorator, was all of dubonnet and silver lamé. A three-foot cellophane frieze around the walls contained the notes of Chopin's "Polonaise Militaire." The total effect "was something like Ali Baba's cave."[8]

Another epoch-making party was the one given by actress Leila Hyams and her husband after the world première of *The Good Earth*. A eucalyptus tree was placed in the front hall with clusters of gardenias replacing its natural foliage, and a great statue of a mandarin princess offered the guests leis of gardenias in its outstretched and benevolent hands. Stuffed white doves, in lifelike postures, were suspended from the ceiling by unseen wires.[9]

The gossip columns offer a running account of the social festivities of Hollywood. Here are some samples of a prosaic season, as plucked from the files:

> The huge gates of Pickfair swung wide for a huge tea and cocktail party which Mary and Buddy Rogers gave for the Grand Duchess Marie, and later for our own celebrated columnist and lecturer, Dorothy Thompson.

> We were greeted by the guests of honor, Lily Pons and Andre Kostelanetz . . . and the tall, blond and handsome Dalies Frantz, the "Titian of the Piano" and MGM actor, who, my dears, is simply an anomalous combination of musical virtuosity and masculine pulchritude. . . . Having acquired a golden tan at Lake Arrowhead, Jeanette [MacDonald] was a vision in golden hues. Her intriguingly bedraped chiffon gown featured a deep shade of *copa de ora*. From a matching turban gracefully fell a scarf, and all was made scintillating by a wide necklace of topaz and old gold.[10]

> Hitting only the high spots of the very large evening . . . roasted pheasant topped the gustatory sequence; gowns and feminine beauty that caught your breath floated by. . . . Host and hostess . . . were Darryl and Virginia Zanuck . . . welcoming Elsa Maxwell's house guest, the Duchess of Westminster, to Hollywood. In the party were the effervescent Elsa, Gilbert Roland and Constance Bennett, Dolores del Rio and Cedric Gibbons, Marlene Dietrich and Erich Remarque . . . [etc., etc.] [11]

The parties with which Marion Davies celebrates William Randolph Hearst's birthday rank among the most spectacular events in Hollywood. An enormous striped tent dominates the garden, and the decorations, favors, menu, beverages, and guest list leave little to be desired. By long tradition, and to the unfailing delight of Mr. Hearst, everyone appears in costume.

Hollywood is often credited with the shindigs of persons who, for one reason or another, are out to crash the scarcely obstinate social gates of the movie colony. In January, 1941, Rex St. Cyr, an elderly gentleman of mysterious career and riches, threw a party in honor of Cobina Wright, Jr., of which the *Hollywood Reporter* wrote:

> Many of the things you have read about in the fan magazines, all that glamour and tinsel that has been pinned on Hollywood in the past, came to life last night at the mask costume ball given by Rex St. Cyr at Ciro's. Everyone of Hollywood's "Who's Who" was there, dressed in varied costumes, and never in the history of the town was there so much color, beauty and magnificence as was on display at the affair. It was a supper dance, and everyone, including the orchestra, captains, waiters, and bus boys, were in costume.[12]

A partial list of the celebrities at this immortal gathering ran to no less than 305 names.

Masquerade parties, it may be said parenthetically, seem to exert a fatal attraction on the wealthy everywhere. Those who have exhausted the ordinary pleasures which wampum affords find new sensations in impersonating the sovereigns, pirates, or courtesans of an earlier day. The *bal masqué* opens new vistas for competitive display and spending. The love of disguise in the United States, so strong in our fraternal societies, reaches its climax in a penchant for royal costumes, which seem to compensate for our lack of an official aristocracy. (In aristocratic England, the fad was to dress up as cooks, butlers, and chambermaids.[13]) In the great day of American plutocracy, "no one would have dreamt of anything so plebeian as modern fancy dress; we had all to be kings and queens and courtiers. Princes of trade could represent none lower than princes of the blood; it was like children playing some fascinating game of make-believe."[14] It is easy to see why costumes would appeal to Hollywood.

The trend in Hollywood is away from what Lucius Beebe called "fall-of-Babylon parties." The heyday of festal extravagance seems to be over, and the very sharpness with which the

Rathbone and the Davies levees stand out in the movie colony suggests their departure from the more modest order of the day. Pretentious and grandiose parties do sprout up, but they are considered a bit passé; and at their most majestic they do not duplicate, in either magnitude or frequency, the Lucullan antics of the good old days. Most of the big parties of the past three years have been launched in connection with movie premières, and in many of these shindigs the expenses (provender, drink, night-club space, entertainment) were footed by the studio, which advertised its commodity and flattered the movie reviewers, who were invited in wholesale lots. And now Hollywood is outlawing lavish premières.

The more ambitious parties of Hollywood are built around a very long roster of guests, alarmingly novel décor and entertainment, and columnists who will report the festivities with appropriate awe. (Louella Parsons, Hedda Hopper, Jimmie Fidler, and Ella Wickersham are the journalists most favored with invitations.) At some parties, professional magicians, horoscopists, or palm readers appear after the repast, to entertain the notables. Many producers have installed private sound and projection systems in their homes to show their guests the latest films.

The popularity of cards, games, charades, and other puerile diversions betrays the necessity for social artifices where the creation of a natural social rapport offers problems too great to be tackled manfully. Bette Davis recently confessed to an interviewer that she had never drunk liquor until she came to Hollywood: "I had to do *something* to enjoy those parties." [15] One hostess said that her next party would be held in a dozen rooms, each with its own *special* divertissement. "The trouble with Hollywood parties," she lamented, "is that people who don't like each other are thrown together."

It is the solemn opinion of this writer that Hollywood parties are profuse in devices designed (1) to distract the attention of the guests from each other; (2) to defer the crisis of conversation.

The movie colony is split into fairly well defined social strata; and the night life of Hollywood tends to revolve around cliques of persons of approximately the same social rank. The top producers and executives compose a powerful in-group into which lesser producers, stars, and outstanding directors are frequently welcomed, but to which they do not actually belong. This group entertains on a scale befitting its responsibilities; its interests and conversation are concentrated on the movie business, movies, horses, poker, and pinochle. "There are one or two of these masters of destiny whose social charm lies largely in their power to make finding a job difficult for anyone who fails to be impressed by their wit and culture." [16]

The actors and actresses are divided into a number of small social circles. There is the British colony, led by men like Ronald Colman and C. Aubrey Smith, and given to gentle sociality, tea, garden parties, and war relief. There is the robust Celtic colony of James Cagney, Pat O'Brien, Spencer Tracy, Frank McHugh, William Gargan, and other gregarious men. There is the stage and concert coterie cultivated by Jeanette MacDonald. There is the brittle, cosmopolitan clique of Constance Bennett, Marlene Dietrich, *et al.* There is the serious, politically active group captained by Melvyn Douglas and Helen Gahagan. There is the night-club crowd—actors, actresses, agents, producers, and undomesticated persons in search of a hilarity which only overcrowding, noise, and calisthenics on a waxed floor seem to induce. There are several dozen clans of directors and writers of different income and screen-credit levels. There is the bright young set, disciples of *le jazz hot,* barbecues, and violent exercise. And there is the socially ambitious, swanky crowd to the generalship of which the Basil Rathbones have hacked their way with steely resolve.

The comparatively small number of night spots in Hollywood never fails to surprise visitors. Movie people do not patronize any night club consistently enough to insure its success, and the community is strewn with the wrecks of enterprises which foundered on the rocks of Hollywood's inconstancy. The famous Trocadero, for years the hub of Hollywood's night life, changed hands three times in two years and is now closed. One restaurateur took the Trocadero over after several predecessors had given up the ghost, remodeled it from stem to stern, improved the dinners, hired *three* excellent orchestras for non-stop dancing, and went out of business in five months. This, it should be noted, despite the fact that the Trocadero fought off the death-rattle with daring novelties, one of which was a "Bank Nite" at which Hollywood's *crème de la crème* sat enchanted at the prospect of winning bottles of perfume, gold cuff links, and other knickknacks the value of which could scarcely have excited the customers had they paused to regard the matter in a calmer light. It was a rare, baffling sight to watch $3,000-a-week actresses, or the wives of $5,000-a-week producers, spring up ecstatically when they won five dollars' worth of gewgaws.

The current sensation in Hollywood's night life is Ciro's, an ultra-swank spot backed by several movie magnates and "Billy" Wilkerson. Strikingly decorated and expertly managed, Ciro's has won immense popularity—but one looks at the record of other ventures of this order and waits for Hollywood's fickleness to hit its stride. The Victor Hugo, one of the landmarks of Beverly Hills, had a career of violent ups and downs, went into receivership, and is now closed.

The movie people patronize only those places which charge high enough prices to exclude the *hoi polloi*, which serve quality food and drink, and which offer superior orchestras and entertainers. But they do not patronize these places consistently enough to cover the huge operating expenses which their tastes demand. Hence, the only centers of night life which endure year after year are fine eating houses or hotel ballrooms which cater to a non-movie clientele as well as to Hollywood. Of the restaurants, the following deserve mention: The Brown Derby (four establishments), Dave Chasen's, the Cock and Bull, Perino's, Don the Beachcomber's, Somerset House, Bit of Sweden, and half-a-dozen places on "the Strip" and in Beverly Hills. Of the dine-and-dance emporia, one notes the new Mocambo, the Ambassador Hotel's Cocoanut Grove, by now an *idée fixe* in the movie colony, Club Bali, the Biltmore, and the Beverly-Wilshire. Other fashionable spots to which the movie people flit from time to time are The Berries, in San Fernando Valley, Lake Arrowhead's High Hat, the Glass Slipper in Malibu, La Venta at Palos Verdes, the Hut in Palm Springs, and the Pine Cone in Monterey. Hollywood's night spots are far inferior to those of New York or Chicago or San Francisco, in both number and quality. One observer remarked, "You could drop all of Hollywood's people, parties, and night clubs in New York—and no one would ever notice them."

Hollywood's parties and night life are a godsend to the wives of the movie makers, who are excluded from the professional life of their husbands. Parties give the movie wives publicity, enhance their social standing, and relieve the boredom of an existence of utter nonresponsibility. Most members of the subtler sex have virtually nothing to do in Hollywood except buy, dress, entertain, and be entertained. Chauffeurs take care of their shopping, cooks prepare their meals, governesses shepherd their children, and pictures tyrannize their husbands. The life of the Hollywood wife slowly drifts into a routine of buying, auctions, luncheons, bridge clubs, and parties. In parties there is at least surcease from the encompassing boredom. One news photographer in Hollywood receives expensive gifts from movie wives for photographing them and their gatherings in the most flattering fashion. At least two women in the film colony have built their husbands' careers by a relentless series of parties at which potential employers were dined, wined, and flattered.

It is a striking feature of a Hollywood party that immediately upon the conclusion of dinner an automatic segregation of the sexes takes place. The men huddle together to talk shop, exchange gossip, or swap anecdotes; the women spend the evening in the time-honored discussion of clothes, children, servants, and food. A Hollywood living room, movie fans will be saddened to learn, bears a marked resemblance to a Quaker meeting.

The popularity of stag parties and "nights out with the boys" is another manifestation of the devaluation of wives in Hollywood. Despite her beauty, clothes, and social application, the Hollywood wife remains an appendage to careers—useful, but not participant. The intensity with which women in movie circles plunge into their own social activities, attend the races, or augment their wardrobes, suggests a rivalry with their husbands which is fostered, in part, by their exclusion from the pulsating experience of movie making. Hollywood wives, as a social type, are no different from the wives of American businessmen as a whole.

The wife, in our civilization, has long been a perambulating vehicle for the exhibition of her husband's wealth and success. (The *nouveau riche* ladies of Colonial days used to powder their hair with gold and silver dust to display the wealth of their husbands.[17]) The Hollywood wife, like the American wife, has ceased to be simply a woman; she is required to be a lady.*

The new kings of trade might work at their offices twelve, fourteen hours a day, but their wives would have something to show for it. Festoons of priceless jewels draped ample bosoms, yards of historic lace-

---

* Women's styles, so delicate and revealing a social weathervane, reflect the change. When women became symbols of wealth whose social function is the vicarious consumption of leisure (in Veblen's vocabulary), the romantic concept of the Lady took hold and the stereotype of feminine charm stressed thin waistlines, small hands and feet, and a slenderness which bordered on undernourishment.[18]

rimmed under-petticoats, the greatest dress designers of Europe vied with one another to create costumes that would grace some splendid ball for one night and then be thrown away. . . . Different dresses for every occasion, eighty or ninety in a season, worn once or twice and put aside.[19]

The quotation is from a Philadelphia socialite's diary, the time was thirty or forty years ago, but the moral might hold for Hollywood today. The women of the movie colony have the means and the need to find a purpose in existence by an assiduous application to parties and clothes. Hollywood's wives are engaged in a continuous battle against the doldrum of disutility; they are occupied with activities which try to deny and disguise the boredom of a life without responsibility. They bring to mind the plaint of Evalyn Walsh McLean: "The one continuing problem in my life has always had the shape of just one question: what amusing thing can I do next? It is not only me it bothers, so I notice; it affects all my friends. . . ." [20]

Hollywood, which is given to extremes in most things, is characterized by either very elegant or very informal dress; there are no hard and fast rules governing the decorum of clothes. Mink coats are worn over lounging pajamas, ermine jackets over shorts.

The first time I was invited to a big party—it was a barbecue supper at Victor McLaglen's La Cañada estate—I asked a more experienced columnist's wife what I should wear. I wasn't altogether convinced when she said, "Anything—absolutely *anything* at all." But she was right. Mrs. McLaglen received her guests in a tweed suit. Constance Bennett was gowned in a stunning afternoon frock. Janet Gaynor was wearing slacks. Myrna Loy was strolling about in a bathing suit. Toward evening Buster Keaton turned up in his land yacht wearing an admiral's uniform. It is literally true that every sort of costume appears at every sort of social function.[21]

At one formal party, half a dozen women turned up in slacks; this, one might imagine, would turn a hostess' hair white, but the ladies were not frowned upon, for they had been wearing formal evening gowns before the cameras for five days running and it was an understandable relief for them to "dress up" by changing into slacks. The fact that actresses report for work at 9 A.M. in ermine, evening gowns, and jewels, and that actors spend long working days encased in white tie and tails, deserves attention as a determinant of Hollywood's styles. The distaste for formal dress in the movie colony has further logic if one considers the climate and the informality it encourages. There is an infectious freedom in Hollywood's attire.

Clothes do not, of course, make the man; but gentlemen contend that they make the gentleman. The Hollywood male would ignore the distinction. The garb of the movie men emphasizes ease rather than rectitude, color instead of conservatism, dash rather than propriety. Slacks, sport jackets, sport shirts, neckerchiefs, sleeveless sweaters (instead of waistcoats), these give Hollywood the atmosphere of an all-year country club. Men in film circles eschew the *de rigueur;* they prefer jackets and trousers of contrasting colors, and they defy the conventional by appearing in tweeds and slacks even when their wives are in long dresses.

On swanky occasions, Hollywood's actors and actresses are expected to dress up, with all the trimmings. The pressure of fashion is great and insistent; stars get publicity with and through their clothes, and their "glamour" suffers if the clothes are not striking. So it is that at the big parties or premières Hollywood's samurai turn out in a display of furs and gowns which dazzle the eye. Some actresses have won careers greater than their histrionic talents would justify simply through their ability in transporting elegant clothes. Among the actors, William Powell and Adolphe Menjou were first accorded recognition because of their haberdashery; certain actors are favored for sophisticated parts because of the ease with which they wear formal dress.

Fashion is a method of adjustment to that group pressure which enforces some degree of conformity among its members, and styles are devices which permit the expression of individualism and competitiveness within the defined boundaries of fashion. The need to distinguish one's self is visible wherever you look in Hollywood. The fact that newspapers will print items such as this: "Arline Judge stunned socialites at a swank shindig last week when she sported, atop her turban, a stupendous emerald and diamond clip," [22] is one reason why Miss Judge appeared that way.* When I. Magnin's, the fashion hub of Hollywood, moved to new quarters, the aristocracy of Hollywood turned out in great numbers for a "preview party," with dancing following a regal tour of inspection.

Clothes attract attention to the wearer, and in Hollywood, where uniqueness is a cult, wardrobes are an arena for competitive exhibitionism. The John Frederics or Lilly Daché hats which the movie Delilahs wear cost anywhere from $35 to $125; the Saks or Magnin gowns range from $75 to $350.† The function of clothes as an index of conspicuous costliness has never been demonstrated more neatly than by Paulette Goddard, who appeared at a party in a wrap-around white sarong with ten-dollar bills stuck nonchalantly around the waistline to complete the decoration.[23]

The people of Hollywood parade their fortune in clothes for ancient reasons. The *nouveaux riches* have always devoted too much attention to their dress, as if to gain by fashions what they lacked in titles. And there is a significant relation between dress and status, between the magnificence of clothes and the pecuniary aspects of prestige. Miriam Beard points out that the

---

* This reminds one of the dowager who "progressed 'to her loge at the Opera kicking a great uncut sapphire or ruby attached to her waist by a rope of pearls." [24]

† No movie queen can hope to rival Mrs. William B. Leeds, with her $40,000 allowance *per annum* for wardrobe; or Jessie Woolworth Donahue, who owns the Romanov crown jewels and a sable wrap estimated at $75,000; or Delphine Dodge Baker, whose pearl necklace is valued at $800,000.[25]

Florentine bankers and merchants vied with one another in their dress for very practical reasons:

This peacock rivalry was not the mere expression of vanity. . . . It was necessary for even the busiest man to display his credit upon his person. . . . Gossips in the Exchange were only too ready to pass rumors of approaching bankruptcy, if a broker happened to come to dinner in too simple a frock or an outmoded hat. . . .[26]

The point applies to Hollywood, too.

Several hundred years ago Guicciardini, the Venetian ambassador to Antwerp, wrote: "Men and women of every age make much ado about clothing to show off their position and fortunes, always in the newest and most magnificent fashion, but not seldom far more costly than decency and morals bid." [27]

There is something familiar and derivative about even the most sumptuous parties Hollywood flings. The most daring movie producer's party pales by comparison to the annual Dorrance revels in Philadelphia, which cost between $75,000 and $150,000; *Fortune* described one of them as featuring "hundreds of live macaws and toucans and cockatoos and parakeets and birds of paradise in cages, and showers of rose petals falling pinkly on the dancers out of an electrically activated sky." [28] When a movie hostess converts a restaurant into a cathedral she is, whether she knows it or not, imitating such social pioneers as James Stillman, who transformed his dining room into an artificial forest and served a "picnic supper" under a fabricated waterfall.[29] When Carole Lombard hit upon the idea of taking over "Fun House," she probably did not know how short her efforts fell of those of Nancy Leeds, who took a whole house party on her yacht and sailed to Rocky Point, where the entire amusement park had been reserved; or of a Clarence Mackay who, when he married Anna Case in 1931, brought the entire Philadelphia Symphony orchestra to Long Island for the nuptials.[30]

Even the Homeric fêtes of Hollywood are but poor imitations of, say, the Bradley Martin ball at the Waldorf-Astoria (cost, $200,000); or of the parties of the mighty Stotesburys, who brought hundreds of guests to Philadelphia in a special train, ensconced them in hotel suites especially decorated in gold and rose, and banqueted them in the Bellevue-Stratford ballroom, which had been transformed into Venice—gondolas, lanterns, Italian singers and all (cost, almost half a million dollars).[31] Even Mrs. Basil Rathbone's far-famed "Night at St. Moritz" must bow to more grandiose predecessors—and contemporaries. This triumph of hoopla, given for charity, took place on the grounds of the Beverly Hills hotel; a wonderful machine manufactured artificial snow, an ice-skating rink was erected over the tennis courts, there was a toboggan slide with sleds, and—for some reason—gypsy fortunetellers. This echoed the fête of certain Eastern socialites in which a ballroom was transformed into an enormous ice-grotto: ". . . as the blocks of ice would melt, they would tumble over each other in charming, glacier-like confusion, giving you winter in the lap of summer; for every species of plant stood around [the] immense floor." [32]

The Leila Hyams adventure in gardenias, reported in this chapter, was a feeble imitation of the Oelrichs *feu d'artifice* at which 48,000 hybrid roses were attached to eight rose trees in the ballroom; or of the wedding in 1935 of Marjorie Post Close Hutton to Joseph E. Davies, later ambassador to Soviet Russia, at which 5,000 chrysanthemums were dyed a bluish pink to match the icing on a 300-pound wedding cake.[33]

One does not wish to denigrate Hollywood's effort, nor disparage the scope and glitter of movie parties. They are certainly the most widely *publicized* parties in the world. But it is necessary to point out that no Hollywood hostess is able to match Mrs. Pembroke Jones, who spent $300,000 each season on entertainment—and the season lasted only six to seven weeks.

In the heyday of Society, one social season in New York City saw some six hundred balls at a total cost estimated to have reached $7,000,000; and the average cost of a suitable dress, *sans* jewelry, was around a thousand dollars.[34]

There is something passé about big-scale parties, and Hollywood suspects it. The supercolossal revels are becoming more infrequent in the movie colony; the high frequency of small parties continues. The search for novelty, for entertainment, for what is at bottom nothing but sheer distraction, suggests the inner poverty of Hollywood, its inability to remain at ease in sustained discussions, its yearning for that mass conviviality which offers refuge from contemplation. The movie makers try to extend the boundaries of escape by giving frequent parties, parties which are full of devices for the conquest of time.

9. OF MARBLE HALLS

IN Hollywood, as in Istanbul or Sioux Falls, the rich hasten to express their wealth, and betray their fitful groping for status, by erecting homes of unnecessary magnitude and splendor. For wealth is a psychological sovereignty, and those within its boundaries live in obligatory palaces. Houses are the most visible and enduring signs of great fortune; in all times and places architecture has served as a primary symbol of social station. The landscape of America, from Baton Rouge to St. Paul, from Baltimore to Hollywood, is dotted with the proud mansions of social ambition. Let us glance at a few of them:

The Woolworth palazzo at Glen Cove, Long Island, was built around a living room which was in itself appraised at $1,000,-000. "Whitemarsh Hall," the E. T. Stotesbury place at Chestnut Hill outside Philadelphia, contains no less than 150 rooms, 45 baths, 14 elevators, and 308 acres of park and gardens. The Nicholas F. Brady house on Long Island contains a dining room where 1,500 guests were served on one occasion. The Samuel Insull estate (4,200 acres) near Chicago cost $9,000,000. On the west coast, the fortress of Samuel Hill, overlooking the Columbia River, contained a throne room with gold furniture from the palace of Queen Marie, and the owner satisfied a little whim by decorating his grounds with a full-scale reproduction of the Druidic monuments at Stonehenge. The whole giddy pattern is epitomized by the merchant prince who expressed a wistful craving for the Great Wall of China.[1] Hollywood offers nothing to compete with these. The biggest of the movie homes would seem puny to the ranking elite of America.

Nor is one mansion, however great and majestic, enough for America's lords of creation, who have country *dachas* in Southampton, Newport, Oyster Bay, Long Island, Palm Beach, Bar Harbor, and along the Hudson. These temples of leisure embrace banquet halls, yacht landings, swimming pools, kennels, stables, greenhouses, race tracks, tennis courts, shooting galleries, bowling alleys, aviaries, and other appurtenances of the good life. One *grande dame* had a fleet of full-sized skeleton ships placed in the bay in front of her home, to create the illusion of a harbor. One coal baron tried to scale Parnassus by reproducing Buckingham Palace at a cost of $5,000,000. And the current hideaways of Doris Duke Cromwell, queen of the multi-mansioned, comprise a manse in Newport, a duchy in North Carolina, a cottage at Antibes, a villa at Palm Beach, and a dream palace in Hawaii which cost $1,000,000 and contains a Delhi marble bathroom inlaid with jade.[2]

No munificence was too great for the American millionaire, no whim too costly, no yearning too infantile. The pavilions of the wealthy are filled with Gobelin tapestries and Tudor chests, sculpture from Greece and balustrades from Venice, medieval armor, Persian rugs, alabaster clocks, walls of enamel and gold. One carved oak-and-ebony bed was inlaid with gold and cost $200,000.[3] The baroque and the pathetic were blended in the taste of the business princes who preceded Hollywood on the much larger stage of fortune; the prodigal and the puerile stalked through the empty opulence of their life.

Hollywood offers no palaces and no furnishings to match those of the Eastern nabobs, but the first batch of movie *arrivistes* made a partial effort to imitate their peers. They built big mansions, fine gardens, and filled their chalets with costly paraphernalia. The hills above Sunset Boulevard, from Holly-wood to the Pacific Palisades, glisten with estates which try to ape the elegance of Long Island or the Riviera. Here are wooded acres, splendiferous homesteads, rambling gardens, ter-races, fountains, tennis courts, and all the accessories of wealth and fame. Here, and in Bel-Air and Holmby Hills, are the homes of Hollywood's elite; here is the movie fan's Valhalla. Here the unpoor of the screen erected their domiciles—French châteaux, colonial mansions, English manors, Italian villas, Spanish ha-ciendas, Cape Cod "cottages." Here rambling driveways and fine brick walls surround homes with a breath-taking view of the hills, the sea, and the whole bright sweep of Los Angeles sprawling across the coastal plain from Sunset Boulevard to Long Beach.

Probably the most imposing dwellings in the film colony are those of Harold Lloyd, Cecil B. DeMille, Mary Pickford, Charles Chaplin, Marion Davies, Winfield Sheehan, and the late Carl Laemmle. The Lloyd estate, an awe-inspiring demesne, is reported to be the most expensive. This architectural *tour de force*, with its terraces and gardens and cascading fountains, its swimming pool and tennis courts, cost well over $1,000,000. The neighboring Laemmle property is almost as impressive, quite as expansive, and nearly as expensive.[4] The Chaplin home contains an atrium described by one visitor as "something like Westminster."

The DeMille manor house tops a hill in Los Feliz, overlook-ing fine lawns, a little park and lagoon, and superb flower beds.* "Pickfair," once renowned as the home of Douglas Fairbanks and Mary Pickford, is a massive gray pile high up in the hills,

* In an article written by a leading California gardener, Mr. DeMille is reported to have spent almost a quarter of a million dollars on his gardens in two estates; this is the nearest Hollywood parallel to the $1,000,000 which Rodman Wanamaker spent for special small-leaf box hedges; or the $25,000 which Pierre du Pont spent, according to *Fortune*, to bring a special bush to his Longwood estate; or the forty gardeners employed by James B. Duke.[5]

set back on ample acreage, with great walls and gates, fine *ameublements,* swimming pool, and gardens.

The three-storied colonial manse of Marion Davies on the sands of Santa Monica overwhelms the eye: its foyer is spectacular, its furnishings lavish, and rooms disemboweled from European castles stand in cool magnificence. The woodwork and chandeliers are worthy of museums; there are van loads of *objets d'art,* innumerable paintings (including a good many of the mistress of the house), and around ninety rooms—most of which, it is said, have telephones connected to the private switchboard. This dovecote contains a long, marble pool (fifty yards from the plebeian Pacific) with a marble bridge bisecting it, à la the Rialto.

The Winfield Sheehan-Maria Jeritza hacienda, one of the showplaces of Beverly Hills, has a lovely sunken garden and a ceiling imported, in the great tradition, from Spain. The fireplace is a maze of tortured seraphim and at one time a cannon rested on the mantelpiece. *Fortune* claims that the Sheehans and their guests dine on golden dishes and drink from golden goblets.[6]

The maintenance costs for these homesteads is, of course, staggering, and the movie people, like the captains of industry, have learned the meaning of the adage that it isn't the cost but the upkeep. "A man builds a fine house," wrote Emerson, "and now he has a master, and a task for life; he is to furnish, watch, show it, and keep it in repair the rest of his days." With the passage of the years, famed movie châteaux have found their way into the lists of the real-estate agents, and their offerings testify to the passing of the old splendor. The 700-acre estate in Rockland County, New York, which Adolph Zukor once called home, is being converted into a realty development with Federal Housing Authority participation.[7]

John Barrymore was impelled to place his $448,000 mansion on Tower Road on the auction block, and refers to it as "that

Chinese tenement." "Frankly," Mr. Barrymore remarked, "it was a kind of nightmare." This celebrated property consists of five acres and two houses joined by "a sort of Turkish pergola." There are *three* swimming pools, one of which is bordered by a water spray; in another, Mr. Barrymore used to keep rainbow trout. "Kept 'em alive for two years and personally fed 'em," he confided to a reporter. "The little guys got to know me." [8] The Barrymore refuge also contains a bowling green, a skeet range, an aviary, two garden houses, a wine cellar, quarters for a dozen domestics, trinkets from the four corners of the world, and a sun-and-moon dial imported from England for the nominal sum of $15,000. The music room is illuminated by a particularly fine chandelier which the greatest Hamlet of his time bought in a moment of weakness from an Austrian archduke for $8,500. In the English tavern room there is a bar which Mr. Barrymore once spied in Alaska and, because of a sentimental attachment, shipped home to his Hollywood hills. [9]

The exotic aerie which Rudolph Valentino built in the hills above Benedict Canyon is another relic of the departed glory. He called it "Falcon's Lair," furnished it with rococo objects, had all the walls painted black, and hung the windows with ebony drapes. It is said that Mr. Valentino had a tinge of heliophobia. The house is now owned by Señor Juan Romero, who built a marble shrine in the garden in memory of the screen's romantic godhead. [10]

These names—Lloyd, DeMille, Chaplin, Pickford, Davies, Barrymore, Laemmle, Sheehan, Valentino, Zukor—are themselves suggestive of Hollywood's past; they are associated with the first era of the movie colony; and the edifices which we have described were built from fifteen to twenty-five years ago.* The naive and flamboyant urges which went into these

---

* This writer could find no Hollywood parallels to W. C. Grunow's $12,000 onyx marble tub, Mrs. Hugh Dillman's gold faucets, Mrs. Seton Porter's black and white marble bathroom, Henry H. Rogers' $250,000 swimming pool, or the tile-pink soil which was imported from France for Mrs. Dodge Sloane's tennis court. [11]

monuments are epitomized with almost deliberate irony in the home currently occupied by Joan Davis, movie comedienne. This basilica, the quintessence of Hollywood's foolish age, is presumably of Moorish design, but the living room is Chinese, the nursery is colonial, one guest room is old English, another is French provincial, the sun room is Hawaiian, and a bedroom, defiantly glamorous, is done all in shiny coral satins.[12]

It is important to recognize the influence of William Randolph Hearst on the movie pioneers. The amazing publisher entered the movie field via newsreels around 1911. Attracted to movies as a hobby, and because they promised profits, his amateur interest turned into professional activity as a means of furthering the dramatic career of Marion Davies. Miss Davies' Santa Monica retreat (the size and furnishings of which show the Hearst touch) became a meeting place for Hollywood and Hearst. The power of the Hearst press, the Hearst magazines, the Hearst radio stations, the Hearst columnists, and the Hearst feature writers insured the aging publisher a welcome in the movie colony. He bought stock in MGM, which released the Hearst *Movietone* newsreels, organized Cosmopolitan Pictures to produce Miss Davies' films, and made deals for the distribution of the pictures, first with MGM and then with Warner Brothers.* Hearst's activities in the Republican party and in California politics brought him closer to the leaders of the movie industry, notably the Messrs. Mayer and Schenck. Hearst's Hollywood correspondent, Louella Parsons, became a plenipotentiary whom no one dared offend. With the years, Mr. Hearst became genuinely attached to the gay, bright picture people and the Hollywood in which they held court.

Hearst opened the portals of San Simeon to the movie crowd, and he dazzled their eyes with the magniloquence of his life and the princely abandon of his expenditure. His baronial castle

---

* The companies which released Cosmopolitan Pictures were given a sixty-day option on stories which appeared in the Hearst magazines.

on the Pacific was a cross between the Palazzo Uffizi and the Hippodrome. His duchy was a domain of such vast dimensions that it could be traversed only in a three-day ride on horseback. His warehouses bulged with $25,000,000 worth of loot—seventy dismantled medieval bedrooms; a monastery from Segovia (dating back to 1141) which Hearst bought for around $500,000 and shipped to New York in 14,000 crates; stained glass valued at $400,000; tapestries assessed at $8,000,000; thirty-four Majolica plates and twenty-nine pieces of silver worth $468,000; thousands of ancient chests and guns and statues and clocks.[13]

The movie parvenus—pretty actresses, ambitious actors, culture-hungry producers—were understandably awed by a man who bestrode an empire of his own making, a man who owned yachts, woods, zoos, lakes, mines, a castle in Wales, and—at San Simeon alone—thirty-five cars! Once the Master chanced to smell a daphne and telegraphed his head gardener to plant a ring of daphne around his palace; the nurseries of California were depleted to comply with this request, at a cost of $12,000. The Lord of San Simeon imported 30,000 trees for his feudality, spent $10,000 in moving two old oak trees thirty feet, and in one inspired planting moved a hundred palms over two hundred miles.[14]

It was Hearst who held the banner of luxury before the early movie magnates. He possessed vast wealth, a Renaissance flair for spending, and an appreciation of the arts. He also bore a name that commanded respect. He was the son of a Senator; he had been a Congressman; he had run for Governor of New York. He consorted with kings, ministers, princes of the church. In William Randolph Hearst, imperial and grandiose, the emerging elite of Hollywood found a modern Croesus. They could scarcely have remained unaffected by his example.

The trend in the movie colony is decidedly away from architectural magnificence. The newer movie homes are not exactly modest, but they strive for comfort and graciousness. Holly-- wood's current generation is less gauche than its predecessors; its taste has certainly improved. It is almost certain that the architectural *faux pas* of the past will not be repeated. The movie people have learned to snicker at Byzantine portals and Moorish patios; they have learned that marble halls and manicured lawns involve exorbitant upkeep, and that taxes, public opinion, and the vicissitudes of movie success conspire to make palaces mock those who built them. There are, of course, the usual and conspicuous exceptions—the Mervyn LeRoy mansion, a white elephant which Mr. LeRoy has for some time contemplated selling, or the elegant domicile of the Jack L. Warners.

About a mile of ocean front at Santa Monica, and slightly less at Malibu Beach, some fifteen miles north, are monopolized by the homes of picture people. These bright plaster villas on the Pacific were built almost on top of each other (as were the mansions of Newport); there is virtually no ground space, neighbors are never more than a few yards removed, and the congestion is almost urban. The houses at Santa Monica, called "Millionaires' Slum" by the caustic, are right on the main highway which runs along the ocean from San Diego to Santa Barbara; on week ends and holidays the stretch is one of the most crowded and noisy arteries in California.

The movie colony is gravitating to areas west and north of Hollywood—Beverly Hills, the sections on or near the Pacific coast, and the San Fernando Valley (around Burbank and Van Nuys).* Low, rambling houses and large grounds are winning daily converts. There is a vogue for the purchase of orange,

* An analysis of the addresses of 305 actors and actresses under contract to Hollywood's studios showed the following distribution: Hollywood, Los Angeles, and West Hollywood, 41.3 percent; Beverly Hills, Bel-Air, Westwood, West Los Angeles, 31.8 percent; San Fernando Valley (Van Nuys, Encino, Burbank, etc.), 14.1 percent; Brentwood, Pacific Palisades, Santa Monica, Malibu, Laguna Beach, etc., 7.9 percent.

lemon, or walnut groves, or acreage where livestock can be raised. This does not, of course, imply a de-emphasis on swimming pools, tennis courts, bars, or fireplaces.

Hollywood is achieving a degree of emancipation from the sillier rituals of upper-class life; it is spreading out, exploiting the space and ease which Southern California offer, passing over the formalistic for the comfortable. The movie homes in Beverly Hills proper, for instance, have modest ground space and are reminiscent of wealthy suburbs rather than musical comedies.

The newer dwellings in the film colony follow the pleasant lines of Monterey, Colonial, Georgian, and Cape Cod architecture. The preference for traditional architecture, incidentally, suggests the lack of certainty about newer cultural forms. Even the best Colonial, Cape Cod, and Georgian houses seem incongruous in Southern California, where Spanish modes and Monterey variations are indigenous. Modern architecture has taken hold in Southern California because of its use of space, light, sun, and outdoor views. The movie people are using fine architects and interior decorators (Neutra, Williams, Spaulding, Frankl) and the professional hand of taste is becoming more and more apparent in their homes. Hollywood's new passion for old things has brought the enduring lines of old English furniture back into wide favor. The houses which the movie makers are building, and the appointments which go into them, are more and more characterized by a harmony which was absent in the gilded mausoleums with which the original children of fortune expressed their sudden wealth. Hollywood is in search of cultural stability.

The west room of the Morgan Library was walled with red silk damask, patterned with the arms of the Chigi family of Rome; on the walls hung splendid Florentine masterpieces of the fifteenth and sixteenth centuries; upon the bookshelves stood a bust by Michelangelo and a rock-crystal bowl said to have been mounted for Queen Christina of Sweden; the mantelpiece and the gilded ceiling had been made for great Italian houses. Morgan sat in a red plush armchair by the fire in this great room, smoking his black cigar and playing solitaire, with a Madonna and Child by Pinturicchio looking down over his shoulder, and Fra Filippo Lippi's altar-piece of St. Lawrence and Saints Cosmo and Damian facing him from the opposite wall. . . . He [Morgan the elder] sat in the red plush chair with the card table before him and slowly puffed on his cigar, and carefully placed the five of clubs on the two, and the eight on the five, and the jack on the eight.[15]

The feverish collection of *objets d'art* generally follows the acquisition of wealth. Collecting is "the thing to do," and the homes of the provident tend to become minor museums for the display of costly properties from the fine arts. In the United States, as in Nürnberg or Paris or Florence, the barons of commerce quickly invaded the marts of beauty and vied with each other in the purchase of old masters, old statuary, and old manuscripts. H. G. Wells tells the story of a London art dealer who finally exclaimed to a rich American client, "If you want a Botticelli that size, you'll have to have it made for you." [16]

Some of our business peers did not know a Holbein from a hatband, but they learned. Others were by nature so allergic to art that they bought only those pictures which "looked real" and spent ransoms on the painted fowl, cows, and battles of this dreary genre. Peter Widener, the Philadelphia street-car magnate, used to buy truckloads of Oriental rugs, Flemish tapestries, and Louis XV commodes on which he had never laid eyes.[17] The trophies of costliness served, in those days as in ours, in St. Louis as in Hollywood, as an outlet for riches, as an expression of the acquisitive instinct, as a method of heightening reputation; and they slaked the thirst for a beauty which was missing from the life of commerce and trade.

Hollywood's homes are not, on the whole, distinguished as repositories of art. The urge to collect is activated by the attainment of a Hollywood income, but the collecting instinct may be satisfied by odd little curios. Joan Crawford collects dolls;

Clark Gable goes in for firearms; Joe E. Brown fancies perfume bottles, of which he is reported to have hundreds. Many movie people accumulate old theatrical programs, original letters, sport objects, historical prints and engravings. Others are attracted to trinkets like little elephants, horses, dogs, or penguins.

The most famous collection of paintings in the film colony is that of Edward G. Robinson, who is said to have spent $300,000 on a splendid group of canvases which embrace Cézanne, Picasso, Dégas, Renoir, Gauguin, Matisse, Daumier, Rouault, Dali, and Grant Wood's famed "Daughters of the Revolution." (Mr. Robinson has framed the original teacup and lace collar used by one of the models.) Thomas Mitchell owns a collection which includes a Picasso, Modigliani, Whistler, and Rouault, and recently purchased a hitherto unknown Rembrandt for $40,000. Ira Gershwin is a connoisseur of contemporary French and American painting, and has some fine examples of African art. Other collectors in the movie colony worth noting are Josef von Sternberg, Charles Laughton, Buddy de Sylva, Jesse Lasky, Gary Cooper, and Raymond Griffith.

Most movie people would not hesitate to spend several thousand dollars on a second or third automobile, a horse, a boat, the furnishing of a game room, or the installation of a Capehart radio-phonograph system which brings melodious noises into every room of a house; but they reject the thought of spending a similar sum for one painting.

The power of learning, to turn to another aspect of culture, is reflected in the fan magazines, which tell the student of Hollywood's mores that "there is little of philosophy, psychology, matters political or sociological, that Bob Montgomery has not read or studied. . . . He can hold his own with scientists, engineers, medical men, learned professors"; or that Deanna Durbin reads "over thirty books a year"; or that Barbara Stanwyck "enjoys serious things—a lake by Corot, a book by Thackeray"; or, even more formidably, that Ray Milland stated: "I like astronomy, love to ponder on the composition and possibilities of the planets. . . . Right now I'm wading through twenty-four volumes of the *Encyclopaedia Britannica.*"[18]

The movie colony boasts a few fine libraries; Charles Boyer's runs to about 3,000 volumes; Carey Wilson, the producer, owns over 5,000 books; Frank Capra, a Leonardo da Vinci admirer, has bought an $8,000 Shakespeare folio and is said to have a library of first editions worth over $50,000; Jo Swerling, movie writer, has a fine collection of first editions; and Walter Wanger has an alarming array of treatises on current politics and international affairs.

Few homes in Hollywood are wholly bereft of reading matter, but the number of homes without a respectable collection of books is depressing. The typical libraries are singularly eclectic. The books in the movie colony fall into three categories: books one "ought" to possess and have visible ("classics," best-sellers, Book-of-the-Month Club selections); books devoted to some upper-class hobby (sailing, dogs, interior decoration, horses); and books devoted to self-improvement (*How to Think on Your Feet, How to Write Effective Letters, The Secret of Business Success*). Volumes on hobbies and self-improvement are especially favored among the movie makers, who also surrender to a weakness for entire sets of books—the *Harvard Five-Foot Shelf*, histories of the world, the world's greatest orations, the world's best literature, and similar short cuts to erudition. Standard sets of O. Henry, de Maupassant, Dickens, and Thackeray, all nicely bound, help to fill library shelves with a minimum of time and decision.

The great number of best sellers one sees in Hollywood's homes is explained partly by the need to read what everyone else is reading, and partly because of Hollywood's unending search for story material; even the reading done after working hours is concentrated on material which may have screen possibilities. The popularity (much smaller) of best sellers in the non-fiction class can be explained by the fact that the movie makers devote too much attention to fiction at a time when fiction has become increasingly irrelevant to political reality, and search for political orientation in a confused and confusing world.

It might be said that in the homes of one sizable slice of the movie colony, most of the books are either quite new or quite old, and that both kinds were purchased recently. Few, that is, are old through steady usage. When homes are built or bought, libraries must be acquired hastily, and since an array of nothing but new books is flagrantly gauche, a healthy percentage of aged books are bought, in sets or by lot. When the library shelves are harmoniously arranged, the purchase of literature drops phenomenally.

Seneca, about 50 A.D., noticed that the *novi homines* of Rome also bought their books in complete sets and never looked into them; and the late John R. McLean, whose daughter is the proud owner of the Hope diamond, left an estate of almost $3,000,000 in stocks, $128,759 in jewelry—and, alas, $471 worth of books.[19]

Let us close this chapter on Hollywood's homes and furnishings, art and libraries, with a quotation from Emerson who, in 1845, long before Hollywood existed, had this to say of the Boston which was the beacon-light of American culture: "One would like to see Boston . . . agitated like a wave with some generosity, mad for learning, for music, for philosophy . . . for art; but now it goes . . . with its hand ever in its pocket, cautious, calculating."[20]

10. HORSES, GIFTS, AND SUPERSTITIONS

The Adoration of the Nag

NO ONE who has been in Hollywood can have failed to be startled by the horse-racing fever which possesses the movie colony; a study of Hollywood which neglected to comment on the role of horses, gambling, and race tracks would be derelict in its duty and incomplete in its insights. The offices, commissaries, stages, and dining-rooms of Hollywood echo with knowing tips and detailed genealogies, with debates, wagers, analyses, and grave references to a dozen dope sheets and racing forms. The more devoted votaries of the turf place wagers all year round, on horses they do not know, running in places they have never visited, in races they never see.

So "natural" has the cult of horses and the obsession with the race track become in Hollywood that the *Hollywood Reporter* and *Daily Variety* regularly print racing charts and bulletins in their pages—as if these represented legitimate news about the motion picture industry. It is difficult to imagine an oil or automobile trade journal giving unabashed space to items on the animal kingdom, but "Today's Santa Anita Consensus" is a customary feature in Hollywood's trade papers during the

212

racing season. In one issue of *Daily Variety*, "Doc Baker's Selections" was featured in a box on page 1, a column called "Stalling Around Santa Anita" was on page 2, the "Chatter" column was full of racing items, and half of page 8 was dedicated to racing dope and tips.[1] Even the movie reviews in trade papers occasionally bear testimony to the power of the equine: "Two entries from the Burbank celluloid stables ran in the money. . . . Breezing home several lengths ahead of the field was *Torrid Zone*, followed by *Flight Angels*." [2] Some anonymous wit once summarized Hollywood's daily life as a span "from track to Troc."

No one knows the size of the toll which the "sport of kings" takes from the movie makers each year. In the first nineteen days of a recent racing season in California, thirty-nine places were won by thirty horses owned by picture people. In one Santa Anita Handicap no less than twenty-seven of the 107 horses nominated belonged to members of the film colony. Movie stars, producers, directors, and agents are active in the business affairs and operation of the Santa Anita, Del Mar, and Inglewood race tracks. They turn out in generous numbers for the races each day; they own stables and horse farms; they hire expert trainers, caretakers, and grooms; they send their thoroughbreds to perform on various tracks throughout the land; they import stallions from England and South America; they go by special train and plane to such rites as the Kentucky Derby or the Saratoga Springs Handicap; they place sizable wagers, from their offices or at the track; they follow the hardly cosmic contests of Santa Anita, Hialeah Park, Narragansett, and Churchill Downs with an intensity which transcends recreation and passes into fanaticism. The time, attention, telephone bills, and sheer distraction-cost which go into Hollywood's adoration of the nag represent a hidden drain on the exchequer and the process of movie making.

It is no secret that studios' telephone bills shoot up fantastically during the racing season. On some sound stages there is a daily letdown of activity after 3:30 P.M., during the racing season, so that the talented and costly persons assembled can get the racing results. One movie executive said: "No one can work Saturday afternoon: if they're not at the track, their mind is. And if it's not the horses, it's the football games." During a conference with labor leaders, one studio representative showed a surprising sympathy for the idea of a five-day week; the illusion of liberalism was dispelled by his confession that he favored a five-day working week because as long as there were races, Saturday mornings were wasted at the studios anyway.

Every company in Hollywood has initiated stern drives designed to cut down the use of studio telephones for calling bookies, laying bets, or getting the latest racing results. This resulted in the wholesale introduction of radios, and orders had to be issued to cope with this crisis. Some fanatics had private telephones on their desks wired directly to bookie offices; the phones were finally removed by official fiat. Hollywood's gossip columns are sprinkled with tidbits such as this: "An important picture was held up for three hours the other afternoon because one of its important players did not show back after lunch. The player had gone over to a bookie joint to hear the running of the fourth race at Narragansett and was caught in a raid." [3]

One movie star bets as high as $15,000 on a big race; one producer established himself as a one-man "winter book" on the Kentucky Derby and took $20,000 worth of bets from colleagues at his studio; one executive rises early during the racing season and goes to his office after several hours at his stable watching his horses work out. "Shooting schedules are often arranged to let stars spend afternoons at the track." [4]

The wide influence of Hollywood's passion for horseflesh is seen in such curios as the Motion Picture Democratic Committee's recommendations for the 1939 Los Angeles primary elections, which were printed as a racing form! Under each nominee's name were parenthetical comments, of which a few are worth preserving for posterity:

1st District............Oscar C. Leach
(A Tough Liberal in a Muddy Race)
2nd District...........Norris J. Nelson
(The Best Man to Beat the Worst Man)
3rd District........No recommendation
(This Race Should Be Scratched)
15th District.............Fred Reaves
(A Great Handicapper)

It is said that Groucho Marx once appeared in the offices of an executive at the MGM studio dressed in a jockey's uniform because, he said, "This is the only way you can get to see a producer these days." The story may be apocryphal, but the point is well taken. It is wearying to recall the time and emotion which adults in the movie colony devote to discussing the speed with which four-legged animals can traverse an elliptical course.

The Nirvana of a goodly share of the movie makers is Santa Anita, some fifteen miles from Hollywood, one of the most beautiful and lucrative temples to racing in the world. The following facts offer some idea of Santa Anita's stature:

The annual $100,000 Santa Anita Handicap is the richest race in the universe; there is a $50,000 Derby and a $25,000 San Juan Capistrano prize as well.

The lowest Santa Anita purse is $1,500; there is at least one $2,000 stake a day; every Saturday there is a $10,000 prize.

In 1939, $1,425,000 was spent by the horsemen and their stable staffs. The total purse in 1939 was $917,000, unequaled anywhere in horse circles.

In the short fifty-three-day season, $36,656,590 was handed through the 304 betting windows.

The State of California annually collects $1,500,000 in taxes from Santa Anita.[5]

215

Santa Anita is also famed for the fact that during its first season (1934), so much money was taken in that the officials of the organization took the unprecedented step of reducing their share of the intake. The length of the season has been reduced on three occasions, and yet the golden tide goes higher.

Santa Anita was born in the mind of Hal Roach, the whilom director and producer of the "Our Gang" comedies, who approached some four hundred people to invest in the stock. Many movie people were on the favored list, but only Bing Crosby, W. S. Van Dyke, and Henry King invested. Wealthy Californians in Los Angeles, Pasadena, and San Francisco came to the rescue and bought into the enterprise. Mr. Roach became the president of the organization.

The glorified race track opened in 1934 with an elegant clubhouse for members, twenty-five beautiful rooms, and twenty bars. The opposition to horse racing from Los Angeles merchants, reformers, and church groups has never abated. But the hotel, apartment, and restaurant people share in the bonanza when thousands arrive from all over America to attend the season. No other race track has so celebrated a clientele. "On an afternoon in the Turf Club, the exclusive section atop the clubhouse, I have seen Warner Baxter, the Walt Disneys, the Fred Astaires, the George Burnses, Cecil B. DeMille, Cary Grant, Spencer Tracy, Joan Crawford, Pat O'Brien, Victor Mc-Laglen, Basil Rathbone, Frank Capra, Florence Rice, Rupert Hughes, and dozens of others." [6] These names scarcely begin to do justice to Hollywood's representation.

Del Mar, eighty miles from Los Angeles, is another race track in which the movie people figure prominently. Bing Crosby is president, guiding spirit, and chief owner of this shrine (in addition to his heavy holdings in Santa Anita); Pat O'Brien is vice-president.

The Hollywood Park Turf Club, at Inglewood, a suburb of Los Angeles, was organized by Harry M. Warner, who pledged collateral for a $1,000,000 loan from the Bank of America and later lent the corporation $250,000 to pay off pressing debts; Jack L. Warner was made chairman of the board. The Hollywood Park track paid a twenty percent dividend for the first two years, added another ten percent in the third year, has repaid its original stockholders seventy percent of their outlay, has paid an excess profits tax of $500,000, and started the 1941 season with $100,000 in the bank and nary a debt or tax obligation outstanding.[7]

The publicity which linked Hollywood, horses, and the race track boomeranged, of course, and a movement of abnegation began when the picture people became more sensitive to public reaction. Hal Roach resigned the presidency of Santa Anita, Jack L. Warner resigned as chairman of the board of Hollywood Park, movie directors Raoul Walsh and Alfred E. Green withdrew from the same board, and other film figures began to play down both their horses and their race-track investments.

The horse owners in Hollywood are a proud legion. The biggest and most famed are Bing Crosby, L. B. Mayer, and H. M. Warner, and the roster includes William LeBaron, Raoul Walsh, Mervyn LeRoy, Spencer Tracy, David Butler, Howard Hawks, Barbara Stanwyck, Robert Taylor, John Considine, Jr., George Raft, Zeppo Marx, Errol Flynn, J. Walter Ruben, Lynne Overman, Myron Selznick, Don Ameche, John Cromwell, Robert Riskin, Joe E. Brown (who paid $20,000 for a South American horse), and William Goetz.

Bing Crosby was one of the first and remains the most famous of Hollywood's horse owners. He owns a formidable stable and, with the son of the owner of the celebrated Seabiscuit, possesses a profitable animal named Ligaroti. (Mr. Crosby is an energetic golfer, fisherman, tennis player, and ice-skater as well; he promotes one of the leading golf tournaments in the land.) Louis B. Mayer, a late convert, has plunged into racing with characteristic vigor, now owns over eighty horses and a stable esti-

217

mated at almost half a million dollars, and nominated seven horses for the Santa Anita Handicap of 1939.[8] The Warners and Mervyn LeRoy jointly own a fine stable and practice track at the Warner Calabasas ranch, where some thirty thoroughbreds are groomed in faultless surroundings.

Some of the movie people maintain that their horses are simply a business investment, bred and raced for profit; this makes it possible to deduct the expenses for horses and stables from taxable income as a "business loss." One of the rationalizations which is used to defend the great cost of a racing stable is that "the government would take most of our money anyway."

It is also suggested that those whose hearts are on the turf are motivated simply by a love of horses. This is not convincing; affection does not require competitive testing. Those who love their families are not in the habit of racing their wives or betting on their children. We do, of course, "groom" our wives and show glee over Johnny's report cards; but we have not yet invented institutions for pitting our loved ones against each other as a candid end in itself.

The movie people who own stables and wager substantial sums on selected animals have created new outlets for their competitive impulses. When Mr. Crosby's mare noses out Mr. Roach's mare, for example, Mr. Crosby wins *personal* kudos— even though he neither ran the race nor rode the beast. Mr. Roach, in turn, suffers a rebuff which pleases not only Mr. Crosby, but all the other horse owners, bettors, or general antagonists of Mr. Roach. Mr. Crosby has demonstrated a symbolic superiority over Mr. Roach, and over all the other proprietors whose quadruped chattels sweated to win the contest. The element of vicarious aggression involved here, as well as the competitive joys and the demonstration of superiority, should not go unnoticed. (The verb "beat" refers to physical blows as well as to victory in contest.)

It is also suggested that Hollywood's mania for horses is an innocent one which harms nobody, and that racing is a commendable pastime which refreshes the soul and does not interfere with work. The influence of the equine on the spiritual poses a problem beyond this writer's province; but it is foolish, on the face of it, to assert that a daily preoccupation with horses does not interfere with the production of movies. Grave economic and administrative burdens are involved when shooting schedules are arranged so that the favored can spend the afternoon at the races, and there is no evidence that a studio's personnel are improving their skill or attending to their chores by sitting at Santa Anita during working hours for which they are being reimbursed. The business of movie making suffers when the minds of movie makers are on the track or the stables. There are executive offices in Hollywood in which radios are turned on to catch the "fifth at Inglewood," in which bets are placed all afternoon, in which there is more concern over a horse's rheumatism or the condition of the track than over the day's shooting schedule. It is a well-known fact in the movie colony that the fanatical engrossment in racing presents serious hindrances to movie production during the racing season. Hollywood's output suffers from the conflict—especially in the upper ranks—between the duties of creation and the echo of the race track.

Psychologically, racing represents an artificial crisis which imparts fresh excitement to jaded spirits. "It's a shot in the arm," one of Hollywood's leading horse addicts explained to this writer. "It's the only thing that can take my mind off my troubles. I tried golf, but I'd be thinking of my work in the middle of a stroke. I tried bridge, but my doctor advised me to get more sleep and get out in the open. There's nothing like the races."

Racing is more than a recreation in Hollywood; it is a new show window in which screen celebrities can appear and in which they can win social favor. Horses and aristocracy go hand in hand; the cultivated affection for thoroughbreds is allied to

219

the struggle for prestige.* Isabel Dodge Sloane, like certain movie magnates, was "frightened of horses and unable to ride" but "she nevertheless [maintained] a magnificent stable, hoping to usurp the crown of Mrs. Payne Whitney as the first lady of the turf of the Republic." And Oliver Belmont, one of the social lions of his day, considered his stables the most important part of his estate.[9]

At the races, as at the opera, those who attend to see also attend to be seen. At Santa Anita, which has been expertly publicized, much of the populace comes to see the stars as well as the horses. Hollywood's actors, in turn, can scarcely resist the conspicuousness of the setting. Once the stars and producers have, by their patronage, put the seal of station on racing as a top-drawer avocation, attention is focused, the imitative process begins to operate, and soon half of the studios are making hopeful phone calls to bookies.

The races bring a distinguished and cosmopolitan set to Hollywood, and this has strengthened the ties between Hollywood and the scions of the East. The Whitneys, du Ponts, Vanderbilts, and Donahues come to California for the racing season, and participate in the social gaieties of the circles which revolve around the turf. The Los Angeles Turf Club Ball, which closes the Santa Anita "meeting" each year, is a brilliant fête which compares favorably to the more glittering social events of the nation; it is a meeting ground for Hollywood, Pasadena, and Southampton.

There is another aspect to the role of the races in Hollywood—gambling. The popularity of gambling in the United States as a whole suggests that it is more than a marginal phase of our civilization.† Gambling is an integral part of our culture, and

---

* For comments on the popularity of dogs in Hollywood, see Appendix G.

† According to a Gallup poll, 29 percent of the adult American population have participated in church lotteries—a greater number, incidentally, than the 23 percent who have played slot machines, the 21 percent who have played cards for money, the 19 percent who have bet on elections, the 13 percent who have held sweepstakes

it rests upon potent sanctions. Business is itself a species of gambling; business negotiations are contests backed by wagers; investments are gambles on unpredictable future events. In 1835 the percipient Alexis de Tocqueville wrote:

> This perpetual change which goes on in the United States, these frequent vicissitudes of fortune, accompanied by such unforeseen fluctuations in private and in public wealth, serve to keep the minds of the citizens in a perpetual state of feverish agitation, which admirably invigorates their exertions, and keeps them in a state of excitement above the ordinary level of mankind. The whole life of an American is passed like a game of chance, a revolutionary crisis, or a battle.[10]

Hollywood's people are geared to an industry which is especially subject to sudden changes—which is, in fact, a highly organized attempt to guess what the public will want and when. "Making movies is like shooting dice all day," said a producer. It is not surprising that the profession is implemented by forms of recreation which offer new tensions to those who thrive on them.

Gambling, apart from the sums wagered on horses, has attracted distinguished disciples in Hollywood. For years the Clover Club on Sunset Boulevard, and the Dunes in Palm Springs, catered to that part of the movie colony which enjoys roulette and other games of chance. Tia Juana, just across the Mexican border, Agua Caliente, and the great hotel at Ensenada used to be patronized heavily by film folk devoted to gambling and races, until the Mexican government abolished gambling.*

Poker is particularly popular in the top circles of the movie

tickets, the 10 percent who have bet on horse races (*sic!*), or the 9 percent who have fallen for the charms of the numbers game. (The percentages would be even greater today; the Gallup poll was taken in 1938.) Pinball, punchboards, and slot machines take in from a half to three-quarters of a *billion* dollars annually—as much as the total business in all the shoe stores of the nation.[11]

* Joseph M. Schenck had $403,000 invested in the Compañia Mexicaña del Agua Caliente's vast hotel, casino, clubhouse, dog track, and golf course; he sold his holdings for $50,000 after the Mexican government outlawed gambling.[12]

colony. Hollywood's trade papers carry a heavy amount of gossip on poker games and losses. At one Santa Monica home, $15,000 has often changed hands in an evening of card play. There is no reason to be alarmed at the figure; no one of those who sat around the bitter table earned less than $2,500 a week. Joe Schenck, Hollywood's biggest and best liked gambler, suffered gambling losses of $30,905 in one day, and his losses for one year (1937) totaled $64,894.15. In another year he lost over $20,000 (including $12,190 to Herbert Bayard Swope, $4,711 to Harpo Marx, $2,400 to Darryl Zanuck) and won $15,000 in election bets. In one painful experience, Chico Marx lost around $7,000 and found it necessary to borrow $3,000 to make good his debt.[13]

But there is no evidence that Hollywood's stakes have ever scaled the heights of those games, famed in the annals of New York, where James Buchanan Brady won $180,000 in a night, or where "Bet-a-Million" Gates, in concert with coffee tycoons, coke barons, and sulphur giants, exchanged $750,000 in a night between them. The movie colony cannot produce gamblers like the Donahue who, according to *Fortune*, has lost $900,000 at the gambling tables in Florida.[14]

Gambling is a violation of our moral creed, which rests on the axiom that property and power are *earned*, not won. But the rich have generally given gambling wide license in their ranks. For the rich are familiar with wealth which is derived not from skill, thrift, and virtue—the cardinal middle-class virtues—but via sheer luck—inheritance, "contacts," nepotism, or lucky investments. The fortunes of the rich are in greater or lesser measure testimonials to the role of good luck, and it is not surprising that they try to court the factor more widely.

In Hollywood, where careers are made overnight, where success can depend upon a profile or a voice, where the accident of contacts, relatives, or the omnipotent "break" are in evidence, luck is a prime attribute of living. Where the pursuit of luck can be joined to the augmentation of prestige, and where it offers opportunities for personal triumph at the expense of others, then one sees the full flowering of the sport of kings—or aces.

Gifts

Gifts are a hallowed institution in Hollywood and the gift givers are legion. Presents, like compliments, are dispensed widely, impulsively, and expensively in the movie colony. It is something of a tradition for stars to reward their co-workers with costly offerings upon the completion of a picture. Mae West distributed a truckload of fine luggage to everyone connected with one of her films, down to the electricians and prop boys; she gave her director a diamond and sapphire studded wristwatch, and saddled her producer with a sumptuous gold and chromium desk set of which he remained fearful for the rest of his career. Norma Shearer passed out bottles of perfume, assessed at between twenty and thirty dollars an ounce by connoisseurs, to the female principals in one of her pictures. Samuel Goldwyn sent a Hammond organ to a screen writer who had worked on a difficult script. Hedy Lamarr expressed appreciation to her maid by giving her a new coupé. And Joseph M. Schenck, one of the most openhanded gentlemen in Hollywood, sent flowers regularly to a battalion of friends, and spent $6,336 on Christmas gifts in one year.[15]

There is genuineness in these gestures; generosity and sentimentality are as much a part of show business as superstition. When show people possess wealth, and in addition face income taxes which provide the rationalization that things don't *really* cost so much because the government would get a big slice of the money anyway, then generosity may be expected to flourish. In Hollywood, the birthdays, anniversaries, shooting schedules, and holidays are occasions for the presentation of imposing objects of various degrees of disutility.

The benefactions of the movie colony also serve as symbolic bribery, as they do in most businesses. "Good will" and a congenial rapport with persons with whom it is profitable to curry favor are cemented with material expressions of gratitude. Christmas is the season of personal hauls for movie people as well as department-store buyers. Hollywood's agents are particularly energetic in distributing presents. The deeper purposes of such offerings are concealed from both the recipient and the donor by artful expressions of gratitude: "To Joe, for his understanding . . ."; "To Harry, a real pal. . . ." In some instances, moist sentiment triumphs over good English: "To Jack, for your gratefully acknowledged co-operation. . . ."

The undistributed-profits tax has strengthened generosity by providing a realistic motive for largess. The coffers of some movie companies are opened at Christmas for gifts to a variety of persons whom it is wise to propitiate. Newspapermen and columnists are especially strategic targets for affection, and their vestibules are piled high on Christmas morn with cases of liquor, leather clocks, cigarette cases, desk sets, and other trophies of good will. The wife of one newspaperman recently stated:

. . . The Christmas before we arrived, we were told, every newspaper and magazine writer in Hollywood had received from five to 17 electric clocks. They were new then and they appealed to many donors as an interesting novelty. For our first Christmas, however, the studios agreed mutually to cut down expenses by eliminating all such gifts. So we received nothing from the studios, but oddly enough on Christmas Eve someone from the publicity department at Paramount dropped around with a package. "The studios aren't doing it this year, pal, but this is just a little personal remembrance from me to you for friendship's sake."

That Paramount arrived first was merely by accident; before the holiday was over, a "pal" had appeared from every major studio. The next year they all quietly went back to sending out official gifts. . . . The houses of the most famous and most feared [big-name columnists] look at Christmas like well stocked gift shops, for no important star would dare overlook them.[16]

It should be said, in justice to the Fourth Estate, that some journalists make it a practice to return offerings of excessive value.

The Yuletide loot of one female columnist is as familiar to Hollywood as the monument in Forest Lawn Cemetery. No studio, and few intimates, dare risk offending a lady whose column of chatter is in a hundred papers, who makes personal-appearance tours throughout the land, who runs important radio programs, and who exercises an immeasurable, if declining, influence in the movie colony. One Christmas the automobile of this plump scrivener was robbed by some disrespectful ruffian who appropriated all the booty; the lady's anguish was assuaged when the studios replaced the stolen objects. This brings to mind the statute in Roman law, the *Lex cincia* (204 B.C.), which restricted gifts in cases where the donee was in a position to use undue influence on the donor.

Superstitions

Show people are notoriously superstitious; show business and abracadabra seem to run hand in hand. Hollywood, true to its heritage, has an abundance of persons who attach mystical significance to certain objects, dates, or rites believed capable of influencing the universe of events with beneficent results. Clairvoyants, palm readers, astrologers, and the seers of ludicrous cults flourish in the movie colony. There is a fourteenth but not thirteenth edition of the *Players Directory*, published by the Academy of Motion Picture Arts and Sciences; the trade paper which stated that fifteen hundred actors called up to protest against the ominous number probably exaggerated it, but the fact remains that a fourteenth edition followed the twelfth, to the wide relief of all.[17]

In a special column devoted to superstitions, a Hollywood columnist announced: Edward G. Robinson attributes magical value to an old silver dollar; Barbara Stanwyck always wears a gold medallion around her neck; Henry Fonda crosses his fingers whenever he sees a dwarf; Fred Astaire always has a lucky old plaid suit laid out upon beginning a picture; Joan Blondell appeases fate by using a ten-cent basket as a make-up box; Claude Rains places great faith in an intaglio ring which, lost for two years, caused every play in which he appeared to flop (everything has gone well since the ring was found).[18]

Faith in special lucky practices also abounds among directors. Anatole Litvak tries to have at least one staircase with thirteen steps on his set. William Wyler generally plays a French lullaby on the fiddle before he begins shooting a new picture. Mervyn LeRoy gets the number "62" into his pictures, as an address, a license plate, or a ticket. William Dieterle always wears white gloves, is in constant touch with his astrologer, and prefers to start a picture or a scene only after his mentor has analyzed the disposition of the firmament. Mr. Dieterle shot a scene for *Juarez* three weeks ahead of schedule because the zodiac was so propitious. Mr. Dieterle is also hypersensitive to faces to which he does not "vibrate," and is said to have ordered their possessors off his set.[19] Some directors use certain extras in every picture, convinced that bad luck will swoop down if they don't.

These superstitions may appear to be trivial, but they add to the already complicated problems of movie production, and they do their bit to increase costs. One of the leading directors in the business kept an entire outdoor company waiting for an hour and a half because the "astrological time" wasn't favorable; when it was, he jumped up and set the cameras turning, even though several planes overhead ruined sound reception.[20] On another occasion, superstitious anxiety resulted in the loss of several hours of valuable time, and shooting began at a "psychological moment," even though there was a sudden downpour of rain. One actor refused to stage a fall down a flight of stairs because it had thirteen treads; he held up production for an hour while a false landing was removed. Then the actor took the fall—and sprained his wrist. This proved his point: "If there had been thirteen steps, I'd have broken my neck!" [21]

The gossip columns and movie magazines are full of references to Hollywood's pet astrologers and horoscopists. Myra Kingsley, the high priestess of horoscope, is regarded with awe in some circles in the film colony. A gentleman named Norvell has done well enough with his divinations in Hollywood to own a showplace outfitted with Oriental rugs and Italian antiques. Blanca Holmes, another film favorite, gets frequent space in the movie columns. One Los Angeles *shaman* takes a drop of blood from his movie clients and instructs them to phone him when headaches, depression, or bad luck sets in. He then places the drop of blood under a secret "power-giving" machine and bombards it with "health rays" which supposedly soar through the ether into the body of the troubled customer. This medicine man is revered for his genius by his movie clientele. Another learned gentleman, who claims to be a psychiatrist, treats serious neurotic cases by methods ranging from hortatory to grotesque masks.

H. L. Mencken once commented upon "the virulence of the national appetite for bogus revelation." The earnest souls in Hollywood who react to the crises of life by mumbo-jumbo or who swear allegiance to the stars, the palms, or the bumps on the head, are not alone in their predilections. Our aviators, who use the finest scientific instruments, cling to a set of ceremonies to bring them luck; William Jennings Bryan hearkened to a conclave of astrologers when he ran for the Presidency; Commodore Vanderbilt was a devoted client of a spiritualist in

Tompkinsville, Staten Island, and was sure that homeopathic magic could be wrought with a lock of hair; James Gordon Bennett was a disciple of owls, and had them painted on the panels of his house, yacht, and bathrooms; Collis P. Huntington could never be persuaded to live in his $2,000,000 palace in New York because of his faith in the saying that men build homes only to die in them; and Edith Rockefeller McCormick presided over a cult in Chicago Society in which theosophy, Rosicrucianism, *yogi,* and the more mystic concepts of Jung flourished.[22]

The shibboleths of Hollywood, like those of our civilization, differ only in detail from those of more primitive societies. It is doubtful whether a Martian would see much difference between a Masonic rite, a Hollywood preview, and a Trobriand fête. We can better understand the weakness of the movie people for superstitions if we remember that their entire careers have sprung from talents which are unique, obscure, mysterious— talents which defy exact analysis. "Inspiration" is a phenomenon difficult to dissect; and the inspired periods of movie acting or writing or directing fall into the category of trance.

The mechanisms of magic, Freud has pointed out, are remarkably close to those of obsessional neurosis; neither is rare in Hollywood.

Two

THE MOVIE MAKERS

11. THE PRODUCERS: I

WHAT is a producer? The answer to this question must be, "Which producer?" What does a producer do? Again, we must ask, "Which producer?"

Let us take an imaginary producer, Mr. Stone, and let us follow his production of one motion picture. Mr. Stone has three stars under contract: Joan de Roche, Robert Fortescue, and Valerie Masters. He has just read the story department's synopsis of *Dark Rendezvous,* a dramatic story of the war. It's a gripping tale. There is a fine part in it for Joan de Roche; the sister role could be built up for Valerie Masters. Robert Fortescue isn't the type for the leading man—too old; Mr. Stone might be able to hire the free-lance actor, James Fenton. (Fenton gets $100,000 a picture, but he's worth it: the women flock into the theaters when his name is on the marquee.) With Joan de Roche, Valerie Masters, and a popular leading man, Stone will have a "name" cast with strong box-office appeal.

But is *Dark Rendezvous* the kind of picture the public will pay to see eight months from now, when Mr. Stone may be able to release the film? The "screw-ball" pictures are packing them in; Mason's *Wives on Leave* is cleaning up, and Wolf's *Alexander Hamilton,* a fine historical dramatization, stands to lose $200,000. The New York office and the exhibitors say that anything "heavy" is murder at the box-office. Mr. Stone figures that in eight months the public will be tired of "screw-ball" comedies. The cycle is due to be reversed; *Dark Rendezvous* would be a natural at that time. Anyway, the role of the sergeant can be developed for comedy relief; Georgie O'Connor would panic them in the part. (O'Connor gets $1,850 a week; he's worth it.)

Dark Rendezvous is a *human* story; human stories never miss. Mr. Stone will give *Dark Rendezvous* top production. He'll get one of the top directors in the business, La Marche to design the sets, Karling to compose the score, Canolgo for cameraman (Canolgo is terrific for a blonde like Joan de Roche; knows how to bring out her left profile and underlight her chin). These men run up into big money. Mr. Stone figures he can hold the costs down by faking some of the battle scenes; he'll rearrange the extras, use the props from *Bomb Squadron,* re-dress the big *Love in London* set. He can use newsreel shots for the convoy sequence. Including overhead and all, he might be able to bring the picture in for $925,000.

Ray Duell is perfect to write the script. His last two pictures cleaned up. But $2,500 a week for writing costs. . . ! Maybe James Brock can do it. His *Flanders* was a swell job—same kind of story. He's $650 a week less than Ray Duell. Joe Russell is the man to direct, all right. He missed on his last job—but he was handed a punk story, and by that madman Sidney Thorne. (You can't tell what a director's got when he's working for Sidney Thorne; he'd paralyze Capra.) Joe Russell could do a terrific job with a dramatic story like *Dark Rendezvous.* Right up his alley. Remember *Powerhouse?* (Joe Russell gets $4,000 a week; he's worth it.)

The story department says that the agent is asking $40,000 for *Dark Rendezvous.* Mr. Stone offers $15,000. Warners offers $18,500. Mr. Stone tells his story editor to go up to $25,000 if necessary. They get *Dark Rendezvous* for $22,500; the trade papers announce $35,000 as "the reported price."

Mr. Stone lays out a budget, cuts it down, and hires Brock

to write a treatment. They discuss the "basic story." Mr. Stone thinks the opening is slow, the hero too tender, the major too heavy. He tells Brock: "Build up the middle. Give more play to the girl." Mr. Stone has a great idea: tie Joan de Roche into the second half more closely by having her follow the hero to the battlefield (you can play some great scenes there). Maybe she enlists as a nurse—yes, that's it—*against her father's will!*

Brock works up an outline in ten days. Mr. Stone thinks the opening is fine. But the fight between the interceptor planes and the glider troops is too expensive to produce. The Joan de Roche part needs a lot of work—more scenes with the hero. Brock rewrites. He sends the scenes to Mr. Stone. What's happened to the comedy sergeant? Brock hasn't made him come off. Mr. Stone finds four good spots in which to build up the sergeant. Mr. Stone and Brock go into a story huddle for two days. Brock does another treatment. Mr. Stone thinks they need a sock finish. Brock devises a new finish. Mr. Stone thinks the treatment is rough, but tells Brock to start the script: "Work it over as you write it."

Brock begins presenting sequences. The lines for de Roche are stiff. The hero is a dope—no humor. Mr. Stone thinks Brock has gone stale. He releases Brock and hires Donald Miller. (He wrote *Fantasy in White*—$2,000 a week, but he's worth it.) Miller throws out the middle of Brock's script, builds up the two girls, and rewrites most of the hero's lines, making him more of a Clark Gable character. That means he has to reconstruct the opening. Mr. Stone says he doesn't like "the third act"; Valerie Masters isn't "resolved" as a character.

Miller gets a sensational idea for a new ending. That makes the script forty pages too long. Mr. Stone decides to reduce five sequences in the middle to a montage—then dissolve right from headquarters to the submarine. That leaves a big hole in the story, but Mr. Stone covers it with an insert of the girl's diary to explain what happened. (Miller will have to plant the diary.)

Mr. Stone tells Miller to push the script into shape for the director. Joan de Roche is waiting around—on salary.

All through these weeks, Mr. Stone has been attending to a hundred other matters connected with *Dark Rendezvous*. He patched up a truce between Joan de Roche and director Joe Russell (old feud). He signed Russell after a long fight with Russell's agent, who tried to make a flat picture deal. Mr. Stone couldn't get John Borden from RKO for the male star; he made a deal with Paramount for William Dormel. (Mr. Stone gave them Robert Fortescue for one picture.) Mr. Stone, conferring with director Russell and his casting director, also signed up the rest of his cast. He has held conferences with Joe Russell and the art department, the cameraman, the special effects man, the process department, the composer, the publicity office. The picture will cost $1,189,000 as it now stands. Mr. Stone has to cut that down plenty. He wins Joe Russell over to cutting out the typhoon and a lot of extras. Miller works over the script again.

Valerie Masters complains about her part: "I can't put myself into this kind of a dame. I ought to play a girl with a sweeter side." Miller sweetens up the character. Now de Roche complains: "Masters is so sweet that I'm made out to be a harpy. Let *me* offer to drive the ambulance when the major is dying." Miller objects to Russell's cutting out the submarine stuff. Russell thinks that Miller isn't sympathetic to his point of view. Mr. Stone gets an attack of indigestion. Russell urges Mr. Stone to hire Ben Vail to rewrite the comedy scenes. (Vail is great on sophisticated comedy.) Mr. Stone releases Miller and hires Vail ($2,500 a week, but he's worth it). Vail polishes the love scenes. That makes the melodrama seem phony. Mr. Stone tells Vail to work over William Dormel's role: "That guy can't carry a part that calls for all that emotion." More conferences. More discussions. Russell and Vail have a violent quarrel. Vail quits. Mr. Stone makes peace. In two more weeks the script is done.

Okayed by Russell, okayed by Mr. Stone. Mr. Stone is putting the heat on. He has to deliver that picture in sixty days. He's made commitments with the theaters.

The script has gone to the art department for scene sketches; to the costume designer for wardrobe sketches; to the production department for a shooting schedule and budget breakdown. Mr. Stone sends a crew to March Field for background shots.

Shooting starts on Stage 5 (scene 93, page 41). Mr. Stone orders crews to work in three shifts on the big set (Stage 1) so Russell can move on in five days. Mr. Stone sees the first rushes. De Roche is going swell; Dormel is unsteady; you can see Valerie Masters is still unsatisfied with her part. (She's been getting dizzy spells on the set; Mr. Stone has a doctor on the set.) Vail rewrites her lines. Mr. Stone gives Valerie Masters a long pep talk: "This is the strongest part I've ever given you, Valerie; it'll make you a whole new public." Dormel's hay fever gets worse. The shooting schedule is rearranged so they can "shoot around" Dormel. Rain holds up the crew shooting at March Field. The stunt men refuse to do the trick parachute jump for the original price.

Mr. Stone sees more rushes. The sound man is having a hard time with de Roche's voice; she strained it in the scene in the air shelter. Four extras are injured when the prop dugout collapses. The trained dog, O'Connor's mascot in the big comedy scene, stalls the shooting for three hours because he keeps jumping out of focus.

A suggestive story about Joan de Roche gets into Selma Gorman's gossip column. Mr. Stone calls Selma, and begs her to lay off. "I've got over a million tied up in the picture." Joe Russell's wife is taken to the Good Samaritan Hospital for an appendectomy; Russell can't keep his mind on the picture. He runs up thirty-one takes on the medium shot in the Salvation Army scene. Dormel and de Roche have a big fight. Mr. Stone rushes over to Stage 4 and conciliates. Masters and Joe Russell are beginning to get on each other's nerves. The picture is a week behind shooting schedule now. The costs on the masquerade ball run up to $28,000 instead of $22,000. They need a hundred extras for six days instead of three. Joan de Roche refuses to play the scene in the auto: "It makes me a disagreeable character." Mr. Stone has Vail rewrite the scene. That throws one of the earlier shots off base. They re-shoot the sequence. Mr. Stone's eczema flares up.

At last, after fifty-eight days of shooting, all the scenes are finished—thirteen days over schedule. Joe Russell disappears for three days. Mr. Stone locates him at Lake Arrowhead. The film editor finishes a rough cut. It's 800 feet too long and slow in getting started. Mr. Stone starts the final cut. Fritz Karling has begun working on the score. Mr. Stone spends five days and nights in the projection room with the film editor, cutting the picture. The fades, dissolves, and inserts are put in. He takes three minutes out of the first reel, two out of the third, and re-cuts all the sequences in reel seven. He cuts out forty feet where Dormel is mugging in the scene with de Roche. (Joan would be *fu*rious.) He trims several long love scenes; he throws out three close-ups of Valerie Masters (she'll be *fu*rious); that makes de Roche stand out more. Mr. Stone has cut 600 feet out of the film. He has lost eight pounds. The score is recorded.

A sneak preview is held at Long Beach. It's a tough audience. Lots of sailors. The audience is restless during the hospital scenes. A throw-away line of Dormel's on the train gets such a snicker that you can't hear de Roche's follow-up line, which is an important plot point. The major looks silly in the court-martial sequence. (It looked fine in the projection room.) Georgie O'Connor is getting the laughs. Seven preview cards charge that the ending is a straight steal from *Men at Sea*, which played in the theater the week before.

Mr. Stone takes the picture back to the projection room. He spends two more days cutting. The hospital stuff goes out. He calls director Russell back to do some re-takes. Dormel has to be rehired at a special weekly rate. They rescore the scene where the dirigible explodes. The picture is $213,000 over budget. Mr. Stone's sinuses begin acting up. New York calls to say that the exhibitors think the title, *Dark Rendezvous*, will keep the customers away in droves—too gloomy; too high-brow. Mr. Stone offers $100 for the best new title submitted. Vail suggests *Heart of Stone*. A messenger in the mail section comes through with *Two Under Fire*. Mr. Stone changes it to *Three Under Fire*.

There is another sneak preview, in Glendale. The audience reaction is good. Mr. Stone tells the publicity department: "Play up the romantic angle. Play down the realist stuff. In the stills and art work, emphasize Joan in that evening gown in the masquerade ball scene." Publicity arranges the world première for Houston, Texas—a special train for the press and the picture mags. Three governors and an admiral accept invitations. Publicity wangles Joan de Roche an honorary commission in the Texas Rangers, a scroll from Sheridan College ("for her contribution to the art of the cinema"), and a spot on Jimmy Orton's radio show—with several strong plugs for *Three Under Fire* worked into the script.

At the première in Houston a pair of sixteen-year-old twins faint on the sidewalk in front of Joan de Roche. When revived they say: "We're in love with her. She's our ideal." (The twins' mother, a friend of the publicity director's, reported to the police, a week earlier, that the boys were missing from home. They almost worked up a nationwide search.)

Mr. Stone flies to New York to give the sales office a pep talk about *Three Under Fire*. He sees *Single Hour*, the farce by an English playwright. Mr. Stone thinks it would make a great picture. All it needs is a stronger first act. It has wonderful parts for Robert Fortescue and Joan de Roche. He could build up the climax, make it a terrific chase. There's a good spot in it for Michael Barnes. (Barnes gets $3,000 a week, but he's worth it.) They're asking $125,000 for *Single Hour;* Mr. Stone thinks he might be able to buy it for $60,000. It would take little re-writing. . . . He could get Mike Winslow for the script, and Sam Norris to direct. He might be able to bring the picture in for $900,000. It's a very funny story. Nothing big, but plenty of laughs. It can't miss. In six months the public will be sick of all these *human* stories and war stuff—and a picture like *Single Hour,* with a "name" cast . . .*

The hypothetical adventures of Mr. Stone attest to the fact that a producer has it within his power to improve or ruin a picture at a hundred different points. Some producers guide a movie sanely and skillfully from the inception of the first bare idea to the final two-million-dollar commodity, and they stamp it with a single personality and purpose. There are other pro-ducers whose contributions to a movie lie chiefly in irritating the directors by their interference, stifling the writers by their demands, destroying the freshness, consistency, or dramatic logic of a movie by arrogant decisions from which there is no appeal.

The producer should possess the ability to recognize ability, the knack of assigning the right creative persons to the right creative spots. He should have a knowledge of audience tastes, a story sense, a businessman's approach to the costs and me-chanics of picture making. He should be able to manage, pla-

---

* This sketch of the *sturm und drang* of the producer's activity is by no means exaggerated; on the contrary, Mr. Stone may have been engaged in the simultane-ous production of three or four or five pictures, and *Three Under Fire* could easily have been the one which presented the fewest problems.

cate, and drive a variety of gifted, impulsive, and egocentric people.

. . . In his hands lies the supervision of every element that goes to make up the finished product. These elements are both tangible and intangible, the control of human beings and real properties as well as the control of the artistic temperament, the shaping of creative forces and the knowledge of the public needs for entertainment. . . .[1]

"The producer," says Jesse Lasky, "must be a prophet and a general, a diplomat and a peacemaker, a miser and a spend-thrift. He must have vision tempered by hindsight, daring governed by caution, the patience of a saint and the iron of a Cromwell."

. . . his decisions must be sure, swift, and immediate, as well as subject to change, because conditions change continuously in the motion picture industry. . . . The producer's resources must be such that no contingency can stop him from finding [a] star, soothing the director like a super-Talleyrand, or, in all-night conference in shirt sleeves and heavy cigar smoke, "doctoring the scripts by his own creative power." [2]

The late Sidney Howard remarked that there are only two kinds of movie producers: those who produce pictures which their directors and writers create for them, and those who try to be both director and writer, without competence as either.[3] The first type of producer is respected by writers and directors. The second type of producer, the man who tries to out-write the writers and out-direct the directors, Mr. Howard compares to the Australian kiwi, which has wings but cannot fly. It is this species of producer against which most of the directors and writers in Hollywood rebel—the producers who emasculate stories, stifle creative talents, and destroy the integrity of movies with meretricious decrees.* They are arbitrary and dogmatic.

* Every group in Hollywood complains about the producers. In reply to the question, "What are your chief complaints about working as a director?" over a third of the movie directors (35.4 percent) wrote protests about "stupid," "inexperienced," or "interfering" producers and supervision; almost a third (30.8 percent) complained about the scripts and stories over which they (the directors) have no

They provoke an understandable bitterness in those who are compelled to adjust to their Philistine and pedestrian mentalities. They are the men who wreck pictures as surely as sledge hammers wreck wrist watches—only the evidence is not so concrete.

Several years ago the most distinguished movie directors in Hollywood circulated a brief and eloquent statement which, among other things, made these pointed comments:

> No director questions the need of executive supervision, nor are the Directors endeavoring to tell the producing companies how to run their businesses . . . no Director questions the contribution of many individual producers who have given prodigiously to the Industry . . . we have no words but praise and recognition for their accomplishments.
>
> We speak here of the army of the inept, who have been promoted to positions of authority for which they are unqualified, inexperienced and utterly lacking in creative ability. . . . They have little respect for the medium, less respect for their audiences and excuse their lack of imagination by ridiculing it in others.[4]

There are few in Hollywood who would not concur in the attack on "the army of the inept." A few examples are damning and hilarious enough to underscore the point:

> There is the producer who rejected a script "because Bing Crosby falls in love with the girl. In his last two pictures, the girl fell in love with Crosby! The public won't go for Bing falling in love with the girl."
>
> There is the producer to whom a writer, in telling a story, used the word, "frustrated." The producer requested an explanation, and the writer resorted to this analogy: "Take a bookkeeper, a little man earning twenty-five bucks a week. He dreams of getting a big, beautiful boat and sailing to the South Seas. But he can't fulfill his dreams—so he's frustrated." To which the producer cried: "I like that! Put a boat in the picture."
>
> There is the producer who, at the climax of an argument about a story, called his writer to the window and said: "You see that big black car

control. Over a third (35.3 percent) of the directors of photography specifically complained about supervision. The reasons for the antagonism to producers are discussed in chapters 13 to 15.

down there—the seven-passenger Lincoln with the chauffeur. That's mine. Which one's yours?" The writer pointed to a coupé. The producer said: "A Plymouth, huh? Okay, we'll do the story *my* way."

There is the producer who urged a writer to criticize a script "absolutely frankly; don't pull your punches; I want the truth!" When the writer began to comment, the producer cried, "Why, that's just your personal opinion!"

There is the producer who for years has refused to allow any of the characters in his films to speak German: "If they really *are* Germans, have them speak French."

There is the producer who—when the writer said, "The hero is walking down a dark alley; he has a terrible sense of disaster; he's frightened!"—declared that the audience wouldn't understand the hero's fright because "anything I don't see I'm not afraid of."

There is the producer who kept remarking that a director was stubborn. The director objected, "What do you want me to do—be a yes-man?" The producer replied, "No, no, no—but you could at least agree with me."

There is the executive of whom an associate said, "If he understands what you're talking about, he thinks he thought of it himself."

There is the producer who wouldn't allow his director to show a character entering a room without removing his hat (even reporters, detectives, etc.), because "the women in the audience resent it."

There are, in short, producers who are incompetent and uncultured, men obstreperous in manner, narrow of vision, obtuse in mentality. And there are the other kind.

In the words of the movie directors, there are producers "who have given prodigiously to the Industry." A David O. Selznick deserves high praise for a long and distinguished cavalcade of films: *Rebecca, Gone with the Wind, A Star Is Born, Bill of Divorcement, David Copperfield, Anna Karenina.* It was Mr. Selznick who selected the story, the screen-writers, and the directors for these films, and he brought good taste, story sense, and a unifying harmony to their production. It was Mr. Selznick who took three years to make *Gone with the Wind* and spent almost $4,000,000 on it; the picture will probably exceed $25,-000,000 in gross box-office receipts.*

A Samuel Goldwyn, much lampooned as the inheritor of Mrs. Malaprop's mantle, deserves high commendation for *Wuthering Heights, The Little Foxes, These Three, Dead End, Dodsworth.* These were fine stories done with admirable judgment and faultless "mounting," and they reflected the uncompromising search of the producer for pictures that would not betray their subject matter.† Alva Johnston concluded that Goldwyn

. . . has turned out distinguished pictures over a long period. Hundreds have collaborated with him, but [he] has been able to place his unmistakable mark on all his work. The greatest tribute to him is that the phrase "the Goldwyn touch" is part of the vocabulary of Hollywood. "The Goldwyn touch" is not brilliance or sensationalism. It is something that manifests itself gradually in a picture; the characters are consistent; the workmanship is honest; there are no tricks or short cuts; the intelligence of the audience is never insulted. Goldwyn ran away from his home in Poland at the age of eleven and arrived here alone in the steerage at the age of thirteen. His education in English was a year at night school. With his background, the most impressive fact about him is his development of taste and artistic conscience.[5]

Each studio has a personality; each studio's product shows special emphases and values. And, in the final analysis, the sum total of a studio's personality, the aggregate pattern of its choices and its tastes, may be traced to its producers. For it is

---

* Mr. Selznick worked with eighteen different writers in translating Margaret Mitchell's book into a screenplay. He rejected every first-rank Hollywood actress for the role of Scarlett O'Hara. He spent months in screen-testing stars and finally selected (amidst much criticism) the relatively unknown Vivien Leigh for the part. He worked with three different directors, and a battalion of other creators, stubbornly maintaining *his* conception of a story that—for all its defects—filled the screen with a dimension and force the movies had rarely touched since David Wark Griffith.

† The background of *Wuthering Heights,* to take one example, is revealing. A complete script by Ben Hecht and Charles MacArthur had been knocking around Hollywood for over a year. The Brontë story had been turned down by most of the studios as being "too morbid." The script was purchased by an independent producer who, after months of consideration, decided *Wuthering Heights* had little chance of success at the box-office and sold it to Goldwyn, warning him it was a beautiful property but a hazardous investment.

the producers who establish the preferences, the prejudices, and the predispositions of the organization and, therefore, of the movies which it turns out.

The films which open with the lion of Metro-Goldwyn-Mayer, for example, owe much to the personality and strategy of Louis B. Mayer. MGM prefers epics to tales, drawing-room comedies to dramas, elegant backgrounds to simple ("dreary") locales. All this is to a large degree the work of Mr. Mayer, a shrewd, gifted showman and a hard-driving executive, who has emphasized Personalities and Production ever since MGM was formed (1924). For fifteen years Mr. Mayer has devoted himself to the augmentation of a battery of stars whose box-office value by far surpasses that of any other studio in Hollywood.* Mayer has made the entire MGM organization revolve around the hub of Personalities. The stories and production of MGM's pictures are geared to the studio's stars and, more than in any other studio in Hollywood, are subordinated to the final goal of star-appeal.

Warner Brothers emphasizes drama and melodrama, fast-moving stories with hard-surfaced characters in muscular situations. The Warners' pictures aim at the powerful rather than the pleasant. The Warners' roster of stars suggests the characteristics of its output: James Cagney, Bette Davis, Edward G. Robinson, Pat O'Brien, Ida Lupino, John Garfield, Humphrey Bogart, and, for many years, Paul Muni; even the studio's "glamorous" personalities—Errol Flynn, Ann Sheridan—thrive in violent rather than genteel locales. Warners specializes in emotions, not manners; the studio produces virtually no sagas of the boudoir. All this means that the actors whom Warner Brothers

---

* MGM Stars: Clark Gable, Greta Garbo, Spencer Tracy, Hedy Lamarr, James Stewart, Joan Crawford, Mickey Rooney, Myrna Loy, Robert Taylor, Norma Shearer, William Powell, Wallace Beery, Jeanette MacDonald, Lionel Barrymore, Greer Garson, Judy Garland, Robert Montgomery, Eleanor Powell, Melvyn Douglas, Rosalind Russell, Margaret Sullavan, Robert Donat, Nelson Eddy, Robert Young, Lana Turner, and others.

features, the stories which the studio buys, the mood and tempo which are injected into the direction and the production, reflect the judgment and the likes of the top producers, Jack L. Warner and Hal B. Wallis.

The films of Twentieth Century-Fox, to take a last example, testify to the implacable influence of Darryl F. Zanuck, "the greatest nickelodeon mind in America," a man with prodigious energy and a compulsion to supervise everything in a film from costumes to sound effects. With the rare exception of a *Young Abe Lincoln* or *The Grapes of Wrath*, for which Mr. Zanuck merits acclaim, Twentieth Century-Fox uses formula plots with clever variations—the characters are stereotyped; the motivations are shallow; the movement is swift and economic; the conflicts are unsubtle and the dénouements are "pat." It is significant that the women stars of Twentieth Century-Fox are ingenues and the male stars are juveniles.*

If one must generalize about the producers in the movie colony, it is best to follow the comment of Gilbert Seldes:

Moving pictures are made by a great variety of men, some intelligent, some ignorant, some with the desire to make good money no matter how contemptible their product may be, some with the desire to make good pictures and to make good money, nearly all of them . . . with no great knowledge of the people in the world around them, most of them encased in their wealth and prestige, intimidated by the investment of money . . . and terrified by the prospect of failure.[6]

A brief historical résumé of the producers in motion pictures will explain their power and skills. The producers who emerged from the infancy of the film industry were hard-driving, competent, and versatile. They had to be. The first producers—men like Zukor, Lasky, Fox, Lubin, Selig—took an active part in every department of movie making. They raised money, borrowed cameras, and rented "studio" space. They thought up

* Tyrone Power, Alice Faye, Don Ameche, Linda Darnell, Betty Grable.

plots and wrote subtitles; they created characters; they invented gadgets; they painted sets and set up lights. They sometimes developed their own film and generally edited their reels. They ran the entire threadbare business of making mutilated images which moved jerkily on imperfect film, and they sold their product to penny arcades and nickelodeon parlors. These men were artisans as well as businessmen, craftsmen as well as promoters. They had to be. They combined the talents of bankers and circus barkers. They possessed immense drive, resourcefulness, and an almost maniacal capacity for work.*

The original movie producers personally assumed the financial risk entailed in manufacturing movies, and took a continuous part in every aspect of the production and the merchandising of films. Neither point is true today. The motion picture industry became large, complex, and specialized. With each step in the expansion of the movie business—as a business, a technique, a craft, an institution—the all-inclusive role of the producer was delimited. Financing became a problem distinct from administration; the production of a movie became quite a different thing from the operation of a big business. All this is to say that as the motion picture industry grew, as the market for movies expanded, as the making of pictures became a process requiring an increased division of labor, specialists began to replace prima donnas in every department of movie making —except production. The producers were free to remain prima donnas; who could say them nay?

The quality of movies changed; the taste for movies improved. And the producers whose esthetic judgment had been adequate for the penny-dreadful narratives which once dominated the screen found themselves expressing penny-dreadful judgments on Pulitzer Prize novels and plays. It was no wonder that the directors and writers who moved into Hollywood came

---

* See William Fox's statement—"for thirty years I avoided carrying a watch"—in chapter 3.

to chafe under the decrees of their superiors. The artists began to rebel against men who were, they said, "prostituting" the screen.

Hollywood made more and more pictures, in larger organizations, at higher costs, with an immensely ramified division of labor. And the producers found it necessary to create lieutenants and sublieutenants in the growing army of movie makers—assistant producers and associate producers, supervisors and story supervisors, A producers and B producers. The profits sanctioned the reckless expansion of production staffs.

In June of 1938 the Screen Directors Guild published an illuminating report on Hollywood's output. In 1937, the analysis said, Hollywood had used 220 producers to make 484 pictures; ten years earlier, in 1927, Hollywood had used only 34 producers to make 743 pictures. In other words, 800 percent more producers were used in 1937 to make 40 percent fewer pictures than in 1936! (The change in the number of directors over the same period was negligible; 234 received screen credit in 1937, as against 246 in 1927.[7])

It was a significant revelation, for it demonstrated with figures what gossip had long been charging—that the ranks of the producers were inflated; that the number of producers was wasteful; that most producers had fairly easy jobs and received, therefore, unnecessarily large salaries. ". . . uncertainty, duplication, and waste characterizes the present 'system of production.' "[8]

There will always be producers of movies, just as there will always be managers in factories or captains on steamships. Making pictures is a business—a business involving great costs, elaborate equipment, and complex interrelationships among gifted and temperamental people. A business is run for profit, and in any business the criteria of efficiency, rather than of art, must prevail. This is especially irritating to the artists who become part of a business, for artists are primarily concerned with their creation and not with the cost or the profit potential it represents.*

Any business must use some yardstick for measuring efficiency. (Profits are an empirical test of efficiency.) That is why there will always be producers for motion pictures. They may be wiser, more competent, more sensitive than the producers in Hollywood today. They may be writers or directors ascended to producer rank. They may accept a more sharply defined function. But they will be producers. For there will always be someone to decide, someone to handle the personnel and operate the administrative mechanics of movie making. (That is why there are producers even for documentary movies which are not made for profit.) There must, in short, be someone to conciliate the inevitable conflict between the artists and the businessmen of Hollywood, between the art and the business of movie making. For there *is* an inevitable conflict between art and business in enterprises which must use artists in order to make profit; the beautiful is not necessarily the popular, the profitable is generally not beautiful, and popular art is as much despised by artists as "intellectual art" is despised by businessmen.†

The producer is an employer—in fact or in symbol. He is identified with the company and the company's point of view. His job is to make pictures which bring in net earnings. But the paradox lies in the fact that it is the producers in Hollywood today who are often the worst offenders against efficiency and moderation. They are often the very people who increase costs by foolish decisions, who negate economies by extravagant im-

* This accounts for many of the conflicts between directors and producers, and writers and producers. See chapters 13 and 14.

† At a recent convention of exhibitors in Hollywood, Charles Pettijohn of the Motion Picture Producers and Distributors Association castigated the "intelligentsia" in the movie colony, and remarked that intellectuals "are people educated beyond their intelligence." This sortie was greeted with appreciation by the assembled non-intellectuals.[9]

pulses, who "over-produce" a film which does not justify the costs poured into it. The opinion of the movie directors is worth citing once more:

There is no desire on our part to absolve the Director of some of the responsibility. . . . But we must emphasize that the larger responsibility rests with those in executive positions of power. The Director finds himself very often actually carrying on wasteful and costly practices because of the present system. . . . When a script is finally handed to a Director, he often finds in it an accumulation of writing done to order with little clarity or entertainment value, which he must attempt to infuse with life without changing a line, a scene or coming in behind schedule . . . minor executives [are] unfamiliar with dramatic construction for the purpose of motion pictures, unfamiliar with the physical problems and possibilities of actual production, and divorced from the spontaneous life of story, actors and directors. . . .[10]

The producer is in a position which fosters willful demands. Power, in motion pictures as in politics, intoxicates those who possess it. The producer, like the dictator, often falls victim to the delusion that authority mysteriously endows its possessor with a range of competence which reaches from dramaturgy to economics. The producers of Hollywood have been indulged in the expression of their own taste, their own vanities, their own unrestrained—and often impractical—impulses. They are possessed by competitiveness, and they compete with each other in the elegance and scope of the films they make.

The producer, steeped in the Hollywood tradition, headstrong with authority, often makes decisions which are psychologically gratifying rather than economically wise. Million-dollar movies are sometimes an expression of a producer's ego rather than his business judgment. For it is profoundly satisfying to produce movies on an immense and dazzling scale. Reputations in Hollywood are made by movies, not balance sheets.*

* Producers, like book publishers, occasionally present the public with a product which has little chance of financial success but does hold forth the promise of succès d'estime. The Long Voyage Home, Make Way For Tomorrow, Abe Lincoln in Illinois, Escape, A Midsummer Night's Dream are outstanding examples.

Besides, when a producer pours money into a film it is easy to rationalize the expenditure by insisting that the extra costs increased the probability of higher returns. In a field where objective criteria are missing, who can say with certainty whether or not a producer's decision to spend another $250,000 was wise? If the picture makes a profit, he will contend that it would have taken a loss had he not put the extra $250,000 into it; there will be no way of proving that he might have made a greater profit—or a higher percentage of profit—had the $250,000 not been expended.

Grandiosity is part and parcel of the personality of the impresario—and the producers are, above all else, impresarios. The movies gratify the narcissism of their producers. Samuel Goldwyn, for example, is temperamentally opaque to the sharing of glory. He parted with Arthur Hornblow, once his associate producer, because Hornblow wanted credit on the screen for pictures on which he worked as associate producer. "Sam's reaction to this was like that of Henry IV when he caught the Prince of Wales trying on the crown; he was wounded to the heart. . . . He was ready to give [Hornblow] more money, a European vacation, or anything except participation in the Goldwyn fame." [11]

The producers' penchant for self-dramatization provoked this outburst from the chairman of the Allied States Association of Motion Picture Exhibitors:

. . . use of the power invested in [the producers] for self-aggrandizement goes beyond the mere lining of pockets. It extends to personal publicity of the most blatant kind. A year or so ago one executive caused his company to insert many pages of advertising in the trade papers devoted to self-glorification in connection with an anniversary which he was celebrating. Another recently astonished theatregoers by causing his name to appear in letters several feet high in the introduction to one of his pictures. Sales drives and playdate drives are conducted, not in the name of the company or on the merit of the product, but in the name and for the glory of some company executive. Scarcely a week passes that a luncheon or a dinner is not promoted in the honor of some executive. . . .[12]

The public has been fed on Hollywood's lavishness for two decades, and the long succession of films produced with utter extravagance has established an audience demand for sumptuousness. The public has come to expect "the Ziegfeld touch" three times a week, and regards million-dollar pictures as part of the natural order. It is not surprising that such a public reacts to simple, moving stories, simply told, with the disappointment of Holy Rollers at a Quaker service. The moviegoer may not know what is meant by "production values," but when he praises a movie because "it's got Spencer Tracy, Jeanette MacDonald, all those beautiful scenes, that nice music, and that realistic earthquake," he is casting his ballot in favor of the very factors which send the costs of production into the stratosphere. The crowning poser lies in the fact that, having had their taste corrupted by the producers' preference for the colossal instead of the convincing, the public is providing the producers with exactly the arguments which justify more and more costly production.

The president of the Independent Theater Owners Association, Harry Brandt, recently took a two-page advertisement in a trade paper to hurl a heated challenge:

"Why are pictures still being made with mounting costs and no increase in quality?

"Why don't they [the producers] do something about eliminating the extravagant waste in Hollywood?

"Why don't they start cutting down the fabulous salaries?

"Because the present crop of big brains doesn't know what the public wants.

"Because the $3,000 and $5,000-a-week executives, who should be trying to cure this industry of its ills, are lethargic, have got into a rut and are too firmly entrenched while actually they are gradually being entombed.

"Because they are afraid of any change that might upset their heretofore pleasant routine." [13]

The mighty salaries of Hollywood's production staffs, which we shall explore in the next chapter, are by no means an easy pill for the Eastern movie executives to swallow. Three New York executives, in different movie companies, told this writer (1) that the men in charge of production in Hollywood are extravagant, reckless, or "crazy"; (2) that they (the New York executives) would be only too happy to replace them by sound administrators, but did not know of sound administrators who also had movie talent; (3) that the only way to solve the problem was to try to get bigger profits by persuading or forcing "the mad producers" to "restrain" themselves. The most cogent opinion, from a famed financier with large movie holdings, ran along these lines: "The men on the West Coast are paid preposterous salaries because they have the kind of mad genius that's needed to put out films. I'd like to find executives who can cut Hollywood's costs without strangling the creative talents of the men who keep sending costs up. The moving picture industry needs men who can understand a balance sheet and a three-ring circus."

The conflict between the studios and the corporations, between the producers and the financiers, between Hollywood and New York, is worth discussing here. When the motion picture industry began its mushroom growth, in the 1920s, the movie companies needed money—money to erect bigger studios, build more theaters as outlets for their product, make bigger pictures. This financing came from bankers and investment groups; and the executive-producers became responsible to the men who provided them with money. By 1928 the financial houses of the East had gained wide influence and control in Hollywood's production. But the costs of making pictures soared, the pattern of extravagance in movie production continued, and economic crisis gripped the industry from 1929 to 1932. The financiers began to check the authority and the independence of the producers. Giant organizations—Paramount,

251

Fox, Universal, RKO—were reorganized either in bankruptcy or just on the verge of it.* Representatives of Eastern banking houses moved into Hollywood "to keep an eye on production," to cut costs, to reorganize studio operations, to temper grandiose ideas with business fiats.

For a time it appeared that movies would never again be made on so reckless and sumptuous a scale, that the decisions of businessmen would take priority over the impulses of movie men. But the financiers could not make profitable movies. Their representatives could not understand, manage, or adjust to Hollywood's people and problems. The directors of the motion picture corporations discovered that, unlike other businesses, it was suicidal to institute sudden and severe changes in movie personnel. In the ordinary business world, it seemed natural for a Sewell Avery to move from the presidency of a gypsum company to the presidency of a mail-order house, and it was natural for him to remain a director of meat-packing, gas, coke, and railroad companies as well. But in motion pictures, the bankers learned, it was impossible to replace the talents of "the wild men of Hollywood" without courting disaster. The "geniuses" of the movie colony might be checked; they might be guided; but they could not be replaced with any degree of confidence in the outcome.

The case of Paramount offers a striking example and moral on this point. In a last-minute effort to head off receivership, the old Paramount-Publix Corporation brought in John Hertz as a director and chairman of the finance committee (in 1931). He cut salaries, discharged inefficients, attacked nepotism. He

* In 1933, the Paramount-Publix Corporation filed a petition in bankruptcy; it was reorganized in 1935 under Section 77B of the bankruptcy act and emerged as Paramount Pictures, Inc. The Radio-Keith-Orpheum Corporation went into bankruptcy in 1933, and was reorganized after seven years in the federal courts. The Fox Film Corporation was reorganized voluntarily in 1931 and again in 1933 (with the consent of its creditors and the holders of its securities), and in 1935 merged with the Twentieth Century Company (Joseph M. Schenck and Darryl F. Zanuck) to become the Twentieth Century-Fox Film Corporation.[14]

sliced annual telephone and telegraph bills from $800,000 to $400,000. He took $5,900,000 off the theater-lease burden. He reduced $600,000 insurance premiums 25-35 percent. He reduced Paramount's annual payroll by no less than $9,300,000, and cut the annual operating expenses from $133,000,000 to $100,000,000.[15] No Hollywood studio had experienced so violent a shake-up. Then Hertz and Adolph Zukor, the founder, chairman, and godhead of Paramount, had a falling out. Hertz resigned. Trustees in receivership were appointed. Another reorganization followed.* And still Paramount failed to show a healthy pulse-beat.

In 1936, the weary board of directors hired Joseph P. Kennedy to find out what was wrong. Mr. Kennedy (later United States Ambassador to the Court of St. James) was a businessman of ability and a financier of repute; he had, besides, been associated with such movie enterprises as Pathé and FBO (Film Booking Office, later absorbed by the Radio Corporation of America). Kennedy went to Hollywood, watched, studied, listened, examined records, and presented a report. This is what he said was wrong with Paramount:

1. Producers held exorbitant contracts, and there was no relationship between a producer's salary and the box-office success of his pictures.
2. Stars were poorly handled.
3. Overhead was indefensibly high.
4. The constant turnover of the production head of the studio was disastrous.
5. Authority was not clearly defined.
6. Scenario costs were excessive.
7. The "write-off" on stories and contracts was enormous.

* By a group headed by Harold Fortington (representing the Royal Insurance Company and certain British investment trusts), Lehman Brothers, Electrical Research Products, Inc. (ERPI), Hallgarten and Company, White, Weld and Company, and the Atlas Corporation. They elected their men to the new board of directors and put in John Otterson, former president of ERPI, as president of the company. An investigation of the company's affairs had resulted in a score of law suits, one of which was a trustees' suit for $18,000,000.[16]

8. Shooting schedules were disregarded; scripts were not ready when shooting began.
9. Budget estimates were not complete or accurate when shooting began. Picture budgets were a joke, since they were exceeded with impunity.
10. There was glaring extravagance in the number of "takes."
11. The ERPI contract for sound licenses was excessive.
12. The conflicts within the board of directors caused confusion, uncertainty, and weakened morale in the production branch of the organization.[17]

And to cap the analysis, Mr. Kennedy concluded that there had been *too much "business" interference* with the production of movies. He recommended that a "picture man" (a Hollywood producer, in other words) be appointed chief of production, with authority to proceed without interference from the bankers' representatives and the investment houses. It was a striking acknowledgment that movie production demanded movie producers—men with a flair for showmanship and an instinct for dramaturgy, men who could orchestrate the sound and fury with which pictures are made.

The New York executives learned that orthodox business practices may destroy "unorthodox" intangible assets: the creative urge, the sense of being indulged. They had instituted routine economies without understanding that Hollywood's producers, actors, directors, and writers do not get fabulous salaries for their daily output, or their measurable diligence, or the decorum of their methods, or the regularity of their working hours. They forgot, in the words of the financier quoted earlier, that they needed to temper their knowledge of balance-sheet costs with an understanding of three-ring circuses. "They learned," an executive told this writer, "*why* Hollywood producers get fabulous salaries."

Moods rule Hollywood, not data. Financial statements, business indices, even box-office returns are used, when they are used at all, not to guide changes in method and policy, but as metaphorical whips on energy and expectations. When box-office revenues nosedive and the Eastern offices begin issuing frantic orders, Hollywood surrenders to the jitters. There are changes in studio management, wholesale lay-offs, slashes in budgets; options are not exercised; the free-lance market freezes overnight; and minor panic sweeps the town. But Hollywood soon plunges into more excited efforts, and geometric enthusiasm grips the studios. One always hears fervent incantations of "smash hits" just around the corner.

Hollywood is temperamentally incapable of caution; the stakes go to the venturesome; the premium is on daring and novelty. Showmanship is itself a synonym for grandiosity. Besides, movie making is not a systematized process in which ordered routine can prevail, or in which costs can be absolute and controlled. Too many things can and do go awry, every day, every hour, during the manufacture of a movie. Movies are made by ideas and egos, not from blueprints and not with machines. Every story offers fresh and exasperating problems; every actor, director, writer carries within him curious preferences and needs; and the omnipresent hand of a mutable public throws sudden switches in the traffic of ideas through which the making of movies flows. The movie business moves with relentless speed; change is of the essence, and Hollywood must respond to change with short-spanned flexibility.

In Hollywood, the vagaries of show business are repeated, embellished, and cherished by the men who make movies until they are convinced—or convince themselves—that nothing in pictures is normal, nothing predictable, that all is a succession of intuitive stabs into an unknown, tantalizing future. Benjamin B. Hampton concluded that "conventional" practices have generally proved disastrous in Hollywood, and that it was the reckless, gambling producers who survived:

. . . so again in 1918, the producers who hesitated lost ground in the struggle . . . [for] industrial survival, and those who disregarded common business prudence and rushed ahead on a showman's hunch saved their skins. The reckless producers mercilessly consigned their war stories to the scrap heap . . . and poured their available capital, plus all the money they could borrow, into the feverish filming of new plays dealing with nothing but romance and adventure. . . . It would seem as though whenever the movie-makers become conservative they lose money; this is a field in which the daring win.[18]

A new solution for the problem was tried in the case of Universal Pictures. Nathan J. Blumberg, on taking over Universal in 1937-1938, reorganized the studio by placing two executives in charge of Hollywood production who had been reared and trained in *exhibition*—movie selling, buying, distribution, and theater operation. Clifford Work and Matthew Fox, like Mr. Blumberg, knew nothing about making pictures, but they knew a great deal about the movie market. They knew what and who the public would pay to see, and where. They knew which stars or stories were "right" for which theaters or theater-areas. They knew, therefore, how much it was wise to spend on given pictures. The "exhibitor boys" took over the studio with the intention of making pictures for *definite markets*. They were prepared to sacrifice art, egos, Academy Awards, or *kudos* from reviewers, for box-office results. It was a revolutionary venture in Hollywood.

The Blumberg-Fox-Work combination set up iron budgets, and enforced a firm, if flexible, discipline. They did not try to interfere with the creative afflatus, though they subjected creators to a *blitzkrieg* of administrative control. They did not tell their directors how to direct, or their writers how to write. They did not "make a Marlene Dietrich picture." They said, "We'll make a Marlene Dietrich picture for $600,000." Then they found the kind of story in which they' believed Dietrich could attract an audience, and they insisted on making a picture from that story for the amount of money which, in their judgment, a Dietrich film justified as a cold business investment. They never spent more, and they usually spent less.

They cut costs mercilessly. They fired temperamental talents which could not submit to shooting schedules. They substituted short-term deals for long-term contracts. When they hired high-priced actors they squeezed the roles into a short shooting schedule, and finished with the actors in three weeks instead of six. They lured top-flight actors (whom they could not afford to hire) into their fold by giving the star a percentage of the profits. They even persuaded some stars to invest money in their pictures (Bing Crosby, W. C. Fields).

They scoured the Universal stock of unused scripts, and filmed stories which had been collecting dust in the files. They went through Universal's film and newsreel vaults for action shots (forest fires, air battles, oil fires, floods) and put writers to work fabricating stories around the stock scenes. They invented titles which sounded popular, and ordered stories written around them (*Tower of London, Frankenstein's Daughter*). They re-issued old successes (*Frankenstein, Dracula*) to raise quick money, and when necessary they pasted new scenes onto old classics (*All Quiet on the Western Front*). They bought the movie rights to popular comic strips and radio characters, and made cheap movie serials for the Southern market.

They made action pictures, horror pictures, farces, cheap musicals. As one Universal executive said, they were delighted when the New York *Times* movie critic panned one of their films, because that generally meant that the critic for the New York *Daily News* would praise it. "Compare the circulation of the two." They intrigued the public with "reverse casting" (James Stewart as a sheriff and Marlene Dietrich as a saloon entertainer in *Destry Rides Again*). And they used to the full the one great star they had inherited, Deanna Durbin, by letting her producer, Joe Pasternak, handle the gold mine he had discovered.

The monetary consequences to Universal Pictures were startling. In three years (1938-40, inclusive) the "exhibitor boys" whom Hollywood had regarded with some disdain increased the gross sales of their organization from $18,150,876 to $27,677,627. In three years, said the chairman of Universal's board of directors, they converted a net loss of $1,084,999 into a net profit of $2,390,772.* The record is all the more remarkable if we remember that these were the years in which the motion picture industry faced the end of its world market; World War II was on, foreign markets were collapsing, film money was being impounded abroad. . . .

The final point, for the purposes of this chapter, is that the salaries paid to the Universal executives and executive-producers pale by comparison with the dazzling remuneration of producers at MGM or Twentieth Century-Fox or Paramount.† The executive-management group at Universal received new contracts, in 1941, which gave them annual salaries ranging from $62,400 to $91,000 for two years, and would then range from $75,400 to $117,000.‡

The introduction of exhibitor-executives into Hollywood represents, to the mind of this writer, the most striking and signifi-

---

* Universal's record since 1935:

1935	$ 677,186	deficit
1936	1,988,524	deficit
1937	1,084,999	deficit
1938	591,178	deficit
1939	1,153,321	net profit (consolidated)
1940	2,232,805	net profit (consolidated)
1941	931,280	net profit for first 17 weeks [19]

† One MGM producer and supervisor recently signed a new long-term contract, retroactive to March 5, 1939, and extending to December 31, 1945. "Under the deal, he receives $4,000 a week plus seven percent of the combined Loew annual net profits in excess of $2,745,744, after a dividend of $2 a share has been deducted on the common." [20]

‡ There was also additional "incentive compensation": a profit-sharing plan under which the executives receive from one-half of one percent of operating income up to $2,500,000, and from one to two percent of operating earnings in excess of that amount. Each of the five vice-presidents was to receive, each year, warrants to purchase 3,000 shares of Universal Corporation common stock at $10 a share, the chairman and president of the organization receiving 5,000 such warrants. The warrants already held by members of the executive group, which ran for five years and gave them the right to buy stock at prices ranging from $8-$10 a share, were to be exchanged for the longer term warrants at the higher purchase rate. [21]

cant development of recent years in the production policy of Hollywood.* Two things are certain: (1) the power given exhibitor-trained men over production in Hollywood is one solution New York is trying for Hollywood's recurrent problems; (2) the exhibitor-executives have not improved the quality of motion pictures, but they have increased the profits of their companies. It remains to be seen if the trees will continue to bear golden fruit.

* Paramount sent Y. Frank Freeman, a theater man from Atlanta, to Hollywood in 1938 as vice-president in charge of production. In 1938, RKO placed George J. Schaefer, a former sales manager, film-exchange booker, distributor, and film salesman, in charge of its organization. (At MGM, Al Lichtman and Sam Katz have for several years been important in the studio's operation; both are drawn from the theater and sales fronts of the motion picture industry.) RKO's record, at the date of this writing, fails to show any marked improvement. But Paramount's net profits are decidedly on the upgrade; Paramount's total net profit for 1940 was more than $2,500,000 above 1939. Paramount's consolidated earnings for 1939: $2,737,533 (after $70,000 provided for contingencies). The discount on the purchase of debentures, and the net share of undistributed earnings of partially-owned subsidiaries, would bring the 1939 total net earnings to $3,874,944. Consolidated earnings for 1940 were $6,304,064 plus $98,066 discount on the purchase of debentures. Total earnings: $6,402,130. Paramount's earnings for 1940 were announced at $7,633,130. This included $1,231,000 net interest in the combined undistributed earnings of partially-owned subsidiary companies.[22]

12. THE PRODUCERS: II

"PRODUCER" is a term which covers several meanings. There are producers who head small companies, executive-producers of large motion picture corporations, producers who work on a salary, producers who get a percentage of the profits. There are producers who are employers, and producers who are employees.

It is difficult to make categorical distinctions about the producers in Hollywood, because their functions are not clearly differentiated and their jurisdiction varies from studio to studio. But it will be convenient to distinguish seven types of producers among the 159 working in the movie colony.*

1. *The Executive Head of a Studio.* In four motion picture corporations the president or chairman of the board works in and from the studios in Hollywood:

Twentieth Century-Fox	Joseph M. Schenck	Chairman of the Board
Warner Brothers	Harry M. Warner	President
RKO Radio	George Schaefer	President
Columbia Pictures	Harry Cohn	President

The Messrs. Schenck, Warner, and Schaefer are primarily con-

* Our analysis of the movie companies, and of the credits on 1,141 movies produced in three years (1937-39, inclusive) by the major studios, found 159 producers, executives, and associate producers active in Hollywood in 1939-40. Director-producers (see Chapter 13) are not included.

260

cerned with the business, finance, theaters, and trade problems of their respective organizations; the actual *production* of movies, with all its attendant problems, is delegated to executives in charge of production (see below). Harry Cohn heads Columbia Pictures as a corporation, and is in charge of the production of its films as well.*

The executive head of a studio is exactly what his title implies; he is the Commander-in-Chief. He passes upon finances, administration, costs, and policies. He is the final authority and the ultimate power. The executive in charge of production, described below, is his Chief of Staff.

2. *The Executive in Charge of Production.* The executive in charge of production (or the executive-producer) is generally the vice-president of a motion picture corporation. He is responsible for the operation of the studio, whereas the executive head is concerned with the operation of the corporation. The executive-producer supervises forty to sixty feature pictures a year, plus those short subjects (one or two reels) which may be part of his studio's program. (Some shorts, and all newsreels, are made in New York.) He generally shares in the profits of the studio.

The executive-producer has a staff of producers working under him. He allocates picture budgets, purchases stories, and passes upon scripts and films. He hires and fires; he assigns his producers, actors, directors, writers, technicians to their tasks. He combines the functions of administrator, impresario, and roving quarterback. Movies are what the executive-producers encourage or *allow* their battery of creative talents to make of them. The executive-producers for the major studios in Hollywood are:

* For the other major studios, the presidents reside in and operate from New York: Nicholas M. Schenck, president of Loew's Incorporated (MGM); Sidney Kent, president of Twentieth Century-Fox; Barney Balaban, president of Paramount Pictures; N. J. Blumberg, president of Universal Pictures.

Loew's, Inc. (MGM)	Louis B. Mayer *	Executive in Charge of Production
Paramount	Y. Frank Freeman	Vice-President
Warner Brothers	Jack L. Warner	Vice-President
Twentieth Century-Fox	Darryl F. Zanuck	Vice-President
RKO Radio	Joseph I. Breen	Vice-President †
Columbia	Harry Cohn	President (see category above)
Universal	Clifford Work	Vice-President

3. *The Independent Producers.* The independent producers are presidents of their own (and small) corporations who get or provide their own financing, and release their product through a major studio. Unlike the executive-producers, the independent producers put out only a few pictures a year (one to five). They have no staff of producers and need maintain only a few actors, directors, and writers under contract. They are not subject to the elaborate administrative and political problems which beset the head of a large studio. United Artists—which produces no pictures itself—is the organization which *distributes* the films produced by the leading independent producers: Charles Chaplin, Samuel Goldwyn, David O. Selznick, Walter Wanger, Alexander Korda, Hal Roach, James Roosevelt, Edward Small, and others.‡

The men described thus far—executive heads, executive-producers, and independent producers—are Hollywood's cabinet

* Louis B. Mayer is, for some reason, not an officer of Loew's, Inc., but is listed in the corporation's records as "executive employee" or "executive in charge of production." Metro-Goldwyn-Mayer uses the most elaborate production scheme in Hollywood. The executive in charge of production is Mayer, but he tends to share responsibility with Edgar Mannix (vice-president) and a staff of executive producers (Lichtman, Katz, Thau, Cohn).

† In June, 1941, Mr. Breen resigned as administrator of the Production Code Administration, a post he had held from its inception in 1934, and became vice-president in charge of production for RKO-Radio Pictures.

‡ "Independent producers" is often used in Hollywood to designate the organizations which are not among the eight major motion picture corporations; e.g., Republic Pictures (rapidly becoming a powerful and profitable studio), Monogram, Condor, the producers who occupy "Poverty Row," and so on. This study is concerned with the eight major organizations, and by "independent producers" we shall mean the men named in the text above.

and general staff. They are the spokesmen of the motion picture industry's production branch. As members of the Association of Motion Picture Producers (a California corporation nominally independent of the Hays office, which is called the Motion Picture Producers and Distributors of America) they determine Hollywood's policy and practices with reference to wage scales, labor disputes, the talent guilds, and the labor unions. They are what is generally meant in Hollywood when the term "the producers" is used to mean those who govern and dominate the production of movies. Their known annual salaries range from $106,000 to $688,369.*

4. *The Producer in Charge of A Pictures.* The A producer is in charge not of a studio's entire production, as is the executive-producer, but of twenty to thirty A pictures. ("A" pictures means quality pictures, generally pictures which cost over $500,000.) He works with and under the executive-producer, and supervises a group of associate producers under him.

The top A producer has a narrower area of authority than the executive-producer. He is given a budget for his pictures, or is obliged to have his budgets approved. He has less authority in hiring and firing, in contracting for talent or building personalities. He is concerned with the actual production of pictures, and not with the problems which an executive-producer faces: payroll, studio administration, labor problems, personnel, and so on.

Hal B. Wallis of Warner Brothers and Buddy de Sylva of Paramount offer good examples of the producer of A pictures. (At Twentieth Century-Fox, the functions of the executive-producer and the A producer are combined in the same man, Darryl F. Zanuck.) The top A producers receive from $106,000 to $260,000 a year.

* The salaries of producers (all categories) are given in pp. 383.

5. *The Producer in Charge of B Pictures.* The producer of B pictures (roughly speaking, pictures which cost under $500,-000) is a subordinate of the executive-producer, and, in some cases, of the producer in charge of A pictures. His job is to turn out from twenty to thirty pictures a year with speed, economy, and a stern disregard of esthetics or prestige. He uses inexpensive stories and talents. He may remake old movies, use stories discarded by other producers, or have cheap scripts made to order. He is the foreman of a production line which manufactures commodities of varying degrees of palatability. He must have a talent for cutting corners, for he is held to small budgets. His job, in the words of one veteran of the ranks, is to "knock off new pictures like clay pigeons." Bryan Foy of Warner Brothers (sometimes called "King of the B's") and Sol Wurtzel of Twentieth Century-Fox are the best-known producers in this category. The top B producers in Hollywood receive from $109,000 to $182,000 a year.

6. *The Producer (or Associate Producer).* * The producer (or associate producer) works under the A producer, and is actively engaged in the production of from one to six pictures a year. He works in the closest relationship to these films. He supervises the writers on story and script. He works with the director in planning the emphases and "key" of a story, the handling of the cast. He is in direct contact with all the technicians and departments entering into the making of the film. But he has no jurisdiction over any pictures save those which he is given to produce. He has no authority, that is, over the picture program of a studio, or the budgets, policies, and administration. He is

---

* At Warner Brothers all the producers except Hal B. Wallis and Bryan Foy are called "associate producers." At MGM no producers are classed as "associate producers." At Twentieth Century-Fox all the producers except Darryl Zanuck and Sol Wurtzel were termed "associate producers" from 1935 to 1941, when a change in policy gave to the associate producers the status of producers, with more autonomy on their pictures. At some studios the term "associate producer" is reserved for B picture supervisors.

an employee. The producers earn from $200 a week to over $300,000 a year, depending upon the duties they perform, their reputation and record, and the studio at which they work.

7. *The Producer-Director.* The man who directs a movie works for the producer; but the director who has achieved sufficient importance to be given full production authority on the pictures which he directs is a producer-director. He selects his own writers, cast, cameraman, and so on. After his budget has been approved by the executive-producer, and his basic story has obtained executive approval, he has full freedom to shape and fashion the film. The director-producer may make from one to three pictures a year.

There are about thirty producer-directors in Hollywood, of whom the best known are Frank Capra, John Ford, Ernst Lubitsch, Gregory La Cava, John Stahl, Wesley Ruggles, Lewis Milestone. A director-producer such as Cecil B. DeMille or Frank Lloyd is head of his own corporation, releasing his pictures, through a major studio which finances them in part or in full. Producer-directors earn from $90,000 to $294,166 a year.

We have discussed the functions and powers of Hollywood's producers. Let us now analyze them as a professional group. The facts about the producers and executives in the movie colony will cast light upon men who are for the most part unknown; the facts will subject some popular misconceptions to the test of objective evidence.

Age. The producers and executives in the movie colony range in age from 26 to 65 (as of 1940). The median average age for 112 producers and executives is 44.* This might be compared

---

* The 112 comprised 92 producers and 20 executives. The median average age for 92 producers is 43; for 20 executives, 45; for the combined 112, 44. The materials on producers in this chapter were taken from many sources: *Who's Who in America, Motion Picture Almanac, Film Daily Year Book;* extensive data were collected first-hand, in prolonged interviews, and much was provided by producers.

to the median average age for directors (43), writers (37), actors and actresses (34). The age distribution of producers and executives is interesting:

1.8 percent are under 30 years of age.
27.7 percent are 30-39 years of age.
45.5 percent are 40-49 years of age.
25.0 percent are 50 years of age or over.

In other words, more than a fourth of the producers are under 40; less than half are between 40 and 50 years old; a fourth are 50 years old and over.

Let us compare the material on producers to 595 cases drawn from other professional groups in Hollywood:

Age	112 Producers and Executives (Percent)	595 Cases * (Percent)
Under 30	1.8	12.4
30-39	27.7	36.8
40-49	45.5	26.7
50-59	23.2	17.3
60 and over	1.8	6.7

The proportion of producers over 50 years of age (25 percent) is almost identical with that prevailing in the professional circles of the movie colony (24 percent). There are far fewer producers under 40 (29.5 as compared to 49.2 percent), and far more producers between 40 and 50 (45.5 as compared to 26.7 percent).

Hollywood often apologizes for its errors and its excesses by pointing to the relative immaturity of its people. The plea is more tenable for the writers or actresses in the movie colony than for the producers; only 34.9 percent of the actresses and 42.4 percent of the writers are over 40 years old, as we shall see; but 70.5 percent of the producers are over 40 years old, and 91.9 percent are 35 years of age or older.

* 271 actors, 66 directors, 120 writers, 41 first-film editors, 79 assistant directors, 18 directors of photography. See Appendix D.

266

Birthplaces. There is a popular impression that most pro-ducers are "foreigners." The facts contradict this belief. Out of 132 producers and executives, 82.6 percent were born in the United States, and 17.4 percent were born abroad. If we include 4 Canadian-born among the American-born, we find that 85.6 percent of the producers in Hollywood were born in the United States or Canada, and 14.4 percent were born abroad.*

How does the number of foreign-born producers compare to other groups in the movie colony? A much smaller percentage of the producers (17.4) were born abroad than actors (25.3) or directors (28.7), but a larger percentage than writers (13.9).† For the four leading professional groups in Hollywood as a whole (555 cases), 78.2 percent were born in the United States and 21.8 percent were born outside our national territory.

Education. Another stanch assumption about the movie colony is that the producers are almost entirely illiterate. Alva Johnston expressed the common conception neatly when he wrote:

. . . [In Hollywood] the university alumni are working for the high-school alumni, and the high-school alumni are working for the grammar school alumni. You can roughly measure the importance of a man in the movie industry by the number of stories told about his ignorance.[1]

But the facts about the educational record of the movie pro-ducers will occasion surprise. Out of 121 producers and execu-tives for whom data were available: ‡

* Another interesting figure: 109 producers were born in the United States, 4 in Canada, 7 in Great Britain, 1 in Ireland. This total is 121 (91.7 percent); only 11 (8.3 percent) of the producers were born in continental Europe. See Appendix D for complete tabulation.

† The proportion of producers in the movie colony born outside of the United States is exactly the same as the proportion of foreign-born whites in Minneapolis or in Oakland, California; it is considerably smaller than the percentage of foreign-born whites in Boston (29.4), Chicago (24.9), Cambridge, Mass. (28.4), Rock-ford, Ill. (21.2), Providence, R. I. (25.5), Cleveland or Detroit (25.5), and so on.[2]

‡ 100 producers and 21 executives; this writer could not find information for 34 producers and 4 executives. The educational record of our group would prob-ably be brought downward if data for the missing 38 were available.

HOLLYWOOD: THE MOVIE MAKERS

9.9 percent had no formal education beyond the grammar-schoo level.
33.1 percent went only to high-school.
57.0 percent went to college.
    13.8 percent received college degrees.*
    12.4 percent received college degrees and went on to graduate work.

The number of producers with college training (57 percent) indicates that illiteracy is not rampant in Hollywood's upper strata. The popular stereotype stems from the circumstance that the less cultivated producers are the ones about whom the press and the public hear most often. This is made clear if we separate the producers from the *executives* and examine the difference in educational background between 100 producers and 25 executives. Only 5 percent of the producers did not proceed beyond the grammar-school level, as compared to 33.5 percent of the executives; and 61 percent of the producers went to college, as compared to only 38.1 percent of the executives. The differences are striking.

Let us now compare the educational record of Hollywood's producers to that of the other professional groups in the movie colony. An analysis of 706 cases shows:

	Total Cases	Number Who Went to College	Percent
Producers and executives	121	69	57.0
Actors	251	125	49.8
Directors	66	35	53.0
Writers	133	107	80.5
Directors of photography	17	7	41.2
Assistant directors	79	44	55.7
First film editors	39	16	41.0

The conclusion is extremely interesting: A higher percentage of the producers (57.0) attended college than did actors, directors, directors of photography, assistant directors, or first film

* The 22 who received college degrees collected 19 bachelor degrees, 2 masters' 3 doctorates, of which one was an honorary LLD.

editors. As a *group*, only the writers in the movie colony are working for their academic inferiors. If we again separate the producers from the executives, we find that the percentage of movie *executives* who went to college (38.1) is smaller than that for any other professional group in the movie colony; the producers' college record still remains higher (61 percent) than that of the other groups with the exception of writers.

Frederick Lewis Allen points out that of ten "overlords" of American financial power—J. P. Morgan, George F. Baker, James Stillman, E. H. Harriman, John D. Rockefeller, William Rockefeller, H. H. Rogers, J. H. Schiff, William K. Vanderbilt, and James R. Keene—only one, Morgan, had a college education.[3] Hollywood's executives are not *sui generis* in their academic nondistinction.

University training [says Alva Johnston] is an essential to the old, standard professions, but is apparently a handicap in a new, changing, experimental calling in which imagination and judgment are more important than specialized knowledge. The semi-literates often seem to have a vehemence, decisiveness, and single-mindedness which are commonly educated out of college men.

It is sometimes said that Hollywood does not appreciate educated men, which is like saying that the Olympic Games do not appreciate inferior athletes. . . . The advantage possessed by the uneducated man or half-educated man seems to be that he is forced at an early age to face his own problems, to accept responsibilities, to make decisions.[4]

Experience. When the name of a movie magnate is uttered, one of the first associations to spring into the mind of the listener is "tailor" or "button-hole maker." The implicit assumption, as was pointed out in the first chapter of this book, is that in one fell swoop a pants-presser jumped from a loft on West 37th Street to an office in Hollywood. This is an interesting stereotype (and a reflection upon Hollywood's publicity); but it obviously ignores the total career-line of the men who produce movies, the stages by which their experience was gained, their wits sharpened, their proficiency acquired.

An analysis of the biographies of 102 producers and executives revealed long and impressive backgrounds in professional movie making:

PROFESSIONAL EXPERIENCE IN HOLLYWOOD

102 Producers and Executives

Number of Years	Percent
25 and over	14.7
20-25	15.7
15-20	16.7
10-15	11.8
5-10	28.4
5 or less	12.7

In other words:

30.4 percent of the producers have worked in motion picture organizations *in Hollywood* for 20 or more years.
47.1 percent have worked in Hollywood for 15 or more years.
58.9 percent have worked in Hollywood for 10 or more years.
41.1 percent have worked in Hollywood for less than 10 years.

It should be noted that "experience in Hollywood" does not include experience in motion picture distribution, sales, theaters, publicity—an apprenticeship which many producers have undergone.

The *nature* of the producers' experience is significant. Information was found in this field for 144 producers and executives; it revealed the movie work performed by the producers *other than* and prior to their present jobs in Hollywood:

Production in other studios	102
Executive positions in other motion picture organization	62
Writing (movie)	52
Distribution	29
Direction (movie)	21
Advertising and publicity (movie)	19
Story departments	13
Assistant directors	12
Acting (movie or other)	11
Film editing	8

On the whole, the professional experience of producers has been long, practical, and varied. That experience has unquestionably given the producers a knowledge of costs, shooting schedules, casting, technical production problems. It has not necessarily supplied them with insights, taste, or creative judgment. The number of experienced incompetents in Hollywood's corps of producers (to which most producers will testify) brings to mind the observation of the elder Pitt: "[I] content myself with wishing that I may be one of those whose follies may cease with their youth, and not of that number who are ignorant in spite of experience." [5]

Marriage and Divorce. The marital record of 79 producers and executives shows that 2.5 percent have never married, 74.7 percent have been married once, 20.3 percent have been married twice, 2.5 percent have been married three times. In other words, 22.8 percent of the producers have been married more than once. Let us now look at the probable distribution of divorces: *

> 69.7 percent of the producers have *not* been divorced.
> 24.1 percent have probably been divorced once.
> 5.0 percent have probably been divorced twice.
> 1.2 percent have probably been divorced three times.

In all, accordingly, 30.3 percent of the producers in our sample have probably been divorced. This is a slightly higher percentage than is found among the directors in the movie colony, 29.1 percent of whom seem to have been divorced, but it is lower than the proportion found among Hollywood's actors, 35.5 percent of whom, apparently, have been disespoused. The producers' divorces may also be compared to a group of 378 movie makers † (for whom data were available), of whom 24.9

---

* The divorce data cannot be exact, for reasons suggested in chapter 5. The problems involved in obtaining information on divorces, and the several methods used to ascertain and check the material, are set forth in Appendix E.

† 200 actors, 55 directors, 63 assistant directors, 48 film editors, 12 directors of photography.

percent have been divorced. The combined group of 457 (*i.e.,* including the 79 producers) shows that 24.5 percent of the professional groups in the movie colony have probably cut their connubial bonds on one or more occasions. (3.9 percent seem to have been divorced twice, and 1.3 percent three times.)

Salaries. Everyone knows that the producers receive prodigious salaries. The lists made public each year by government agencies have placed Hollywood's executives and producers in the spotlight of public attention.* Suppose we begin our exploration of producers' earnings by tabulating the salaries of fifty-four producers and executives in Hollywood who received over $75,000 in 1938. (1938 figures are used because they are the most recent complete data available; Hollywood's salaries have not been lowered since 1938; in many cases they are higher today than they were then.)

EXECUTIVE AND PRODUCER SALARIES OVER $75,000 (1938)

	Executives	Producers	Total
$75,000-$100,000	1	11	12
$100,000-$150,000	4	16	20
$150,000-$200,000	5	8	13
$200,000-$250,000	3	1	4
$250,000-$300,000	1	1	2
$300,000-$400,000		2	2
$600,000-$700,000	1		1
Total	15	39	54

The executive in the movie colony, as would be expected, receives substantially more money than the producer. Exactly two-thirds of the movie executives (in Hollywood) received annual salaries *over* $150,000, as compared to 30.8 percent of the producers; 69.2 percent of the producers received remunera-

* Louis B. Mayer, for instance: In 1937 he received $1,296,503; in 1938 he received salary and bonuses amounting to $893,000; in 1939 he received $688,369; in 1940 he got an aggregate remuneration of $697,049 (of which $541,049 was said to represent a share of the profits of Loew's, Inc.).[6]

tion *under* $150,000, as compared to 33.3 percent of the executives.

Who are the movie executives who are so handsomely rewarded? The roster which follows presents the salaries (for 1938, except in two cases): [7]

Louis B. Mayer	$688,369 *	Harry Cohn	$185,000
Darryl F. Zanuck	265,000	Harry M. Warner	156,000
Edgar J. Mannix	249,481	Jack L. Warner	156,000
Sam Katz	.247,756	Benjamin Thau	136,878
Al Lichtman	229,391	Walter F. Wanger	130,000
Pandro S. Berman †	213,773	Joseph M. Schenck	106,000
David O. Selznick	203,500 (1937)	William Goetz	106,000
Samuel Goldwyn	189,000 (1937)	Hal E. Roach	106,000
	George J. Schaefer	$68,240 ‡	

This is a startling array of remunerative largess. § It demonstrates what Benjamin B. Hampton meant when he wrote, in his *History of the Movies:*

The ability to produce one good photoplay once in a while is rare enough, but to direct the activities of an entire studio requires administrative talents of a high order. Movie corporations have spent millions of dollars in searching for such ability, and not more than a dozen men have been found equal to the task.[8]

* Another published report stated that Mr. Mayer received $893,300 aggregate remuneration in 1938, of which $763;300 ·represented bonuses and shares in profits.[9]

† Now a producer at MGM; Mr. Berman was vice-president in charge of production at RKO in 1938.

‡ According to the registration statement filed with the Securities and Exchange Commission on June 18, 1940, Mr. Schaefer, president of RKO Radio, receives $68,240 a year plus $250 per week for expenses.

§ The roster given above contains only the names of movie executives working in and from Hollywood. If a more inclusive analysis is made, combining the salaries and bonuses of the New York and Hollywood executives of motion picture corporations, we discover that film executives (all corporation officers and directors) received no less than 18.96 percent of the *net profits* (after all charges) of the motion picture companies. Only department stores funnel off a larger percentage of net profits (32.1) to their management and directorial group. The remuneration of film executives comes to 1.59 percent of the *total volume of sales* of the corporations. Only one industry (cement manufacture), among the eighteen for which data were available, paid out a larger percentage (1.61). And, it should be remembered, the motion picture business ranked *eleventh* among the eighteen industries studied in its total assets, and *fourteenth* in its total volume of business. See Appendix B.

What of those producers, the reader may ask, who are not executives of their companies, *i.e.*, who work as employees on salary? The record shows that thirty-nine producers devoid of executive status received over $75,000 in 1938; the following twenty-one producers received over $100,000:

Loew's Incorporated (MGM)		*Twentieth Century-Fox*	
Hunt Stromberg	$328,817	Sol Wurtzel	$182,583
Mervyn LeRoy	300,000	Harry Joe Brown	122,041
Bernard H. Hyman	194,187	Nunnally Johnson	119,166
Robert Z. Leonard	190,083	Raymond Griffith *	117,375
Lawrence Weingarten	170,272	Kenneth MacGowan *	104,333
Sidney Franklin	169,000	Max Gordon *	100,250
Louis D. Lighton	156,166		
Joseph L. Mankiewicz	156,000	*Columbia*	
Harry Rapf	137,339	Sam Briskin	106,000
John W. Considine, Jr.	122,666		
		Universal	
Paramount		Joe Pasternak	119,875
William Le Baron	182,000		
Arthur Hornblow, Jr.	145,166	*Warner Brothers*	
Albert P. Lewin *	114,958	Hal B. Wallis	260,000
Harold H. Hurley	109,416	Robert Lord	134,450
		Bryan Foy	109,916
		Sam Bischoff	104,250

Are the above data representative of all the producers in Hollywood? No. They deal only with the highest salaries (the upper fifth, as we shall see); they do not include those producers who receive stipends which are substantially more modest. Hollywood, like the public at large, probably does not believe that any of its producers earns less than, say, $25,000 a year. But a survey of payroll data at three major studios revealed that a fifth of the men listed as producers, associate producers, or "supervisors" earned under $250 a week, *i.e.*, under $12,500 a year. Three studios opened their payrolls to this writer (Warner Brothers, Twentieth Century-Fox, Columbia), and for

---

* No longer at the studio named.

fifty-two producers of all types the records showed the following weekly salaries:

Weekly Salary (1938)	Producers	Percent	Weekly Salary (1938)	Producers	Percent
Under $250	11	21.2	$1,500-$1,999	8	15.4
$250-$499	7	13.5	$2,000-$2,999	6	11.6
$500-$749	9	17.3	$3,000-$3,999	2	3.8
$750-$999	3	5.8	$4,000-$4,999	1	1.9
$1,000-$1,499	3	5.7	$5,000 and over	2	3.8

This offers several valuable conclusions:

A fifth of the producers (21.2 percent) at three major studios earned under $250 a week, i.e., under $12,500 a year (fifty working weeks).

More than half the producers (52 percent) earned under $750 a week (roughly speaking, $36,000 per year).

Two-thirds of the producers (63.5 percent) earned under $1,500 a week, i.e., under $75,000 a year, and one-third earned over $75,000 a year.*

A fifth of the producers (21.1 percent) earned $2,000 or more a week, meaning $100,000 or more a year.

The median average salary for the producers at three major studios was $500-$750 per week.

No other group in Hollywood can approximate these glittering figures.†

No industry in America pays such high salaries to so many men. The question naturally arises: Are they worth it? The movie executives would say Yes. The movie employees would probably say No. The public would probably murmur, "It's wrong." ‡ How can one measure a producer's value, or the salary which he is worth? The empirical answer is: By the amount he can command in a market in which competitors bargain for

---

* Note that 54 executives and producers in Hollywood earned over $75,000 in 1938. This would mean about one-third of the 159 producers in the movie colony, and this checks the validity of the data obtained from three major studios and given above.

† Compare the earnings of producers to those of directors, actors, writers in chapters 13-15.

‡ Although, significantly enough, polls by Dr. George Gallup revealed that a majority of moviegoers think that Hollywood's stars are not overpaid.[10]

his services. The demand for talent in Hollywood has always been fiercely competitive. "Box-office" personalities have always been few, and the desperate competition for "smash-hit" actors, directors, writers, or producers has kept sending their salaries upward. The studio which wants a certain producer or actor or director knows that that person can obtain a given salary at another studio, and will probably make movies which will make more profit than his princely salary adds to the costs.

The crucial point is that movies have made *enough* profit to endure increasing demands for higher remuneration and ever-increasing costs. Movies have made immense profits for several decades. *Traffic in Souls,* a Universal picture made in 1913, cost $5,700 and grossed $450,000. *Over the Hill,* a 1920 Fox film, cost $100,000 and netted over $3,000,000.[11] In 1938, at one studio, the following four pictures brought in the following gross receipts (approximately 25 percent of the gross receipts should be deducted for distribution, publicity, etc., to determine the net receipts): *

Picture Cost	Gross Receipts
$ 298,493	$ 743,574
603,248	927,595
672,942	1,234,746
1,137,398	1,212,731

William Fox started a career in movies in 1904 with a capital of $1,600. Twenty-five years later he sold out for a sum estimated at $20,000,000. Jesse Lasky, Arthur S. Friend, and Samuel Goldwyn organized their first company in 1913 with $26,500.

---

* The names of the pictures cannot be given; the materials were supplied to this writer in confidence. Not all pictures make money, obviously. The cases of some picture losses might be indicated:

Picture Cost	Gross Receipts
$1,486,087	$1,100,261
1,062,930	737,268
2,066,019	919,207
1,332,654	716,087

In three years Goldwyn sold his stock for over $900,000. The four Warner brothers bought a projector and a print of *The Great Train Robbery* in 1905, and went into roadshow exhibition. In 1937 the net earnings of Warner Brothers Pictures, Inc., were $8,617,000; in 1939 the total assets were $168,618,000.[12]

The movie makers quickly realized the magnitude of the profits of the movies and of their producers. It was only natural that the stars—who knew that their personalities drew people into movie houses—demanded high salaries. The directors—who knew that they really made the pictures—demanded more money. The writers—who knew it was their stories, ideas, and inventiveness which "made" movies—fought for higher salaries. And when the salaries of the top actors and actresses began to approximate astronomical figures, the producers, obviously, scarcely were content to pay themselves less than they paid their employees. The rise in costs on one sector of movie making created a vicious circle from which there was no escape. And as the market widened, as the movies improved, as more and more people developed the movie-going habit, the profits continued to roll in *despite* the mounting pyramid of costs, and the salaries rose higher and higher. There was little bargaining latitude left to the movie executives.

It is easy to rationalize the salaries of Hollywood's producers. An analysis of 39 pictures produced by 16 producers in a major studio shows that of these 39 films 33 made profits. In well over half of the cases, the higher the salary of the producer, the higher the net profits to the studio from the pictures which that producer made. Examples:

Producer A. Salary over $250,000. Produced five pictures; net profits to the studio, $3,056,683.

Producer B. Salary $165,458. Produced one picture; net profit to the studio, $1,212,731.

Producer C. Salary $92,750. Produced two pictures; net profit to the studio, $823,343.

There is another point which accounted for the movement which carried Hollywood's emoluments to stupendous levels. The great profit which movies made could go to either the stockholders or to the managers and movie makers. The question was simple enough: Who shall get the profit? Hollywood, as was suggested in an earlier chapter, has neither the tradition nor the desire to split its profits with a horde of anonymous and "uncreative" stockholders. "What does the stockholder contribute to movies? Why does he deserve big rewards? A few percent interest on his money is all he ought to get." Movie profits went into higher salaries and bonuses. Movie profits were funneled back to the movie executives (in Hollywood *and* New York), movie producers, top stars, top directors, top writers. Movie profits went into higher movie costs.

It was for this reason that a curious and important psychological hiatus was created between the prosperity of a movie corporation and the prosperity of the producers and top-talent groups of that corporation! A motion picture company might suffer net losses for three years—but the people who were making movies in Hollywood had been drawing exorbitant salaries in the same years, and would probably continue to do so.

Who could replace them?

As a group, the producers possess more power than any other group in the movie colony, and they exercise it arbitrarily. They enjoy greater security and more sinecures than any other group in Hollywood. They are given great credit for their successes, and are rarely chastised for their failures. Their position depends more upon friendship and kinship—and less upon demonstrable merit—than that of any other group in Hollywood. Their abilities are praised too highly by their friends and dismissed too easily by their enemies. They are the first to criticize their colleagues, and the first to resent that criticism from an outsider. And they are the most popular targets for Hollywood's hostility and ridicule. To preserve our balance of judgment, it is necessary to observe that in Hollywood, as in other sectors of our society, the most convenient target for all sorts of psychological hostilities is "the boss."

13. THE DIRECTORS

MAKING a movie is telling a story. Superior pictures are pictures which tell superior stories in a superior manner. Poor pictures are pictures which, despite the talent of their actors, the ingenuity of their construction, or the scale of their production, tell a poor story—or tell a story poorly. On the screen, as on the stage or in the novel, the play is still the thing.

Everyone who is engaged in the long process by which movies are made is engaged in the delineation of a story. The writer writes a tale, not just words. The actor creates characters, not just grimaces. The cinematographer underlines moods with light and shadow. The composer uses music to capture emotions. And the movie director is the man through whom the separate creations are translated into a motion picture. The director takes script, actors, cameramen, technicians, and *directs* them, in the literal meaning of the word, fusing the parts into a single pattern with a point, a purpose, a central theme. He controls the pace and rhythm, the overtones and meaning of a screenplay.

The movie director changes that which does not conform to his conception of what the story is, or how it should be told. There is a world of difference between the way a script looks and the way it "acts." There is a world of difference between a mimeographed screenplay and a movie. The movie writer creates a story, but the movie director creates a motion picture.

One of the functions of the director is to save us from the writer enamoured of his own wit; another is to save us from the players enamoured of their own personality; and a third is to save us from the producers . . . who believe they know what the public wants. And all of this means that the function of the director is to understand the chief purpose of the picture he is making, and know what its total effect ought to be, and to see that all other effects, no matter how desirable in themselves, are made secondary to this one. . . . The movie director is the man ultimately responsible for what we actually see on the screen.* [1]

A motion picture is never photographed in continuity. The story is "shot" in pieces. It must be. If you observe a movie you will see that there are "jumps" every minute or so. You see a crowded ballroom; then the camera moves through the dancers until all but four couples are excluded; then you jump closer to one couple; then you see the woman's head, as viewed from over the man's shoulder; then you view the man's head; then you jump to the orchestra leader; then to a courier riding a horse madly; then the courier is in front of the building, leaping off his horse, and runs inside; then you are inside the ballroom as the courier bursts in; then you are very close to his face as he shouts, "Napoleon is Emperor!"; then you are near the chandelier watching the four hundred dancers cheer; then you jump back to the man and women, embracing; then you see her hand letting a rose fall to the ground . . .

Each of these short, separate scenes is a single shot. And each must be photographed with the camera in a different place. The director directs each shot, and fuses all of them into one unified, finished motion picture. He "cuts" (*i.e.*, edits) and assembles the hundreds of separate scenes before the producer edits the picture. He selects the shots (as many as thirty shots may be made of an actress uttering two lines of dialogue and bursting into tears), slices their length, cuts out incidents, rearranges the sequence of events, creates contrasts, movement,

* The directors would demur that it is the producers who are responsible for what finally appears on the screen. See the pages which follow.

climaxes. The director must always preserve a clear conception of the whole, while he directs on the sound stages, while he sits in the cutting room. He must gauge the tempo of scenes in juxtaposition. He must sense the rhythm of episodes so that there is a fluid, continuous line to the unfolding of the story. He must give differentiated emphasis to voices, words, acts, gestures. He and he alone controls the dramatic value and the "story line" of a film.

In the days of silent films, the movie director wrote skeleton scenarios, cut the film, sometimes wrote the subtitles, supervised the lighting and photography—and sometimes acted in the picture. During this era of picture-making, directors and producers worked together informally and continuously, and the director was second only to the producer—for it was the director who actually made the movies. "The mysteries of the movies were locked up in his brain." [2]

The director was indispensable in movie making, and directors received salaries exceeded only by those given to stars. The emoluments of Cecil B. DeMille, whose name became a household word, were second only to those received by the royal triad: Mary Pickford, Charlie Chaplin, and Douglas Fairbanks. The studios at one time tried to publicize their directors in an effort to head off the soaring popularity and bargaining power of their stars; but the public, unfamiliar with a director's tasks (and face), never responded with enthusiasm.*

As the function of the directors rose in significance, Hollywood's producers began to worry about the directors' increasing power and independence. After the revolution of talking pictures, the movie director was forced into an absurd secondary position. In those confused, groping days, directors were ordered to shoot scripts which described every shot, every

---

* Only David Wark Griffith and Cecil B. DeMille made reputations which had demonstrable box-office value. Since then only a few directors—Capra, Lubitsch, Orson Welles—have achieved individual drawing power.

movement of action, every position of the camera. Changes were not permitted, directorial creation was discouraged, interpretation was crushed. Dialogue directors were imported from New York to guide the movie directors; men from Broadway were lured to Hollywood to cope with the crisis of spoken dialogue. The results were what might have been expected: the movies became cluttered with words; stories were buried under dialogue; the essential *movement* of movies was sacrificed to the conceptions and the limitations of the stage.

By 1934, the directors had returned to power. They still knew how to work with visual images. They still knew how to make moving pictures, how to give movies the active, urgent pace which the screen demands. It is significant that in 1938, out of 244 active directors in Hollywood, 136 were movie directors who had won some recognition in silent pictures before the coming of sound; only 21 had been brought to Hollywood directly from Broadway.[3]

In 1938 and 1939 the directors began to assert their strength again. The Screen Directors Guild was recognized by the producers in February of 1939, after a long and stubborn fight, and the directors campaigned for greater creative freedom in their work. The top directors won greater freedom at the expense of the associate producers and supervisors who held power over them. The strongest indication of the trend lay in the increased use of contracts which made leading directors producer-directors in their own right. Until 1938-39, this had been the position of only a few men—DeMille, Lloyd, Lubitsch, Capra; but within three years there were added to the producer-director list such men as Wesley Ruggles, Leo McCarey, William Wellman, Gregory La Cava, Mervyn LeRoy, George Stevens, Mitchell Leisen, John Ford, Mark Sandrich, Orson Welles, and others.

Hollywood's executives are discovering that the directors who know their craft, who are attuned to the requirements of the screen, who work in first-hand contact with actors, scripts, cam-

283

eras, and cutters, who have gone through the story mill of Westerns, potboilers, comedies, action pictures, farces, tragedies, and musicals, are the key men of movies. The leading directors know how to deliver the goods. They are the central craftsmen of the screen. They hold the crucial position between ideas, stories, budgets, actors—and the final movie which appears on the screen.

The critical quality which the director injects into movies can be illustrated by a few examples. The Lubitsch "touch" lies in Ernst Lubitsch's exquisitely witty treatment of bright and essentially insignificant stories (*Ninotchka, Trouble in Paradise, That Uncertain Feeling, If I Had a Million*). Lubitsch's films are preoccupied with sex rather than passion; with manners, rather than emotions. His characters, his inflections, and his stories play exquisite variations on the theme of *liaison intime*. The humor is Gallic, charged with double entendres, rich in urbanity. William Wyler (*These Three, Dodsworth, Jezebel, Wuthering Heights, The Little Foxes, Dead End*) instills tragic intuitions and a sense of nemesis into his movies. The characters are stalked by doom; a brooding uneasiness dominates the scenes and lends tension to the episodes.

Leo McCarey is equally gifted in handling comedy, tragedy, and farce. His work ranges from *Ruggles of Red Gap*, one of the best comedies ever made, to *Make Way for Tomorrow*, one of the finest tragedies the screen has seen, to *The Awful Truth*, a farce of expert construction. McCarey's work is subtle, intricated, exact, and shows immense inventiveness in comic characterization and dramatic "business."

Frank Capra's films are distinguished by the kind of characters and situations into which Capra breathes his special attitude: simple, "human" people in funny but moving predicaments reminiscent of the folk tale. The stories which Capra brings to the screen are remarkably similar, and they can be reduced to a single phrase: the pure in heart always triumph.

Every Capra picture has overtones of aspiration; every Capra character has undertones of frustration. Every Capra picture contains one long, intense sequence in which suffering is maximized: the courtroom scene in *Mr. Deeds,* the stable and race sequences in *Broadway Bill,* the filibuster in *Mr. Smith Goes to Washington,* the ball-park episode in *Meet John Doe.* Capra plunges his characters—and his audiences—into the agony which arises from the persecution of innocents. He is forever telling the story of a symbolic crucifixion: Mr. Deeds, Mr. Smith, John Doe, even Broadway Bill are modern Christs persecuted by the worldly and the corrupt.

It is not the intention of this book to explore the esthetics or technique of movie direction. But a conception of the role which the director plays in movie making is essential to an understanding of the movies and the movie makers. The uproarious nonsense of *My Man Godfrey* rose from the bold manner in which Gregory La Cava handled preposterous situations, and the faultless treatment of a psychopathic problem in *Private Worlds* is directly attributable to the same director. Such films as *The Life of Émile Zola* or *The Story of Louis Pasteur* testify to the dignity of the conception of William Dieterle. And one sees the signature of Frank Borzage in *Man's Castle,* of King Vidor in *The Big Parade* or *The Crowd;* of Sam Wood in *Our Town* or *Goodbye, Mr. Chips;* of Orson Welles in every moment of *Citizen Kane.*

It is the director who *tells* the story, and the story-teller can shape the story to his ends. Given the same story, different directors would emerge with entirely different movies. Take *Cyrano de Bergerac,* for example. In the hands of director John Stahl, the picture would probably be played entirely from the viewpoint of Roxane rather than Cyrano; there would certainly be a death-bed scene in which Roxane, having spurned the pure soul of Cyrano for the empty pulchritude of Christian, awoke—

after endless agony—to the folly of her ways. Leo McCarey would probably have Cyrano marry Roxane in the first reel, to spite Christian, and she would remain in love with Christian for the remainder of the play. A director of B pictures would make Rostand's play a story about "a long-nosed guy" who, at the end, undergoes an operation by the world's greatest plastic surgeon. Frank Capra's Cyrano would be a shy commoner-poet in the service of the aristocrat Christian; Roxane would know that Cyrano is being used for Christian's ends, would collaborate in a cynical deception, and would end in self-purification because of the discovery that she has fallen in love with none other than Cyrano himself. Busby Berkeley would, of course, produce a musical comedy, with Cyrano as a song-writer instead of a poet: Jimmy Durante would be cast in the central role and there would be gigantic dance numbers under the Eiffel Tower; at the end it all turns out to have been a dream. Frank Lloyd might place the entire production aboard a ship. Howard Hawks, fresh from *His Girl Friday* (a remake of *The Front Page*), might make Cyrano a woman. Alfred Hitchcock would toy with the thought of making Cyrano a member of the French intelligence service who sends code messages via poetic recitations: the nose was false all along. And some directors would shoot Rostand's original story—and probably lose a fortune for the studio which risked it.

It is the director who tells the story on the screen.

Let us analyze the directors as a professional group. There are around 250 members of the Screen Directors Guild in Hollywood. The data which follow are based on elaborate questionnaire materials filled out by sixty-nine directors—a sample large enough and representative enough to permit generalization—and on materials collected from many other sources.*

* Complete tables on all the data which follow are in Appendices C through F.

Age. Hollywood's directors (66 cases) range in age from 21
ɔ 59 (as of 1940). The median average age is 43.

>1.5 percent are under 30 years of age.
>31.8 percent are 30-39 years of age.
>50.0 percent are 40-49 years of age.
>16.7 percent are 50 years of age or over.

Exactly one-third of the directors in the movie colony are
nder 40. Exactly half of the directors are between 40 and 50
ears old. Using other intervals, we find 10.6 percent of the
irectors are under 35; 48.5 percent are between 35 and 45; and
4.2 percent are between 45 and 49.

Compared to the producers: about the same percentage of
irectors and producers are under 30; slightly more directors
ɾe between 30 and 39; slightly more directors are 40-49; but
ɪbstantially less are 50 years of age or over.

Compared to Hollywood's writers: far fewer directors are
nder 30 (14.1 percent of the writers; 1.5 percent of the direc-
ɔrs); far fewer directors are 30 to 39 years old (31.8 percent
s against 43.5); twice as many directors are 40-49 years old
50 percent as against 26.6 for the writers), and almost the same
ercentage are 50 years of age or over (16.7 for directors as
gainst 15.8 for writers).

Compared to the actors: a much larger percentage of actors
15.8) than directors are under 30; almost the same percent are
ɔ to 39 years of age; far more directors are 40 to 49 years old
50 percent as compared to 18.0 for the actors); but 35 percent
f the actors are 50 years of age or over as compared to only
3.7 percent of the directors.

Birthplace. Out of 94 directors,* 67 (71.3 percent) were born
ι the United States, and 27 (28.7 percent) are of foreign birth;
1.9 percent were born in the United States and Canada. The

* Birthplace data were not taken from questionnaire replies; the birthplaces of
ɔvie directors were taken from the *Motion Picture Almanac.*

countries from which Hollywood's directors come can be in
dicated briefly:

	Percent
Germany	6.3
Great Britain	5.3
Russia	5.3
Hungary	2.1
Austria	2.1
France, Ireland, Australia, Italy: 1.1 percent each	

The discussion in an earlier chapter explained why, in a
probability, more directors are of foreign birth than actors (25.
percent), producers (17.4 percent), or writers (13.9 percent)

Education. For the sixty-six directors on whom accurate in
formation was available:

10.6 percent had no formal education beyond the grammar schoo
level.
36.4 percent went only to high school.
53.0 percent went to college.
25.7 percent received a college degree.
12.1 percent received a college degree and took post-graduat
work.

Two directors hold doctorate degrees, one is a Phi Beta Kapp;
and one was graduated *cum laude.*

Compared to Hollywood's producers: approximately the sam
percentage of directors attended grammar school only an
high school only, and a slightly smaller proportion of directo
(53 percent as compared to 57 percent of the producers) wer
to college. But almost twice as many directors received degree
(24.6 as against 13.8 percent). The same percentage of dire
tors and producers undertook post-graduate work.

Compared to actors: more directors went to college (53 pe
cent as compared to 49.8 percent for the actors), but far mor
directors have only had a grammar school education (10.6 a
against 2.8 percent). More actors have had high school trainin

clusively (47.4 percent as against 36.4 percent for the direc-
rs).

Compared to writers: directors, like all the other professional
oups in Hollywood, are substantially below the writers in
ademic training. The 53 percent of the directors who went to
llege are overshadowed by the 80.5 percent of the writers.
ut almost the same percentage went on to post-graduate work.

Experience. An analysis of the professional experience of
ollywood's directors shows:

PROFESSIONAL EXPERIENCE IN HOLLYWOOD

69 Directors

Number of Years	Percent
25 and over	20.3
20-25	20.3
15-20	14.5
10-15	21.7
5-10	14.5
5 or less	8.7

other words:

40.6 percent have worked in Hollywood for over 20 years, in one
capacity or another.
36.2 percent have worked in Hollywood for 10-20 years.
14.5 percent have worked in Hollywood for 5-10 years.
8.7 percent have worked in Hollywood for 5 years or less.

Compared to Hollywood's producers: a larger percentage of
rectors have worked *in Hollywood* for 20 or more years (40.6
rcent as against the producers' 30.4); a larger percentage of
rectors have worked in Hollywood for 15 or more years (55.1
against 47.1 percent for the producers); far fewer directors
an producers have worked in Hollywood for 10 years or less
3.2 percent for the directors, 41.1 percent for the producers).

Let us ask a more specific question: How long have the movie
rectors worked *as directors* in Hollywood? Here the facts are
mewhat surprising: more than one-third of the men (67

cases) who are Hollywood's directors today (34.3 percent) began directing pictures since 1935. In other words, although over half of the directors have worked in films in Hollywood for at least 15 years, and over two-fifths for 20 years, more than a third of the directors did not become directors until (years ago. Half of the directors in Hollywood stepped into the directorial ranks after the advent of talking pictures (1928-29) Almost a fourth of the directors (23.9 percent) have been direc tors in Hollywood for 15 years or more. Over a third (34.3 per cent) of the directors active in Hollywood today, *began* direct ing movies in 1935-39. (This is a substantially larger percentage than can be found for any earlier five-year period. The increase in the number of pictures Hollywood produced—because of double features—the replacement of old directors with younger men, and other factors would explain this.)

What is the *nature* of the experience—in Hollywood—which the film directors of the movie colony have had? An analysis of the professional backgrounds reveals that the following movie jobs were held by sixty-six directors *prior to* their present occu pation: *

	Percent
Assistant directors (associate, dialogue, technical)	62.1
Writers	25.8
Actors	16.7
Production (assistant producers, producers, unit managers)	15.2
Cameramen or camera departments	15.2
Property department	12.1
Film editors (cutters, assistant cutters)	10.6
Script clerks	9.1

The high percentage of directors who were assistant director is to be expected. The fact that a fourth of Hollywood's direc

* The percentages are obviously not meant to total 100, since each director ha worked in several fields.

tors were movie writers is significant and unexpected. The relatively small percentage (10.6) of directors who have been film editors is contrary to the general impression held in the movie colony.

What kind of experience did the directors have *before* they came to Hollywood as movie makers?

36.0 percent had had experience in some phase of movies outside of Hollywood before they came to Hollywood.

32.8 percent had had experience on the legitimate stage, but not in movies.

15.6 percent had never worked either in films or on the stage.

15.6 percent had never been employed in any industry except motion pictures.

Now let us ask what job in Hollywood's studios the directors held just before they began directing. In other words, what occupations served as direct springboards to movie direction as a career?

47.0 percent of the directors were drafted from the ranks of the assistant directors, dialogue directors, technical directors, etc.

15.2 percent began their Hollywood careers as directors; *i.e.*, they either started as directors, in the days of silent films, or were brought to Hollywood as directors from the stage or the movie field outside Hollywood.

10.6 percent entered movie direction via film editing.

7.6 percent were actors just before they began directing.*

6.1 percent were working in some aspect of movie production before becoming directors.

4.6 percent were movie writers just before they began directing.

3.0 percent were cameramen.

Earnings. The amount of money paid to movie directors is a potent testimonial to the importance which the motion picture industry attaches to their talents. Even in the silent days, a top film director could command $100,000 for a single picture, and recently Gregory La Cava was paid $150,000 for directing one

---

* This pattern was popular in the days of silent films; it rarely, if ever, occurs today: the director's job has become much more specialized.

film.[4] In replies to questionnaires, 6 out of 67 directors (9 percent) wrote that they have earned as high as $4,000 a week sometime in their careers as Hollywood directors; 4 (6 percent) have earned $5,000 or more a week. When directors attain producer-director status, they can earn as high as $6,000 a week (Mervyn LeRoy's contract at MGM guaranteed him $300,000 a year).

In 1938, forty-five directors earned over $75,000.[*] Thirty-four directors earned $100,000 or more:

Frank Capra	$294,166	William A. Wellman	$136,805
W. S. Van Dyke	216,750	Henry King	133,500
Roy del Ruth	216,741	David W. Butler	133,000
Wesley Ruggles	199,061	George Stevens	130,416
John Ford	196,791	George Cukor	125,883
John Stahl	196,000	Alfred Santel	122,000
Clarence Brown	188,708	Henry Koster	118,916
Jack Conway	182,000	William Seiter	117,583
Lloyd Bacon	179,125	Anatole Litvak	117,857
Michael Curtiz	171,000	Henry Hathaway	115,541
Edmund Goulding	168,916	Mitchell Leisen	115,000
Archie Mayo	167,812	Howard Hawks	112,500
Frank Borzage	166,083	Raoul Walsh	107,083
Victor Fleming	156,000	Irving Cummings	105,000
Norman Taurog	156,000	Rowland V. Lee	104,375
Frank Lloyd	150,749	Gregory Ratoff	104,333
King Vidor	137,666	Gregory La Cava	100,000

Is this formidable array of earnings typical? No, obviously, since it singles out the ranking directors of Hollywood. Let us take a more representative view. Sixty-two directors reported, in questionnaires, that their annual earnings ranged from $1,500 to $200,000 in 1938. The median annual earnings for directors was $16,500![†]

[*] See *The Movie Elite*, p. 60.

[†] Four directors did not work at all, or did not work as directors in 1938; two directors worked as directors only part of the year, and to have used the earnings reported would have been misleading. It is quite probable that our sample is weighted towards the lower end of the earning and income scale: *i.e.*, that a larger percentage of the lower income directors filed their returns than directors in the

ANNUAL EARNINGS (1938)

	Percent of Directors
Under $5,000	12.9
$5,000-$9,999	17.7
$10,000-$19,999	22.6
$25,000-$49,999	16.2
$50,000-$99,999	9.7
$100,000-$200,000	19.3

These figures indicate that:

30.6 percent of the directors who worked in Hollywood in 1938 earned less than $10,000 for the year.
Over two-thirds (69.4 percent) earned $10,000 or more.
45.2 percent earned $25,000 or over.
Well over a fourth (29 percent) earned $50,000 or more.
Over a fifth (22.5 percent) earned $75,000 or over.*
Almost a fifth (19.3 percent) earned $100,000 or more.

At three major studios which provided payroll information to this writer (Warner Brothers, Twentieth Century-Fox, Columbia) the following pattern of salaries prevailed for forty directors:

Weekly Salary (1938)	Directors	Percent
Under $250	3	7.5
$250-$499	8	20.0
$500-$999	11	27.5
$1,000-$1,499	4	10.0
$1,500-$1,999	3	7.5
$2,000-$2,499	3	7.5
$2,500 and over	8	20.0

top income brackets. The former group generally co-operate more than the latter, for obvious reasons: they volunteer information more freely in the hope that they can improve their status by presenting certain facts. High-earning groups, in any occupation, are more content, more defensive about revealing information about their income, less co-operative in filling out questionnaires. It is probable, therefore, that the analysis of earnings based on questionnaire materials presents a less favorable picture of the directors as a group than the facts about *all* the directors in Hollywood, if available, would show.

* The forty-five directors who earned $75,000 or more in 1938, according to the salary lists published by government agencies, constitute about one-fifth of the 235 directors in the Screen Directors Guild. Note how this tends to confirm the representativeness and reliability of the questionnaire data, which showed 19.3 percent of our sample as earning $75,000 or more in 1938.

Weekly salaries are, of course, not indications of actual earnings. A director on a salary of $1,000 a week may work only twelve weeks in the course of the year; another getting $500 a week may work forty weeks and so earn more. Besides, many directors work at more than one studio during the year.

In Hollywood, we have seen, the fluctuations in earnings are violent. This is true of movie directors as well as actors or writers. To emphasize the point, let us look at the earnings for three years of seven movie directors.

ANNUAL EARNINGS

	1936	1937	1938
A.	$ 12,000	$ 12,000	$ 36,000
B.	62,500	7,500	87,000
C.	45,833	143,000	50,500
D.	80,000	40,000	7,000
E.	20,000	16,000	2,500
F.	30,000	75,000	none
G.	238,000	150,000	130,000

In some instances, of course, sharp changes in earnings are the result of the director's decision rather than his misfortune. The directors who earn huge sums per week or per picture often refuse employment on pictures or stories which they do not wish to direct. Some directors, after a particularly successful picture or a particularly successful year, will loaf for a while. Some, aware of the diminishing returns effected by sharply graduated income taxes, do not care to exert themselves after passing $75,000 or $100,000 per annum earnings. In 1938, for example, Leo McCarey received only $77,500; he surely could have received twice as much had he been concerned only with making money. But it is safe to assume that any director who earns under $50,000 a year exercises no choice in the matter.

The questionnaire filled out by Hollywood's directors contained several queries on salary and income which offer extremely interesting information. Let us ask, first: What was the *original* weekly salary which movie directors in Hollywood received? Sixty-eight answers were obtained to this question. The directors in Hollywood began directing at salaries ranging from $50 to $3,500 a week. Almost a fourth of the directors (23.6 percent) received $50-149 a week when they started directing in movies; 30.9 percent received $150-249; 23.5 percent received $250-499; 11.8 percent received $500-999; 10.3 percent got $1,000 and over per week. The median average for first weekly salary as a director was $200.

But weekly salaries, we have said, can be very misleading: How much did the movie directors earn in their first year as Hollywood directors?

11.7 percent earned under $5,000 in their first year as directors.

One-fourth (26.7 percent) earned under $7,500 in their first year as directors.

Exactly half of the directors received under $10,000 a year in their first year as directors; half received $10,000 or more.

Exactly one-fourth (25 percent) earned $20,000 or over in their first directorial year.

8.4 percent of our group earned $50,000-100,000 in their first year as directors.

The median average earnings for the directors in their first year of work as Hollywood directors was $9,900. The range of first annual earnings was, naturally, very great: $2,600-100,000.

What has been the *highest* weekly salary which the movie directors in Hollywood have ever received? The highest weekly salaries ever received, by directors active today, range from $125 to $5,000. The median "highest weekly salary" is $1,000.

Half the directors in Hollywood today have earned $1,000 or more per week at some point in their career.

Almost three-fourths of the directors in our sample (73.1 percent) have earned $500 or more per week.

22.5 percent have earned $3,000 a week or more at some time.

7.5 percent have never earned as much as $250 a week.

An analysis of the earnings-pattern of movie directors shows a constant rise in the trend of weekly salaries. But more directors have *not* received increases in salary over a long span (or have suffered actual decreases from some high point in earlier years) than is ordinarily supposed. Thus:

Three-fourths of the directors (74.5 percent) have received higher weekly salaries since 1935 than in any preceding year.

One-fourth received a higher weekly salary at some time *before* 1935.

The case of certain old-timers is illustrated by the fact that slightly over one-tenth of the directors (11.1 percent) earned their highest weekly salary *before* 1927.*

Marital Status. The analysis of marriage and divorce among the movie makers, including the directors, has been presented in several places earlier in this book.† At this point let us simply recapitulate the salient facts on marital status for the sixty-eight directors who reported:

19.1 percent are single today.

80.9 percent are married today.

Sixty-one directors (89.7 percent) are or have been married. A slightly smaller percentage of directors are married today than producers (88.2 percent) or writers (87.7 percent), but a considerably larger percentage than actors (68.4).

Of the sixty-one directors who are or have been married:

32 have probably been married only once.

12 have probably been married twice.

1 has probably been married three times.

3 have probably been married four times.

13 did not state the number of times they have been married.

---

* These figures should be interpreted with some caution. If a director testified that he received his highest weekly salary, say $500, in 1932 there are two possible interpretations: (1) that he has received under $500 a week since; (2) that he has continued to receive the same amount. He may have meant that 1932 was the year in which he first received $500 and that he has not received more than $500 a week since then.

† Chapters 5 and 12.

Fifty-seven directors reported on the number of children they have had: 17 have no children, 18 each have 1 child, 15 have 2 children, 5 have 3 children, 2 have 4 children.

Attitudes, Preferences, Complaints. In the questionnaire circulated to Hollywood's directors, this question was asked: *"If salary were no consideration,* what position in the industry would you most prefer? . . . Why?" Such a query offers a useful index of aspiration, a gauge by which to measure the individual's adjustment to a professional job. It is important, accordingly, to notice that very few movie directors would prefer to be anything but directors if they could choose their craft. Of sixty-eight directors who answered the question:

> 58.8 percent said they preferred to remain directors.
> 29.4 percent said they would like to be directors who also produced their own pictures (and would therefore have more freedom over their work).

Only 5.8 percent said they would want to be producers alone.*

In other words, 88.2 percent of Hollywood's directors prefer to remain directors. The comments which were written to support the occupational preference were emphatic in stressing the "creative," "exciting," "thrilling" aspects of movie direction. Many directors remarked that they "liked," "loved," or "enjoyed" directing. Many commented on directing as a "medium for self-expression."

A second question presented to the directors offers a valuable insight into their collective attitude: "What are your chief complaints about working as a director?" Here was a wide-open opportunity for the expression of grievances: the question was deliberately formulated in the most general and unsuggestive manner. The answers (65) were illuminating. Few directors complained about the conditions of their work. Few complained

---

* Only one director said he would like to be an actor, and two directors said they would prefer to be directors who also wrote.

about their working hours. Few complained about the irregularity of employment. Few complained about salaries. Few complained about promotional opportunities. What, then, did the directors select as the object of their discontent?

35.4 percent complained (and vigorously) against "stupid supervision," "supervision by inexperienced persons," "producers' stupidity," and so on.

30.8 percent complained (and strongly) about "lack of contact with story," "lack of sufficient story preparation," "inane stories."

29.2 percent complained about a combination of matters which we can lump under the category, "thwarted craftsmanship": insufficient time to do their work, too much pressure during the making of a picture, censorship, the lack of opportunity for initiative and self-expression, and so on.

It is especially noteworthy that 15.4 percent of Hollywood's directors made *no complaints at all*. The directors want greater opportunities for self-expression, for creative freedom, for individuality. They want, in other words, to do more of what they are doing. Even more than the other talent groups in the movie colony, they love their work.

Let us see how this pattern is fortified by the answers to still a third question: "In what specific ways could your working relationship be improved?" Here, again, was an open field for the directors to express their views. The answers (54) were revealing. No directors made suggestions concerning the physical conditions or hours of their work. Only 1.8 percent complained about insecurity and contracts. None complained about materials. Few complained about promotional opportunities. Few complained about nepotism in the studios. But

48.1 percent of the directors asked for "a freer rein in making pictures," "less interference," "making director responsible to one producer alone."

22.2 percent urged that the director be placed in closer working contact with writers, or film editors, or casting directors, asking for greater authority on stories, scripts, cast, sets, and so on.

16.6 percent made suggestions which arise from thwarted craftsmanship: "more time for preparation," more opportunities "to direct
as I see it," and so on.

12.9 percent of the directors made no suggestions at all or remarked
that their relationship to the studios "is perfectly okay."

If we combine the answers to the two questions ("What are
our chief complaints . . . ? In what specific ways could your
working relationship be improved?") we can construct the con-
tellation of grievances and discontents of Hollywood's direc-
ors.

COMPLAINTS AND SUGGESTIONS
(66 Directors)

	Percent
Supervision: kind, quality, or amount	56.06
Relationship to other groups: writing, casting, editing, music, sets	40.91
Thwarted craftsmanship: censorship, pressure of time, lack of preparation, more opportunity for self-expression	34.84
Method of operation or organization	9.09
Salary and related matters (salary rate, vacations, overtime pay)	7.58
Insecurity, irregularity of employment, contracts	4.55
Promotion (opportunity, discrimination, favoritism)	4.55
Hours (long, irregular, week-ends)	3.03
Nepotism	3.03
Physical conditions	none
No complaints	12.12

Directors and Writers. At the suggestion of the Screen Directors Guild the following question was put into the questionnaire circulated to the directors: "Would you prefer to work
with writers in preparing scripts for pictures you want to direct?" The response left no doubt that Hollywood's directors
strongly favor closer collaboration between writers and directors. No less than 82.5 percent of the directors answered the
question affirmatively. (20.2 percent were particularly emphatic

299

and wrote in "Yes! Yes!" "Decidedly!" and so on.) Only on director answered in the negative.

The reasons given by the directors for urging wider collabor tion with writers can be illustrated in a few excerpts: "It is th director who has to translate the script to the screen." "Ver few writers understand how to write action so that it can b photographed." "Want to get my ideas into the story." "Stor problems could be solved *before* shooting began." "Save cos and headaches." "The director has the camera point of view "Would get better relations between directors, writers and pr ducers."

Professional collaboration between movie directors and mov writers is, as a matter of fact, very widely practiced—by th leading directors. (7.3 percent of the directors answered tha they are collaborating with writers now.) But this collaboratio occurs only on the uppermost levels of movie making—whe leading directors can select their stories and their writers, an can work on a screenplay from the first idea to the finished fil The directors want the collaborative method to be used mo often and more widely. Whether the writers do is another ma ter . . .

The movie director and the movie writer are always collab rating—whether they know it or not, whether they prefer it not. The director needs a script to shoot; the writer needs director to put his script on the screen. The way in which director shoots a script—the photographic angles, the inflection the pace, the mood,—is, in effect, a new interpretation of wha the writer has written. Directors cut speeches, change charac ters, revise plot, introduce gags, invent bits of dramatic "bus ness"—in short, they put *their* conception of a story on th screen. The making of a film requires a combination of the skil and insights of both directors and writers.

It would seem that collaboration between movie directors an writers is as natural as co-operation between librettists and com

osers, or architects and contractors. The difficulty lies in the
ict that few directors and writers can work together amicably.
'he creative process and the creative personality do not lend
iemselves easily to partnership. The writers want the directors
> shoot the scripts which the writers write; the directors want
ie writers to write the scripts which the directors want to shoot.
lost directors think there are very few writers who understand
ie screen and the special needs of the screen; most writers
iink that there are few directors who can appreciate a story
'hich departs from the routine. Most directors think that
/riters "fall in love" with their characters and situations, and
)se sight of the moving picture as a technique; most writers
iink that directors want to be writers themselves, cannot resist
ie congenital urge to make changes for the sake of making
hanges, and introduce appalling clichés of characterization and
urpose into stories which aim at freshness and individuality.

Both the directors and the writers are right. The basic point
; that there are few directors and writers who can work to-
ether; there are few whose egocentrism (inevitable in those
'ho live by fantasy) can endure the demands, the rebuffs, and
he concessions which collaboration imposes upon those who
ry it. When a director and writer do perform as a single crea-
ive team, the results are salutary. This writer believes that
lirector-writer teams have produced the best films in Holly-
vood. For example: the films resulting from the collaboration
f John Ford and Dudley Nichols; Frank Capra and Robert
liskin; Alfred Hitchcock, Joan Harrison, and Charles Bennett;
Vesley Ruggles and Claude Binyon; and Leo McCarey, Orson
Velles, Gregory LaCava, Garson Kanin, and whatever writers
hey work with.

The movie director, it should be noted, does not create *ab
nitio:* he works with a script which writers have written; he
lirects actors who strive to interpret roles *their* way; he em-
)loys cameras, lights, sets, music which other creators have

devised. The director is, therefore, in the curious psychological position of being accorded deference which is high—but ambiguous, because of the "synthetic" character of his work. Many directors protest that their importance in movie making is underestimated; they think that writers are given too much praise for the screenplay, that actors get too much praise for their performances. Many directors, that is, are certain that it is *their* direction which lends life and conviction to a script; that it is *their* direction which is responsible for the subtlety or effectiveness of an actor's performance.

There is some truth in this; but there is just as much truth in the fact that no director works miracles: the director needs a script which is competent and actors who can act. Such a top flight director as Garson Kanin has said, "Anybody can direct a good picture if he's got a good script"; and Gilbert Seldes who calls the director the most important figure in movie making, has remarked that "ninety percent of the judgments delivered on the quality of directors is really concerned with the thoughts and ideas presented ready-made for the directors to work on." [5]

Directors and Producers. No less an authority than Irving Thalberg made the statement that it is the director who is responsible for the story which appears on the screen.[6] This is true, *if* the director has had any choice or influence over the story which he is given to direct. In April of 1939, Frank Capra, President of the Guild, wrote an open letter to a movie columnist on the New York *Times* in which he said, "About six producers today pass upon 90 percent of the scripts, and cut and edit 90 percent of the pictures."

. . . there are only half a dozen directors in Hollywood who are allowed to shoot as they please and who have any supervision over their editing. We all agree with you when you say that motion pictures are the director's medium. . . . [But] we have tried for three years . . . to have two weeks' preparation time for "A" pictures, one week preparation

302

time for "B" pictures and to have supervision of just the first rough cut of the picture. . . . We have only asked that the director be allowed to read the script he is going to do and to assemble the film in its first rough form. . . . It has taken three years of constant battling to achieve any part of this.

I would say that 80 percent of the directors today shoot scenes exactly as they are told to shoot them without any changes whatsoever, and that 90 percent of them have no voice in the story or in the editing. . . .*

Hollywood's directors are hostile to the producers because the directors want to do their job in their own way, according to their vision and talent. The producers complain that directors "go off half-cocked," do not watch costs, and sacrifice movie showmanship to "arty" and pretentious shots. The director feels stifled by producers who combine a lack of special skill or general sensitivity with maudlin ideas and mediocre tastes. The producers feel irritated by directors who forget that movies are made (1) to tell a story, (2) to make money.

It is the firm conviction of the Screen Directors' Guild that rehabilitation lies, first in changing the present "system of production" which pervades the Industry, namely, eliminating the involved, complicated and expensive system of supervision which separates the Director and Writer from the responsible Executive Producers . . .

The significant fact remains that even today the best pictures made in the Industry are largely those in which the Director has had real participation in their dramatic and mechanical structure . . . in direct association with the Executive Producers without the interference of intermediaries.

. . . the Directors' Guild earnestly recommends that closer unity be established and maintained between the real Producer on the one hand and the Director and Writer on the other . . .[7]

It is rather surprising to find W. R. Wilkerson of the *Hollywood Reporter* on the same side:

---

* Capra also said, "I believe the blame is as much the director's as it is due to the mass-production system, because directors are prone to sit back and enjoy their fat salaries and forget the responsibilities they have toward the medium they are in.[8]

303

. . . A director . . . must know a lot more about production than the majority of individuals who are now vested with production authority under the common heading of "associate producers" . . . the director [has been] hampered too much, through a system that necessitated [his listening] to people who, in most cases, did not know what they were talking about.[9]

We bring this chapter on Hollywood's directors to a close with a few words on their evaluation of American movies. The invitation to "Comment on American movies today" drew written answers from fifty-three directors. Well over half (54.7 percent) made entirely unfavorable remarks on Hollywood's movies. About a fourth of the directors mingled their criticism with praise. A tenth (9.4 percent) were entirely favorable in their remarks on the content of movies.

The largest number of directors criticized the lack of "originality" or "individuality" in films. The comments clustered around these typical phrases: "too stereotyped," "factory made," "too much reliance on formula," "all carefully treading in each other's footsteps." Over a fifth of the directors (22 percent) criticized run-of-the-mill stories and typical pictures: "weak stories," "too many gangster pictures," and so on. Over a tenth of the directors (12 percent) complained about the manner in which stories were handled: "too much talk," "missing the human element," "not enough action." All the comments apropos the star system, censorship, the quantity production of films, and the economic pressures of the industry were entirely unfavorable.

There were, naturally, many contradictory opinions. Some directors complained that Hollywood is producing "the same old stories done in the same old way"; others said Hollywood "is progressing all the time." Some wrote, "the artistic approach is pretty punk"; others remarked that Hollywood "is rapidly progressing in artistry."

The comments can be summarized in four sentences: Hollywood's directors are critical, above all else, of the amount of originality and imagination in the movies today. They are concerned with the type of story and picture which is in vogue. They rebel against censorship and the factors ordinarily believed to enhance box-office appeal (*e.g.*, the star system). And one-tenth of the directors remarked that the intelligence of the American audience is being underestimated by Hollywood's producers.

14. THE WRITERS

WHEN an author writes a novel or a play, he simply invests his time, energy, and talent. It takes little capital; it entails little risk. But when a writer works for a studio, he becomes an *employee* engaged in the manufacture of an extremely expensive commodity. And there is the key to many of the problems, dilemmas, and agonies of the writer in Hollywood. He is an employee. The roots of the screen writer's discontent lie in the very manner in which a writer works, in the continual rebuffs which he endures in Hollywood, and in the position which he holds in the movie structure—a position for which, by temperament and experience, he is utterly unprepared.

To the writer, the most gratifying part of writing is the absolute sovereignty he enjoys over his work. He possesses irrevocable authority over his characters, plot, and phrases. He is king in the universe of his fantasy. Judgment can be passed only upon his finished work: it can be praised or damned or ignored; but no one can change a word or a mark of punctuation. Writers satisfy the yearning for omnipotence in their work, for in their work they are omnipotent.

All this vanishes when a writer sits down behind a desk in a studio in Hollywood. He is no longer a creator working within the self-bounded, one-dimensional world of self-expression; he is an employee. He is instructed to adapt a novel for which he has little respect. He is handed collaborators whom he dislikes. He is ordered to introduce a tap dancer into a story about an African safari. He is asked to "add a few jokes" to the scene he has fought to keep poignant; or to "speed up the story" at precisely the point where he wanted to develop the characters; or to invent a "smart" but unnatural opening, or a "sock" but phony climax. He is an employee.

The very purpose of Hollywood's producers is opposed to the basic motivation of writers. The producer asks, "Will it make money?" The writer asks, "Will it make sense?" The producer wants to gratify popular taste; the writer wants to improve it. The producer wants to make pictures which make a profit; the writer wants to write pictures which make him feel proud. The producer wants to "entertain" the audience; the writer wants to move, influence, or enlighten the public.

Since the producer is paying the writer to do a job, he expects the writer to do the job or quit. But since the producer has hired the writer to write, the writer expects to be allowed to put *his* conceptions and characters on the screen. The paradox lies in the fact that often the writer's version of what will make money is better than the producer's, and sometimes the producer's showmanship and "hunches" rescue the writer's work from pretentious and static nobility. Since there are no criteria with which to measure the *probable* effectiveness or profitability of a story or a scene, both writers and producers are proved to be wrong in their judgment as often as they are proved to be right. A producer's story slant often makes a picture successful at the box-office; but his interference with the logic and mood of a story more often proves disastrous to its success. The same may be said of writers, who can hardly be objective about their own work. The important point is that the writer is deeply offended because he must accept the authority of someone else over the thing he has created—someone who is not a writer, somone whose manners may be gross, whose instincts may be

307

crude, whose intelligence is too often opaque to subtleties and originality.

The Hollywood writer is not writing prose or producing literature. He is feeding an enormous machine that converts words, faces, sounds, and images into some nine thousand feet of celluloid. His material is thrown into the hopper of movie making, where other men and minds, other preferences and prejudices, grind it into pieces and champ it into a pattern no one of them completely controls or envisages.

Screen writers are compelled to write for a mass market. They often rail against the producers, the directors, the Code, or "the system" when they are, in reality, rebelling against the task of creating entertainment for over 50,000,000 people instead of the select minority for whom they had once written stories or novels or plays.

The clash between creative desires and movie costs arises a hundred times a week. The conflict between the writer's screenplay and the requirements of the sound stage was neatly illustrated by Norman Krasna, writer, co-producer, and author of *The Devil and Miss Jones:*

. . . Jean Arthur walked briskly from the counter, to the pillar, talking to Charles Coburn. Sam Wood [the director] traced the walk with the camera, the microphone hovered over the pair. It was a wonderful scene. Suspense, charm, and a touch of pathos. And the best thing about it was that it was the right length.

Miss Arthur walked and talked. When she stopped talking she was four feet from the pillar. Sam Wood turned to the author. . . . Sam wanted more words. No, no, pleaded the author. Couldn't Miss Arthur walk a little faster? Miss Arthur tried. But since she had been walking briskly in the first place, it soon developed that if the author was going to insist on letter-pure, comma-perfect [script], Miss Arthur would play this particular scene at a trot. Shall I be brief? *The Devil and Miss Jones* was not shot letter-pure, comma-perfect, or even close. . . .[1]

The writer who has tasted the joys of independent creation is thrown into abysmal discontent by Hollywood. He wants to write something in which he "believes." He wants to set down his honest conceptions—of people, emotions, events—without making compromises to costs, "business sense," "a fourteen-year-old public," or other demons in the producers' cosmology. The writer rebels against the necessity of inventing people who do not carry conviction, or situations which corrupt the integrity of his work. He becomes steeped in dissatisfaction with the "bilge" he writes to order. He develops a sense of guilt about his "betrayal" of his talents and his intelligence. He finds it hard to cope with the sense of futility which overpowers him in the middle of another story about the heiress and the reporter, the duchess and the jewel thief. He becomes guilty about the amount of money he is receiving for work for which he has no respect. He cannot suppress the self-indicting feeling that he ought to be writing "something significant."

The Hollywood writer is always plagued by the idea that he could write a fine book or play—if only he could break the bonds of Hollywood. Most writers in the movie colony echo the words of Dalton Trumbo: "The system under which writers work [in Hollywood] would sap the vitality of a Shakespeare. They are intelligent enough to know that they are writing trash but they are not intelligent enough to do anything about it." [2] But it is not a question of intelligence; it is a question of power, economics, reality, and personality structure.

The writer, like the composer or the painter, identifies himself with his work. Praise of his work is praise of himself; criticism of his work is a blow to his pride. The producer needs great tact and insight to make a writer feel that displeasure with his story is not tantamount to dissatisfaction with the author; the director who can reject a scene without affronting a writer's ego is rare. And the writer whose work is appraised by a producer or director whom he considers unliterate is in the position of a painter who is told by a blind man that his colors are false. It does not take much reflection to understand the rage generated in a writer by a producer's *obiter dictum* to the effect that "the dialogue don't add up, and the characters ain't refined," or by a director's insistence that "women aren't that way; change the scene."

The fact that words are used to exercise authority intensifies the writer's antagonism. For the writer is an expert in words and feels superior to his superiors when words are used. The writer often complains about the producer's decisions when he really is contemptuous of the producer's vocabulary. In story conferences, the crude personality and the verbal ineptitude of the producer (or the director) goad the writer into hostility—and when he loses his points he saves his pride by a consciousness of his intellectual superiority to the men who have overruled him.

It is significant that the writers who find it easiest to adjust to Hollywood are (1) writers who have served as writer-employees before coming to Hollywood (newspapermen, advertising writers, publicists), (2) writers who have written only for the screen. These men do not invest too much self-esteem in their work; they do not feel personally rebuffed by either the criticism or the manners of producers. They indulge in few illusions about their artistic prerogatives. They accept the *conditions* of screen writing as well as the weekly checks, and recognize the necessary conjunction of the two. "For a thousand a week," one cynical scrivener said, "I'd dramatize the Sears, Roebuck catalogue for a producer who couldn't spell 'cat.'" It is the story-carpenters of Hollywood—tough-skinned, pragmatic—who mock their colleagues in a refrain which is famous in the movie colony: "They ruin your stories. They massacre your ideas. They prostitute your art. They trample on your pride. And what do you get for it? A fortune."

The reader has probably been dazed, at one time or another, by the battery of writers' names which is often flashed on the screen: 310

THE WRITERS

Screenplay
Noel Langley
Florence Ryerson
Edgar Allan Woolf

From the book by
L. Frank Baum

Adaptation
Noel Langley

or:

JUAREZ

Screenplay
John Huston
Wolfgang Reinhardt
Aeneas MacKenzie

From the play by
Franz Werfel

And the Novel "The Phantom Crown" by
Bertita Harding

Most screenplays are constructed by more than one writer. The instance of *Gone with the Wind,* in which seventeen writers were used on the story, has been cited; it is not hard to give other instances. Walter Wanger's *Foreign Correspondent,* which began as Vincent Sheean's *Personal History,* at one time or another used the services of John Lee Mahin, John Howard Lawson, James Hilton, Charles Bennett, Joan Harrison, Budd Schulberg, Ben Hecht, Robert Benchley, and Lester Cole. Alfred Hitchcock's name must be added to the list of writers, since he participated most actively in the construction of the final story and, as in most films which Hitchcock directs, was responsible for many of the melodramatic inventions.

The Hollywood practice of team writing is not due simply to the failure of producers to know what they want—although a good deal of waste is directly attributable to muddle-headed-ness. A movie is an immensely complex narrative, and the technical capacities of camera, cutting, and movie method make it imperative for the ordinary movie to embody four, five, or ten times as much material as a play. Gilbert Seldes is of the opinion that "more dialogue is produced in one year in Hollywood than on the stage in five years. There is simply not enough good dialogue to go round. . . ."[3] Many writers in Hollywood (to say nothing of producers and directors) would agree with the statement that there just are not enough writers in the movie colony who can turn out a complete, competent screenplay single-handed.

Multiple-collaboration tends to rob a writer of his sense of personal relation to a story. How can it be otherwise when the writer knows that he is working on something which another writer has begun, that other writers may be working on it at the same time, and that still others will be called in to alter his work after he is done? This type of patch-quilt creation undermines the writer's sense of individual responsibility. It is utterly alien to his experience and desire. The Hollywood producer or director is generally spared the irritations of multiple-collaboration, which offends the individuality of writers, assaults their vanity as craftsmen, and leads to bitter and perennial squabbles over screen credits. Few writers can remain unperturbed when their names are paired with scriveners whose work they do not respect.

A picture might have more literary integrity, more unity, if only one writer worked on it all the way and followed it through production. . . . But integrity and unity do not reflect box-office returns. . . . A producer in the theater may be willing to risk and able to lose $20,000 to $30,000 on a favored author. With a picture which costs anywhere from $400,000 to $1,000,000 or more to produce, the sponsors cannot afford to take any chances of presenting artistic flops. . . . There is, therefore, only one law to picture people. The picture must make money. . . . Everything the public likes is good. . . .[4]

In Hollywood, most writers make far more money than they can get in New York, but they enjoy far less individual prestige. The authors of books, the playwrights, the magazine contributors are lords in the kingdom of literary deference. But Hollywood's writers are employees, units in a vast and complex manufacturing process. They are "shoved around" by producers and directors; their work is treated like merchandise; their opinions are often disregarded, their conceptions usually violated. The Hollywood writer is given few opportunities to fortify his self-esteem.

The writer—no matter how small his talent or how modest his aspirations—tends to identify himself with a craft which has always enjoyed high intellectual status. Writers have always had an historical place and an historical function. They are, in a sense, the unofficial oracles of society. They shape the dreams of men; they sing for the mute and dare for the timid. They are, as someone said, the "divine skeptics," enemies of intolerance, rebels against flatulence and platitude.* But in Hollywood, they just make movies.

The movie writer does not need to know how to write; he does need a talent for plot contrivance and a sense of colloquial dialogue. This has been true of the movies from the beginning. A "scenario writer," in the early days of films, was essentially a plot-man. He devised a story in the form of rough scenes which were to be photographed. The stories were simple and hackneyed. He wrote subtitles which were flashed on the screen to convey unphotographable information. The subtitles were de-

---

* The respect accorded men who are articulate stems, in part, from the child's veneration for the adult. To the child, words are adult tools; words are a screen between his world and the world of adults. The use of words is the beginning of maturity; the road to adulthood begins with a word. It is not surprising, therefore, that we regard those who use words better than we do as more "adult," more accomplished, more mature. In a competitive society, where argumentation flourishes, dialectical skill and verbal dexterity are powerful weapons in the daily fight for prestige.

signed for audiences which could not make mental bridges over
discontinuous sequences, audiences which could neither read
nor think quickly. ("We'll cut across the prairie and head them
off at the pass!" "I'm taking the 4:15 to Bingsville to tell Mary
I love her!" "Meanwhile, in Dead Man's Gulch, Rinaldo and
his treacherous crew . . .")

When the industry began to make bigger pictures with more
ambitious stories (1918-24), the producers started to import
famous authors to Hollywood. A brigade of illustrious names
moved westward: Maurice Maeterlinck, Rupert Hughes, Mary
Roberts Rinehart, Rex Beach, Elinor Glyn, P. G. Wodehouse,
Gouverneur Morris, Clayton Hamilton, Sir Gilbert Parker. But
only a few of the famed authors were able to understand or
master the requirements of the screen. They retained an attitude of tolerant superiority to Hollywood and movie writing;
they neither studied nor perfected the technique which offered
writers a medium of new scope and mobility.[5] The "big names"
drifted back East. Hollywood's "hack writers" stayed on. They
were attuned to the rhythm and the pattern of movies; they
knew how to keep a scene short, how to juxtapose sequences,
how to "plant" material which paid off in comic or melodramatic
surprise. They could not write saleable stories or books; but
they could construct muscular, intricated screen stories. They
were not really writers; they were plot carpenters and stereotype experts.

When sound revolutionized the movies, history repeated itself. Hollywood was desperate for actors who could read lines
without looking ludicrous, and utter noises that were not in-
human. Hollywood was desperate for writers who could write
dialogue which was fit to be spoken. The producers frantically
bought up Broadway's plays and photographed them with nervous fidelity.

The more faithfully the stage play was photographed, with its dialogue
left almost word for word, the greater was the disappointment of spec-

314

tators for whom the essential appeal of the screen lies in its pageantry and rhythms. When on the other hand changes were made in the interests of screen needs, the literary groups were equally disappointed. . . . The very people whom the producers hoped to bait . . . were the ones most disgruntled at the changes.[6]

The producers were caught without a supply of writers who could turn out polished, swift, and effective dialogue. They lured playwrights and authors to Hollywood in droves. But the producers learned that famous authors and accomplished playwrights did not necessarily adapt themselves to the dimensions and the propelling activism of the screen. The literary scribes wrote beautiful lines and witty repartee. They created three-dimensional characters and subtle situations. They elaborated a counterpoint of plot and people. But their stories did not *move*. Their stories groaned under a massive load of talk. The men new to Hollywood were writing plays, not screenplays. They were working in the fine tradition of the stage; they were not making movies. And so the producers teamed the playwrights with scenario writers or "plot constructionists." The scripts of distinguished playwrights were cut, edited, and arranged into stories stripped of verbiage and driven by action. Dialogue writers, plot constructionists, "additional dialogue" writers, story doctors, "joke men," gag men labored on the scenarios of litterateurs and tried to recapture movie speed and excitement in pictures which could talk. It was not unusual to have six, eight, a dozen writers working on the same picture. At this stage, one producer declared:

We are forced back on the conclusion that we have got to have picture and dialogue that go together, that contribute each to the telling of the story, that together make a complete artistic unity. A whole army of men both here and in New York are trained to write silent pictures, but there are none trained to write talking pictures. Playwrights are doing it, and so are screen-writers; but they are all fumbling in the dark.[7]

The talking picture had to find a form of its own, a form in which dialogue and sound effects would complement, rather than sacrifice, the unique breadth and movement of movies. The Hollywood writers—graduates of the westerns and the two-reel comedies, masters of the chase, the "pratt-fall," the "gimick," the artifices of movie construction—kept the movies moving. They added pace and plot, bold contrasts and brittle contrivances, to the rounded characters and the polished language of the playwrights. They shaped the modern screenplay —swift, complicated, colloquial—into a medium for telling a story with camera *and* dialogue.

The introduction of distinguished authors to Hollywood did an enormous amount for the prestige and compensation of movie writers. An industry and a medium which used the talents of Nobel and Pulitzer Prize writers (Shaw, O'Neill, Sherwood, Howard) could no longer be dismissed for its infantilism or its vulgarity. Bit by bit it became apparent that the movies, for all their banalities and beginnings, were achieving higher—and often admirable—stature. The movies began to win a place among the arts, a place in contemporary culture. In 1937, Clifford Odets, the most touted young playwright in America, apostle of the socially significant and white hope of "the new theater," hearkened to Hollywood's call and joined the ranks of the writers in the movie colony. He signalized the end of two decades of disdain when he announced: "The movies have taken over the field of entertainment in this country. The theater, which once had a potent and powerful voice, has dwindled to a little squeak that sometimes, but not often, sounds like something cultural." [8]

I was once asked, "What do you think is the indispensable requirement for a good picture—the star, the director, the producer, or what?"
I answered, "The author."
A great picture has to start with a great story. Just as water can't rise higher than its source, so a picture can't rise higher than its story. The bigger the stars, the director and the producer, the harder they fall

on a bad story. Not even Clark Gable and Myrna Loy, excellent as they are, could carry the story of Parnell. The picture was an echoing flop.

—SAMUEL GOLDWYN [9]

That Hollywood attaches great importance to the Story is no news, although few producers seem to be as cognizant of its decisive importance as Mr. Goldwyn. The prices which Hollywood pays for popular plays and novels are prodigious, as a few recent examples will show:

Lady in the Dark	$285,000
The American Way	250,000*
The Man Who Came to Dinner	250,000
Abe Lincoln in Illinois	225,000*
My Sister Eileen	225,000
Tobacco Road	200,000*
Arsenic and Old Lace	175,000*
Saratoga Trunk	175,000†
For Whom the Bell Tolls	150,000

But the respect of Hollywood's producers for writing is quite different from their attitude to writers. The producers have not handled their writers with a conspicuous understanding of the writers' problems and grievances. For many years the high-handed practices of certain producers left the movie writers at the mercy of men who were neither ethical in their methods nor reliable in their promises.

A producer . . . frequently calls in from three to five writers and hands them a book to read, with instructions to come back in a few days with a story idea. The writers may put in two days digesting the book and two to three times that long preparing a story idea. When they come back, they say, the producer may take possession of all the ideas, and a short time later turn the story over to still another writer to develop under his guidance. They say the writer drawing the assignment accepts the job innocent of any knowledge that the ideas were developed by fellow scriveners. The other five have worked anywhere from four days to two weeks on spec [speculation], and received nothing for their efforts.[10]

* With certain royalty provisions.
† With rights to revert to Miss Ferber after the story is filmed.

The blithe technique of picking a writer's brains, using his time, or lifting his ideas was not infrequently reported in Hollywood's gossip columns:

That writer who was given plenty of air at one of the majors is now in quite a "het." It turns out that all those hot ideas he had been telling his producer, all of which were tossed back to the writer, are now being unfolded by the producer in the weekly production meetings, and will win him a new contract. And to add to the writer's woes, he has nothing to prove the ideas were his.[11]

Until the producers' agreement with the Screen Writers Guild was consummated, in 1941, Hollywood's writers—unlike Hollywood's directors or actors, stagehands or electricians—worked under conditions which lacked basic standards of equity or collective bargaining rights. For two decades the movie writers in the low salary brackets (of whom there are plenty) were not given the protection of minimum wages or minimum periods of employment. They were discharged with no advance notice; their employment was sporadic and their tenure short-lived. They were laid off for short-term periods, under contract but without pay. They worked on stories on which other writers were employed, without knowing who their collaborators (or competitors) were. Their right to screen credits was mistreated by certain producers who allotted credit to their friends or relatives or—under pseudonyms—to themselves. They were frequently offered the bait of speculative writing without either guarantees or protection in the outcome.

The obstinacy and indiscretion with which the producers opposed Hollywood writers in their fight for recognition, basic working conditions, and a code of fair practices, is one of the less flattering commentaries on the men who control movie production. The National Labor Relations Board charged that the producers had conspired to carry out "a plan of interference" with the writers' attempt to organize themselves and choose their bargaining representatives; that the producers had used pressure on writers in an effort to force their resignation from the Screen Writers Guild; that the producers had circulated propaganda among the Guild's members; that certain producers had made speeches to their writers—in studio commissaries, on studio time—in which the leaders of the Guild were mentioned in "opprobrious, vile, and defamatory terms"; that producers had threatened to fire and blacklist Guild members; that the producers had "conspired" with Screen Playwrights, Incorporated, a rival organization to the Guild, at a time when the producers *knew* that the Playwrights did not represent the majority of writers in Hollywood.* [12]

It was not until June, 1941, after more than five years of negotiation and acrimony, and three years after the Screen Writers Guild had been certified as the legal representative of screen writers in Hollywood, that the producers capitulated.† They had hurled challenges, uttered threats, issued fiats, employed long and costly maneuvers of opposition. It would take years for the bitterness and suspicion (on both sides) to die away. The producers, for all their vigor and showmanship, were still insensitive to the meaning of public relations. In their dealings with the writers, as in their earlier negotiations with the actors and directors of Hollywood, the producers demonstrated that they had no workable concept of employee relations.

* In August, 1938, the National Labor Relations Board had supervised an election of the writers in Hollywood; the Screen Writers Guild had won by a vote of 267 to 57 and was designated by the Board as the legal collective bargaining agency for writers.

† The screen writers won a seven-year contract which provided: A minimum wage of $125 a week; a minimum of $1,500 for all flat deals for movie stories; the elimination of speculative writing; an 85 percent Guild shop for the first three years of the contract, a 90 percent Guild shop thereafter; a minimum period of two weeks' employment for writers receiving $250 or less a week and a minimum of one week for writers receiving $250-500 a week; one and two weeks' notice of termination of a contract (depending on writer's salary and length of employment); the arbitration of disputes; a committee to settle differences arising under the contract; control of screen credits by the Guild; writers, upon request, to be informed when other writers are assigned to work on the same material.

We turn to an analysis of the movie writers as a group. What has been their experience, education, professional background? How old are they and how much do they earn? What do they think of movies? . . .

Age. Hollywood's writers range in age from 23 to 63 (as of 1940). The median average age for 120 writers who gave the year of their birth in questionnaires is 37. The movie writers are substantially younger than the movie producers, actors, or directors. This can be demonstrated in a table of percentages:

Age	Writers	Directors	Actors	Producers
Under 30	14.1	1.5	15.8	1.8
30-39	43.5	31.8	31.2	27.7
40-49	26.6	50.0	18.0	45.5
50 and over	15.8	16.7	35.0	25.0

Almost a third of the movie writers (31.7 percent) are under 35; 57.6 percent are under 40; and 70.9 percent are under 45.

Birthplace. An examination of the biographies of 108 movie writers showed that 86.1 percent were born in the United States and 13.9 percent were born outside the United States. (87 percent were born in the United States and Canada.) A smaller percentage of movie writers are foreign-born than actors (25.3 percent), producers (17.4 percent), or directors (28.7 percent). Over half of the writers born outside the United States come from England (8.33 percent); Ireland, Canada, Germany, Hungary, Russia, and Australia have each contributed less than one percent to Hollywood.

Education. As a professional type, the writer is to a large degree dependent upon education for the acquisition and refinement of his skills; as a personality type, the writer is drawn to books, words, and scholarship (in one form or another). The academic record of 133 Hollywood writers shows:

2.2 percent had a grammar school education only.
17.3 percent went to high school but not college.
80.5 percent went to college.

48.6 percent are in possession of college degrees
(including 7 master's degrees and 2 PhD's).
12.8 percent undertook post-graduate work.

'he educational background of Hollywood's writers, as we ob-
erved earlier, is far superior to that of other movie makers.
'he proportion who attended college is substantially larger for
vriters (80.5 percent) than for directors (53 percent), actors
49.8 percent), producers (57 percent), directors of photog-
aphy (41.2 percent), film editors (41 percent), or assistant di-
ectors (55.7 percent). The percentage of movie writers holding
ollege degrees (48.6) is much higher than directors (24.6),
roducers (13.8), or actors (17.6).

Experience. In certain ways, movie writing is more special-
zed than movie directing or producing. The analysis which
ollows shows that fewer screen writers drifted into writing from
ther fields of movie making; more writers began their Holly-
vood careers *as* writers (72.5 percent) than producers began
s producers, or directors as directors (29.6); and a substantial
roportion of the other jobs held by screen writers lay in fields
losely related to movie writing (*e.g.*, story and scenario depart-
nents) or in fields which involved word-use and word-skill
publicity, advertising).

WRITERS' EXPERIENCE IN HOLLYWOOD
135 Writers

No jobs other than writing	71
Story department (reader, story editor, etc.)	27
Production (producer, associate producer, shorts, assistant to executive, etc.)	21
Direction (director, assistant director, dialogue director, etc.)	15
Publicity and advertising	13
Acting	11
Film editing (cutter, title editor, etc.)	9

Less than 5 writers worked in each of the following departments: casting, clerical, property,
music, research, script clerk, censorship, laboratories, sound.

It is striking that out of 138 writers for whom data were available, 100 (72.5 percent) were writers in their *first* Hollywood job; only 27.5 percent, that is, began their movie careers in a field other than screen-writing. That screen-writing can be a step to movie directing or production was seen in the chapters on producers and directors, which showed that 36.1 percent of Hollywood's producers and 25.8 percent of Hollywood's directors have worked as writers.

Movie writers are being given more opportunities to produce movies. Among Hollywood's producers, Nunnally Johnson, Robert Lord, Gene Markey, Mark Hellinger, Joseph L. Mankiewicz, Gene Towne, Bruce Manning, Graham Baker, Dore Schary, Jerry Wald, and others were movie writers not so long ago; among the directors, Preston Sturges, Vincent Sherman, and John Huston stepped into the directorial ranks from screen writing.

Earnings. The size of the movie writers' earnings is often confused with the staggering amounts which Hollywood pays for novels or plays. The top movie writers are very well paid; but they are by no means as well paid as Hollywood's directors, actors or producers.

In the chapter called "The Big Money" we saw that at least 17 Hollywood writers earned $75,000 or more (1938) as compared to 80 actors, 54 producers and executives, 45 directors, and 4 musical directors. The 17 writers who landed in this majestic category were:

Robert Riskin	$180,125	Walter de Leon	$89,475
Ben Hecht	159,996	John L. Balderston	88,500
Preston Sturges	143,000	Anita Loos	87,500
Claude R. Binyon	100,000	Casey Robinson	85,666
Talbot Jennings	96,333	John Lee Mahin	80,833
Jules Furthman	95,266	Laurence Stallings	79,208
Sidney Buchman	92,750	Sonya Levien	77,066
Vincent Lawrence	91,333	Jack Yellen	76,800

William A. McGuire $76,250

These names were taken from the salary lists published by the Treasury Department. The list is incomplete on several scores: the published data were admittedly not complete for writers; and the names and salaries were taken from individual studio payrolls. Since many writers work at more than one studio in the course of a year, and often sell original stories during the periods when they are not on salary, the listing does not give a representative picture of the high-earning writers in the movie colony. Such men as Gene Fowler, Morrie Ryskind, Dudley Nichols, and Jo Swerling, for example, are not included, and their incomes are unquestionably among the first fifteen in the ranks of movie writers.

But there are well over 800 writers in Hollywood—of one class or another; and employment for writers is notoriously uneven, short-termed, and unpredictable. Many writers are unemployed for long periods; many work on a "picture deal" basis; many have long-term contracts which, because of studio options, are not so long or so binding.

An analysis of the salary lists for the four largest studios in Hollywood (MGM, Paramount, Warner Brothers, Twentieth Century-Fox) shows that 535 producers, actors, directors, and writers received $15,000 or over in these four studios in 1937: 237 actors, 165 writers, 77 directors, 56 producers (excluding officers of the corporation). The analysis showed that 67 writers at MGM, 44 writers at Paramount, 33 writers at Twentieth Century-Fox, and 21 writers at Warner Brothers each received $15,000 or more. The 165 writers constituted 30.8 percent of the total number (535) who received $15,000 or over (but see below).

The median average for the 165 writers was approximately $25,000. (Half of the writers *who earned $15,000 or more* received under $25,000; half received over $25,000.) About a fourth of the writers received $35,000-$50,000. Few writers received $80,000, and very few received $100,000 or more. These figures should be compared with the median average for the other groups which earned $15,000 or more: actors ($35,000), directors ($55,000-$60,000), producers ($70,000-$75,000). About a fourth of the 237 actors who earned $15,000 or more received over $70,000; about a fourth of the 77 directors received over $105,000; about a fourth of the 56 producers received over $125,000. Hollywood writers, it is clear, are paid substantially less than Hollywood's actors, directors, or producers.

The 1938 payrolls at three major studios (Warner Brothers, Twentieth Century-Fox, Columbia) disclosed an interesting pattern. In these three studios, 228 writers were employed at the following weekly salaries:

Weekly Salary	Number	Percent
Under $250	93	40.8
$250-$499	52	22.8
$500-$749	36	15.8
$750-$999	17	7.5
$1,000-$1,499	16	7.0
$1,500-$1,999	10	4.4
$2,000 and over	4	1.7
Total	228	100.0

According to the payrolls of three major studios, therefore:

40.8 percent of the employed movie writers received under $250 a week.
59.2 percent received $250 or more a week.
36.4 percent received $500 or more a week.
20.6 percent received $750 or more a week.
13.1 percent received $1,000 or more a week.
6.1 percent received $1,500 or more a week.

The data would undoubtedly show higher writer-earnings if MGM and Paramount were included.

We cannot, unfortunately, compare the data given above to

information from questionnaires, which would give a more comprehensive and a more representative picture of the earnings and *employment* of Hollywood's writers. Questionnaires were mailed to the entire membership of the Screen Writers Guild, but the significant materials were withheld by the executive board.*

Marriage and Divorce. Of 129 screen writers in Hollywood, 71.3 percent are married today and 28.7 percent are divorced. There are no data available on the number of marriages, divorces, or children.†

The Writers' Writers. The members of the Screen Writers Guild were asked to "indicate the screen writer whose work you most admire." The poll may be of interest: ‡

* Questionnaires (anonymous) were mailed to the membership of the Screen Writers Guild after this writer had consulted with the executive board, addressed a mass meeting of the Guild, and formulated a questionnaire in collaboration with a special committee of the Guild appointed for that purpose. On the first returns, 143 questionnaires were received. But before the follow-up letter could be mailed (as was done for actors, directors, and eight other groups in Hollywood), and before a second copy of the questionnaire could be circulated to enlarge the sample, the executive board of the Guild ordered a stop to the inquiry. This was due to the fact that several members of the executive board fought the effort to make an objective analysis of screen writers along the established lines of social science research. The reasons for their opposition were never made clear. After several months of negotiation, in which this writer again appeared before the executive board, the first 143 questionnaires were made available to the Motion Picture Research Project for analysis. But the questionnaires had been sliced up, and all information pertaining to salaries, divorce, and other points was deleted. The materials which were released by the Guild are analyzed in this chapter. In 1940, the Guild published a pamphlet which asserted that 50 percent of the screen writers earned less than $120 per week in 1939. Unfortunately, none of the data in the Guild's survey can be accepted as reliable: the analysis violated accepted statistical methods and practices; writers not employed at Hollywood studios were included; would-be writers on agents' lists were included. Writers who had earned nothing from screen work were included in the array from which average earnings were extracted. A "trend analysis" was given for three years (1937-1939), but data on 1938 were omitted; the class-intervals used distorted the real distribution of earnings; and so on.
† The answers to the question on "number of marriages" was deleted by the executive board.
‡ The poll indicates the number of references to the ten leading writers named. Many writers wrote in more than one name. Half a dozen writers, whose names do not appear, received less than five mentions each.

Dudley Nichols	56	Lillian Hellman	12
Robert Riskin	44	John Lee Mahin	10
Donald Ogden Stewart	21	Jo Swerling	10
Claude Binyon	14	Nunnally Johnson	8
Ben Hecht	13	Frances Goodrich and	
(Hecht & MacArthur)	7	Albert Hackett	7

Comment on American Movies. The questionnaire sent to the screen writers contained this query: "Comment on American movies today." The response of 141 writers, who made 169 remarks about content, shows:

> 133 comments were entirely unfavorable.
> 25 comments were entirely favorable.
> 11 comments were neither favorable nor unfavorable.

The largest proportion of the movie writers' criticism, like that of the directors, was directed against the "dishonesty" or lack of "initiative" or "originality" of movies, or their lack of relationship to life and reality today (18.9 percent of the 169 comments). There were 20 criticisms (11.8 percent) of censorship; the same number criticized the kind of stories ("formula," "boy meets girl") which are, for the most part, filmed. (If we combine the criticism of movie stories with the criticism of the movies' "lack of initiative or originality," we would have 51 comments out of 169.) There were 13 unfavorable remarks apropos producers and supervisors ("stupid," "dumb"); 9 comments questioned excessive attention to box-office appeal; 6 comments complained about B pictures; 9 comments praised the artistry and technique of movies.

The writers are the most articulate and incisive critics of movies in Hollywood. It is not hard to understand why. The writer is a story-teller, and his comments on movies are those of a story-teller commenting on stories. The writers, of all the groups in the movie colony, feel most frustrated by the constricting demands of producers, the public, and censorship. The writers, of all the groups in Hollywood, want to create stories different from those being told on the screen today—stories with deeper motivation and wider purpose, stories with relevance to our times, stories with characters freed from the vacuum of stereotypes, stories with dramatic situations rooted in a reality which is largely ignored in the contemporary film. But whether such stories would be popular with the public is dubious; whether they would make enough money to cover the costs of production, much less return a profit, is still more debatable. It is no happy fact that some of the finest films Hollywood has produced have done miserably at the box-office, and some of the most maudlin and trivial pictures have reaped fortunes.*

The movie writers, let us repeat, are employees engaged in the manufacture of high-cost merchandise which must be sold to a market of enormous proportions. The movie industry, which operates with huge costs, and the multitudinous movie customers, who are not distinguished by esthetic sophistication, impose inescapable limitations which Hollywood's creative talents will forever dislike and against which they will forever discharge the antagonism born of frustration.

* For example, the following films either lost money or made a disappointing profit: *Abe Lincoln in Illinois, Our Town, The Long Voyage Home, Juarez,* and many others. The scarcely salutary pictures in which Jeanette MacDonald, Wallace Beery, Nelson Eddy, Alice Faye, Don Ameche, Dorothy Lamour appear have generally made a great deal of money. The relative apathy of movie-goers for such films as *Confessions of a Nazi Spy, Escape, Mortal Storm*—each an honest, courageous effort and an excellent movie—is reflected in their moderate or disappointing reception at the box-office. In 194 separate surveys made by Dr. George Gallup, it was found that only New York audiences seem to want pictures with political content involving Hitler and the Nazis.[13]

15. THE ACTORS

HOLLYWOOD means movies and movies mean stars. No group in Hollywood receives as much attention from the public as the men and women whose personalities are featured in films and around whom entire movie organizations have been geared. Of all the movie makers, it is the actors—publicized, romanticized, idealized—who are most potent in attracting people to the theaters. One of the first questions raised in every-day discussions of a movie is "Who's in it?"

The interest of the public in movie actors and actresses was manifested at the very beginning of motion picture history, and has never lost its force and fervor. Long before the names of actors even appeared on the screen, in advertising, or on theater marquees, the movie-goers clamored to pay homage to their favorites. The actress named Gladys Smith (Mary Pickford) who appeared in the early Biograph films was quickly identified by movie patrons as "Little Mary" or "the little girl with the curls." The patrons who liked western pictures asked for "Bronco Billy." [1]

The producers did not welcome this at first; they preferred to establish their own names, or the name of the company, in the public mind—but they never succeeded. The public's selection of movie personalities was of great importance in the rise of the motion picture industry; for when the public began to prefer one face to another, they also began to distinguish among the films which competed for their money. The choice of personalities led to the expression of opinion concerning the kind of stories or pictures in which those personalities appeared, and then the public began to patronize those theaters which showed the pictures in which popular actors were featured. By 1915, the movie producers began to offer the theaters groups of films, seven or eight to a lot, which featured one star. By 1919, the system of building stories, productions, and advertising around a few selected personalities was the very heart of the motion picture industry.

Hollywood learned that pictures with stars make money, and that those without stars do not—or do not make as much as they would if they featured popular personalities. Almost every factor in movie making was subordinated to the needs and talents of those actors who had a faithful ticket-buying public. The star system was hailed as the foundation of movie prosperity.[2]

A star, we have said, is a monopoly. A Charles Boyer or a Claudette Colbert has a monopoly on those graces of voice, eyes, manner, attitude which constitute the individual personality. There is only one Clark Gable, only one Bette Davis, and although Hollywood is fond of thinking in typologies and attempts to build up a "Gable type" or a "Davis type" the public is not won over to synthetic substitutes. The public makes the stars. (Note the public's apathy for some personalities who were highly touted and widely publicized: Anna Sten, Francis Lederer, Grace Moore, Walter Huston, and others.)

The uniqueness of a personality, it is easy to see, places that personality in an almost unchallengeable bargaining position. The producers' competition for stars whose pictures earn profits has always bordered on the frenetic. The movie magnates paid astronomic sums to the movie stars because they had to. Those who wanted stars had to pay the price for them, and the stars who commanded the highest salaries also made the highest profits for their employers. The producers who paid exorbitant sums for talent prospered; those who did not, or could not, lost out. As motion pictures made greater profits, the stars demanded more money; the producers were able to pay it.

The competition of producers for movie stars was scarcely voluntary: the dazzling salaries which the producers paid out were not evidence of insanity, poor business judgment, or recklessness. This was demonstrated in the thirties when Paramount and Universal, under reorganization, tried a partial abandonment of the star system in the effort to cut costs. The "sensible" businessmen did cut their movie costs by letting the high-priced stars go—but they cut their profits (or increased their lack of profits) even more. And the stars which Paramount and Universal dropped—or who were lured away by Warner Brothers' or MGM—kept bringing the big money into the coffers of the studios for which they worked.

The salient importance and profitability of stars can be seen in such cases as Shirley Temple, Sonja Henie, or Deanna Durbin. Shirley Temple is reported to have earned over $20,-000,000 for Twentieth Century-Fox in the bright years of her pre-adolescence. Miss Henie, an ice-skater with no film experience, made many millions for the same studio overnight. Deanna Durbin is said to have saved Universal from disaster in 1938-39. Every Durbin picture has earned huge sums; none has made a net profit of less than a quarter of a million dollars. An executive of Universal told this writer that Durbin's box-office power was so powerful and her future value so great that the company would not take $10,000,000 for her contract.

One final example: when David Selznick prepared to make *Gone with the Wind* he discovered that Clark Gable was not only the perfect personality to play Rhett Butler but that the popular demand for Gable in that role was so great that any other choice might prove detrimental to the film's success. Selz-

ıick was forced to make extraordinary concessions to MGM in
ırder to obtain Mr. Gable's services: the picture had to be dis-
ributed and released through MGM (instead of United Artists,
vhich had released earlier Selznick-International films) and
MGM leased the film to the movie theaters for seventy percent
ıf the box-office intake (the highest percentage ever received).
MGM's share of the profits from *Gone with the Wind* will prob-
ıbly be as great as Selznick's. Selznick could not get Gable for
he role unless he met MGM's terms; the terms were very high;
ıut Selznick found it profitable—and necessary—to meet them.
Gone with the Wind will gross over $25,000,000; some reports
:redit it with having passed the $30,000,000 mark in 1941.[3]

The actors in the movie colony have been discussed through-
ıut the chapters of this book. We have referred to their place
n Hollywood and in movie making; we have analyzed their
manners, their homes, their superstitions, and their earnings.
[t is not necessary to elaborate on that discussion here.

The professional problems of Hollywood's actors are of a
ıimpler character than those of Hollywood's producers, directors, and writers. For the actor is a talented mime or a beautiful
person who is given a part and directed in the performance of
that part. The decisions which actors make are relatively un-
complicated; their power to influence a story is relatively subordinate. Many stars in Hollywood do have "story approval"
clauses in their contracts, and can refuse to appear in roles
which seem unsympathetic or unflattering. But in that event,
another actor is hired for the part. . . . The actor cannot shape
the content of a film to the *degree* that a director or writer or
producer can; the actor's power to affect the structure or the
implications of a movie, or to exercise control over the point or
the meaning of a film, is negligible. Even the actors' interpretations are to a large extent controlled by the director, the script,

331

the cutting of the film, and the producer's decisions about th
story and the actor's place in it.

Before we analyze the actors as a professional group one com
ment should be added. Actors thrive on praise, but praise to ai
actor for a performance is, in a sense, criticism of the actor as ;
person. When you compliment an actor for the way in whicl
he played a part you underline his sense of insufficiency, fo
you are congratulating him for his skill in imitating someon
else. Actors are forever dubious of the worth of their own per
sonality: their talent lies in identifying themselves with anc
acting as *other* personalities. This writer cannot forget the over
tones in the words of a celebrated Hollywood actor, who musec
aloud: "God, what a part I've got in this picture! What a mar
to play—scientist, scholar, fighter, one of humanity's greates
benefactors. And me"—a shrug—"I'm just a ham." There are few
actors who are not overcome by the thought that their talents
though unique, are not "significant," that their work, though
entertaining to millions, is not "important," that their personalities—so inflated in publicity, so idolized by fans—are, by thei
own inner cognizance, empty, vain, and shallow. The readiness
and frequency with which actors call other persons "phony"
suggests the fear that they may be phony too. . . .

The analysis of movie actors which follows does *not* include
the extras, of whom there are some 7,000 in Hollywood. The
extras lead a different life, do different work, and have entirely
different problems from the actors with whom we shall be concerned. The extras never play a character in the movies; they
do not speak lines; they do not really "act"—except in the broad-
est sense. (A group of extras may be instructed to dance, walk,
look happy, sad, or "natural.") In the movies the extras are
important *en masse*, not as individuals. Their names are never
mentioned on the screen. The extras have for many years presented a perplexing economic and social problem to the motion

picture industry; a study of the movie extras is a complete and complicated task in itself.* Since this book is concerned with the movie makers, as contrasted to what has been called the movie workers, Hollywood's extras do not fall into the sphere of our inquiry.

The data which follow were gathered in collaboration with the Screen Actors Guild. Questionnaires were mailed to the 1,753 class A actors (extras are class B members). A total of 309 returns was received, about 18 percent of the A players in Hollywood. The sample of 309 (212 actors, 89 actresses, and 8 whose sex was not given) is more than large enough and is representative enough to justify generalization.†

Age. An analysis of 271 actors' questionnaires reveals that Hollywood's actors range in age from 18 to 76; the median age is 42.

> 15.8 percent are under 30 years old.
> 31.2 percent are 30-39 years old.
> 18.0 percent are 40-49 years old.
> 20.6 percent are 50-59 years old.
> 12.2 percent are 60-69 years old.
> 2.2 percent are 70 years of age or over.

About a third (32.9 percent) of the class A actors in Hollywood are under 35; almost a third (32.1 percent) are between 35 and

* An intensive study of the extras was made by the Standing Committee of actors and producers. The report of the Central Casting Bureau for 1940 showed that out of the entire class B membership of the Guild, only 9 extras earned as high as $2,500-$3,000; 423 extras earned $1,000-$1,500; 155 earned $1,250-$1,500; only 192 earned $1,500-$2,000; only 45 earned $2,000-$2,500. Only 3.1 percent of the available extras in Hollywood averaged $150 or more a month from movie work in 1940. (Many extras derive income from other part-time jobs.) The average annual earnings for 7,050 extras who worked in Hollywood in 1940 was $350; in 1939, the average earnings for 9,849 extras were $317; in 1938, the average for 8,875 was $320; in 1937, the average for 15,900 was $187; in 1936, the average for 22,914 extras was $105. These figures support the recommendation made by the Standing Committee, a recommendation later approved by a vote of the extras themselves (2,704 to 434): that the only solution to the extra problem lies in a sharp reduction of the extra rolls.[4]

† See Appendix D for a detailed analysis of the size and representativeness of the sample, including the representativeness of the proportion prevailing between actors and actresses.

333

50; and slightly more than a third (35 percent) are 50 years or over.

The popular impression of the actors' youthfulness is due to the fact that it is the younger stars who are best known to the public and most featured in films; the numerous middle-aged or elderly "character" actors in Hollywood are generally ignored. The romantic roles around which most movies are built puts youthful actors at a premium in Hollywood, and gives them constant prominence in the public mind.

Hollywood's actresses, incidentally, are decidedly younger than Hollywood's actors. The median average age for actresses is 34; for actors it is 46. Over a fifth of the actresses (21.3 percent) are under 25 years of age, as against only 2.1 percent of the actors; 37.6 percent of the actresses are under 30, as against 6.8 percent of the actors; and 65.1 percent of the actresses are under 40 as compared to only 39.4 percent of the actors.[*]

The strong variation in ages may be explained by the fact that there are many more male than female "character" actors, and that the female "romantic leads" in movies are much younger than the male romantic leads. Actresses like Linda Darnell, Lana Turner, Nancy Kelly, Betty Grable, Priscilla Lane, Gene Tierney, Laraine Day, Olivia de Havilland, and others are featured in romantic parts opposite men who may be ten to twenty years older. The reverse is rarely true. (Very few, if any, of Hollywood's leading male actors are as young as the actresses just mentioned.) Movie actors are more mature than movie actresses, and they retain their popularity longer. The romantic stereotype permits a much wider range, for casting purposes, to male than to female thespians; the older male actors appear in young (or temporally ambiguous) roles far more often than actresses of the same age-group.[†]

[*] Data from 271 questionnaires: 80 actresses, 190 actors, 1—sex not given.

[†] The following male stars are forty years of age or over: Ronald Colman, Fredric March, William Powell, Gary Cooper, Clark Gable, Spencer Tracy, Charles Boyer, Melvyn Douglas, Nelson Eddy, Walter Pidgeon. None of the ranking female stars is

Birthplace. An examination of the birthplaces of 221 actors revealed that 74.7 percent were born in the United States and 25.3 percent were born outside the United States; 76 percent were born in the United States and Canada.* The foreign-born actors were largely drawn from Great Britain (8.1 percent) and Ireland (3.6 percent). Germany, Austria, France, Russia each accounted for 1.4 percent, and Hungary, Sweden, Australia, Japan, Norway, Mexico, India, China accounted for less than 1 percent each. We have noticed that the percentage of actors born outside the United States (25.3) is smaller than the percentage of directors (28.7) but larger than the percentage of producers (17.4) or writers (13.9).

Education. An analysis of the educational record of 251 Hollywood actors shows:

2.8 percent had only a grammar school education.
47.4 percent finished high school but did not attend college.
49.8 percent went to college.
21.0 percent have had four or more years of college.
17.6 percent received degrees.
5.6 percent have done graduate work.

The percentage of Hollywood's actors who attended college (49.8) is lower than the percentage for directors (53.0), producers (57.0), or writers (80.5). The proportion of actors who received college degrees (17.6) is higher than the proportion of producers (13.8), but lower than directors (24.6), and much lower than writers (48.6).

The male actors are better educated than the females: 57.6

forty; the following are 35-37 years old: Norma Shearer, Irene Dunne, Claudette Colbert, Myrna Loy, Marlene Dietrich. Dr. Harvey Lehman of Ohio University made a statistical analysis and concluded that the "success" age-curve for most actresses runs 25-29, but for most actors it runs 30-34. The implication, which our data confirm, is that the popularity of actors may run five years longer than that of actresses.[5]

* Birthplace information was derived not from questionnaires but from actors' biographies in the *Motion Picture Almanac*. The complete list of class A actors and actresses under contract to the major studios in 1940 (228) was examined; no information was available for 7 actors.

percent of the actors in our sample attended college, as compared to 30.6 percent of the actresses. And only 7 percent of the actresses have had four or more years of college training, as against 26.6 percent for the actors. The more complete educational background of male actors can be explained by the fact that (1) actresses embark upon their careers at an earlier age than actors, as we have seen; (2) the assumption, in society at large, that women do not need as much learning as men.

Experience. One of the cherished legends about Hollywood is the one about the extra who jumps to stardom. It is a pretty story, but unfortunately it is not supported by the facts. Actors and actresses often mount Hollywood's ladder with striking rapidity—but *not* from the ranks of the extras. An analysis of the movie careers of 309 actors and actresses shows that only 1.9 percent have been extras; in other words, only one out of every fifty class A actors has come up from the extra ranks. There are, of course, the conspicuous exceptions; here are several case-studies of actors who emerged from the vast sea of extras:

Actor, 34 years old. Hollywood extra in 1928. Became a player in 1933, at $800 a week. Earned $40,000 in 1936, at $2,000 a week. But earned only $13,000 in 1937, $14,000 in 1938, and $9,500 in 1939.

Actress, 29 years old. Sang in vaudeville, night clubs, radio. Began her movie career as an extra in 1929. In 1930, received $75 a week. In 1933, earned $350 a week. Highest annual earnings occurred in 1932, when she earned $5,560. Has worked intermittently since 1932; only nine weeks of work in 1938, only six weeks in 1939. Annual earnings: $3,000 in 1938, $2,000 in 1939.

Actor, 35 years old. Hollywood extra in 1928. In 1929 was given a bit part at $100 a week. By 1934 was playing leads, at $1,000 a week. Since 1935, has been a co-star, at a salary which began at $1,500 a week and has run as high as $6,500. Highest annual income: $180,000, in 1940. Now receives $3,000 a week or $52,000 a picture.

Two other actors who began their Hollywood careers as extras advanced to featured-player parts; the highest amounts they have ever earned in Hollywood are \$6,500 and \$16,500 a year respectively.

It is clear that very few extras become leading players, still fewer become stars, and those who do ascend to high movie rank do not necessarily earn the high salaries identified with Hollywood's top actors.

Let us examine the larger pattern of professional experience which is found among the actors in the movie colony. How many years have the actors spent in movie work (of any kind) in Hollywood? The evidence of 304 questionnaires reveals the length of movie experience for the actors:

PROFESSIONAL EXPERIENCE IN HOLLYWOOD

304 Actors

Number of years	Percent
25 and over	4.3
20-25	7.2
15-20	6.6
10-15	17.4
5-10	30.9
Under 5	33.6

In other words, a third of the actors in Hollywood have worked in movies for less than five years, and almost two-thirds (64.5 percent) for ten years or less. This is a very short record of professional experience, if compared to the movie producers, directors, or writers (*q.v.*).

The great number of actors who have had limited experience in Hollywood testifies to the influx of young people on a scale much greater than could be found among the producers, directors, and writers; it also indicates that far less experience or training is *necessary* for movie acting. The age of an actor (or, even more, of an actress) is a basic career component. The highest earning and employment periods for Hollywood's actors are, in general, directly related to age; and whereas the careers of producers, directors, or writers tend to assume a cumulative pattern, the careers of actors reach the point of diminishing returns much sooner and decline more swiftly. (This is one reason that the actors, their agents, and their business agents fight to get the big money "while the gettin' is good.") The director or producer or writer adds to his value and strengthens his career with each year of experience; but while the actor is learning how to act, he is becoming progressively older; and he must, in effect, start a new *kind* of acting career—as a character actor, an older "type," and so on.

The male actors in the movie colony have had considerably longer movie experience than the females.

Hollywood experience	210 Actors (Percent)	88 Actresses (Percent)
20 years or more	14.7	4.5
10-20 years	28.0	15.9
Less than ten years	57.3	79.6

The differences are striking: 42.7 percent of the male actors have worked in Hollywood for ten or more years as against only 20.4 percent of the actresses; 79.6 percent of the actresses have worked in movies for *less* than ten years, as compared to 57.3 percent of the male actors.

This supports the analyses which showed that movie actresses are much younger than movie actors; they would be expected to have had a shorter span of popularity. The male actors, we have seen, continue to get leading roles when the actresses begin to drop out of pictures: this is inferentially supported by the table above.

What kind of experience have the actors had as a group? Earlier chapters have shown us that Hollywood's directors have been writers, cameramen, film editors, and assistant directors; that the producers have been engaged in distribution, publicity, direction, writing, and so on. But this diversity of background is not to be found among the members of the acting profession.

Of 309 actors and actresses in Hollywood no less than 87.4 percent have held *no other job* in pictures; 7.1 percent have worked as directors (or assistant directors, dialogue directors, etc.); only 4.5 percent have been writers; and less than 1 percent have been engaged in production, in camera departments, in film laboratories, in casting, and so on. This supports the view that the talents of actors for other kinds of movie jobs are not too pronounced: their skills are not easily transferable; their movie experience outside of acting has been limited.

What were the *first* jobs held in Hollywood by the actors? The evidence of 309 questionnaires shows that no less than 95.8 percent of the actors began their Hollywood careers *as* actors.* This is an overwhelming majority; it is far greater than the proportion of movie directors who began as directors (29.6 percent), or writers who began as writers (72.5 percent). It suggests, once again, the higher degree of occupational concentration which prevails among actors.

How much theatrical experience have Hollywood's actors had aside from movie work? † Our sample shows that 84.7 percent had some theatrical experience *before* coming to Hollywood; if we add those actors who had stage experience *after* their movie debuts, we find that 87 percent, in all, have worked in entertainment fields outside of the motion picture industry. Approximately 20 percent of the actors have had radio experience at one time or another.

Earnings. In no other field of movie making do the big salaries offer as misleading a conception of the earnings of the *group* as in the case of actors. The salaries of Hollywood's leading stars

---

* Only 1 percent began as directors, 1 percent as assistant directors, and less than 1 percent each as writers, laboratory technicians, cameramen, publicity, or property department.

† Theatrical experience was considered to include any and all appearances before an audience—stage, vaudeville, night clubs, concerts, opera, circuses, etc.; but not radio work, which was analyzed separately.

are undeniably enormous; the weekly salaries of feature players, bit players, comedians, supporting leads are undeniably
striking. The top salaries are publicized in Hollywood and to
the world: big sums, like big names, are always news. But the
fallacy of the impressions created by the publicity is expressed
by the actor who remarked, "Sure, I get $500 a week. But I
worked four weeks last year, six weeks the year before, and
three weeks the year before that."

The actors with personal box-office power won huge salaries
from Hollywood as far back as thirty years ago. A few striking
cases will illustrate how much money the producers found it
profitable to pay the stars, and at how early a point in movie
history. In 1912, Mary Pickford was getting $40,000 for each
picture in which she appeared. By 1914 she was earning $60,-
000 per picture. In 1917-18 she received $10,000 a week from
Paramount, a percentage of the profits, and a bonus of $300,000
for signing the contract. In 1919 she was earning $500,000 a
picture at First National. From 1919 to 1924, when she was a
star, producer, and part-owner of the United Artists group,
Mary Pickford was making as much as $1,200,000 from each
movie in which she appeared. So great was the Pickford name,
so enormous her drawing power, so devastating her competitive
value, that when Adolph Zukor failed to hire her away from
United Artists he then offered to pay her $1,000 a week for
five years (a quarter of a million dollars) if she would retire
from the screen for that period! It was worth that much to
Paramount not to have to face the competition of Pickford
films.[6]

There were other dazzling personalities who commanded
dazzling salaries. Charles Chaplin, "the one universal man of
modern times," got $150 a week in 1913 and a year later was
getting $1,250 a week. In 1915 Mutual Films paid him $10,000
a week plus a $150,000 bonus.[7] When Chaplin joined the United

THE ACTORS

Artists group as a member-owner, with a share in the profits of both his pictures and the United Artists corporation, his movies netted him well over two million dollars each; one film is reported to have earned four million dollars for Chaplin. Gloria Swanson received $20,000 a week from Paramount, in the early twenties, and Tom Mix is said to have received $19,000 a week during his heyday. Stars like Thomas Meighan, Colleen Moore, and Pola Negri received $7,000 a week and over.

In 1931 a public which should have been inured to Hollywood's algebraic emoluments learned that Constance Bennett had a contract for $300,000 "for ten weeks' work"—supposedly the highest straight weekly salary ($30,000) ever paid.[8] Actually, the figure was misleading: Miss Bennett was getting $150,-000 a picture for two pictures. Cary Grant, Carole Lombard, Ronald Colman get $150,000 per film, and Mae West received $300,000 a picture at the height of her spectacular but short-lived career.

We have seen that in 1938 at least 80 Hollywood actors and actresses earned $75,000 and over. If we break this down we discover the following array:

TOP ACTOR EARNINGS: 1938

Annual Earnings	Actors
$ 75,000-$100,000	26
$100,000-$150,000	23
$150,000-$200,000	12
$200,000-$250,000	5
$250,000-$300,000	5
$300,000-$400,000	6
$400,000-$500,000	3
Total	80

This means that 54 actors received $100,000 or more; 31 got $150,000 or over; 19 earned $200,000 or more; 14 received $250,000 or over; 9 got $300,000 or more.

Who were the blessed who landed in the realm of six-digits?

The following fifty-four actors received $100,000 or over in 1938:*

ACTORS' INCOMES OF $100,000 OR OVER: 1938 [9]

Name	Earnings	Name	Earnings
Claudette Colbert	$426,944	Deanna Durbin	$174,916
Bing Crosby	410,000	Fanny Brice	166,500
Irene Dunne	405,222	Joe E. Brown	165,000
Charles Boyer	375,277	Robert Burns	155,952
Wallace Beery	355,000	Robert Young	148,916
Cary Grant	340,625	Nelson Eddy	146,416
Shirley Temple	307,014	Bette Davis	143,458
Joan Crawford	305,384	Basil Rathbone	140,833
Norma Shearer	300,000	Myrna Loy	140,666
Warner Baxter	279,807	Pat O'Brien	140,333
Clark Gable	272,000	Jean Arthur	136,666
Greta Garbo	270,000	Lionel Barrymore	136,584
Fred Astaire	266,837	Fredric March	136,311
Jack Benny	250,000	Marlene Dietrich	130,000
Victor McLaglen	248,082	Jeanette MacDonald	125,000
James Cagney	243,000	Fernand Gravet	121,242
Spencer Tracy	212,000	Freddie Bartholomew	118,166
Robert Montgomery	209,750	Barbara Stanwyck	117,291
Ginger Rogers	208,767	Tyrone Power	117,083
Katharine Hepburn	195,160	Oliver Hardy	116,850
Douglas Fairbanks, Jr.	194,270	W. C. Fields	115,000
George Raft	186,964	Sonja Henie	112,500
Robert Taylor	184,833	John Barrymore	105,833
Fred MacMurray	183,333	Henry Fonda	105,000
Frank Morgan	182,895	Jack Holt	103,461
Errol Flynn	181,333	Ronald Colman	102,083
Loretta Young	175,060	Edward G. Robinson	100,000

It should be pointed out that the discussion thus far rests upon *salaries* only. Some actors derive additional incomes from

* The list was constructed from information released by the Treasury Department and the Securities and Exchange Commission. Some actors (Gary Cooper, *e.g.*) are not represented in the list because those motion picture companies which do not have stock open to public purchase (Goldwyn and other United Artists producers) are not required to report their high salaries.

a variety of "side-line" enterprises. Bing Crosby, we have seen in chapter 4, draws heavy amounts from radio work, phonograph records, race track dividends, and different real-estate holdings. Such movie-radio stars as Bob Hope and Jack Benny earn almost as much—or more—from their work on the air as they get for appearing before the cameras. There are no authentic data for the total incomes of Hollywood's leading actors and actresses. We can, however, supply some random information.*

W. C. Fields and Jeanette MacDonald are each reported to get around $5,000 for a radio appearance; Burns and Allen received $10,000 a week in radio one year and added $92,000 to that sum from movie work. Fred Allen's earnings from radio work ran $416,000 in one year; he appears in pictures infrequently, but picks up around $60,000 each time he does. The Messrs. Walter Winchell, Rudy Vallée, and Ben Bernie have garnered lucre in Hollywood to swell their radio royalties. Edgar Bergen has filled his coffers through radio and films, *via* Charlie McCarthy.

Some stars are blessed with incomes from a curious variety of commercial enterprises. Bob Burns made $85,000 in one year by permitting his name to be used on a musical contrivance called the "bazooka." The Disney animals and the Charlie McCarthy character have poured enormous sums into the laps of their creators, who lease the name and visage of their brainchildren to manufacturers of dolls, dresses, sweat shirts, comic strips, drinking mugs, plates, flashlights, and other novelties. Shirley Temple is said to have earned fifteen times as much from her sponsorship of by-products as from her acting.[10]

But let us descend from the Olympian heights, where the air is giddy, the inhabitants limited, and the statistics vaguely un-

---

* An analysis of the records filled in on questionnaires by 298 actors and actresses indicated that from 1938-40 (inclusive), about 70 percent worked only in movies; 21.1 percent did some stage work concurrently or intermittently along with movie work; and 11.7 percent reported occasional radio assignments.

real. Let us consider the larger, more representative aspect of Hollywood's actors as a group. What is the monetary pattern which includes the big stars and the run-of-the-mill actors? What is the relationship between weekly salaries and annual incomes? What is the pattern of employment and unemployment for movie actors in Hollywood?

We turn to the facts offered by 292 actors * in the movie colony who answered several detailed questions on their annual earnings for three years (1938-40 inclusive), their weekly salaries, and their employment in 1939. First, how many actors worked in movies in 1939?

5.5 percent were totally unemployed.
4.5 percent had had no jobs in the movies, in Hollywood.†
90.0 percent had some work in movies in 1939 (if only for one day).

What were the weekly salaries of the actors who reported some employment for 1939? The salaries ranged from $75 a week to $12,500 a week (the salary which may be deduced for an actor who received $125,000 per picture).

WEEKLY SALARIES: 1939

262 Actors and Actresses ‡

Weekly Salary	Percent	Weekly Salary	Percent
Under $250	10.3	$1,500-$1,999	3.8
$250-$499	32.4	$2,000-$2,499	1.1
$500-$749	25.6	$2,500-$4,999	3.1
$750-$999	10.7	$5,000 and over	1.9
$1,000-$1,499	11.1		

From this table we learn that 79.9 percent of the actors receive under $1,000 a week, that 20.1 percent receive $1,000 or more a week, and that 6 percent get $2,000 a week or more.

* Seventeen did not answer, or gave answers which were unclear or illegible.
† Some actors in this group arrived in Hollywood (from the stage, little theaters) during 1939 and had just begun their quest for movie careers.
‡ 16 unemployed, 14 did not work in movies in Hollywood, 17 did not answer. Total cases: 309.

Nothing exposes the fallacy of Hollywood's *salaries* as an index of welfare so much as the contrast between weekly figures and the total amount which actors find they have earned at the end of the year. What were the actual annual earnings of the actors? A careful check of the evidence provided by 253 actors * revealed that the annual earnings for 1939 ranged from "less than $50" to $300,000. The median average was $4,700. This offers a startling contrast to the prodigious weekly figures which we have been examining; it means that half of Hollywood's class A actors earned $4,700 or less in 1939 and that half earned $4,700 or more. The violent exaggerations which are induced in the public mind by the $200,000 and $300,000 salaries of the most illustrious movie stars are deflated by a recognition of the meaning of the $4,700 a year median for Hollywood's actors—*excluding* the extras. There is a difference between the median annual earnings of male actors ($4,700) and females ($4,150).

The range in the annual incomes of actors is so gigantic (under $50 to $300,000) that it is difficult to handle the data with clarity unless we divide the actors into groups, to avoid the distortion which results from great extremes. It will be simple and revealing to divide the actors into four groups, according to their weekly salaries in 1939 (253 cases):

Weekly Salaries	Median Annual Earnings (1939)
Under $500	$ 2,000
$500-$999	6,075
$1,000-$1,999	20,000
$2,000 and over	103,500

Now let us see how many actors earned how much from movie work over a three-year period (1937-39 inclusive):

* Eliminating those who had been totally unemployed in 1939; those who had not worked in any movie studio; nine actors who were employed but did not answer the question.

ANNUAL INCOMES: ACTORS *

Annual Income	1939 (Percent)	1938 (Percent)	1937 (Percent)
Under $2,000	25.7	22.2	18.8
$2,000-$3,999	19.4	20.4	20.6
$4,000-$5,999	9.5	10.6	10.0
$6,000-$7,999	9.9	13.9	8.8
$8,000-$9,999	4.3	2.8	5.9
$10,000-$19,999	14.6	12.5	18.8
$20,000-$39,999	9.1	9.3	6.5
$40,000-$59,999	2.8	2.3	4.1
$60,000-$99,999	.8	1.4	3.0
$100,000 and over	3.9	4.6	3.5

The median annual earnings for actors in 1939, as we have seen, was $4,700. In 1938, it was $5,000. In 1937, it was $6,000.

The sharp decline in the earnings of Hollywood's actors from 1937 to 1939 reflects the general decline of the movie business in the same years, and of the volume and profitability of American business at large.† The vast expenditures of the defense program in 1940 and 1941 did not inflate movie earnings to anywhere near the degree that it helped other enterprises. The withdrawal of a million young men to army camps, the reduction of the monthly wages of those men to $21, the dislocations effected by moving defense workers into new areas where housing (and theaters) were limited—all were reflected in box-office disturbances for 1939 and 1940 which brought lamentation from movie executives. The psychological effects of the war, and the recurrent crises in international affairs and American diplomacy, also seem to have encouraged a public apathy to films.

Let us bring this discussion of the earnings of Hollywood's actors to a close by asking two questions: What was the *first*

* 253 reports for 1939, 216 for 1938, 170 for 1937.
† An analysis of the net earnings of seven major motion picture companies for the same years shows earnings of $36,926,000 in 1937, $21,577,000 in 1938, and $19,-110,000 in 1939. The net earnings of the movie companies fell off 41.6 percent from 1937 to 1938, and 11.4 percent from 1938 to 1939. See the tables in Appendix B.

weekly salary which the actors received in their first jobs as movie actors in Hollywood? What are the *highest annual incomes* which the actors have received?

FIRST WEEKLY SALARIES AS ACTORS

239 Cases

Salary	Percent
Under $250	44.4
$250-$499	29.3
$500-$749	10.9
$750-$999	7.1
$1,000-$1,499	5.8
$1,500-$1,999	1.3
$2,000 and over	1.2

This indicates that less than half of the class A actors in Hollywood (44.4 percent) *began* their movie work at a weekly salary under $250; over half of the actors (55.6 percent) began on a salary of $250 or more a week; and over a fourth (26.3 percent) began at a weekly salary of $500 or more.

The second question we raise will correct any misconceptions which may arise from the favorable record presented in the array of first weekly salaries. What are the *highest* annual amounts earned in Hollywood by the actors who are in the movie colony today?

HIGHEST ANNUAL EARNINGS

239 Cases

Highest Annual Earnings	Percent *
Under $2,000	6.8
Under $4,000	18.6
Under $6,000	27.0
Under $10,000	45.6
Under $20,000	69.2
Under $30,000	80.2
Under $60,000	90.7
Under $100,000	93.7

* The percentages do not total 100; the categories are progressively inclusive.

A listing of the highest annual earnings ever received from movie work by the film actors reveals a median average of $10,500. In other words, half the class A actors in Hollywood today have never earned $10,500 a year from their movie work, and half have earned $10,500 or more at some time in their careers before the camera.

Marriage and Divorce. The analysis of the actors' marital and divorce record, and of the rambunctious publicity assigned to this side of Hollywood's mores, was explored in "Eros in Hollywood," chapter 5. Let us recapitulate the data briefly.

How many actors are single or married (as of 1940)? The record for 294 actors who answered shows that 201 (68.4 percent) are married and 93 (31.6 percent) are single. There is a pronounced difference between the current marital status of male and female actors: 45.3 percent of the women were single in 1940, as against 25.9 percent of the men. The difference is to a large degree explained by the great variation in the ages of male and female actors. It is also worth noticing that 80 percent of the male actors reported that they were or had been married, as compared to 64 percent of the actresses.

How many times have how many actors been married? The *probable* number of marriages for the leading 200 actors and actresses * may be set forth:

18.5 percent have probably never been married.
54.5 percent have probably been married only once.
20.5 percent have probably been married twice.
5.5 percent have probably been married three times.
1.0 percent have probably been married four times.

In other words, 73 percent have probably been married either once or not at all; 27 percent have probably been married two or more times.†

* See Appendix E for the method used.
† It is quite possible that the leading 200 actors and actresses have been married and divorced more frequently than would be true for the actors in Hollywood as a group.

How many actors have been divorced, and how many times? Here again the material represents the *probable* pattern, according to the most reliable information available for 200 actors and actresses:

> 64.5 percent have probably never been divorced.
> 26.0 percent have probably been divorced once.
> 8.0 percent have probably been divorced twice.
> 1.0 percent have probably been divorced three times.
> .5 percent have probably been divorced four times.

In other words, 35.5 percent of the actors have probably been divorced and 64.5 percent have probably not been divorced.

How many children do the actors have? From 157 replies * to questionnaires, we find:

> 40 have no children.
> 67 have 1 child.
> 22 have 2 children.
> 20 have 3 children.
> 5 have 4 children.
> 1 has 5 children.
> 1 has 6 children.
> 1 has 8 children.

Complaints. The complaints of 198 actors were analyzed from their answers to two questions: "In what specific way could your working conditions at the studios be improved?" and "Suggestions for the Screen Actors Guild." The largest proportion, 49.5 percent, complained about factors relating to security and employment; the questionnaires showed a steady, strong refrain asking for "more work," "steady employment," "a regard for seniority," "a better chance for unknowns," "bigger play to bit players."

A fifth of the actors (19.2 percent) protested about the num-

* Of the 309 cases, 157 answered the question "Number of children"; 73 actors were single and had never been married, 63 did not answer the question on number of children, and 16 did not answer the questions on either marital status or number of children.

ber of hours they work and asked for shorter working hours, a definite working day, less night work. Many of these complainants remarked that in addition to a long working day the actor must spend at least half an hour in the morning applying make-up and the same amount of time, after the working day, in removing make-up. Many actors requested a strict eight-hour day, and several suggested a five-day week.

A fifth of the actors (19.2 percent) expressed grievances which arise from what may be called thwarted craftsmanship: they asked for more time to study their roles, more rehearsals with the cast, more opportunities to read the entire script (rather than their parts alone), a greater diversification in the roles they are given, and so on.

Some 12.6 percent made suggestions revolving around the actors' relationship to other movie crafts: more co-operation from and with assistant directors, better casting practices, better stories from writers and producers, and so on. Only 2 percent complained of favoritism or nepotism.

It is significant that no less than 19.7 percent of the actors specifically remarked that they had *no* complaints, that working conditions are satisfactory, that, in the words of several respondents: "To an actor of the old days, working conditions are heaven"; "Studios are treating actors very well since Guild shop went into effect"; "I've worked in all kinds of show business and have never been treated better than in Pix."

The Actor and the Movies. The actors were invited to "Comment on the content of American movies today," and 189 actors made 293 comments.

Sixty-five actors made comments of a general character: 51 were favorable in their remarks; 12 were unfavorable; 2 were neither favorable nor unfavorable. Those who praised Hollywood's movies were ambiguously laudatory: "wonderful," "getting better," "best in world," "best entertainment." Those who were derogatory remarked that movies were "largely drivel," or "eighty percent trash," or "too little footage to cheer for." One of the 2 neutral commentators said, "The content of any popular art is exactly what the whole body of folkways makes it."

Fifty-eight actors commented on the kind of pictures and stories which Hollywood produces; 35 were critical in their remarks, 23 were favorable. Those who criticized Hollywood's output mentioned "too many gangster films," "too many pictures have trifling plots," "too much gag humor," "same old stories," and so on. Those who praised the movies remarked that "pictures are getting down to earth," "becoming more adult," "each year our pictures are improving."

Thirty-nine actors' comments revolved around the treatment of a story or theme: 30 were critical ("too spectacular," "maudlin," "conventional direction," "more action, less dialogue") and 9 were favorable ("growing maturity," "instructive").

Twenty-nine actors commented on "originality" or "initiative": 25 condemned formula pictures or "shoddy material"; 3 remarked that Hollywood was beginning to be "honest" and "free." (These 29 comments can be combined with the 58 adverse comments on the kinds of pictures and stories being filmed; if so, then 70 actors out of the 189 who commented were critical of Hollywood's stories, pictures, initiative, and originality.)

Twenty-one actors commented on artistic factors: 14 actors made favorable remarks on the artistry of movies (photography, sets, technical factors, costumes, music); 7 criticized the movies on esthetic grounds: "too extravagant," "should use more color," and so on.

Twenty actors specifically mentioned the role of the box-office, and were almost equally divided in their comments. Some deplored the potency of the box-office, but stated that considering this handicap "the producers are doing a good job." Others said the American film underestimates the box-office level of intelligence and that the producers would meet popular taste more adequately by improving the movies. There was a marked absence of agreement in the comments which pertained to box-office factors and the movies.

Sixteen actors mentioned B pictures and quantity production; all sixteen were condemnatory.

Eleven actors mentioned the star system, and all of them denounced it ("worn out," "too much footage to 'glamour,'" etc.). The comments undoubtedly came from actors who were not stars.

Ten actors condemned censorship; none defended it.

What conclusions can we extract from these 293 comments? Simply that Hollywood's actors do not accept either Hollywood or the movies uncritically; and that, as a group, actors are more critical than contented with the character and substance of American movies today.

Three

16. THE LONG ARM OF HOLLYWOOD

"IN the four corners of the globe, who reads an American book, or goes to an American play, or looks at an American picture . . . ?"
—SYDNEY SMITH, 1820.

Lord Northcliffe called motion pictures "the fifth estate." It is a valuable phrase. The frequency with which we hear the cliché "press, radio, and movies" testifies to the recognition that Hollywood is one of the key symbol-centers of the world. The influence of Hollywood is immense and pervasive. It is an influence which transcends differences in language or custom, age or creed. It is an influence which ranges from slang and songs to the export of typewriters or the pattern of women's coiffures. It is an influence which, to repeat a Frenchman's comment, threatened a colonization of the world by the American culture whose films are its most potent and energetic carriers. It is an influence which springs from two sources: the movies and the movie stars.

The long arm of Hollywood reaches into every province of the manners and the mores of our time; it does not, except obliquely and occasionally, touch the ideologies of our day. The movie makers are beholden to a mass market; they are saddled with enormous costs; they know that ideas attract

355

controversy; and they shape their stories into fables which testify to the proposition that maximum profits reward maximum innocuousness.

The extraordinary significance of the movies is illustrated by the fact that of all the contemporary arts—and businesses—it was the movies which were singled out for discussion in a special papal encyclical devoted to that purpose (Pius XI, July 2, 1936). And the potency of films, the threat to national policies or private interests which they can be assumed to represent, is demonstrated by the astonishing variety of protests which pour into Hollywood week after week. The expostulations against movies, from governments, foreign offices, business groups, religious orders, trade associations, fraternal societies, or professional bodies, are nothing short of cosmic in their range and in their substance.

The Japanese censors, for example, strongly objected to a Hollywood version of *Madame Butterfly* because Sylvia Sidney, in kissing Lieutenant Pinkerton (the scene was handled with pathetic caution), placed her arms around his neck in such a manner that her elbow was bared. This, apparently, was tantamount to nudity in Japan. A national billiard association voiced hot protest because pool rooms, in the movies, are shown as unkempt places where disreputable characters congregate. The late Polish Government barred *Show Boat* because the song, "Ol' Man River," was "proletarian propaganda" likely to incite the Polish masses to rebellion. The American Newspaper Guild objected to the prevalence of impolite, intoxicated, or unscrupulous reporters on the screen.

The British regularly censor those movie scenes in which animals so much as *appear* to be suffering, even though Hollywood's studios offer affidavits from humane societies proving that the effects were achieved quite without pain to our Darwinian cousins. The Glass Bottle Blowers Association complained that the movies were giving free advertising to canned beer, and a group in the canning industry insisted that the movies are spreading the gospel of bottled beverages. France (1939) compelled Hollywood to change the villain of *Beau Geste* from a Frenchman to a Russian.

An organization of silver fox breeders expressed their indignation because in one picture a Negress was seen wearing a silver fox. The Audubon Society voiced a complaint concerning a story which was being considered by a studio because the plot required that an eagle carry off a child. It is easy to extend this Domesday Book to chilling proportions, but let us end this array of hurt feelings by citing the letter which denounced a movie because it "maligned and burlesqued" the Master Plumbers of America, a group, it was insisted, "which has done more to protect the health and comfort of the American people than any other group or industry." *

No matter what the intentions of the movie makers may be, no matter how unconscious they may be of the effects of their product, no matter how reluctant Hollywood may be to manipulate the subtle and persuasive power at its disposal, the movies exert an influence which is vast and profound.[1]

In a world convulsed by catastrophe and change, Hollywood sells the oldest of allegories in its simplest and most consoling outlines: Boy Gets Girl. Those who berate the movies for their enslavement to Boy Meets Girl—Boy Loses Girl—Boy Gets Girl forget that this theme has been sovereign in the novel and the play for several thousand years, and in cultures ranging from the Greek to the Chinese. They forget that the unhappy ending was unpopular even in enlightened Athens. They forget that no less an authority than Aristotle declared that one of the primary

---

* The cases are taken from an extensive analysis of the files and correspondence of the Production Code Administration. Copies of the letters or documents making each of the criticisms are in the possession of this writer.

functions of the artist is to serve his audience, that the only art of political importance is popular art: "the poet is guided in what he writes by the wishes of his audience." [2] They forget that T. S. Eliot, surely no apostle of the flesh-pots, observed that the movies have supplanted the stage in serving the public with melodrama and concluded that "melodrama is perennial and . . . the craving for it is perennial and must be satisfied." [3]

In the recondite naïveté of Hollywood's movies, life is a simple game between love and misunderstanding, between the pure in heart and the other kind. Optimism is basic, romance is of the essence, crises are rarely more than personal. In the movies, problems are solved by mere love, sheer will, or expiatory gestures; that is, by virtue, luck, or divine intercession. In the norms of the silver screen, virtue, luck, and divine intercession are incomparably more important than skill, intelligence, or reality. The Greek dramatists, it will be remembered, lowered an actor-Jove from the top of the stage so he could settle the destiny of the characters whenever the plot became too complicated for the author; Hollywood's *deus ex machina* is nowhere as crude: he resides in the very content of the movies, in the structure and values of the movies themselves.

In the movie story of mankind, the man who writes to Mother, steps aside for his friend, or places his sweetheart's happiness above his carnal desires is pretty sure to end as the ecstatic bridegroom, the president of the company, or the composer whose genius the audiences at Carnegie Hall acclaim by beating their palms into a pulp. The cad who kicks a dog, cheats at cards, betrays a friend, or attempts to seduce a maiden, is headed straight for the Big House, death, and eternal perdition beyond. To movie heroes, of course, death is no more than the passport to eternal joy, its occurrence usually being accompanied by a majestic chorus of unseen angels hurling triumphant hosannahs at the audience while the screen swarms with moving clouds. It is surely consoling to discover that in the special logic of the movies, self-sacrifice always ends in successful (if unplanned) self-aggrandizement; and that selfishness is utter folly, doomed to a terrible fate.

All this means that in the moral lexicon of Hollywood, honesty is always rewarded, evil is always punished, and crime—in an exquisite reflection of the pragmatic emphases of our world—does not *pay*. The Lord Chief Justice of Great Britain, Lord Hewart, dismissed the contention that the movies help to "make" criminals, in this happy line: "If virtue triumphed in actual life as regularly as on the films, this world might be an easier place both to police and to understand." [4]

Hollywood's racial typologies are forever dismaying. To the movie addict, Negroes are lazy, light-hearted mortals who tap dance on the slightest provocation and are prone to burst into spirituals during a thunderstorm. Italians seem to be a singularly specialized species, either childishly happy or dreadfully brutal; their talents, by some anthropological curse, are limited to restauranting or crime. Swedes, of course, are slow-witted behemoths dedicated to either the sea or the basement. In the realm of higher learning, teachers are depicted as frustrated, if female, or emasculated, if male. And the moviegoer knows that a happy woman is one who enters a room with her arms full of packages. An entire social philosophy is reduced to that one classic image.

It is fitting to ask how a generation which has been inoculated with the inclusive romanticism of the movies—a romanticism which encompasses everything from individual amour to social issues—will cope with an increasingly hard and unpretty reality. To those intoxicated by the champagne of the film, everyday life and love may represent the deflation of periodically inflated expectations. One may be excused for wondering what are the consequences to psychological security when clerks are encouraged to believe in high destiny, when buck-toothed ingenues dream of Errol Flynn. True, there were Fairy Princes and Princesses long before celluloid was invented; but were they ever so real, and did they actually talk and kiss and sing?

The emphasis of the films upon action, violence, and brash conduct necessarily involves a devaluation of the thoughtful and the contemplative. This can hardly avoid influencing the manners of a society already predisposed to the physical solution of disputes, the mentality of a society most of whose inhabitants are more respectful of Hugh Johnson than John Dewey.

This is not meant to imply that Hollywood creates its *own* values, or that Hollywood invents stereotypes with single-handed omnipotence, or that Hollywood *causes* the public acceptance of banal homilies. The movie makers are in many ways compelled to feed a popular diet to a public which is in firm possession of deplorable tastes—tastes derived from sources far older, deeper, and more potent than Hollywood. The very success of Hollywood lies in the skill with which it *reflects* the assumptions, the fallacies, and the aspirations of an entire culture. The movie producers, the movie directors, the movie writers, and the movie actors work with the stereotypes which are current in our society—for they, too, are children of that society; they, too, have inherited and absorbed the values of our world. But Hollywood, through the movies, *reinforces* our typologies on an enormous scale and with overpowering repetitiveness. Whether the movies imitate life or whether life imitates the movies is for others to decide; this writer believes that like missionaries on a desert island, they begin to convert each other. Some critics say that audiences complain about the movies because the movies do not reflect reality; it is this writer's suspicion that more people lament the fact that reality does not reflect the movies.

The long arm of Hollywood can be seen in any home or department store, or by glancing into the nearest mirror. Indirect lighting, modern furniture, and resplendent bathrooms, those landmarks of man's ascent from barbarism, owe much to the silver screen. The off-the-face hat, invented to keep shadows off the faces of movie Lorelei who are paid for their unshadowed features, swept the feminine world in the past decade and re-established a style which is two thousand years old. The movies helped to undermine the taboos which fought off a cosmeticized world. The short-vamp shoe, the decline of the American custom of eating peas with a knife, elegant feminine underthings, the popularity of Scotch and soda, and smoking by adolescents and women—all may be traced in some measure to Hollywood's persuasive power.

The impact of Hollywood on speech, song, and gesture is even more obvious. In Bombay or Oslo or Hong Kong the boys who worship James Cagney, George Raft, or Edward G. Robinson incorporate machine-gun noises and impudent gestures into their play. (In 1939, five thousand police chiefs in the United States voted their annual award to Mr. Cagney as the person who had done most to discourage crime in our land.[5]) The song hits of Shanghai and Dayton are often the same, and Alice Faye or Dorothy Lamour probably introduced them. When Edmund Lowe and Victor McLaglen hurled "Sez you!" at each other as a deadly riposte at regular intervals in one of their film sagas, the phrase became a part of our language for years. The chief constable of Wallasey, a suburb of Liverpool, sadly remarked in one of his annual reports:

> I cannot refrain from commenting adversely on the pernicious and growing habit of . . . youths to use Americanisms, with nasal accompaniment, in order to appear, in their own vernacular, *tough guys*. On one of my officers going to search him, a young housebreaker told him to *"Lay off, cop."* Oh-yeahs are frequent in answer to charges, and we are promised *shoots up in the burg [sic]* and threatened to be *bumped off*.[6]

Women have taken an increasingly important place in modern society; in no realm of endeavor has the stronger sex risen to the prominence it occupies in the movie colony and the film industry. No business can match Hollywood's female personnel for influence; there are, indeed, no counterparts to a Lombard, a Shearer, or a Colbert. In the index of fame and fortune, the illustrious names of the stage, opera, or letters must yield to the imperial queens of the screen. It should occasion no surprise to learn that when a questionnaire was submitted to girls in one section of New York, asking them what they wanted to be, two-thirds of the lasses replied—movie actress.[7]

The movie idols have usurped the role of Society in establishing styles. Today, Society's fashions are more imitative of Hollywood's than the other way around. Marlene Dietrich's affinity for slacks, for example, was a major factor in the rise of a new article of feminine disguise. The hat which Greta Garbo wore in *Susan Lennox* put thousands of milliners to work on a style which was hailed as revolutionary. Jean Harlow's platinum-dyed hair started a vogue which has not yet, unfortunately, abated. Norma Shearer's bob, for *Romeo and Juliet*, altered women's hair-do for over a year and brought bitter conflict into a million boudoirs. In men's apparel, slack suits, polo shirts, Tyrolean hats, and roll-collar shirts are inescapable evidence of Hollywood's influence. It is a familiar but ever-impressive fact that when Clark Gable disrobed in *It Happened One Night* and was revealed to be *sans* undershirt, he sent the men's underwear business into a decline which, glassy-eyed manufacturers estimated, cut their business from forty to fifty percent within a year.

Hollywood has lured some of the finest designers and couturières in the world into its bailiwick. Movie previews are attended by style copyists who rush their drawings back to the East so that a Crawford gown, mass-produced and cheaply priced, can stream to the women of America with a minimum of delay. There are over fifteen "style-reporting" agencies in Los Angeles which act as style scouts for department stores all over the world; they send out weekly bulletins, sketches, samples, and tips on who is wearing what. Buyers are especially susceptible to Hollywood's styles: it is easier to sell a "number" which has been featured in a film seen by millions of consumers, and sales arguments are fortified by references to the fact that "Ginger Rogers wore this very dress in Palm Springs." Besides, department store buyers like to come to Hollywood: the weather, sports, and the carnival atmosphere make their stay pleasant; and the opportunity of seeing movie stars in the flesh, apart from being exciting in itself, enhances prestige at home to a staff in awe of those who saw the mighty in their habitat. Los Angeles is a booming fashion and clothes-manufacturing center; in sportswear, it has become almost unrivaled.*

We have seen that over twenty years ago English, German and French merchants began to complain to their governments about the influence of Hollywood's movies on their commerce. Audiences which see American typewriters, furniture, automobiles, radios, or clothing in the expertly photographed films of Hollywood show an understandable preference for American merchandise. Any visitor to Europe is impressed by the Americanization of clothes, homes, and habits.

The role of the movies in heightening the public's taste for the perquisites of wealth was even more striking. During the roaring Twenties, the American appetite for luxuries spread and deepened: the war years were over, the 1919 depression had been endured, and the glittering, if spurious, prosperity of a decade had begun. Money was god, money-making a cult, spending a glorious adventure. In cars and clothing, houses and services, the pleasure-bent pursued their desires. The interest in etiquette, beauty creams, and democratic snobbery, mile-

* See Appendix A.

stones on the road to Sophistication, was evidenced in the rush for books, magazines, and tutors in the esoteric arts of decorum. Above all, a fast-living, high-riding middle class was possessed by curiosity to know how the rich and the sophisticated lived. The movies taught them. *Nouveaux riches* movie makers projected *nouveaux riches* values into the films. Hollywood presented the *nouveau riche* as a more understandable and sympathetic social type.

It was Cecil B. DeMille who sensed the public demand and, with his own special genius, turned the movies into a medium which satisfied the public's desire for knowledge about the mores of acquisition. DeMille gazed upon life and came to the conclusion that the brotherhood of man was primarily interested in only two things—money and sex. The DeMille boudoir epics blended money and sex with incomparable showmanship. The master brought celebrated designers, interior decorators, hairdressers, and brassière experts to Hollywood. He shattered the fashion monopoly of Paris by putting glorified fashion shows on the screen; he gave shop girls ringside seats at dress salons for the price of a movie ticket:

DeMille showed them the object of their dreams in actual use. . . . He knew to a hair the value of over-emphasis and over-elaboration . . . his interiors, exaggerated as they often were, were nevertheless convincing; any one of them might have been in the home of a multi-millionaire, and many of them undoubtedly were after DeMille pointed the way. . . . He withdrew the curtains that had veiled the rich and the fashionable, and exhibited them in all the intimate and lavish details of their private lives.[8]

The DeMille influence has persisted in movies for the simple reason that the lavish is perenially attractive to the populace and perenially profitable to the film companies. Apparently the only rival to money and sex (in the movies) is action, and the content of Hollywood's movies may be encompassed by those three symbols.

Magazines in a dozen languages feed the fan world which is hungry for a glimpse within the wondrous halls of Hollywood. The Italian movie publication *Film, after* the boycott of American movies by Mussolini and the actual withdrawal of American movies from Italy, was loaded with photographs of Hollywood's godlings. In one issue, page one featured Merle Oberon, Louis Hayward, and Sally Eilers; on page four, there was Douglas Fairbanks, Jr.; part of page five displayed Ann Miller; page seven was occupied by a massive photograph of Fred MacMurray; page nine was graced by Lola Lane; and page twelve aimed at posterity with an action shot of Mickey Rooney. More than twice as much space was devoted to Hollywood's stars as to their Italian and European rivals.[9]

Even where there is revolt against Hollywood's dominion, the unconscious aping of Hollywood testifies to the enormity of its influence. *Filmindia,* Bombay's fat fan magazine, conducts a relentless crusade against Hollywood's "disgusting libel of the Indian people . . . disgraceful pictures . . . insidious anti-Indian propaganda. . . ." Only pictures of native stars fill its pages; nary a note or picture of a Hollywood luminary is allowed. And yet, in the same issue in which the quotation cited above occurs (March, 1939), there is a page of photographs in which Indian sirens in American dress cavort in a penthouse (!); one picture shows a lovely Hindu actress using a Flit gun; there is a full page of pictures of native Don Juans in polo shirts, sport jackets, bow ties, felt hats, and ascot scarves (and only one turban); and there is a closeup of a beauteous Hindu maiden with her hat pulled low over her eyes, aiming a gun at the camera in the approved Hollywood mode.

Dr. George Gallup and his American Institute of Public Opinion conducted surveys for two years on the reading habits of Americans in all walks of life and different sections of the land; one of the striking facts "that is scored and underscored in these studies is the tremendous influence of Hollywood on reading tastes." Gallup points out that Hollywood boosts the classics of literature into new and extraordinary popularity. When the movie *David Copperfield* was being publicized, the Cleveland Public Library ordered over 125 extra copies of the book to meet the probable rise in demand; and although the library had over five hundred copies of the book, the shelves were bare of *David Copperfield* and other Dickens novels for weeks. The film *Wuthering Heights* served as a remarkable boomerang to the book's popularity. Four publishing houses sold out all their editions of the work in a short time, and book stores and public libraries could not cope with the rediscovery of the Brontë masterpiece.[10]

The hand of Hollywood shapes the fiction we read in books and magazines. American writers can scarcely escape being influenced by the brisk structure, tempo, and dialogue of the film; and the golden purse of Hollywood has created a legion of scriveners who write with one eye on screen possibilities. Bennett A. Cerf, publishing head of Random House and the Modern Library, recently announced:

. . . Until a sweeping readjustment takes place . . . in the motion picture world, writers will not be interested enough in either books or book publishers to regard them as very much more than little way-stations on the royal road to Beverly Hills. . . . How can a sense of proportion be preserved when a lot of worn-out old hacks who haven't written an honest word or thought an honest thought for ten years can still draw a couple of thousand dollars a week turning out scenarios, and newcomers whose first novels are still wet from the presses are offered contracts that make their total earnings from the book rights look like a lunch check at the Automat. . . . The thing that an author wants most from his publisher these days is a letter of introduction to Darryl Zanuck.[11]

The phenomenal rise of Hollywood as a radio center is another manifestation of the film capital's accentuated influence. The radio industry comes to Hollywood for comic, crooning, or histrionic personalities: the size of radio's investment in Los

Angeles is exceeded only by its investment in New York, and a University of Southern California study estimates that over fifty percent of the most popular national radio programs originate in Hollywood.[12] The union of movies and radio has deepened and widened the influence of Hollywood.

The Lynds have pointed out, in *Middletown in Transition*, that adolescents not only enjoy the movies, but "go to school" in the movie houses. They model themselves after movie stars; they repeat movie jokes and gestures; they learn the subtleties of free behavior between the sexes; they develop surprisingly sophisticated manners; and they pattern their lives not on those of their parents, but on "the sharp figures of the silver screen which present gay and confident designs for living."

All of our institutions, with the important exception of the movies, are cautious about sex and its treatment for adolescents; it is only natural, therefore, that the influence of the movies becomes proportionately greater in this delicate sphere.[13]

In one community in New York City which was studied intensively:

. . . the movies [were] not only the most universal form of recreation, but a major source of ideas about life and the world in general. . . . Movie attendance had become practically universal. . . . The neighborhood movie house was an important feature of the life of the community. . . . The glamour which surrounded the movie and entertainment world . . . was positively dazzling to young people.[14]

Sociologists have commented on the role of the motion picture in reshaping our attitudes to marriage and divorce, our methods of courtship, our reaction to the problems of family life. The movies, with their uniformity of content, bridge the ancient gap between the urban and the rural, and undermine the provincialism of non-metropolitan life. The movies are a source of excitement and substitute experience, a potent agency of non-formal education, a dramaturgic genie who stimulates and gratifies fantasy. The movies put vicarious romance in our laps; they set up ideal stereotypes for love and ideal norms of success. To men everywhere the movies are as inexpensive and universal an avenue of escape as our world offers. An advertisement in the *Saturday Evening Post* sang Hollywood's praises in these lyrical words:

Go to a motion picture . . . and let yourself go. Before you know it you are *living* the story—laughing, loving, hating, struggling, winning! All the adventure, all the romance, all the excitement you lack in your daily life are in—Pictures. They take you completely out of yourself into a wonderful new world. . . . Out of the cage of every-day existence! If only for an afternoon or an evening—escape! [15]

The movies have extended the dimensions of leisure. They have opened new horizons in education. They have created new foci of public attention. The influence of talking pictures produced for a mass market, distributed world wide, and exhibited simultaneously in hundreds of cities and towns, is at once too immense and too subtle for exact appraisal. It seems self-evident that Hollywood represents a challenge to the sovereignty of church, school, and family in the realm of values. The philosopher, the politician, the publicist, or the student may well agree with Mortimer J. Adler when he observes that the movies are "more than any other art the social and political problem of our day." [16]

APPENDICES

A. THE MOVIES AND LOS ANGELES

I. A Note on Industrial Los Angeles

Since 1880, and more especially since 1920, Los Angeles' rate of growth—in population, industry, wealth—has surpassed that of any of the leading ten cities in the land, and its record raises the eyebrows of students of urbanism. From 1850 up to 1930, the population more than doubled itself every ten years. By 1940, Los Angeles had become the fifth largest city in the United States, with an official population of 1,504,277. Los Angeles County is America's aircraft center, is second only to the Detroit area in automobile assemblage and to Akron in tire production, is third in oil refining and in furniture manufacture, is fourth in the manufacturing of women's clothing. In recent years, Los Angeles has led the country in the number of building permits issued, and the County has had a greater number of real estate *transactions* than any in the country.* And in the ownership and use of automobiles—a necessity in the Gargantuan expanse of a city with 450 square miles—Los Angeles County stands unchallenged: over 1,076,000 automobiles, five automobiles for every four families, more in this one county than in all but six states in the Union. A Department of Labor study showed that wage-earners in Los Angeles spend more money on automobiles than on clothes.†

II. Why the Movies Came to Hollywood

Hollywood maintains its supremacy as movie capital of the world long after the conditions which led to its original choice have disappeared.

* "Facts About Los Angeles County Market," published by *Los Angeles Times*, May, 1938, pp. 3, 7, 9. For figures on population growth and manufacturing see *Statistical Abstract of the United States*, 1939 and 1940, and *World Almanac*, 1940.
† *Los Angeles Times*, March 25, 1939, p. 11.

APPENDIX A

The men who set up their cameras in Hollywood over thirty years ago were trying to escape from the Motion Pictures Patent Company, a powerful and rapacious New York trust which beat down independent competition by strong-arm methods; the early producers were also evading Federal court injunctions and prosecutions of cases involving infringements on the trust's pool of monopolized patents.* Southern California was close enough to Mexico so that harassed producers could hop across the border when marshals of the United States courts drew too close. The Lasky studios came to Hollywood quite unintentionally: a crew had been sent to Flagstaff, Arizona, to get shots for a Western thriller but found Flagstaff snow-bound, went on to California, and landed in a sleepy hamlet called Hollywood.

Southern California had steady sunshine, a necessity in the days when movie-shooting took place out of doors; and cheap labor, cheap extras, and free attractive backgrounds brought other film pioneers to the West Coast. It was discovered that within two hundred miles of Los Angeles there were splendid geographical substitutes for every phenomenon from the Sahara Desert to the Khyber Pass. These were primary advantages; when added to the Wild West locales in which California abounded, and which the early movies required for the major part of their output, Southern California was unrivaled as a film center. The movie men—producers, actors, directors, cameramen, cutters, scenarists—flocked to Los Angeles, and soon the skill-market was concentrated there; the eastern studios in New York, Chicago, and Long Island went into a deseutude from which they never recovered.

* Benjamin B. Hampton, *History of the Movies*, p. 79.

B. PRODUCTION COSTS, ANALYSIS OF MOVIE COMPANIES, COMPARISON WITH OTHER INDUSTRIES

I. Data on Movie Production and Production Costs in Hollywood

1. NUMBER OF PERSONS EMPLOYED IN MOVIE PRODUCTION IN HOLLYWOOD

Between 27- and 33,000 persons, in all, are engaged in the production of films in Hollywood, according to the official records of the California Department of Employment.* The state Division of Labor Statistics declares that there are around 13,000 wage-earners a month (meaning skilled and unskilled labor) in movie production in California. In December, 1940, 12,391 persons were engaged in movie *production* in California.† The biennial census on movie production cited 30,405 persons, in all, as engaged in making movies in the Los Angeles industrial area in 1937: 14,007 were salaried employees and officers of the companies; 16,398 were wage-earners.‡

* "A Study of Seasonal Unemployment in California," California Department of Unemployment, Unemployment Reserves Commission (1939), p. 125.
† *California Labor Statistics Bulletin*, No. 197, published by Division of Labor Statistics and Law Enforcement, State of California.
‡ United States Department of Commerce, *Biennial Census: 1937, Motion Pictures*, January, 1939, p. 3. See also *Statistical Abstract of the United States*, 1939, p. 834.

2. SOME OF THE CRAFTS EMPLOYED IN MOTION PICTURE PRODUCTION IN THE MAJOR STUDIOS

January 1-December 31, 1938

	Total Number Employed	Total Payroll
Carpenters	2,906	$3,099,938.96
Second and Assistant Cameramen	314	906,295.58
Electricians (Gaffers, Best Boys, Operators)	1,695	2,669,642.85
Grips (Foreman, First and Second Grips)	1,312	2,280,707.67
I.B.E.W. (Electricians, Journeymen, Class 2 Soundmen)	428	886,145.51
Laborers (Laborers and Class B Grips)	2,174	1,789,517.78
Machine Shop Workers (Welders, Foundrymen, Platers, Buffers, Blacksmiths, Sheet Metal Workers, Foremen)	271	306,395.32
Precision Machinists	88	197,877.82
Drapers and Upholsterers	134	152,596.36
Makeup and Hairdressing Men	136	472,895.96
Nurserymen, Gardeners, etc.	378	272,404.76
Painters (Foremen, Color Mixers, Sign Writers, Painters, Apprentices, Marbelizers, Furniture Finishers)	957	1,364,696.36
Projectionists	217	634,451.82
Property Men (Prop Men, Foremen, Florists, Swing Gang)	710	961,356.89
Prop Makers	948	1,151,950.92
Scenic Artists	82	136,811.19
Sound Men (Class 1, 2, 3, 4, Film Loaders)	533	1,556,121.01
Modelers, Plasterers, Mould Makers, and Apprentices	376	358,628.98
Still Department (Enlargers, Developers, Retouchers, Printers, Still Cameramen)	278	652,694.52
Auto Mechanics	22	42,256.02
Drivers (Autos, Trucks, Horsemen)	747	1,115,369.82
Wardrobers (Class 1, 2, 3, 4)	299	375,527.58
Plumbers	92	167,859.79

Source: Analysis of major studios' payrolls, a continuing study made by Mr. Fred Pelton of the Association of Motion Picture Producers. Data made available to this writer by Y. Frank Freeman and Fred Pelton.

APPENDIX B

3. HOLLYWOOD'S TOTAL PRODUCTION COSTS, BIENNIALLY, 1921-37

Year	Cost of Production	Percent Change From Preceding Year
1921	$ 77,397,000	. . .
1923	86,418,000	+11.7
1925	93,636,000	+ 8.4
1927	134,343,000	+43.5
1929	184,102,000	+37.0
1931	154,436,000	—16.1
1933	119,343,000	—22.7
1935	161,865,000	+35.6
1937	197,741,000	+22.2

Sources: Census of Manufactures, 1929 and 1933, "Motion Pictures, not Including Projection in Theatres." *Statistical Abstract* (1939) for 1935 and 1937 data; *Statistical Abstract* (1940), p. 864.

4. BREAKDOWN OF TOTAL PRODUCTION COSTS: 1939

Salaries	$ 89,884,841
Wages	41,096,235
Supplies, film, fuel, energy	31,118,277
Contract work	2,023,529
Other expenses	22,726,089
Total	$186,848,971

Source: United States Department of Commerce, Bureau of the Census, *Sixteenth Census of the United States: 1940.* February 28, 1941, Preliminary Report, p. 2.

5. PICTURE COSTS: 1938 *

Company	Over $1,000,000	$500,000 to $1,000,000	$250,000 to $500,000	Under $250,000	Total Number of Pictures
A	2	2	4	10	18
B	5	18	5	22	50
C	6	16	8	11	41
D	3	5	6	29	43
E	1	4	3	39	47
F	2	15	14	21	52
Total Pictures	19	60	40	132	251
Percent of Total	7.6	23.9	15.9	52.6	100.0

* From information supplied by six major studios in Hollywood. Because the information was given in confidence, the studios cannot be identified.

APPENDIX B

II. Analysis of Motion Picture Production Companies in Hollywood

1. TOTAL ASSETS
SEVEN MAJOR MOTION PICTURE COMPANIES *
1939

Company	Assets	Percent of Total Assets
Warner Brothers	$168,618,000	27.03
Loew's	157,333,000	25.22
Paramount	109,575,000	17.57
R.K.O.	95,965,000	15.39
20th Century-Fox	58,828,000	9.43
Columbia	18,560,000	2.98
Universal	14,856,000	2.38
Total	$623,735,000	100.00

Source: The data for all companies except R.K.O. are taken from the Securities and Exchange Commission Survey of Listed Corporations, Volume II. The R.K.O. figures are from Standard Statistics, November 1, 1939, p. 441.

2. VOLUME OF BUSINESS: 1935-1939
EIGHT MAJOR MOTION PICTURE COMPANIES

Volume of Business (Thousands of Dollars)

Company	1935	1936	1937	1938	1939
Loew's	$ 85,033	$ 94,805	$107,822	$108,892	$112,489
Paramount	90,581	102,821	104,186	100,928	96,183
20th Century-Fox	42,448	51,671	56,172	58,201	53,752
Warner Bros.	84,476	90,204	99,864	102,206	102,083
Columbia	15,995	17,499	19,066	20,102	19,414
Universal	14,317	14,711	16,396	18,555	23,879
R.K.O.	45,480	49,180	52,921	56,275	51,451
United Artists	10,555	9,708	12,909	11,747	13,478
Totals	$388,885	$430,599	$469,336	$476,906	$472,729

Percent of Total Volume of Business

	1935	1936	1937	1938	1939
Loew's	21.88	22.02	22.97	22.84	23.80
Paramount	23.29	23.88	22.20	21.16	20.35
20th Century-Fox	10.92	12.00	11.98	12.20	11.37
Warner Bros.	21.72	20.95	21.28	21.43	21.59
Columbia	4.11	4.06	4.06	4.22	4.11
Universal	3.68	3.42	3.49	3.89	5.05
R.K.O.	11.69	11.42	11.27	11.80	10.88
United Artists	2.71	2.25	2.75	2.46	2.85
Totals	100.00	100.00	100.00	100.00	100.00

Source: Data for all companies except R.K.O. and United Artists taken from Securities and Exchange Commission Survey of Listed Corporations, Volume II, June, 1939. R.K.O. figures from Standard Statistics, November 1, 1939, p. 441. United Artists data reported in Boxoffice as part of replies to Department of Justice interrogations, February 24, 1940.

* Data not available for United Artists.

APPENDIX B

3. NET EARNINGS, SEVEN MAJOR MOTION PICTURE COMPANIES: 1935-1939

Net Earnings (Thousands of Dollars)

Company	1935	1936	1937	1938	1939
Loew's	$ 7,626	$10,584	$14,334	$ 9,918	$ 9,538
Paramount	653	6,012	6,045	2,866	2,758
20th Century-Fox	3,090	7,723	8,617	7,252	4,147
Warner Bros.	674	3,177	5,876	1,930	1,741
Columbia	1,815	1,569	1,318	183	2
Universal	(677)*	(1,835)*	(1,085)*	(591)*	1,153
R.K.O.	685	2,486	1,821	19	(229)*
Totals	$13,866	$29,716	$36,926	$21,577	$19,110

Percent of Total Net Earnings

	1935	1936	1937	1938	1939
Loew's	55.00	35.62	38.82	45.97	49.91
Paramount	4.71	20.23	16.37	13.28	14.43
20th Century-Fox	22.28	25.99	23.34	33.61	21.70
Warner Bros.	4.86	10.69	15.91	8.94	9.11
Columbia	13.09	5.28	3.57	.85	A (Less than $\frac{1}{10}$ of 1%)
Universal	(4.88)*	(6.18)*	(2.94)*	(2.74)*	6.03
R.K.O.	4.94	8.37	4.93	.09	(1.20)*
Totals	100.00	100.00	100.00	100.00	100.00

Percentage Change in Net Earnings

	1935-36	1936-37	1937-38	1938-39
Loew's	+ 38.8	+35.4	—30.8	— 3.8
Paramount	+820.7	+ .5	—52.6	— .4
20th Century-Fox	+149.9	+11.6	—15.8	— 42.8
Warner Bros.	+371.4	+45.9	—67.1	— 9.8
Columbia	— 13.5	—16.0	—86.1	— 98.9
R.K.O.	+262.9	—36.5	—99.0	—110.0
Universal †	. . .	. . .	. . .	. . .
Percent change for seven Companies	+114.3	+24.3	—41.6	— 11.4

Source: Data from all companies except R.K.O. taken from Securities Exchange Commission Survey of Listed Organizations, Volume II. R.K.O. figures from Trustees Report in Reorganization Proceedings, June 17, 1940.

* Parentheses denote red figures.
† Net Losses for each year except 1939.

APPENDIX B

III. *Comparison of Motion Picture Industry with 17 Other Industries*

An exhaustive analysis was made of all the data published by the Securities and Exchange Commission for corporations registered under the Securities and Exchange Act of 1934. The materials published by the Securities and Exchange Commission give detailed statistics for eighteen industries, but do *not* comprise a complete survey of American corporations, or American business as a whole. The SEC publications do not include, for example, public utilities, communications, railroads, textiles, insurance companies, bank holding companies, banks and trust companies, bond holders' protective committees, and the industries listed as "miscellaneous" in the census of manufactures. It is obvious that a large and significant part of the American economic structure is not touched.

In other words, our comparison of the motion picture industry with seventeen other industries does not show the position of motion pictures in the entire economic structure of American business, nor are the seventeen other industries listed necessarily the *leading* industries in the country. The analysis simply covers all the materials published by the Securities and Exchange Commission up to 1940. It should be emphasized that when comparable data are available on all American industries, motion pictures will rank far lower than is indicated in the following tables.

The Securities and Exchange Commission publications used in the analysis are reports Nos. 1 to 18 in the series entitled

SELECTED INFORMATION ON (NAME OF INDUSTRY)

Registered Under the Securities Exchange Act of 1934

At June 30, 1938

A partial report on the census of American listed corporations, A Works Progress Administration Project sponsored by the Securities and Exchange Commission. (Project Nos. O. P. 65-21-5049, 265-97-6003, and 365-97-3-19.)

1. Ranked according to volume of business in 1937, the eighteen industries are:

Industry	Volume of Business
1. Oil Refiners	$4,122,155,556
2. Steel	2,847,988,476
3. Meat Packing	2,719,084,404

APPENDIX B

Industry	Volume of Business
4. Automobiles *	2,604,667,667
5. Mail Order Houses	1,038,598,068
6. Chain Grocery—Food	1,028,195,100
7. Department Stores	1,003,406,953
8. Cigarette Manufacturers	938,922,674
9. Chemicals and Fertilizers	934,084,497
10. Tires and Rubber Products	784,723,113
11. Chain Variety	782,866,328
12. Agricultural Machinery	598,196,252
13. Containers and Closures	455,371,874
14. Motion Picture Producers †	**406,855,095**
15. Office Machinery	224,814,755
16. Sugar Refining (Cane)	182,117,253
17. Sugar Refining (Beet)	70,508,360
18. Cement Manufacturers	56,553,454

2. In terms of size of total assets, the industries ranked as follows in 1937:

Industry	Total Assets
1. Oil Refiners	$6,880,858,481
2. Steel	4,181,765,978
3. Chemicals and Fertilizer	1,688,231,343
4. Automobiles	1,525,435,062
5. Meat Packers	825,807,223
6. Cigarette Manufacturers	734,231,460
7. Tires and Rubber Products	724,271,752
8. Agricultural Machinery	691,658,262
9. Department Stores	662,421,723
10. Mail Order Houses	544,720,716
11. Motion Picture Producers	**529,950,444**
12. Chain Variety	517,596,667
13. Containers and Closures	500,763,151
14. Office Machinery	272,739,839
15. Chain Grocery—Food	227,786,488
16. Sugar Refining (Cane)	218,684,648
17. Cement Manufacturers	138,594,605
18. Sugar Refining (Beet)	129,506,300

* Excluding Ford. The SEC does not possess data on those corporations whose stock is not listed on the open market as purchasable by the public.

† This includes distribution and exhibition (theaters, real estate, and distribution organizations of the motion picture corporations). Material on United Artists is not included: United Artists is a distributing and theater-owning corporation and not a motion picture producing company: the producers who release through United Artists are incorporated separately and individually, and since none of their stock is' listed in the open market, none of them is included in the SEC material.

APPENDIX B

3. EXECUTIVE REMUNERATION AS A PERCENTAGE OF NET PROFITS * (1937)

1.	Department Stores	32.10%	10. Sugar Refiners (Beet)	5.18%
2.	**Motion Pictures**	**18.96**	11. Chain Stores (Variety)	4.77
3.	Meat Packers	16.11	12. Steel	3.66
4.	Chain Grocery (Food)	15.58	13. Cigarettes	3.63
5.	Cement	14.18	14. Chemicals and Fertilizers	3.60
6.	Rubber Tires	9.31	15. Agricultural Machinery	3.46
7.	Office Machinery	7.99	16. Mail Order Houses	2.97
8.	Sugar Refiners (Cane)	7.65	17. Oil Refiners	1.67
9.	Containers and Closures	6.65	18. Automobiles	1.52

Source: SEC publications listed above.

4. EXECUTIVE REMUNERATION AS A PERCENTAGE OF TOTAL VOLUME OF SALES (1937)

1.	Cement	1.61	10. Chain Stores (Variety)	.36
2.	**Motion Pictures**	**1.59**	11. Rubber Tires	.32
3.	Office Machinery	1.22	12. Cigarettes	.32
4.	Department Stores	.81	13. Steel	.26
5.	Chemicals and Fertilizers	.75	14. Oil Refiners	.20
6.	Sugar Refiners (Beet)	.64	15. Mail Order Houses	.15
7.	Containers and Closures	.62	16. Automobiles	.14
8.	Sugar Refiners (Cane)	.43	17. Chain Grocery (Food)	.13
9.	Agricultural Machinery	.38	18. Meat Packers	.11

Source: SEC publications listed above.

* Net profits after all charges deducted.

C. ANNUAL EARNINGS, WEEKLY SALARIES, AND SPENDING PATTERNS

1. HOLLYWOOD INCOMES OVER $75,000 (1938)

Earnings	Executives *	Producers	Actors	Directors	Writers	Musical Directors	Total
$ 75,000-100,000	1	11	26	11	13	4	66
100,000-150,000	4	16	23	18	2	0	63
150,000-200,000	5	8	12	13	2	0	40
200,000-250,000	3	1	5	2	0	0	11
250,000-300,000	1	1	5	1	0	0	8
300,000-400,000	0	2	6	0	0	0	8
400,000-500,000	0	0	3	0	0	0	3
500,000-600,000	0	0	0	0	0	0	0
600,000-700,000	1	0	0	0	0	0	1
Total	15	39	80	45	17	4	200

Source: Salary lists made available by Department of the Treasury and published by the House of Representatives' Ways and Means Committee.

2. REMUNERATION DATA: 1939 †

Company	No. Persons Receiving over $20,000 ‡	Total Amount Paid Persons Receiving over $20,000	Average
Loew's	236	$16,461,799	$69,753
Paramount	131	6,620,718	50,540
Warner Bros.	139	6,604,101	47,512
Twentieth	130	6,635,803	51,045
Universal	55	3,191,019	58,019
Columbia	47	2,843,138	60,492
Total	738	$42,356,578	$57,394

* In addition to the Hollywood executives included in this table, the following data, for executives in *New York,* may be added to round out the picture for the motion picture industry: 8 New York executives received between·$75,000-100,000, 4 received between $100,000-150,000, 3 received between $150,000-200,000, 1 received between $200,000-250,000, and 1 received between $250,000-300,000.

† From annual reports of companies to Securities and Exchange Commission.

‡ Exclusive of executives and directors of the corporations.

APPENDIX C

3. ACTORS: ANNUAL EARNINGS *

Weekly Salary Rate	Number	Range of Annual Earnings	Average Annual Earnings	Median Average Annual Earnings
		1939		
Under $500	108	$ 50-$ 16,000	$ 3,048	$ 2,000
$500-$999	92	200- 36,000	8,296	6,075
$1,000-$1,999	37	2,000- 90,000	23,119	20,000
$2,000 and over	16	6,000- 300,000	113,344	103,500
Total	253	$ 50-$300,000	$ 14,867	$ 4,700
		1938		
Under $500	89	$ 25-$ 12,000	$ 3,058	$ 2,250
$500-$999	78	475- 32,250	7,457	6,000
$1,000-$1,999	34	3,000- 62,500	22,690	21,175
$2,000 and over	15	12,000- 300,000	113,937	100,000
Total	216	$ 25-$300,000	$ 15,437	$ 5,000
		1937		
Under $500	66	$ 225-$ 12,500	$ 3,056	$ 2,225
$500-$999	70	1,050- 25,000	8,877	7,225
$1,000-$1,999	22	5,000- 60,000	29,175	27,250
$2,000 and over	12	15,000- 300,000	111,667	97,500
Total	170	$ 225-$300,000	$ 16,500	$ 6,000

4. ACTORS' ANNUAL EARNINGS: 1939 †

Annual Income	Number	Percent
Under $2,000	65	25.7
$2,000-$3,999	49	19.4
$4,000-$5,999	24	9.5
$6,000-$7,999	25	9.9
$8,000-$9,999	11	4.3
$10,000-$19,999	37	14.6
$20,000-$29,999	18	7.1
$30,000-$39,999	5	2.0
$40,000-$59,999	7	2.8
$60,000-$79,999	1	.4
$80,000-$99,999	1	.4
$100,000 and over	10	3.9
Total	253	100.0

Annual Earnings Range: $50-$300,000
Average Annual Earnings: $14,867
Median Average Annual Earnings: $4,700

* Data from replies to questionnaire. Question: "Annual income from motion picture acting in 1939 ...... 1938 ...... 1937 ......" The total number of actors giving information on annual incomes varied; see totals of number reporting above.
† Data from questionnaire replies.

APPENDIX C

5. DIRECTORS: ANNUAL EARNINGS *

Income	1936 No.	1936 Pct.	1937 No.	1937 Pct.	1938 No.	1938 Pct.
Less than $5,000	2	3.8	5	8.5	8	12.9
$5,000-$9,999	8	15.1	8	13.5	11	17.7
$10,000-$14,999	11	20.8	11	18.6	5	8.1
$15,000-$19,999	5	9.4	5	8.5	9	14.5
$20,000-$24,999	4	7.5	4	6.8	1	1.6
$25,000-$49,999	4	7.5	8	13.5	10	16.2
$50,000-$74,999	6	11.3	1	1.7	4	6.5
$75,000-$99,999	4	7.5	4	6.8	2	3.2
$100,000-$124,999	3	5.7	5	8.5	6	9.7
$125,000-$149,999	3	5.7	5	8.5	3	4.8
$150,000-$174,999	1	1.9	1	1.7	1	1.6
$175,000-$199,999	..	..	1	1.7	1	1.6
$200,000 and over	2	3.8	1	1.7	1	1.6
Total Reports	53	100.0	59	100.0	62	100.0
Worked only part year	3		2		2	
Not working as director	9		2		4	
No answer	4		6		1	
Grand Total	69		69		69	

	1936	1937	1938
Median	$20,000	$20,000	$16,500
Average	$47,559	$48,000	$43,974
Range	$4,300-$238,000	$4,000-$200,000	$1,500-$200,000

6. WEEKLY SALARIES OF PRODUCERS, ASSOCIATE PRODUCERS AND SUPERVISORS AT 3 MAJOR HOLLYWOOD STUDIOS: 1938 †

	Number	Percent
Less than $250	11	21.2
$250-$499	7	13.5
$500-$749	9	17.3
$750-$999	3	5.8
$1,000-$1,249	1	1.9
$1,250-$1,499	2	3.8
$1,500-$1,999	8	15.4
$2,000-$2,499	3	5.8
$2,500-$2,999	3	5.8
$3,000-$3,499	1	1.9
$3,500-$3,999	1	1.9
$4,000-$4,499	..	..
$4,500-$4,999	1	1.9
$5,000-$5,499	1	1.9
$7,500	1	1.9
Total	52	100.0

* Data from questionnaire: Question: "Annual income from screen directing in 1938 ...... 1937 ...... 1936 ......"
† From an analysis of the payroll data of Twentieth Century-Fox, Warner Brothers, and Columbia Pictures Corporation.

APPENDIX C

7. WEEKLY SALARIES OF DIRECTORS AT THREE MAJOR HOLLYWOOD STUDIOS: 1938 *

	Number	Percent
Less than $250	3	7.5
$250-$499	8	20.0
$500-$749	5	12.5
$750-$999	6	15.0
$1,000-$1,249	2	5.0
$1,250-$1,499	2	5.0
$1,500-$1,999	3	7.5
$2,000-$2,499	3	7.5
$2,500-$2,999	3	7.5
$3,000-$3,499	4	10.0
$3,500-$3,999	. .	. .
$4,000-$4,499	. .	. .
$4,500-$4,999	1	2.5
$5,000	. .	. .
Total	40	100.0

8. WEEKLY SALARIES OF WRITERS AT THREE MAJOR HOLLYWOOD STUDIOS: 1938 *

	Number	Percent
Less than $250	93	40.8
$250-$499	52	22.8
$500-$749	36	15.8
$750-$999	17	7.5
$1,000-$1,249	11	4.8
$1,250-$1,499	5	2.2
$1,500-$1,749	7	3.1
$1,750-$1,999	3	1.3
$2,000-$2,249	. .	. .
$2,250-$2,499	. .	. .
$2,500-$2,749	3	1.3
$2,750-$2,999	. .	. .
$3,000-$3,249	1	.4
Total	228	100.0

* From an analysis of the payroll data of Twentieth Century-Fox, Warner Brothers, and Columbia Pictures Corporation.

APPENDIX C

9. WEEKLY SALARIES (UNDER $1,000) OF ACTORS AT THREE MAJOR STUDIOS: 1938 *

	Number	*Percent*
Less than $50	..	..
$50-$99	228	40.6
$100-$149	62	11.0
$150-$199	38	6.8
$200-$249	34	6.1
$250-$299	45	8.0
$300-$349	23	4.1
$350-$399	18	3.2
$400-$449	17	3.0
$450-$499	4	.7
$500-$549	40	7.1
$550-$599	1	.2
$600-$649	23	4.1
$650-$699	4	.7
$700-$749	1	.2
$750-$799	20	3.6
$800-$849	..	..
$850-$899	1	.2
$900-$949	1	.2
$950-$999	1	.2
Total	561	100.0

* From an analysis of the payroll data of Twentieth Century-Fox, Warner Brothers, and Columbia Pictures Corporation.

10. SPENDING AND SAVINGS: 16 CASE STUDIES

Case	Total Income (1938)	Housing, Household Operations, Food, Furniture, Domestic Help, etc. %	Personal (Husband and Wife) Clothing, Medical, Children, Education, Recreation, etc. %	Dependents, Relatives' Support, etc. %	Automobile, Expenses, Maintenance %	Charity, Gifts, Contributions %	Taxes: Federal, State, Real & Personal Property, etc. %	Occupational Expenses: Agents, Secretaries, Office, Business Manager, Advertising, Publicity, Previews, Business Travel, Dues, Telegraph and Telephone, etc. %	Available for Savings: Savings, Insurance, Annuities, Real Estate, Stocks and Bonds, Other Investments, Payments, etc. %
A	$ 16,721	16.2	13.5	..	2.1	.1	10.0	17.9	40.2
B	19,200	11.5	21.4	1.5	2.6	.5	2.1	13.0	47.4
C	25,589	29.3	7.1	..	1.4	1.5	10.4	28.8	21.5
D	31,484	13.3	10.9	19.2	2.2	1.2	4.7	19.5	28.9
E	38,545	40.9	11.3	7.5	1.1	.5	10.1	19.1	9.5
F	39,307	13.3	22.7	1.9	3.5	.3	9.4	15.1	33.8
G	40,077	26.2	17.9	2.1	..	.7	8.4	19.4	25.3
H	41,997	16.0	23.1	4.3	3.0	.7	16.5	20.2	16.2
I	46,000	10.0	19.6	..	6.1	.4	11.1	12.4	40.4
J	78,250	10.6	10.3	15.3	3.8	.7	10.8	12.4	36.1
K	104,096	3.8	24.6	6.1	.4	1.3	21.7	5.1	37.0
L	105,554	8.6	2.9	3.0	2.2	1.4	7.9	13.2	60.8
M	121,492	15.6	15.5	5.5	4.0	1.1	21.3	11.8	25.2
N	129,000	10.0	6.5	1.0	3.3	1.6	10.4	12.3	54.9
O	134,739	6.9	8.5	..	1.3	1.4	23.7	14.9	43.3
P	220,000	18.8	5.3	.2	2.0	.6	34.1	26.6	12.4

D. SOCIAL DATA

I. *A Note on Data Given in Appendices D to G*

The tables which follow present data on 159 producers and executives, 309 actors, 69 directors, 143 writers, 41 first film editors, 19 directors of photography, 79 assistant directors. The materials for all groups except producers and executives were derived from questionnaires submitted through Guild organizations. (Sample copies of the questionnaires are reproduced at the end of this appendix.)

The questionnaires were checked carefully for reliability. We analyzed the internal evidence of the questionnaires to determine whether the story presented was consistent and coherent. For example, a comparison of the answers to such questions as "Year of first motion picture work in Hollywood," "First salary," "Outline your motion picture experience in Hollywood (with dates and earnings)" served as a check upon the accuracy and consistency of the respondent.

The validity of a sample depends upon two factors: its size and its representativeness. For each of the groups studied, two questions were therefore raised: Is the sample large enough? Is the sample representative? These questions can be answered for each group.

Producers and executives. Our data embrace 159 producers and executives in Hollywood: 134 producers, 25 executives. The producers' data were not obtained from questionnaires, since only 17 producers filled in the questionnaires submitted. A complete list of producers was obtained by taking all of the producers credited on the screen for movies produced by the eight major Hollywood studios during the years 1938-1939 (inclusive) * as listed in the cumulative index of the Academy of Motion Picture Arts and Sciences. The executive producers and the corporation executives operating from and in Hollywood (who do not ordinarily get screen credit), were taken from the corporation personnel as listed in the 1939-40 and 1940-41 *Motion Picture Almanac.* The data for 159 producers were taken from extensive interviews, our files on the movie

---

* 403 pictures in 1937, 362 in 1938, 376 in 1939.

colony, the *Motion Picture Almanac, Who's Who in America, Film Daily Year Book,* and information supplied by the studios. It should be noted that the 159 is not a sample, but represents the *total number* of producers and executives actively engaged in motion picture production in the major studios of Hollywood—and in those subsidiary organizations which *release* (or produce and release) their product through the major studios. In some instances, particular information was not available for some producers; but in every instance material was gathered for well over three-fourths of all the producers in Hollywood. Such a sample is more than large enough and representative enough for generalization.

Actors. Questionnaires were sent to 1753 Class A players * of the Screen Actors Guild; 309 actors replied, or 18 percent of the total number of active and inactive Class A players in the Screen Actors Guild as of April 15, 1940. Is this sample large enough for generalization? Eighteen percent of a group is more than adequate for statistical studies; smaller percentages are used in academic and government surveys. Is the sample representative? We checked the representativeness of the *number* of actors included and the earning groups into which they fell. In both instances, our sample proved to be remarkably representative. The earnings groups of all the A-Players in Hollywood (as reported by the Screen Actors Guild) are compared to similar earning groupings for our sample of 309:

			S.A.G. Earning Figures for All A-Players as of August, 1940	Earning Figures from Questionnaire Sample		
				1939	1938	Average 1938-39
A-1 Class	over	$50,000	8% †	5.9%	6.0%	6.0% †
A-2 "	$15,000 to	$49,999	13%	13.8%	15.7%	14.7%
A-3 "	under	$15,000	79%	80.2%	78.3%	79.3%

The comparison above indicates that our sample of 309 actors is almost identical to the proportions prevailing among the various earning groups included.

The Screen Actors Guild was unable to supply information with respect to the relative number of *male* and *female* actors among the A-players. However, since all A-Players are required to contribute to the Motion Picture Relief Fund, we checked our sample against the number of men and women players contributing to the Motion Picture Relief Fund in 1939:

* As has been explained in chapter 15, extras (Class B members of the Guild) are excluded.

† Note that the Screen Actors Guild figures probably include income from all types of acting. Our tabulations are on the basis of screen earnings alone. As the chief variance is in the upper brackets, where additional earnings (apart from movies) are most likely to occur, the apparent representativeness of the sample is striking.

	Percent Contributing to MPRF 1939	Percent Included in Questionnaire Sample
Actors	71.4	70.4
Actresses	28.6	29.6

Once again, our sample of actors is singularly representative, showing a deviation from the total group of not more than one percent.

Directors. Questionnaires were mailed to the entire active membership of the Screen Directors Guild (232 on November 1, 1939). Sixty-nine replies were received. This represents over one-fourth of the active membership and is more than an adequate sample. As for the representativeness, the 69 directors ranged in age from 27 to 58 (as of 1939); in annual earnings, from 0 to $238,000; in education, from those who did not finish grammar school to those who hold doctorate degrees. It is possible that our sample for directors is weighted toward the lower end of the income scale: *i.e.*, that a higher percentage of the lower-income directors filled out questionnaires than did directors in the top income bracket.

Writers. See the footnote in chapter 14, p. 325. At the time this study was made, the membership of the Screen Writers Guild was between 600 and 700; this included associate members, the latter being members who have not been employed frequently or long enough in Hollywood to be classed as active members. The 143 questionnaire returns comprise a large enough sample for generalization; no adequate verification of the representativeness of the sample was possible. However, the sizeableness of the sample, and the comprehensive range in content of the questionnaires returned, suggests a high degree of representativeness. Information on the birthplaces of writers was obtained (as in the case of producers) from interviews, our files, by analyzing biographical materials in the *Motion Picture Almanac, Who's Who in America,* and other sources.

Extensive reports on Hollywood's film editors, directors of photography, assistant directors, research workers, laboratory technicians, and cartoonists, were also made and submitted to the Guilds representing these groups. The results of the analyses are being published under the editorship of Dorothy B. Jones, executive assistant to this writer on the Motion Picture Research Project, by Western Personnel Service of Pasadena, California—a non-profit agency supported by contributions from several academic foundations and eighteen Western colleges and universities. Copies of these analyses may be obtained by writing to Western Personnel Service. Some of the data on these groups are used in Appendices D through G for comparative purposes; but since this book is primarily concerned with producers, directors, writers, actors, the complete data on other groups is not included.

II. Social Data on Movie Makers

1. EDUCATION

	Grammar School (8 yrs. or less)		High School						College						Graduate Study						Total	Group
	No.	Pct.	1	2	3	4	Tot.	Pct.	1	2	3	4	Tot.	Pct.	1	2	3	4	Tot.	Pct.	No.	Pct.
Executives	7	33.3%	..	..	..	6	6	28.6%	1	2	1	1	5	23.8%	2	1	..	..	3	14.3%	21	100.0%
Producers	5	5.0	1	7	2	24	34	34.0	6	22	7	14	49	49.0	10	1	1	..	12	12.0	100	100.0
Actors	7	2.8	5	16	11	87	119	47.4	20	32	21	38	111	44.2	4	8	..	2	14	5.6	251	100.0
Directors	7	10.6	2	4	7	11	24	36.4	6	7	2	12	27	40.9	4	2	1	1	8	12.1	66	100.0
Writers	3	2.2	2	1	1	19	23	17.3	11	18	14	47	90	67.7	9	3	2	3	17	12.8	133	100.0
Directors of Photography	..	..	2	2	..	6	10	58.8	2	2	1	1	6	35.3	1	..	..	..	1	5.9	17	100.0
Assistant Directors	2	2.5	3	6	5	19	33	41.8	5	14	5	12	36	45.6	6	2	..	..	8	10.1	79	100.0
First Film Editors	..	..	..	4	1	18	23	59.0	3	5	2	4	14	35.9	2	..	..	..	2	5.1	39	100.0
Total *	31	4.4%					272	38.5%					338	47.9%					65	9.2%	706	100.0%

* Data were not available for 39 producers and executives. The following number did not offer information on education in their questionnaire replies: 58 actors, 10 writers, 3 directors, 2 directors of photography, 2 film editors.

2. PLACE OF BIRTH

Place	Executives and Producers No.	Pct.	Actors No.	Pct.	Directors No.	Pct.	Writers No.	Pct.	Total No.	Percent
U. S. (Total)	**109**	**82.6**	**165**	**74.70**	**67**	**71.3**	**93**	**86.1**	**434**	**78.20**
Middle Atlantic	55	41.7	48	21.72	22	23.5	42	38.8	167	30.09
E. North Central	22	16.7	26	11.80	14	14.9	12	11.1	74	13.33
Pacific	9	6.8	10	4.51	15	16.0	9	8.3	43	7.75
W. North Central	6	4.5	23	10.41	3	3.2	8	7.5	40	7.21
New England	5	3.8	15	6.80	6	6.3	9	8.3	35	6.31
Mountain	3	2.3	13	5.90	2	2.1	5	4.6	23	4.15
South Atlantic	5	3.8	10	4.51	2	2.1	3	2.8	20	3.60
W. South Central	..	..	13	5.90	2	2.1	3	2.8	18	3.24
E. South Central	4	3.0	6	2.70	1	1.1	2	1.9	13	2.34
Philippine Islands	..	..	1	.45	..	..	..	..	1	.18
Foreign (Total)	**23**	**17.4**	**56**	**25.30**	**27**	**28.7**	**15**	**13.9**	**121**	**21.80**
Great Britain	7	5.3	18	8.14	5	5.3	9	8.33	39	7.03
Russia	5	3.8	3	1.36	5	5.3	1	.93	14	2.53
Canada	4	3.0	3	1.36	3	3.2	1	.93	11	1.98
Germany	1	.76	3	1.36	6	6.3	1	.93	11	1.98
Ireland	1	.76	8	3.60	1	1.1	1	.93	11	1.98
Hungary	2	1.5	2	.90	2	2.1	1	.93	7	1.26
Austria	1	.76	3	1.36	2	2.1	..	..	6	1.08
France	..	..	3	1.36	1	1.1	..	..	4	.72
Union of S. Africa	..	..	3	1.36	..	..	..	..	3	.54
Sweden	..	..	2	.90	..	..	..	..	2	.36
Australia	..	..	1	.45	1	1.1	..	..	2	.36
Poland	1	.76	..	..	..	..	1	.93	2	.36
Japan	..	..	2	.90	..	..	..	..	2	.36
British W. Indies	..	..	1	.45	..	..	..	..	1	.18
China	..	..	1	.45	..	..	..	..	1	.18
India	..	..	1	.45	..	..	..	..	1	.18
Mexico	..	..	1	.45	..	..	..	..	1	.18
Norway	..	..	1	.45	..	..	..	..	1	.18
Italy	..	..	..	..	1	1.1	..	..	1	.18
"Europe"	1	.76	..	..	..	..	..	..	1	.18
Total Reports	132	100.0	221	100.0	94	100.0	108	100.0	555	100.0
Unknown	27	..	7	..	12	..	91	..	137	
Grand Total	159	..	228	..	106	..	199	..	692	

Source: The material on actors and directors is taken from questionnaire returns; the material on executives, producers, and writers was obtained from *Who's Who in America*, the *Motion Picture Almanac*, and other sources. The large number of writers for whom birthplace information was unavailable is accounted for by the fact that few movie writers are in *Who's Who in America* or (proportionately) in the *Motion Picture Almanac*.

3. AGE (1940): THE MOVIE MAKERS (I)

	Actors		Producers		Executives *		Directors		Writers		Total	
	No.	Pct.	No.	Pct.	No.	Pct.	No.	Pct.	No.	Pct.	No.	Pct.
Under 20	3	1.1	..	..	..	..	..	..	..	..	3	.5
20 to 24	18	6.6	..	..	..	..	..	..	1	.8	19	3.3
25 to 29	22	8.1	1	1.1	1	5.0	1	1.5	16	13.3	41	7.2
30 to 34	46	17.1	6	6.5	1	5.0	6	9.1	21	17.6	80	14.1
35 to 39	38	14.1	19	20.7	5	25.0	15	22.7	31	25.9	108	19.0
40 to 44	18	6.6	26	28.3	..	..	17	25.8	16	13.3	77	13.5
45 to 49	31	11.4	20	21.7	5	25.0	16	24.2	16	13.3	88	15.5
50 to 54	25	9.2	13	14.1	4	20.0	9	13.7	13	10.8	64	11.3
55 to 59	31	11.4	5	5.4	4	20.0	2	3.0	5	4.2	47	8.3
60 to 64	22	8.1	1	1.1	..	..	..	..	1	.8	24	4.2
65 to 69	11	4.1	1	1.1	..	..	..	..	..	..	12	2.1
70 and over	6	2.2	..	..	..	..	..	..	..	..	6	1.0
Total	271	100.0	92	100.0	20	100.0	66	100.0	120	100.0	569	100.0

4. AGE (1940): THE MOVIE MAKERS (II)

	Assistant Directors		Directors of Photography		First Film Editors		Total	
	No.	Pct.	No.	Pct.	No.	Pct.	No.	Pct.
Under 20	..	..	..	..	..	..	..	..
20 to 24	2	2.5	..	..	..	..	2	1.5
25 to 29	8	10.1	..	..	3	7.3	11	8.0
30 to 34	19	24.0	..	..	9	22.0	28	20.3
35 to 39	21	26.6	..	..	13	31.7	34	24.6
40 to 44	16	20.3	6	33.3	10	24.4	32	23.2
45 to 49	6	7.6	4	22.2	3	7.3	13	9.4
50 to 55	7	8.9	8	44.5	3	7.3	18	13.0
Total	79	100.0	18	100.0	41	100.0	138	100.0

* In Hollywood.

APPENDIX D

5. FATHER'S OCCUPATION

Occupation	Actors No.	Pct.	Directors No.	Pct.	Asst. Dir. No.	Pct.	1st Film Editor No.	Pct.	Dir. of Photog. No.	Pct.	Total No.	Pct.
Professional *	142	49.7	21	30.9	24	31.2	15	39.5	4	23.5	206	42.4
Proprietary †	95	33.2	34	50.0	31	40.2	14	36.8	5	29.4	179	36.8
Agricultural	10	3.5	1	1.5	4	5.2	1	2.6	3	17.6	19	3.9
Clerical	19	6.5	1	1.5	5	6.5	2	5.3	2	11.8	29	6.0
Skilled Labor	14	4.9	6	8.8	9	11.7	3	7.9	2	11.8	34	7.0
Semi-Skilled	1	.4	2	2.9	1	1.3	..	..	..	..	4	.8
Unskilled	..	..	..	..	1	1.3	..	..	..	..	1	.2
Retired or none ‡	4	.4	2	2.9	2	2.6	1	2.6	..	..	9	1.9
Unspecified	1	.4	1	1.5	..	..	2	5.3	1	5.9	5	1.0
Total	286	100.0	68	100.0	77	100.0	38	100.0	17	100.0	486	100.0

Source: questionnaire replies. No data available for writers and producers.

* Professional: Actors, accountants, artists, teachers, engineers, newspapermen, physicians, professors, stage, etc.
† Proprietary: Brokers, insurance men, merchants, shopkeepers, real estatemen, contractors, exporters-importers, etc.
‡ Retired: "Sportsmen," "yachtsmen," etc.

III. *Sample Questionnaires* *

QUESTIONNAIRES FOR ACTORS

Your first occupation in motion picture work in Hollywood? What studio? Year?

Estimate the total length of time you have been employed as an actor at each of the following studios (write in studio names if not listed): Columbia? MGM? Paramount? RKO? Republic? Twentieth Century-Fox? Universal? Warner Brothers? United Artists (name producer)? Other studios?

Outline your motion picture experience as an actor and *in all other departments*, as follows: As a supporting actor? As a lead? As a star? In some other acting role (*e.g. an extra, singer, dancer*)? As a director or any other non-acting position (*specify*)? Dates, from —— to —— (for each entry)? Average Annual Earnings (for each entry)?

Outline your professional experience in other branches of the show business: Type of work (for example: *"Vaudeville," "Broadway support-*

* All questionnaires were anonymous. The questions (not format) are given here; adequate spacing was allowed for each question.

ing role," "Radio singer")? Dates, from — to — (for each entry)? Average Annual Earnings (for each entry)?

In what specific ways could your working conditions at the studios be improved?

Weekly salary as Hollywood motion picture actor 1939? 1938? Number of weeks worked 1939? 1938? On contract? Per picture deal? Week to week? Day to day? If you work on per picture deal, how much do you earn per picture?

Annual income from motion picture acting in 1939? In 1938? In 1937? *First weekly salary* as an actor in Hollywood, and year? *Highest weekly salary* as an actor in Hollywood, and year? *First annual income* as an actor in Hollywood, and year? *Highest annual income* as an actor in Hollywood, and year?

Number of years in High School? College? Name of College? Major or special field? Degrees? Honors (*Phi Beta Kappa, awards, etc.*)? Special training?

Single? Married? Number of children? Sex? Year of birth? What was your father's occupation?

Indicate the Studio whose pictures you most admire. Why?

Comment on the content of American movies today.

Suggestions for the Screen Actors Guild.

QUESTIONNAIRES FOR MOVIE DIRECTORS

What studio in Hollywood gave you your first movie job? Year?

Estimate the approximate total length of time you were employed as a director at each of the following studios (write in studio names, if not listed):

Columbia? MGM? Paramount? Independent? RKO? Republic? Twentieth Century-Fox? Universal? Warner Brothers? United Artists (name producer)? Other studios?

Your longest *continuous* period of employment as a director at any one studio?

How many pictures did you direct in 1938?

Outline your complete motion-picture experience, in all departments: Position (*Such as Cameraman, Asst. Director*)? Type of Work (*Comedies and shorts, Serials*)? Years (*1920-25, 1926-30*)? Average Annual Earnings?

List the jobs you held before you came to Hollywood, in chronological order and approximate time of each (*Broadway director, 10 yrs.; vaudeville actor, 5 yrs.; newspaper advertising, 2 yrs.*).

What are your chief complaints about working as a director?

Would you prefer to work with writers preparing scripts for pictures you are to direct?

If so, at what stage should such collaboration begin? Why?

In what specific ways could your working relationship with the studio be improved?

If salary were no consideration, what position in the industry would you most prefer? Why?

Weekly salary as Hollywood director in 1938? Number of weeks worked? On contract? Per picture deal? Week to week?

Annual income from screen directing in 1938? In 1937? In 1936? First weekly salary as a director in Hollywood, and year? Highest weekly salary as a director in Hollywood, and year? First annual income as a director in Hollywood, and year?

Number of years in High School? College? Name of College? Major or special field? Degrees? Honors (*Phi Beta Kappa, awards, etc.*)?

Check: Single? Married? Divorced? Number of times married? Number of children? Year of birth? What was your father's occupation?

What magazines do you read regularly (not trade papers)?

Indicate the studio whose pictures you most admire.

Comment on the content of American movies today.

QUESTIONNAIRES FOR SCREEN WRITERS *

What was your first movie job in Hollywood? Studio? Year?

How did you get into motion picture writing in Hollywood (*e.g., brought out to adapt book, sold original, transferred from N. Y. story dept., relative offered job, etc.*)?

Your longest *continuous* period of employment as a writer at any one studio?

Estimate the approximate length of time you worked as a writer at the following studios: Columbia? MGM? Paramount? Republic? RKO? Twentieth Century-Fox? Universal? Warner Brothers? Other?

List other departments of the industry in which you have worked and approximate length of time (*e.g., Production, 6 mo.; Story Dept., 1 yr.; etc.*).

In which branch of the industry, other than full-time writing, did you work in 1938?

Indicate the *number* of your screen credits: Screen play? Original story? Adaptation? Additional dialogue? Other?

Extent of your published writing and produced plays *before* you became a screen writer in Hollywood (*e.g., 2 novels, 1 play, 15 magazine stories, etc.*)?

Extent of your outside writing, as above, *since* you became a screen writer in Hollywood?

* See footnote, p. 325.

APPENDIX D

List the jobs you held *before* you became a movie writer in Hollywood, in chronological order and approximate time of each (*e.g., salesman, 6 mo.; high school teacher, 2 yrs.; reporter, 2½ yrs.; feature writer, 1 yr.; etc.*).

Which of your previous experience, writing or otherwise, do you consider most valuable for movie writing?

Number of years High School? In College? Name of College? Major or specialization? Degrees? Honors (*Phi Beta Kappa, awards, etc.*)?

Single? Married? Divorced? Remarried? Number of children? Birthdate? What was your father's occupation? Wife's occupation before marriage? After marriage?

What magazines do you read regularly (not trade papers)?

To what clubs, societies, or other organizations do you belong?

Does screen writing permit the expression of your best creative efforts? Why?

What do you consider your special talent in movie writing (*plot, dialogue, etc.*)?

What are your chief complaints about working as a screen writer?

If salary were no consideration: (a) What position in the industry would you most prefer? (b) What career would you most prefer: Screen writer? Novelist? Playwright? Magazine writer? Other? (c) For which studio would you prefer to work as a writer? Why?

Weekly salary as Hollywood screen writer in 1938? Number of weeks worked? *Check:* On contract? Picture assignment? Week to week? Free lance?

Annual income from screen writing in 1938? In 1937? In 1936? First weekly salary as screen writer in Hollywood, and year? Highest weekly salary as screen writer in Hollywood, and year? First annual income as screen writer in Hollywood, and year? Highest annual income as screen writer in Hollywood, and year?

Have you taken a cut in weekly salary (as a writer) since 1936? How much (%)? What year? Reason?

Highest annual income *before* becoming a Hollywood screen writer? Year? Occupation?

Comment on the content of American movies today.

Indicate the studio whose pictures you most admire.

Do you prefer working on a script by yourself? With a collaborator?

Indicate the three screen writers whose work you most admire.

Other comments on motion picture writing? '

Suggestions for the Screen Writers Guild?

E. MARRIAGE AND DIVORCE DATA

I. *A Note on the Method Used*

As was pointed out in chapter 5, there are no reliable published data on marriage and divorce in Hollywood. We could not obtain information on divorce *per se* through a questionnaire: the word "divorce" creates resistance, and any question which used the word would not be answered by enough respondents to warrant generalization, as we discovered in several sample questionnaires. In formulating the questionnaires, therefore, we were compelled to resort to a question on "number of marriages." We knew this would not be wholly satisfactory; but it was the only question we could ask and it provided certain basic facts from which to work. The executive board of the Screen Actors Guild decided against including a question on number of marriages in the questionnaire which went to the actors; the Screen Writers Guild permitted the question to be put, but then withheld the information, as has been explained in chapter 14.

We received fairly satisfactory data on *number of marriages* for the movie directors, assistant directors, directors of photography, film editors. In order to obtain information on marriage and divorce among the actors and producers, the following scheme was set up, tested, and then used. The complete list of actors and actresses under contract to the major studios in Hollywood was copied from the 1939-40 *Motion Picture Almanac;* we added those top-flight actors who are not under contract to any one studio (*e.g.,* Ronald Colman, Fredric March, etc.). This list ran to 278 names. The author then tabulated the number of marriages and divorces for as many of the 278 actors and actresses as possible (from material in our files, from personal knowledge, interviews, etc.). The list of 278 names was then submitted to three persons who have lived and worked in Hollywood for more than ten years each: a producer, an associate producer, a writer. Each of these men is thoroughly conversant with the Hollywood scene. The lists of our three experts, and the list drawn up by this writer, were then checked against each other. (1)

APPENDIX E

Where three or more of the lists agreed exactly in the number of marriages and divorces given for an actor or actress, that information was accepted. (2) Where three or more lists agreed to *minimum* information, that information was accepted: *e.g.*, if two lists stated that an actor was divorced twice, and two lists stated that the same actor was divorced three times, the fact accepted was that the actor was divorced twice. This expert-scoring technique produced agreement, according to the two criteria established, on 200 out of the 278 actors and actresses.

The expert-scoring method was tested for accuracy in the following manner: the questionnaires which had been sent to actors included a question on whether they were married or single today (1940); the answers to this question can be compared to the percent shown to be single or married in our experts' tabulation.

	Percent According to Expert-Scoring	Percent Found by Questionnaire Sample
Married	68.5	68.4
Single	31.5	31.6

In other words, there was a variation of only .1 percent between the questionnaire data and the testimony of the expert panel.* Since this method depended entirely upon the degree to which the actors named and their personal histories were known to the experts, it was easier to obtain results for actors than for the lesser-known groups in Hollywood. The technique could not be used with success for Hollywood's writers or directors.

The marriage and divorce data for producers were obtained from a wide variety of material: biographies, interviews, newspaper clippings, and other sources and materials in our files. Of the 159 producers and executives in the movie colony, tested information was finally obtained for 122.

For the groups other than actors and producers, divorce information was deduced from the questionnaire information supplied on the number of marriages. There is, of course, no exact coincidence between the number of marriages and the number of divorces, since a person may have been married once, divorced, but did not remarry: the divorce would not, therefore, appear in a tabulation of number of marriages. But where *two* or more marriages were indicated, this writer felt it reasonable to infer the existence of one divorce. (This ruled out the possibility that remarriage might have followed the death of, rather than

* It is true that contemporary information (married today or single today) is probably more reliable than information about the past (number of marriages or divorces). Nevertheless, the correlation of questionnaire data with expert-scoring data was so marked as to suggest the high degree of reliability of the tabulation of three experts plus this writer.

divorce from, a spouse; a check showed that for groups as young—relatively—as ours, remarriage following the death of, rather than divorce from, a spouse was so infrequent that our results could not be affected by one percent.)

The divorce data for directors, assistant directors, film editors, and directors of photography, accordingly, are deduced from the questionnaire data on the number of marriages. This offers us what might be called a *minimum* figure, since we would not have a record for a person who was married once, divorced, but did not remarry. It is probably a minimum figure for another reason: so large a number did *not* answer the question on the number of marriages: 13 directors, 16 assistant directors, 7 directors of photography, 16 film editors. This leads to the reasonable conclusion that they did not answer precisely because they had been married more than once and felt reluctant to supply this information, and this would suggest that the data which were received on number of marriages represent a minimum figure.

The tables on marriage and divorce which follow are offered with the reservation that they give the *probable* picture of marriage and divorce.

1. MARITAL STATUS (1940)

Group	Married	Single	Total
Actors	201	93	294
Producers	15	2	17
Directors	55	13	68
Writers	92	13	105
Assistant Directors	54	25	79
Film Editors (Cutters)	67	38	105
Directors of Photography	17	1	18
Total	501	185	686
Percent	73.0	27.0	100.0

2. NUMBER OF MARRIAGES

Group	None	One	Two	Three	Four	Total
Actors *	37	109	41	11	2	200
Producers *	2	59	16	2	0	79
Directors	7	32	12	1	3	55
Assistant Directors	18	31	9	4	1	63
Film Editors	9	34	5	0	0	48
Directors of Photography	1	6	5	0	0	12
Total	74	271	88	18	6	457
Percent	16.2	59.3	19.3	3.9	1.3	100.0

* Probable number. Other data from questionnaires. See note on method at beginning of Appendix E. Also see Table 3, below.

3. PROBABLE NUMBER OF DIVORCES

Number of Times Divorced	Actors Number	Actors Percent	Producers Number	Producers Percent
0	159	64.5	55	69.7
1	52	26.0	19	24.1
2	16	8.0	4	5.0
3	2	1.0	1	1.2
4	1	0.5	0	0.0
Total	200	100.0	79	100.0

4. NUMBER OF CHILDREN

Occupation	None	One	Two	Three	Four	Five	Six	Seven	Eight	Number of Answers
Producers	1	4	6	1	..	..	..	..	..	12
Actors	40	67	22	20	5	1	1	..	1	157
Directors	17	18	15	5	2	..	..	..	..	57
Directors of Photography	1	7	3	2	..	2	..	..	..	15
First Film Editors	6	9	4	1	..	..	..	..	..	20
Assistant Directors	17	17	15	..	1	..	..	..	..	50
Film Editing Department	9	11	5	..	..	..	..	1	..	26
Total	91	133	70	29	8	3	1	1	1	337

400

F. COMMENTS AND PREFERENCES OF MOVIE MAKERS

I. *Comments on American Movies Today*

In the questionnaires submitted to actors, directors, and writers the following question was included: "Comment on American movies today." An analysis of the responses indicated that the movie makers focussed their attention, and concentrated their comments, on items which can be classified under the following nine categories:

1. *Type of picture or story*—Comments or suggestions as to the stories Hollywood is or should be producing.
2. *Originality*—So many referred to originality as a criterion in judging film content that it seemed to call for a separate category—even though it is closely related to "type of picture or story."
3. *Treatment of Theme*—Suggestions or criticism as to the way in which film stories are presented—*e.g.*, the amount of dialogue or action, the type of direction, etc.
4. *Artistry*—Evaluations of the technical aspects of production—the sets, the camera work, the lighting, the acting, etc. All such comments were grouped under the head of "Artistry."
5. *Star System*—Specific references to stars and the star system as influencing movie stories, types of films, movie content, etc.
6. *Censorship*—All references to censorship of the film, the effects of censorship, etc.
7. *Quantity as Related to Quality Production*—Comments about volume production, relative number of B and A pictures, etc.
8. *Box-office Appeal*—All specific references to the box-office as a critical factor in judging film content.
9. *Economics of the Industry*—All suggestions or comments which specifically referred to the economic aspects of the industry in evaluating the product.

The classification given above is, of course, not exact, since the comments were in many instances difficult to categorize with precision. It was, however, necessary to set up classifications for the purpose of making comparisons across group lines, and the classifications given above proved serviceable. In the tables which follow, miscellaneous

401

comments, irrelevant comments, and failure to answer the question are also tabulated.

1. COMMENTS ON AMERICAN MOVIES TODAY
189 ACTORS

Comments	Favorable	Unfavorable	Neutral	Total Comments	Pct. of Actors
1. Initiative, Originality, Honesty	3	25	1	29	15.3
2. Type of Picture and Story	23	35	. .	58	30.7
3. Treatment of Theme	9	29	1	39	20.6
4. Artistry	14	7	1	22	11.6
5. Star System	. .	11	. .	11	5.8
6. Censorship	. .	10	. .	10	5.3
7. Quantity as Affecting Quality (B Pictures)	. .	16	. .	16	8.5
8. Box-Office: Appeal and Influence	8	11	1	20	10.6
9. Economics of Industry	. .	2	1	3	1.6
10. Miscellaneous and General	51	12	2	65	34.4
11. Irrelevant	9	. .	. .	9	4.8
12. None	. .	. .	11	11	5.8
Total	117	158	18	293	

2. COMMENTS ON AMERICAN MOVIES TODAY
50 DIRECTORS

Comments	Favorable	Unfavorable	Neutral	Total Comments	Pct. of Comments	Pct. of Directors
1. Initiative, Originality, etc.	2	23	. .	25	29.4	50.0
2. Type of Picture and Story	3	7	1	11	12.9	22.0
3. Treatment of Theme	1	5	. .	6	7.1	12.0
4. Artistry	2	3	. .	5	5.9	10.0
5. Star System	. .	. .	3	3	3.5	6.0
6. Censorship	. .	. .	2	2	2.3	4.0
7. Quantity as Affecting Quality (B Pictures)	. .	6	. .	6	7.1	12.0
8. Box-Office Appeal and Influence	. .	10	. .	10	11.8	20.0
9. Economics of Industry	. .	4	. .	4	4.7	8.0
10. Miscellaneous and General	9	2	2	13	15.3	26.0
Total	17	60	8	85	100.0	

3. COMMENTS ON AMERICAN MOVIES TODAY
141 WRITERS

Comments	Favorable	Unfavorable	Neutral	Total	Pct. of Total Comments
1. Initiative, Originality, Relation to Life Today	..	31	1	32	18.93
2. Type of Picture and Story	..	20	1	21	12.4
3. Treatment of Theme	1	9	..	10	5.92
4. Artistry and Technique	9	1	..	10	5.92
5. Star System	..	2	..	2	1.2
6. Censorship	..	20	..	20	11.8
7. Quantity As Affecting Quality (B Pictures)	1	6	..	7	4.1
8. Box-Office Appeal	4	9	1	14	8.3
9. Economics of Industry	..	5	..	5	3.0
10. Miscellaneous and General	10	17	5	32	18.93
10a. Supervision: Producers-Executives	..	13	..	13	7.7
11. Irrelevant	..	..	1	1	.6
12. None	..	..	2	2	1.2
Total	25	133	11	169	100.00

II. *Occupational Preferences*

The questionnaires contained the following question: "*If salary were no consideration,* what position in the motion picture industry would you most prefer? . . . Why? . . ." Some of the answers have been given in the text. The answers given by other groups may be summarized.

Assistant directors: 52.7 percent of the assistant directors would prefer to be directors. 24.3 percent said they would prefer to be producers. 8.1 percent said they would prefer to be producer-directors. 4.1 percent said they would like to be exactly what they are—assistant directors. 2.7 percent said they would prefer to be writers.

Film editors: 42.1 percent would prefer to be directors. 15.8 percent would prefer to be producers. 15.8 percent would prefer to remain film editors. 7.9 percent would prefer to be producer-directors. 13.2 percent would prefer to be writers: "It gives your imagination a chance," "a more flexible mode of expression." Only one would prefer to be an actor.

Directors of photography: 35.3 percent said they would like to remain directors of photography. 29.4 percent said they would like to be directors because it offers "more chance to create," "it enables one to combine beauty and human relationships into a finished product." 5.9 percent said they would prefer to be director-producers because "it's the only way to make pictures with an individuality." 5.9 percent preferred to be producers because of the greater authority for picture-making involved.

G. DOGS, YACHTS, RESORTS

I. Dogs

Dogs are widely owned and proudly displayed in the movie colony. Terriers, Chows, Dachshunds, and Police Dogs are as much a part of Hollywood as Capeharts. The fashion in dogs, as in games or station wagons, runs in cycles. The Terrier market had a great boom, then leveled off; the Dachshund craze swept the colony, but has declined sharply. The alliance of esthetics and costliness is shown in the love for particularly homely animals who, because they are expensive, are considered to possess a peculiarly beautiful ugliness.

The annual Beverly Hills Charity Dog Show, to which movie stars donate most of the 300 trophies, is a gala event in Hollywood's social life. At the most recent show of the Kennel Club in Beverly Hills, 600 dogs of fifty-five different breeds were on majestic promenade, including the prize Afghan hounds of Jack Oakie, the famous Chihuahua of Lupe Velez, and the rare Rhodesian lion hounds of Errol Flynn. At the Harbor Cities Kennel Club All-Breed Dog Show at Long Beach, sponsored by Miss Bette Davis's Tailwaggers and the Film Welfare League, 1287 animals were exhibited, and attracted over fifteen thousand persons; the show leaped from eighty-sixth to fourth place in the United States. The editor of *Dog World* considers California "the doggiest state in the Union," with forty shows a year—one-seventh of all the shows in the country.

Dogs in Hollywood, as in other citadels of wealth, are an essential part of the good life. Owning a dog is one of the things which are "done." The pure-bred dog is a symbol of position, associated with the hunt and other English prestige-criteria. The dog is also the classic friend of man—an utterly servile beast who flatters man's ego and accepts his sovereignty in the minor kingdom of the home. We have commented in an earlier chapter on the attraction of pedigree to those whose own ancestry is undistinguished. Let us add that thoroughbred dogs are costly to buy and expensive to maintain. This greatly enhances their desirability.

APPENDIX G

One Great Dane, owned by a prominent actor, consumes no less than three pounds of round steak daily, two quarts of milk, and special vitamin preparations. The food costs alone for this animal average five dollars a week, and the dog requires veterinarian supervision, expert bathing, and special care which bring the total maintenance bill to fifty dollars a month. Lupe Velez's Chihuahua, which weighs just seven ounces, cost her mistress an estimated seven hundred dollars.*

It would be unfair to suggest that dogs have no useful function. They serve as watchmen and protectors—a necessity not to be scorned by picture people, who live in fear of blackmailers, psychopaths, burglars, and kidnappers. The fame and wealth of the movie people are standing invitations to the criminal and the deranged: threatening mail or nuisance telephone calls are not uncommon in Hollywood. Many movie people acquire dogs to guard their children and their homes; those who do not have children find dogs substitutes for affection.

Hollywood's devotion to dogs verges on the maudlin. The extraordinary advertisement which follows was printed on the entire last page of the *Hollywood Reporter* on July 3, 1941.

DEAR MR. AND MRS. HOLLYWOOD:

We are the cats and dogs, Persian and alley, pedigreed and mutts, pets and homeless, whose little hearts beat fast in panic and fear as the great Fourth of July approaches.

Last year so many of us became homeless, we ran terrified from the noise, from the large and small crackers that were thrown at us in fun, sometimes in deviltry. We ran miles away and became lost. Some of us were killed as we blindly crashed against auto wheels. Some of us went insane. Some hid in dark holes, afraid to ever come out into the light again—and died of starvation.

Hundreds of us ended at the pound, unclaimed, unwanted—and were put away. But we didn't want that. We wanted our homes again, the young and old masters we loved, the milk, the cushions, the slippers to chew. We wanted to purr, to wag tails; but so many of us are gone now—forever. Victims of terror, victims of the thoughtlessness of boys and girls who ordinarily wouldn't hurt a dumb animal for anything in the world.

Please—we are writing you and other friends and begging for a few words of consideration on our behalf. Won't you speak for us and tell the boys and girls that we can't speak for ourselves?

Thank you.

II. *Yachts*

The yachts in the movie colony include the *Sirocco* of Errol Flynn and Lili Damita, the *Seaward* of the Cecil B. DeMilles, the *Panacea* of the

---

* Irving Hoffman, *Hollywood Reporter*, April 4, 1938, p. 3.

Charles Chaplins, the *Athena* of Rena and Frank Borzage, the *Melinda* of Gene Markey and Hedy Lamarr, the *Dolphin* of the Frank Morgans, the *Zoa III* of the Preston Fosters, George Converse and Anita Stewart's *Junalaska*, the *Araner* of the John Fords, the *Stardust* of Isabel Jewell, and lesser ships—from that of Joseph L. Mankiewicz's to the 36-foot sloop of the young actor Frankie Thomas. Ronald Colman, Lewis Stone, and James Cagney also own yachts. Joseph M. Schenck took a $35,000 loss when he sold his boat *Martha*. The sailing is excellent along the Pacific Coast, and trips to Santa Barbara or Catalina Island are no rare treat. The movie seamen belong to the Emerald Bay Yacht Club at Catalina, and have an annual regatta and Commodores' Cruise which begins at Catalina and reaches its climax in a fleet formation sailing to Avalon. The grand finale is a dinner dance with the fleet anchored off the Hotel St. Catherine at Santa Catalina, at which the movie commodores wear much gold braid and insignia. The La Conga club at Catalina has a private dock for the varied skiffs owned by movie people who sail across for a cocktail, a dinner, or a rhumba.*

The movie yachts can in no way compare with the boats owned by the elite of the East. See the compilation of material on boats in Ferdinand Lundberg's *America's 60 Families*, pp. 433-437.

III. Resorts

Week-ends in Southern California are the occasion for intense vacationing. The state is emphatically motorized; highways are superlative and distances seem to offer no problem to week-end escapologists.

Hollywood is as devoted to the week-end habit as the British are. Some movie makers own a beach house, ranch, country place, or lodge (in addition to their ordinary homes). Others frequent the many resorts near Hollywood. Palm Springs on the desert, just over a hundred miles from Los Angeles, is the most popular winter resort. The El Mirador Hotel and the Desert Inn are heavily patronized by movie people. The popularity of Palm Springs is indicated by the fact that Magnin's and Bullock's stores have opened branches in the desert oasis. *Variety*, the *Hollywood Reporter*, and dozens of fan magazines crowd the Palm Springs news-stands.

Harold Lloyd, Edward Goulding, George Brent, Joseph Schenck, Glenda Farrell, and other celebrities own homes near Palm Springs, and

* For the above see Ella Wickersham's columns in the *Los Angeles Examiner:* September 7, July 20, June 12, April 10, August 6, September 7, July 13, 1939.

several dozen filmites rent places in the vicinity for the three month season. La Quinta, twenty miles beyond Palm Springs, is newer, quieter and now more fashionable. Here the movie makers hobnob with (to take a few random press clippings) Mrs. Cornelius Bliss, Jr., the Eliot Wadsworths of Boston, and Templeton Crocker of San Francisco.

Lake Arrowhead, in the mountains two hours from Hollywood, is a popular summer resort. The North Shore Tavern is heavily patronized by film folk, and the shores of Lake Arrowhead are dotted with homes belonging to members of the film colony. The new Arrowhead Springs Hotel, controlled by Schenck, Zanuck, Goetz, and Paley, is a luxurious and modern retreat decorated by Dorothy Draper, who is reported to have received $20,000 for her services.* Forty minutes from this fine hostelry is a mountain ski course, owned and operated by the Arrowhead Springs Hotel.

Catalina Island is too over-run with tourists and middle-class vacationers to be as popular with the Hollywood group as it once was; but there are some who sail or fly to Catalina and put up at the old-fashioned but expensive St. Catherine Hotel. Coronado Island (off San Diego), Santa Barbara, Monterey, and the smaller towns along the Pacific Coast, attract some members of the film colony.

The resort and pleasure extremities of Hollywood do not begin to rival the sumptuous recreational areas of the Eastern elite; Malibu Beach is not to be compared to Miami Beach; Palm Springs cannot rival Hot Springs. Nothing in or near Hollywood compares to Newport, where the line of marble villas—whimsically called "cottages" by their proprietors —stretch along the cliffs and over Ochre Point like palaces, built by men who "thought nothing of spending ten million dollars for a house in which they lived for six weeks in a year." †

* *Hollywood Reporter*, October 7, 1939, p. 2.
† Elizabeth Drexel Lehr, *"King Lehr" and the Gilded Age*, p. 115.

H. FAN MAIL

I. *A Note on Fan Mail*

Interviews were held with the heads of the fan mail departments of all the major studios in Hollywood, who made the following generalizations. A major studio receives between 18,000 and 45,000 fan letters or postcards a month. January and February are the biggest months for fan mail; December appears to be the worst month. About 90 percent of all fan letters come from persons under 21; between 85 and 90 percent come from girls. (See analysis below.)

The age of the writers of fan letters seems to vary with the age of the actors to whom the letters are addressed. The great majority of letters to a young star come from young people; the majority of letters to a middle-aged or character actor come from more mature fans. The older the star and the more mature the roles in which the star appears, the smaller is his fan mail. The young, handsome, "romantic" stars receive most of the fan mail—probably because most of the writers of fan mail are under 21 years of age.

The heads of fan mail departments assert that they can tell when a new actor or actress has "clicked" with the public from the kind of fan letters which begin to come into the studio: letters asking why the player was not given bigger roles. Much of the fan mail in this category contains the expression: "Who was the man [or girl] who played the part of so and so?" When an actor or actress begins to receive fan mail from a substantial number of fans over an extended period of time, the studios think that the actor has "caught on." Very few of the stars answer their fan mail themselves.

Most fan letters include a request for a photograph. At one time the studios mailed free photographs to persons writing in for an actor's picture. This developed into a very costly practice: it is said that in one year in the 'Twenties, a Hollywood studio sent out over a million and a half photographs. The studios today impose a nominal charge for photographs, to cover the cost of postage, handling, and wrapping.

This has caused a sharp decline in the number of pictures sent out, and in the number of requests for pictures. The estimated cost of a photograph, mailing, packaging, etc., is around six cents.

Movie fans object to any change in the physical appearance of their favorites. If an actress changes her coiffure, or an actor removes his mustache, the fans respond in protest. Fans object when certain actors or actresses are seen drinking in movies, if this violates a previously established stereotype of virtue.

There are many fan clubs in the United States, each dedicated to the exaltation of one star. Most of these clubs are run by housewives or business girls with a vague desire to get to Hollywood themselves (as their correspondence finally reveals). The membership of the clubs shows great overlapping: the members of one club appear in the membership lists of nearly all the others.

II. *Comment on 1,821 Fan Letters and Postcards*

An analysis was made of all the fan mail received by a major Hollywood studio in one month (January, 1939) for one ranking male star and one ranking female star. The female star received 1,149 letters and postcards; the male star received 672. The statistical analysis of the 1,821 items of fan mail will be found below.

Most of the fan letters (about 90 percent) ask for an autograph or a photograph. Many request employment, assistance to friends, cast-off clothing, money, and so on. Many ask for advice on personal problems. Many fans indicate a marked desire to unburden their ambitions and unhappiness.

Those letters which contain more than a request for a photograph or autograph, make comments praising the physical qualities or the acting ability of the star. There is wide use of the phrase, "You're my favorite actor (or actress)." There are many comments on recent movies in which the star has appeared. Many fans write that they have seen a picture six or seven times; one young movie addict said he had seen one movie (in which his idol appeared) 130 times.

One is impressed, in reading the fan mail, by the earnestness and naïveté of the effort to make the star seem more "real" to the fan writers. There is a pronounced desire to make the fantasy of movie experience less of a fantasy and more of a reality. There are many efforts to support the conception that the star is a personal friend. Many fans offer elaborate details about their life, family, work, and hopes, and urge the star to reciprocate with similar information. A small proportion of the letters are pathological in content and make pathological requests.

Among the requests made of two movie stars by 1,821 fan writers were the following specific items:

Cake of soap
Piece of fur
Paper lipstick tissues
Banjo
Spoon
Salt and pepper shaker set
"Piece of gum you have chewed"
Bicycle
3 hairs
Hairpin
Shoe or stocking
Wrist watch
Beads
"Close, shose, and hat"
Handkerchiefs
Offer to mortgage life or services for cash
Telegram to cousin on birthday

Match covers
Aviator's helmet
"Piece of (your) horses' tail or lock of (your) hair"
3 page order blank to Sears Roebuck
Offer to say prayers
Cigarette butt
Picture of star in step-ins
11 pages of "I love you" written 825 times
Button from coat
"Wait for me"
Named pet flea after star
$1,000,000 in movie money
Autographed pair of shorts
Collar button
Offer to take place of star's dog
Blade of grass from star's lawn

III. Analysis of Fan Mail Received by Movie Actor

1. BASIC BREAKDOWN ON ONE MONTH'S FAN MAIL (JANUARY, 1939)

	Number	Percent
Total number of postcards received	449	66.8
Total amount of letters received	223	33.2
Total amount of fan mail	672	100.0
Sex of fan writers:		
Female	598	89.0
Male	67	10.0
Unknown	7	1.0
	672	100.0
Approximate age of fan writers: *		
Under 13 years	356	53.0
13 to 21 years	287	43.0
Over 21	29	4.0
	672	100.0

* Note: Most writers state their age, or it can be inferred from references in the letters, internal evidence, handwriting, etc.

APPENDIX H

	Number	*Percent*
Geographical distribution:		
United States	588	87.5
Foreign	84	12.5
	672	100.0

2. GEOGRAPHICAL DISTRIBUTION OF FAN MAIL RECEIVED BY ONE MALE MOVIE STAR (JANUARY, 1939)

UNITED STATES

New York	89	Massachusetts	17
Illinois	76	Connecticut	17
California	70	Texas	14
New Jersey	52	Kentucky	11
Pennsylvania	49	Iowa	10
Ohio	40	Missouri	9
Michigan	26	Alabama	8
Indiana	19	Minnesota	7
Wisconsin	18		

(5 letters each from Maryland and Washington; 4 from Rhode Island, Louisiana, Mississippi, Utah, Georgia, South Carolina; 3 each from Virginia, West Virginia, Kansas, North Carolina; 2 each from Nebraska, Oklahoma, District of Columbia, Hawaii; 1 each from Arkansas and Colorado.)

FOREIGN

Great Britain	39	British West Indies	5
Canada	15	Ireland	4
Brazil	13	New Zealand	2

(1 letter each from: Australia, Bahamas, Portugal, Bulgaria, Rumania, Mexico.)

IV. *Analysis of U. S. Fan Mail Received by Movie Actress*

1. BASIC BREAKDOWN ON ONE MONTH'S FAN MAIL (JANUARY, 1939)

	Number	*Percent*
Approximate age of fan writers: *		
Under 13	194	22.1
13 to 21 years	574	65.2
Over 21	112	12.7
	880	100.0

* Breakdown is for United States only.

412

APPENDIX H

	Number	Percent
Sex of fan writers: *		
Female	761	86.5
Male	119	13.5
	880	100.0
Total number of letters received *	419	47.6
Total number of postcards received *	461	52.4
	880	100.0
Total letters and postcards from U. S.	880	
Total letters and postcards from		
foreign countries	169	
	1,149	

2. GEOGRAPHICAL DISTRIBUTION OF FAN MAIL RECEIVED BY ONE FEMALE MOVIE STAR (JANUARY, 1939)

UNITED STATES

New York	111	Texas	18
Illinois	102	Kentucky	17
Pennsylvania	89	Alabama	15
California	71	Iowa	14
New Jersey	60	Washington	14
Ohio	44	Rhode Island	12
Michigan	40	Wisconsin	12
Massachusetts	30	Georgia	11
Indiana	26	Louisiana	11
Missouri	20	Florida	10
Connecticut	20	Maryland	10

9 letters and postcards from Virginia; 8 from Arkansas, Kansas, North Carolina; 7 from Minnesota and Vermont; 6 from Maine; 5 from Mississippi, North Dakota, West Virginia, and the District of Columbia; 4 from Arizona, South Carolina, Tennessee, and Oklahoma; 3 from Colorado, South Dakota, Utah; 2 from Nebraska, New Hampshire, Oregon, Hawaii, and the Philippine Islands; 1 each from Idaho, Montana, New Mexico, Canal Zone. Unknown: 11.

FOREIGN

Brazil	74	Ireland	4
Great Britain	46	Belgium	3
Canada	23	Portugal	2
New Zealand	7	India	2
Malta	6	Germany	2
Mexico	4		

One each from: Egypt, Austria, Uruguay, Cuba, Dutch Guiana, Malaya, Java, Venezuela, Dutch East Indies, Spain, Dominican Republic, Norway, and Palestine.

* Breakdown is for United States only.

413

REFERENCE NOTES

Part One

1. THE HOLLYWOOD LEGEND

1. Investment figures for the motion picture industry are taken from *Standard Trade and Securities, Motion Pictures Basic Survey*, Part I, June, 1939; *Statistical Abstract of the United States*, 1939; *Biennial Census, 1937, Motion Pictures* (United States Department of Commerce, Bureau of the Census, January, 1939). Number of theaters per population, box-office receipts, and average amounts spent on entertainment per family in the United States are from *Places of Amusement: the United States—1939*, Department of Commerce, Bureau of the Census press release, February 18, 1941. The figures for banks, hotels, and cigar stands are for 1935, the latest year for which data are available (except for number of theaters), and are taken from the *Statistical Abstract*, 1940, pp. 255, 880, 887, 890. Figures on movie attendance were compiled by Dr. George Gallup and are reproduced in the *Hollywood Reporter*, June 19, 1941, p. 1. Dr. Gallup's figures are the most reliable known to this writer; they are the only figures based upon an empirical and systematic survey: according to an article in *Time*, July 21, 1941, p. 73, the figures are based on 194 separate surveys. Similar figures on movie attendance, based on earlier surveys, were given in a letter to this writer from Dr. Gallup.
2. Figures on the number of persons employed in Hollywood's movie industry and on the annual payroll are from the *Biennial Census, 1937, Motion Pictures* (Department of Commerce, Bureau of the Census, 1939). Costs of manufacturing movies are from the Department of Commerce, Bureau of the Census, Census of Manufactures, 1937, *Motion Pictures, Not Including Projection in Theaters*, released February 28, 1941. Figures on the proportion of the world's movies, and of movies made in the United States, which are produced in Hollywood, are from *Motion Pictures Abroad*, Motion Picture Division of the Department of Commerce, January 15, 1939, and *An Economic Survey of Hollywood*, University of Southern California Bureau of Business Research, 1938, Part I, p. 102.
3. There are 504 accredited newspaper and magazine correspondents in Washington. See Leo C. Rosten, *The Washington Correspondents* (Harcourt, Brace, 1937), p. 3.
4. *Filmindia*, March, 1939. Anzac soldiers item: *Time*, January 13, 1941, p. 27.
5. Frederick Lewis Allen, *Lords of Creation* (Harper, 1935), p. 84. The Andrew Mellon item is from Dixon Wecter, *The Saga of American Society* (Scribner's, 1937), p. 141.
6. *Hollywood Reporter*, May 19, 1941, p. 6. See also the full page of pictures in the *Hollywood Reporter*, May 20, 1941, p. 12.

REFERENCE NOTES

7. *Los Angeles Times,* June 5, 1941, p. 1.
8. The Paulette Goddard and Myrna Loy items are from Sidney Skolsky's column in the *Hollywood Citizen-News,* copies of which are in the author's files; Victor McLaglen's statement and the Louis Hayward item were quoted in Ella Wickersham's column, *Los Angeles Examiner,* October 31, 1939; the information concerning Cecil B. DeMille comes from Charles Gibbs Adams, "Gardens for Stars," *Saturday Evening Post,* March 2, 1940, pp. 18-19, 74; the Norma Shearer item is from Sidney Skolsky's column, *Hollywood Citizen-News,* December 18, 1939; the George Raft incident is described in the *Hollywood Reporter,* April 17, 1939, p. 2; the producer citation is from Louella O. Parsons' column, *Los Angeles Examiner,* November 20, 1939.
9. Michael Costello, "They Pronounce it Pre-meér," *Reader's Digest,* February, 1941, pp. 88-92.
10. *Los Angeles Times,* April 28, 1941, p. 4.
11. N. W. Ayer & Son, *Directory of Newspapers and Periodicals,* January, 1939.
12. Hollywood Coordinating Council of Social Agencies, Annual Report, November, 1937, p. 2.
13. Benjamin B. Hampton, *A History of the Movies* (Covici-Friede, 1931), p. 210.
14. Will Durant, *The Life of Greece* (Simon and Schuster, 1939), pp. 232-33; Mrs. John King Van Rensselaer (in collaboration with Frederic Van de Water), *The Social Ladder* (Holt, 1924), p. 147.
15. Hampton, *op. cit.,* p. 285. See also Claude Archer Shull, *The Suitability of the Commercial Entertainment Motion Picture to the Age of the Child,* Ph.D. dissertation, Stanford University, September, 1939.
16. Information given to author by one who was a newspaperman in San Francisco at the time; and Hampton, *op. cit.,* pp. 284-87.
17. Hampton, *op. cit.,* p. 287.
18. *Ibid.,* pp. 352-61.
19. Shull, *op. cit.,* pp. 103-04, 111, 343.
20. Terry Ramsaye, *A Million and One Nights* (Simon and Schuster, 1926), Vol. II, p. 816.
21. Shull, *Wid's Year Book,* 1921 (New York: Wid's Films and Film Folk, Inc.), p. 191.
22. Hampton, *op. cit.,* p. 296.
23. *Ibid.*
24. *Publishers' Weekly,* quoted in *World Almanac,* 1941, p. 556.
25. Douglas Churchill, in Churchill and Frank S. Nugent, "Graustark," *We Saw It Happen,* edited by Hanson W. Baldwin and Shepard Stone (Simon and Schuster, 1939), p. 113.
26. *Statistical Abstract of the United States,* 1940, p. 864.
27. *The Screen Actor* (published by the Screen Actors Guild), September, 1940, p. 8.

2. THE MOVIE COLONY

1. Special report of Central Casting to Screen Actors Guild; figures reproduced in the *Hollywood Reporter,* May 13, 1941, p. 11. Data also given this writer from study conducted by Fred Pelton of the Association of Motion Picture Producers.
2. "Rambling Reporter" column, *Hollywood Reporter,* January 11, 1939, p. 2.
3. Thomas Wood, "The First Lady of Hollywood," *Saturday Evening Post,* July 5, 1939, p. 9.
4. Vernon Louis Parrington, *Main Currents in American Thought,* Vol. III: *1860-*

REFERENCE NOTES

1920, The Beginnings of Critical Realism in America (Harcourt, Brace, 1930), p. 10.
5. Frank S. Nugent, in Churchill and Nugent, *op. cit.*, p. 127.
6. Jimmie Fidler, *Los Angeles Times*, December 3, 1940, p. 7.
7. Nugent, *op. cit.*, pp. 133-34.
8. William James, *Psychology* (Holt, 1899), Chap. 12.
9. William C. DeMille, *Hollywood Saga* (Dutton, 1939), p. 298.
10. Van Rensselaer, *op. cit.*, pp. 238-39.
11. Upton Sinclair, *Upton Sinclair Presents William Fox* (Upton Sinclair, 1933), p. 5.
12. Margaret Mead, "The Manus of the Admiralty Islands," in *Competition and Cooperation Among Primitive Peoples*, edited by Margaret Mead (McGraw-Hill, 1937), pp. 217, 218, 238.
13. *Statistical Abstract of the United States*, 1940, pp. 19, 22-32.
14. Quoted in Miriam Beard, *A History of the Business Man* (Macmillan, 1938), p. 505.
15. Van Rensselaer, *op. cit.*, p. 236.
16. Miriam Beard, *op. cit.*, p. 759.

3. THE MOVIE ELITE

1. Temporary National Economic Committee, Monography No. 43 (1941): *The Motion Picture Industry*, by Daniel Bertrand, p. 12.
2. For figures on the value of feature pictures, see National Recovery Administration, Division of Review, Industry Studies Section: *The Motion Picture Industry*, prepared by Daniel Bertrand, February, 1936. The figures on volume of business and film rentals are from TNEC Monograph No. 43, p. 9.
3. TNEC Monograph No. 43, p. 13.
4. The figures on investment in exhibition are from Standard Trade and Securities, *Motion Pictures Basic Survey*, Part 3; TNEC Monograph No. 43; NRA Division of Review, *op. cit.* The theater statistics are from TNEC Monograph No. 43, p. 11.
5. Allen, *op. cit.*, pp. 6-7.
6. DeMille, *op. cit.*, pp. 300-01.
7. *Hollywood Reporter*, July 15, 1939, p. 1.
8. See Adam Smith, *The Wealth of Nations* (Random House, 1937), p. 460.
9. Allen, *op. cit.*, p. 94.
10. Elizabeth Drexel Lehr, *"King Lehr" and the Gilded Age* (Blue Ribbon Books, 1935), p. 170.
11. Parrington, *op. cit.*, p. 12.
12. Sinclair, *op. cit.*, p. 5.
13. Bernard Shaw, *Nine Plays* (Dodd, Mead, 1935), p. 488.
14. Alva Johnston, *The Great Goldwyn* (Random House, 1937), p. 54.
15. Harry Alan Potamkin, "The Cinematized Child," *Films*, November. 1939, p. 5.
16. Thorstein Veblen, *The Theory of the Leisure Class* (Vanguard, 1932), p. 128.
17. Plutarch, *Lives of Illustrious Men* (Reading, Pennsylvania: The Spencer Press, 1936), pp. 163-64.
18. Charles A. Beard and Mary R. Beard, *The Rise of American Civilization* (Macmillan, revised one-volume edition, 1933), Vol. II, p. 392.
19. Van Rensselaer, *op. cit.*, p. 246.
20. Arthur Livingston, "Theory of the Gentleman," *Encyclopedia of the Social Sciences* (Macmillan, 1930), Vol. VI, p. 619, col. 1.

REFERENCE NOTES

21. Adam Smith, *op. cit.*, p. 746.
22. Van Rensselaer, *op. cit.*, pp. 48, 49, 50.
23. The Fisk and Erie Railroad items are from Matthew Josephson, *The Robber Barons* (Harcourt, Brace, 1934), pp. 318, 135, 134; the Astor parties are described in Lehr, *op. cit.*, p. 84.
24. The details concerning Oliver Belmont, the president of the Baltimore and Ohio, and Joseph Leiter are from Lehr, *op. cit.*, pp. 146, 123-24, 151; the items about the wife of a former publisher of the *Washington Post* are from Evalyn Walsh McLean, *Father Struck It Rich* (Little, Brown, 1936), pp. 252, 264; the Walter P. Chrysler anecdote is from an article by Inez Calloway in *Cosmopolitan*, quoted in *Reader's Digest*, November, 1940, p. 114.

4. THE BIG MONEY

1. *Hollywood Reporter*, December 16, 1940, p. 1.
2. The Roy McCardell item is from Hampton, *op. cit.*, p. 30; Ben Hecht's earnings are given in George Jean Nathan, "Theater," *Scribner's*, November, 1937, p. 66.
3. Interview by Frederick C. Othman with John Stahl in the *Hollywood Citizen-News*. Clipping in author's possession.
4. Mary C. McCall, Jr., "Hollywood Close Up," *Review of Reviews*, May, 1937, p. 44.
5. *New York Times*, May 9, 1941, p. 18.
6. Ferdinand Lundberg, *America's 60 Families* (Vanguard, 1938), p. 16.
7. Pitirim Sorokin, "American Millionaires and Multi-Millionaires," *Journal of Social Forces*, May, 1925.
8. Lundberg, *op. cit.*, pp. 17, 20, 29, 30; "Richest U. S. Women," *Fortune*, November, 1936.
9. For 1938 salaries, see *Los Angeles Times*, June 31, 1940, p. 1. For 1937 salaries, see *Hollywood Citizen-News*, April 7, 1939, p. 1.
10. Quoted in *Hollywood Reporter*, January 21, 1939, pp. 1, 5.
11. John Calhoun Baker, *Executive Compensation and Bonus Plans* (Harvard University Bureau of Business Research, 1939), pp. 28, 34.
12. For figure on Mr. Mayer's income tax in 1937, see *Hollywood Reporter*, April 10, 1939, p. 1. For Nicholas Schenck's statement, see *Hollywood Citizen-News*, December 19, 1938, p. 1.
13. *Time*, April 7, 1940, p. 94.
14. *Hollywood Reporter*, January 27, 1941, p. 1.
15. Vernon D. Wood, "That's Where Their Money Goes," *Detroit Free Press*, Screen and Radio Section, July 9, 1939, pp. 6-7.
16. Walter O. Heinze in *Hollywood Reporter*, October 8, 1940—item that the clients of one business manager save forty percent of their incomes. The revelation concerning the actress-client of another business manager is from Vernon D. Wood, *Detroit Free Press*, *loc. cit.*
17. See *Variety*, March 12, 1941, p. 8; *Los Angeles Times*, March 6, 1941, page A; March 13, 1941, p. 1; March 15, 1941, p. 2; March 27, 1941, p. 5.
18. *Los Angeles Times*, March 25, 1939, p. 11.
19. *Los Angeles Times*, December 4, 1940, p. 5.
20. *Screen Actor*, September, 1940, p. 6; April, 1941, p. 12.
21. *Hollywood Reporter*, January 30, 1939, p. 1.
22. See, for example, *Variety*, June 5, 1940, pp. 3, 46.
23. Gilbert Seldes, "Diamond Pin Money," *Photoplay*, February, 1938, p. 22.
24. *Variety*, March 12, 1941, p. 8.
25. *Time*, April 7, 1941, p. 94.

REFERENCE NOTES

5. EROS IN HOLLYWOOD

1. Will Durant, *op. cit.*, pp. 380, 606.
2. Quoted in Wecter, *op. cit.*, p. 61.
3. Robert Coughlan, "Victor Mature," *Life*, April 7, 1941, pp. 65, 74.
4. Vilfredo Pareto, *The Mind and Society*, Vol. IV, *The General Form of Society* (Ed. Arthur Livingston; Harcourt, Brace, 1935), p. 1869, footnote.
5. Jimmie Fidler, *Los Angeles Times*, December 21, 1940, p. 14.
6. *Ibid.*
7. *Hollywood Reporter*, March 1, 1939, p. 2; *ibid.*, March 15, 1939, p. 2.
8. *Los Angeles Times*, December 30, 1940, p. 4.
9. Frederick C. Othman's column, *Hollywood Citizen-News*, April 5, 1940.
10. Ed Sullivan's column, *Hollywood Citizen-News*, March 25, 1940.
11. Sidney Skolsky, *ibid.*
12. Ed Sullivan, *Hollywood Citizen-News*, September 12, 1940, p. 8.
13. Jimmie Fidler, *Los Angeles Times*, June 26, 1941, p. 16.
14. Thomas Wood, *loc. cit.*, p. 47.
15. The group of unspectacular star-marriages is described in Douglas Churchill's article, "When Movie Stars Marry," *New York Times Magazine*, August 27, 1939.
16. Ella Wickersham's column, *Los Angeles Examiner*, August 10, 1939.
17. Gilbert Seldes, *The Movies Come from America* (Scribner's), p. 62.
18. Churchill, "When Movie Stars Marry," *loc. cit.*
19. Quoted in Jimmie Fidler's column, *Los Angeles Times*, June 27, 1940.
20. Livingston, *op. cit.*, p. 616, col. 2.
21. *Ibid.*
22. *Statistical Abstract of the United States*, 1940, p. 97; *World Almanac*, 1941, p. 527.
23. Van Rensselaer, *op. cit.*, p. 239.
24. *Ibid.*, pp. 239-40.
25. U. S. Bureau of the Census, *Special Report on Marriage and Divorce, 1867-1906*, Part I, 1909; reproduced in Joseph Kirk Folsom, *The Family* (John Wiley & Sons, 1934), p. 385.
26. E. W. Burgess and Leonard Cottrell, Jr., *Predicting Success or Failure in Marriage* (Prentice-Hall, 1939), Chapter IX.
27. Folsom, *op. cit.*, p. 375. It is significant that in 1891, Dr. Walter F. Willcox, on the basis of limited materials available at that time, predicted the divorce rate for 1930 almost exactly. (*Ibid.*) The divorce rate in the United States has more than doubled since the beginning of this century. The latest figures available show that there were 175 divorces per thousand marriages in 1937, as compared to 131 in 1922, 81 in 1900, 62 in 1890. In the last year for which such data were available (1932), Wyoming had a divorce rate of 770 per thousand marriages; Nevada, 563; Idaho, 528; Iowa, 418; Ohio, 377; Texas, 354; and California (seventh on the list), 326. (*Statistical Abstract of the United States*, 1939, pp. 96-97.) It is surprising that Iowa and Ohio rank higher on the divorce rolls than California; this may be explained, in part, by the fact that California has a higher proportion of Catholics in its population than either Iowa or Ohio—roughly, a half for California as against a fifth for Iowa and a third for Ohio. (*World Almanac*, 1939, p. 279.)
28. Frank H. Hankins, "Divorce," *Encyclopedia of the Social Sciences*, Vol. V, p. 179.

REFERENCE NOTES

6. POLITICS OVER HOLLYWOOD

1. The journalist's comment is from *Time*, November 12, 1934, p. 16. The effect of the Sinclair campaign on the stocks of California companies is described in *Time*, October 15, 1934, p. 61.
2. *Ibid.*
3. Cited in Upton Sinclair, *I, Candidate for Governor and How I Got Licked* (Farrar & Rinehart, 1934), pp. 151-52.
4. *New York Times*, November 4, 1934, p. 5, Drama section; and Sinclair, *I, Candidate for Governor*, pp. 127-28.
5. Quoted in Sinclair, *I, Candidate for Governor*, pp. 152-54.
6. *Ibid.*, pp. 155-56.
7. Louella Parsons' column, *Los Angeles Examiner*, September 16, 1936.
8. Martin Dies, "The Reds in Hollywood," *Liberty*, February 17, 1940, p. 48.
9. *Hollywood Reporter*, December 1, 1938, p. 1.
10. Dies, *loc. cit.*, p. 48.
11. Quoted by Irving Hoffman, *Hollywood Reporter*, November 27, 1939, p. 3.
12. Dies, *loc. cit.* pp. 48, 50.
13. *Ibid.*, pp. 49-50.
14. Cf. *Variety*, August 21, 1940, p. 22.
15. Quoted by John C. Lee in *Screen Actor*, September, 1940, p. 4.
16. Manchester Boddy's column, *Daily News*, Los Angeles, October 6, 1940.
17. *Ibid.*
18. *Variety*, July 20, 1938, p. 1.
19. Quoted in *Variety*, August 21, 1940, p. 22.
20. *Daily News*, Los Angeles, August 22, 1940, p. 6.
21. *Ibid.*
22. *Ibid.*
23. Quoted in the *Los Angeles Examiner*, August 16, 1940, pp. 1, 8.
24. Both the Freeman and Dies statements are quoted in *Variety*, August 21, 1940, p. 22.
25. Lee, *loc. cit.*
26. See the *San Francisco Herald*, August 21, 1940, p. 4; *Variety*, August 21, 1940, p. 22.
27. *Hollywood Reporter*, November 7, 1940, p. 1.
28. *New York Herald Tribune*, August 23, 1940.
29. Carl Sandburg, *Abraham Lincoln: The War Years* (Harcourt, Brace, 1939), Vol. II, p. 511.
30. Dies, *loc. cit.*, p. 50.
31. *Ibid.*
32. Quoted in Morton Thompson's column, *Hollywood Citizen-News*, April 4, 1939.
33. Printed in *Town Meeting*, March 3, 1941, pp. 16-17.
34. Quoted in *Daily News*, Los Angeles, August 21, 1940, p. 6.
35. Nugent, in Nugent and Churchill, *op. cit.*, p. 130.
36. *Ibid.*
37. See Harold D. Lasswell, *Psychopathology and Politics* (University of Chicago Press, 1930), and *World Politics and Personal Insecurity* (McGraw-Hill Book Company, 1935).
38. The figures on Hollywood's preference for Roosevelt are from the *Hollywood Reporter*, October 8, 1936. The donations to the Democratic campaign in 1936 are listed in *Variety*, March 10, 1937.

REFERENCE NOTES

7. THE FIGHT FOR PRESTIGE

1. *Hollywood Reporter,* January 27, 1941, p. 4.
2. *Reader's Digest,* February, 1941, p. 89.
3. The Fugger item is from Miriam Beard, *op. cit.,* p. 240. The Ward McAllister quotation is from Van Rensselaer, *op. cit.,* p. 197.
4. DeMille, *op. cit.,* p. 96.
5. Lloyd Pantages, "1939 Society Goes Hollywood," *Cosmopolitan,* January, 1939, p. 90.
6. Wecter, *op. cit.,* p. 1.
7. Allen, *op. cit.,* p. 105; Wecter, *op. cit.,* p. 411-12.
8. Wecter, *op. cit.,* p. 465.
9. See *Fortune,* December, 1937.
10. See *Town & Country,* February, 1940.
11. Wecter, *op. cit.,* p. 34.
12. Ed Sullivan's column, *Hollywood Citizen-News,* December 13, 1938.
13. *Ibid.*
14. Wecter, *op. cit.,* p. 183.
15. DeMille, *op. cit.,* p. 298.
16. *Hollywood Citizen-News,* November 17, 1939, p. 5.
17. R. H. Tawney, *The Acquisitive Society* (Harcourt, Brace, 1921), pp. 159-60.
18. Dixon Wecter's statement is from Wecter, *op. cit.,* p. 11. John Fiske's findings concerning the origins of leading families: *ibid.,* p. 35.
19. The description of John Jacob Astor is from Allen, *op. cit.,* p. 100; and Josephson, *op. cit.,* p. 12. The description of him as "a jovial good-for-nothing butcher" is from Parton and is quoted in Wecter, *op. cit.,* p. 113. The details concerning Commodore Vanderbilt come from Wecter, *op. cit.,* p. 134; Allen, *op. cit.,* p. 100; Josephson, *op. cit.,* p. 329. The Fisk ancestry is discussed in Josephson, *op. cit.,* p. 65, and that of the Goulds in Allen, *op. cit.,* p. 44.
20. *Cf.* Hampton, *op. cit.,* for these details by name.
21. *Reader's Digest,* November, 1940, Peggy McEvoy's column.
22. The malapropisms of the Washington dowager and of the lady from a Western city are recounted in Wecter, *op. cit.,* p. 145; the misstatements of John Kelsey are from Malcolm Bingay, "When Detroit Roared Like a Mining Camp and the World was Remade," Part 2, *Saturday Evening Post,* July 6, 1940, p. 2.
23. Wecter, *op. cit.,* p. 46.

8. THE NIGHT LIFE OF THE GODS

1. Quoted in Miriam Beard, *op. cit.,* p. 248.
2. Constance Bennett, "Good Manners and Hollywood Society," *Liberty,* June 24, 1939, p. 65.
3. *Hollywood Reporter,* July 22, 1939, p. 2.
4. *Hollywood Citizen-News,* June 15, 1939, p. 2; Lehr, *op. cit.,* p. 226.
5. Lehr, *op. cit.,* p. 226.
6. Irving Goldman, "The Kwakiutl Indians of Vancouver Island," *Competition and Cooperation Among Primitive Peoples,* pp. 191-92.
7. *Time,* February 26, 1940, Cinema section.
8. *Ibid.*
9. Lucius Beebe, "Party Lines," *Photoplay,* December, 1937, pp. 26, 78.
10. Ella Wickersham's column, *Los Angeles Examiner,* July 7, 1939.
11. *Ibid.,* May 13, 1939.

REFERENCE NOTES

12. *Hollywood Reporter,* January 27, 1941, p. 4.
13. Miriam Beard, *op. cit.,* p. 689.
14. Lehr, *op. cit.,* p. 68.
15. *Look,* July 2, 1940, p. 41.
16. DeMille, *op. cit.,* p. 298.
17. Wecter, *op. cit.,* p. 106.
18. Veblen, *op. cit.,* pp. 146 ff.
19. Lehr, *op. cit.,* pp. 69, 139.
20. McLean, *op. cit.,* p. 288.
21. Anna Mary Wells, "Newspaper Wife in Hollywood," *The Family Circle* (Los Angeles magazine), June 2, 1939, p. 2.
22. *Hollywood Reporter,* July 25, 1939, p. 3.
23. Hedda Hopper's column, *Los Angeles Times,* June 24, 1940.
24. Lehr, *op. cit.,* pp. 71, 147.
25. *Ibid.,* pp. 69, 139; Lundberg, *op. cit.,* p. 415.
26. Miriam Beard, *op. cit.,* pp. 173-74.
27. *Ibid.,* p. 248.
28. Lundberg, *op. cit.,* pp. 411-12.
29. Allen, *op. cit.,* pp. 109-10.
30. Lehr, *op. cit.,* p. 228; Lundberg, *op. cit.,* p. 415.
31. The description of the Bradley Martin ball is found in Josephson, *op. cit.,* p. 339; for description of the Stotesbury ball, see Lehr, *op. cit.,* pp. 271-72.
32. Ward McAllister, quoted in Wecter, *op. cit.,* p. 181.
33. *Town & Country,* March, 1940, p. 87; Lundberg, *op. cit.,* p. 413.
34. Pembroke Jones item from Lehr, *op. cit.,* p. 138; cost of balls and dress described in Wecter, *op. cit.,* p. 106.

9. OF MARBLE HALLS

1. Value of the Woolworth living-room: from *Saturday Evening Post* series on the Woolworths, February 3 to March 16, 1940. The Stotesbury estate is described in a real estate advertisement in *Fortune,* July, 1939; the home of Nicholas Brady, in Lundberg, *op. cit.,* p. 431; the Insull estate, *ibid.,* p. 430. The Samuel Hill item is from *Time,* May 20, 1940, p. 47; and the merchant prince item is from Miriam Beard, *op. cit.,* p. 631.
2. For information on the country homes of the rich see, for example, Jack Alexander, "Golden Boy: the Story of Jimmy Cromwell," *Saturday Evening Post,* March 23, 1940, pp. 9-11, 119 ff. The homes of Doris Duke Cromwell are also listed in the above article. The item about the *"grande dame"* is from Lehr, *op. cit.,* pp. 228-29, and that concerning the coal baron who reproduced Buckingham Palace is from Miriam Beard, *op. cit.,* pp. 644-45.
3. For description of the period see Parker Morell, *Diamond Jim* (Garden City Publishing Company, 1934), pp. 146-52; and Jerome Davis, *Capitalism and Its Culture* (Farrar & Rinehart, 1935), p. 442.
4. Frederick C. Othman, *Hollywood Citizen-News,* December 23, 1938, p. 4.
5. The data on DeMille's gardens are from Charles Gibbs Adams, *loc. cit.,* pp. 18, 74 ff. The Wanamaker, du Pont, and Duke items are from Lundberg, *op. cit.,* p. 430.
6. *Fortune,* May, 1930, p. 108.
7. The offerings of real estate agents are described in *Variety,* October 30, 1939, p. 3. The Zukor item is from the *Motion Picture Herald,* May 31, 1941, p. 9.
8. Quoted in the *Hollywood Citizen-News,* January 14, 1939, p. 3.

REFERENCE NOTES

9. *Ibid.*
10. *Los Angeles Examiner*, November 9, 1939.
11. Data quoted in Lundberg, *op. cit.*, pp. 416-18.
12. Harry Crocker, *Los Angeles Examiner*, December 29, 1939, p. 12, sec. 1.
13. See Oliver Carlson and Ernest Sutherland Bates, *Hearst: Lord of San Simeon* (Viking, 1936), *passim*. For items on Hearst's warehouses, see Geoffrey T. Hellman, *New Yorker*, February 1, 1941, pp. 29-35.
14. Charles Gibbs Adams, *loc. cit.*
15. Allen, *op. cit.*, p. 134.
16. Quoted in Wecter, *op. cit.*, p. 470.
17. Josephson, *op. cit.*, p. 431.
18. Quoted in Margaret Farrand Thorp, *America at the Movies* (Yale University Press, 1939), pp. 81-82.
19. Miriam Beard, *op. cit.*, p. 47; McLean, *op. cit.*, p. 227.
20. Quoted in Wecter, *op. cit.*, p. 471.

10. HORSES, GIFTS, AND SUPERSTITIONS

1. *Daily Variety*, January 18, 1939.
2. *Boxoffice*, May 11, 1940, p. 41.
3. "Rambling Reporter" column, *Hollywood Reporter*, May 18, 1939.
4. *Life*, July 10, 1939, p. 32.
5. *Look*, February 14, 1939.
6. *Ibid.*
7. Harry M. Warner, quoted in *Hollywood Reporter*, November 5, 1940, p. 5.
8. Ed Sullivan's column, *Hollywood Citizen-News*, February 10, 1939.
9. The Isabel Dodge Sloane anecdote is from Wecter, *op. cit.*, p. 148; the Oliver Belmont item, from Lehr, *op. cit.*, p. 145.
10. Alexis de Tocqueville, *Democracy in America*, Vol. I (The Colonial Press, 1900), p. 432.
11. Cited in Frederick Lewis Allen, *Since Yesterday* (Harper, 1940), pp. 151-54.
12. *Los Angeles Times*, March 18, 1941, p. 3.
13. *Los Angeles Times*, March 12, 1941, p. 1; April 9, 1941, p. A.
14. Morell, *op. cit.*, p. 111. Bet-A-Million Gates' exploits are described in Miriam Beard, *op. cit.*, p. 631 and in Allen, *Lords of Creation*, p. 25. Donahue's losses are mentioned in Lundberg, *op. cit.*, pp. 415-16.
15. *Los Angeles Examiner*, January 1, 1940, cinema section; Joseph M. Schenck's gift-giving is described in the *Los Angeles Times*, March 27, 1941, p. 5.
16. Anna Mary Wells, *loc. cit.*, p. 16.
17. *Hollywood Reporter*, July 21, 1939, p. 1.
18. Ed Sullivan, *Hollywood Citizen-News*, January 14, 1939.
19. Hedda Hopper, *Los Angeles Times*, January 17, 1939, p. 9.
20. *Hollywood Reporter*, July 12, 1939, p. 2.
21. *Long Beach Press Telegram*, March 4, 1939.
22. The Bennett item is from Lehr, *op. cit.*, pp. 281-82; Collis Huntington's superstitions are described in Josephson, *op. cit.*, p. 133. Mrs. McCormick's adventures in mysticism: *ibid.*, pp. 146-47.

REFERENCE NOTES

Part Two

11. THE PRODUCERS: I

1. Jesse L. Lasky, "The Producer Makes a Plan," *We Make the Movies*, edited by Nancy Naumberg (Norton, 1937), p. 5.
2. *Ibid.*, pp. 1, 5-6.
3. Sidney Howard, "The Story Gets a Treatment," *We Make the Movies*, p. 44.
4. "An Analysis of the Motion Picture Industry, by the Screen Directors Guild, Inc.," pp. 1-2, 4-5. (Mimeographed; copy in author's possession; July 18, 1938.)
5. Alva Johnston, *The Great Goldwyn* (Random House, 1937), pp. 22-23.
6. Seldes, *The Movies Come from America*, pp. 10-11.
7. Screen Directors Guild Report, *op. cit.*, p. 3.
8. *Ibid.*, p. 1.
9. *Hollywood Reporter*, June 12, 1941, p. 4.
10. Screen Directors Guild, *op. cit.*, pp. 1, 2, 4, 6, 6-7.
11. Johnston, *The Great Goldwyn*, pp. 86-87.
12. A. F. Meyers' speech to the Twentieth Century Club, April 26, 1938, p. 3.
13. *Hollywood Reporter*, June 11, 1941.
14. United States vs. Paramount Pictures, *et al.*, pp. 43-44.
15. *Survey of Listed Corporations*, 1939-40, Part I, pp. 81-84.
16. *Ibid.*
17. Kennedy report, a copy of which was examined by this writer.
18. Hampton, *op. cit.*, p. 202.
19. J. Cheever Cowdin, in the *Hollywood Reporter*, March 5, 1941, p. 1. Universal's profit and loss figures for 1935-1939 are given in *Variety*, January 8, 1941, p. 25; for 1940, in the *Motion Picture Herald*, February 15, 1941, p. 33; for the first seventeen weeks of 1941, in the *Motion Picture Herald*, May 3, 1941, pp. 35-36.
20. *Boxoffice*, January 20, 1940.
21. *Hollywood Reporter*, March 5, 1941, p. 1.
22. *Film Daily*, April 28, 1941, pp. 1, 7; Motion Picture Herald, May 3, 1941, p. 35.

12. THE PRODUCERS: II

1. Alva Johnston, "Darryl F. Zanuck, the Wahoo Boy," *Profiles from the New Yorker* (Knopf, 1938), p. 362.
2. *Statistical Abstract of the United States*, 1939, pp. 20-25.
3. Allen, *Lords of Creation*, p. 85.
4. Johnston, "Darryl F. Zanuck, the Wahoo Boy," pp. 362, 363.
5. Pitt's reply to Walpole, March 6, 1741, in *Bartlett's Familiar Quotations*, Morley and Everett ed. (Little, Brown, 1937).
6. *Hollywood Citizen-News*, April 7, 1939, p. 1; *Boxoffice*, March 11, 1939, p. 32; *Film Daily*, May 9, 1941, p. 8; *Los Angeles Times*, May 9, 1941, p. 12.
7. 1938 figures from Treasury Department data, *Los Angeles Times*, July 1, 1940, pp. 1 ff. Figures for 1937 are from the list reported by the Ways and Means Committee of the House of Representatives, as printed in the *Hollywood Citizen-News*, April 7, 1939, p. 1.
8. Hampton, *op. cit.*, p. 311.

9. *Boxoffice*, March 11, 1939, p. 32.
10. *Time*, July 21, 1941, p. 73.
11. *Traffic in Souls* figures, *Film Daily Year Book*, 1941, p. 123. *Over the Hill* figures are from Sinclair, *William Fox, p.* 59.
12. The William Fox item is described in Sinclair, *William Fox*, p. xii. The Goldwyn item is from Johnston, *The Great Goldwyn*, pp. 39, 47. The information concerning the Warner Brothers is from the *Film Daily Year Book*, 1941, p. 123, and the *Survey of Listed Corporations*, Vol. II.

13. THE DIRECTORS

1. Seldes, *The Movies Come from America*, pp. 82, 72.
2. Hampton, *op. cit.*, p. 216.
3. DeMille, *op. cit.*, p. 283.
4. *Hollywood Citizen-News*, January 31, 1940; *Variety*, January 31, 1940, p. 1.
5. Seldes, *The Movies Come from America*, p. 74. Garson Kanin's statement was printed in *Time*, July 28, 1941, cinema section.
6. Clara Beranger, "The Story," *Introduction to the Photoplay* (University of Southern California, 1929), p. 75.
7. Screen Directors Guild, *op. cit.*, pp. 1, 5, 6.
8. *New York Times*, April 2, 1939, Drama section, p. 2.
9. *Hollywood Reporter*, March 2, 1939, pp. 1-2.

14. THE WRITERS

1. Norman Krasna, "Some Authors Die Happy," *New York Times*, May 18, 1941, Drama section.
2. Dalton Trumbo, *Forum*, February, 1933, p. 118.
3. Seldes, *The Movies Come from America*, p. 82.
4. Herman Mankiewicz, in M. Eustice, "Additional Dialogue, Scribblers in Hollywood," *Theatre Arts Monthly*, v. 21: 452, June, 1937.
5. Beranger, *op. cit.*, pp. 71-72.
6. Frances Taylor Patterson, "The Author and Hollywood," *North American Review*, v. 243-244, pp. 80, 81, August, 1937.
7. Benjamin Glazer, "The Photoplay with Sound and Voice," *Introduction to the Photoplay*, p. 46.
8. Quoted by George Jean Nathan, "Theater," *Scribner's*, November, 1937, p. 68.
9. Samuel Goldwyn, "Hollywood is Sick," *Saturday Evening Post*, July 13, 1940, pp. 48-49.
10. *Daily Variety*, April 14, 1941, p. 5.
11. *Hollywood Reporter*, May 4, 1939, p. 2.
12. NLRB pamphlet: United States of America, before the National Labor Relations Board in the matter of Metro-Goldwyn-Mayer studios and Motion Picture Producers Association, *et al.* and Screen Writers Guild, Inc. Cases No. R400 to R420 inclusive. Decided June 4, 1938, pp. 30 ff. Also see producers' comments in *Weekly Variety*, January 28, 1939, p. 1.
13. *Time*, July 21, 1941, p. 73.

15. THE ACTORS

1. Hampton, *op. cit.*, pp. 85-86.
2. *Ibid.*, p. 213.

REFERENCE NOTES

3. *Film Daily*, April 2, 1941, p. 1. *Hollywood Reporter*, April 30, 1940, p. 1.
4. Data combined from the Guild's report, *Daily Variety*, August 12, 1940, pp. 1-4; *Film Daily*, April 22, 1941, pp. 1, 6; *Screen Actor*, September, 1940, p. 8; and Central Casting's report as reproduced in the *Hollywood Reporter*, May 13, 1941, pp. 1, 11.
5. Speech to the American Association for the Advancement of Science, quoted in *Daily Variety*, December 31, 1940, p. 1.
6. Hampton, *op. cit.*, pp. 149, 234; DeMille, *op. cit.*, p. 235.
7. Seldes, *The Movies Come from America*, pp. 37, 29; Hampton, *op. cit.*, p. 156.
8. *Magazine of Wall Street*, August 22, 1931.
9. Treasury Department data, as published in *Variety*, July 1, 1940; *New York Times*, July 1, 1940; *Los Angeles Times*, July 1, 1940.
10. For data on earnings received in addition to movie work, see Seldes, "Diamond Pin Money," *loc. cit.*

Part Three

16. THE LONG ARM OF HOLLYWOOD

1. See *Motion Pictures and Youth*, a series of twelve studies made under the auspices of the Payne Fund, for which W. W. Charters was chairman. The studies were published in five volumes by Macmillan from 1933 to 1935. See also the penetrating criticism of the methods used, and conclusions drawn, in the above series, by Mortimer J. Adler in *Art and Prudence* (Longmans, Green, 1937), pp. 231-457.
2. Adler, *op. cit.*, pp. 35-36.
3. *Ibid.*, p. 29.
4. *London Times*, December 15, 1936.
5. *Hollywood Reporter*, July 19, 1939, p. 2.
6. H. L. Mencken, *The American Language* (Knopf, 1938), p. 70.
7. Caroline F. Ware, *Greenwich Village* (Houghton Mifflin, 1935), p. 350.
8. Hampton, *op. cit.*, p. 222.
9. *Film*, March 23, 1939.
10. *David Copperfield* item from *New York Times*, Book Section, January 15, 1939, article by George Gallup, "The Favorite Books of Americans." *Wuthering Heights* item is from the *Hollywood Reporter*, April 24, 1939, p. 4.
11. Quoted in the *Hollywood Reporter*, January 9, 1941, p. 3.
12. University of Southern California Bureau of Business Research.
13. Robert S. Lynd and Helen Merrell Lynd, *Middletown in Transition* (Harcourt, Brace, 1937), p. 169.
14. Ware, *op. cit.*, pp. 367-68.
15. Quoted in Robert S. Lynd and Helen Merrell Lynd, *Middletown* (Harcourt, Brace, 1929), p. 265.
16. Adler, *op. cit.*

INDEX OF SUBJECTS

INDEX OF SUBJECTS

INDEX OF SUBJECTS

431